ALEXIS IN AMERICA

Alexis at age seventeen. Reproduced from Iosif Starkovskii, *Aleksei Aleksandrovich, velikii kniaz' kratkii istoricheskii ocherk piatideciatiletiia, 1850–1900* (St. Petersburg, 1900)

ALEXIS IN AMERICA

A RUSSIAN GRAND DUKE'S TOUR, 1871–1872

LEE A. FARROW

✚

LOUISIANA STATE UNIVERSITY PRESS

BATON ROUGE

Published by Louisiana State University Press
Manufactured in the United States of America
First printing

Designer: Barbara Neely Bourgoyne
Typeface: Sina Nova
Printer and binder: Maple Press, Inc.

Portions of chapter 7 first appeared in the essay "Grand Duke Alexis in Memphis and the Reconstruction of Southern Identity during Reconstruction," *West Tennessee Historical Society Papers,*
59 (2005): 20–36, and are used with permission. Portions of chapters 7 and 8 first appeared in the
essay "Grand Duke Alexei and the Origins of Rex, 1872: Myth, Public Memory, and the Distortion
of History," *Gulf South Historical Review* 18.1 (Fall 2002): 6–30, and are used with permission.
Portions of chapter 5 first appeared in the essay "Grandeur amidst the Ashes: The Chicago Visit
of Russian Grand Duke Alexis, 1871–1872," *Journal of Illinois History* 11.1 (Spring 2008): 2–16,
and are used with permission.

Library of Congress Cataloging-in-Publication Data are available at the Library of Congress.

ISBN 978-0-8071-5839-5 (cloth: alk. paper) — ISBN 978-0-8071-5840-1 (pdf) —
ISBN 978-0-8071-5841-8 (epub) — ISBN 978-0-8071-5842-5 (mobi)

To Sam Ramer, mentor and friend

CONTENTS

Illustrations follow page 114.

ACKNOWLEDGMENTS

As is always the case with a project of this size and scope, I have many people to thank and I ask that I be forgiven if I have overlooked anyone. First, I need to begin by thanking the institutions that made much of this research possible. A grant from the Kennan Institute at the Woodrow Wilson Center allowed me to conduct research in Washington, D.C., while several Faculty Research Grant-in-Aid awards from Auburn University at Montgomery funded trips to the many other cities Alexis visited while in North America. I also used the Blitz Information Center several times to order and obtain copies of documents in Russian archives when I could not visit myself. Finally, the Interlibrary Loan Department at AUM's library has been a tremendous help in obtaining books and documents from around the United States. Thank you, Carolyn Johnson and Karen Williams. This project required research in many places, in the United States, Russia, and Canada. I cannot list everyone by name, but I am enormously grateful to all those library and archival workers who helped me obtain materials. I encountered many people with a passion for history and a willingness to help; they cannot be thanked enough for their efforts. I particularly need to thank Ann Case, university archivist at Tulane University, and Kevin Fontenot, formerly of Tulane University. Kevin actually pointed me to the topic of Grand Duke Alexis when we were graduate students together; he deserves credit for helping me find this fascinating and entertaining topic. I would also like to thank the *West Tennessee Historical Society Papers, Gulf South Historical Review,* and *Journal of Illinois History* for granting me permission to reprint material that previously appeared in article form.

I have also been fortunate enough to have two graduate students who assisted me by compiling lists of possible sources and proofreading my notes—Samantha McNeilly and Brittnee Ward—and one graduate student who did a careful reading of the first draft of the manuscript—Ken Stephens. I am grateful for their help. I would also like to thank Michael Samerdyke, an old friend I met in Moscow in 1994, who read the entire manuscript and gave me very thoughtful and useful feedback. I appreciate his comments and his regular correspondence. Finally, I appreciate the suggestions of the outside readers, whoever they are; their suggestions made this a better book, as well.

On a more personal level, there are many people to whom I owe immense gratitude and thanks for their support. I would like to thank all my colleagues at AUM, particularly the members of my department, and my dean, Michael Burger. Many friends across campus have been excited and enthusiastic about this project, particularly Brad Moody, Elizabeth Woodworth, Kim Brackett, and Dana Bice. I also have many wonderful friends scattered across North America, all of whom have encouraged me along the way. Special thanks must go to Pam Kachurin, Angela Mitchell, Karen Racine, and Heather Thiessen-Reily, four women I wish I saw more often. I am also grateful for the support of the good people at the Lion's Club in Hayes Center, Nebraska, and the various "living historians" and visitors there, who enthusiastically embraced me at the Grand Duke Alexis Rendezvous. Thanks also to Jim Crain, who has shared his collection of ephemera with me; Douglas Scott, Peter Bleed, and Stephen Damm, who corresponded with me about their archaeological research on the Grand Duke Alexis buffalo hunt site; and Byron Stewart, a librarian at Missouri State University, who had collected information on Alexis for years and selflessly mailed a thirty-four-pound box of notes and photocopies to me. I also thank Elizabeth Sverbeyeff Byron, the great-granddaughter of Grand Duke Alexis, who not only met with me and allowed me to interview her, but also read the manuscript in one of its earlier versions.

Finally, I have to thank my family. My parents, Adeline and Leroy Verda, and in-laws, Marilyn and Hank Farrow, are always supportive and appreciative of my professional successes and have listened to me talk about Alexis for years. My husband Ben has not only been a great support, both during the research and writing stages, but he has also read the manuscript in all its various stages and given a great deal of helpful feedback. Finally, my truly wonderful children: Sophia, who is always with me in spirit, and Benjamin and Camille, who have traveled with me for much of this research and have cheered me on and celebrated each little victory along the way. Though I did not take their suggestions to add vampires and zombies to the story to improve my sales numbers, they have always been with me through this process. I hope they are proud of their mom.

ALEXIS IN AMERICA

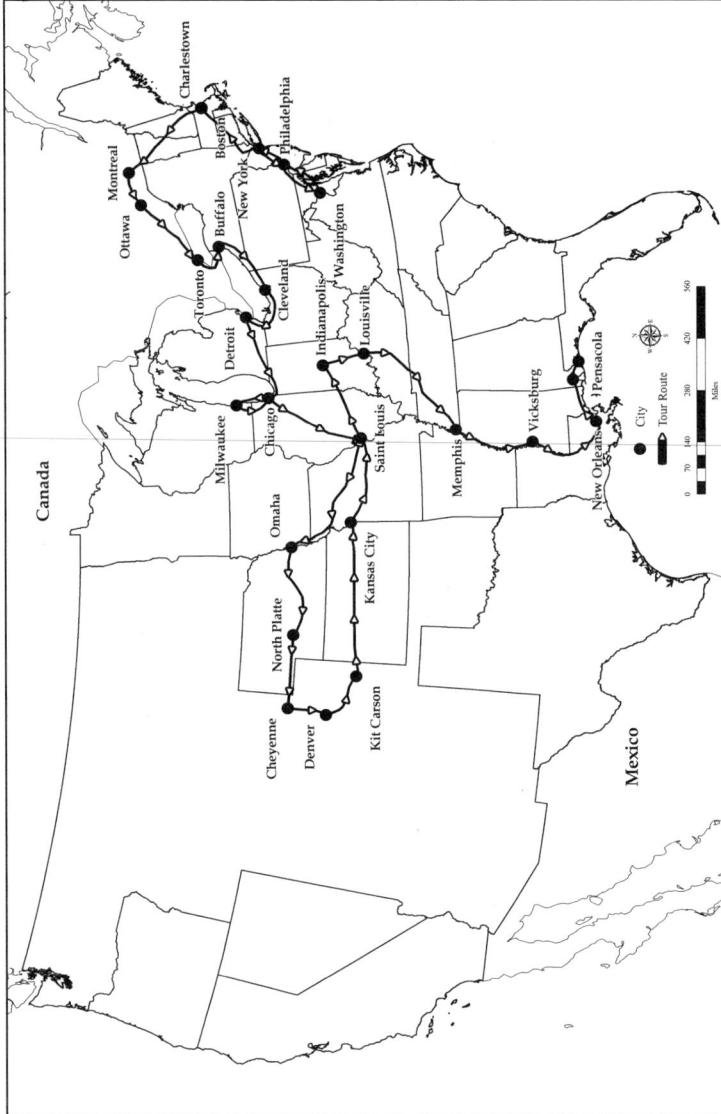

An overview of Alexis's journey.
Map by Christopher Blair.

INTRODUCTION
The Eagle, Today, Nestles Close to the Bear

O N NOVEMBER 14, 1871, Grand Duke Alexis awoke somewhere on the Atlantic Ocean to face another heartsick, interminable day. Traveling on board the Russian frigate *Svetlana*, bound for the United States, Alexis had already been at sea for several weeks, forced to leave behind his country, his family, and the woman he loved. As the tsar's son, Alexis understood on some level that his duties to family and country took precedence over his own personal desires, but it was a difficult reality to accept for a young man. Only twenty-one years old, Alexis was passionately in love and chafed under the restrictive expectations of his family and society. The object of his affection, Alexandra Zhukovskaya, was six months pregnant when he left Russia, and though his parents had forbidden him from continuing the unsuitable relationship and had sent him abroad on a journey of undetermined length, he pined for her. Unbeknownst to Alexis, on that very day, as the *Svetlana* continued on its path for New York, Alexandra gave birth to his son in Salzburg, in the Austro-Hungarian Empire, and named him Alexis. Five days later, on November 19, the *Svetlana* steamed past the bar at Sandy Hook and into the Lower Bay of New York, commencing Alexis's grand tour of the United States and Canada.

———◆———

Alexis's arrival in late November 1871 had actually been several years in the making. In 1865, the U.S. government had invited Grand Duke Constantin to visit, but the invitation was declined. Then in 1867 the U.S. minister to Russia, Cassius Clay, wrote to Secretary of State William Seward that the Grand Duke Alexis was contemplating a tour of the United States. Clay's report was likely a mistake or a misunderstanding, since Alexis was only seventeen years old, but

1

the U.S. government had been hoping for several years to convince a member of the Russian royal family to come for a visit. Only in early 1870 did the United States receive some promising indications that a meeting might actually occur, and by March 1870, it seemed that Alexis would be that person. A year later, however, even the Russian minister in Washington, Constantin Catacazy, was unsure about the exact timing of the fleet's departure. Catacazy's lack of certainty about the grand duke's plans frustrated Secretary of State Hamilton Fish, leading him to appeal to the American minister in St. Petersburg, Andrew Curtin. On June 9, 1871, Fish wrote Curtin, "Is there reason to expect that the Grand Duke is coming to this country[?] We cannot believe what the Minister [Catacazy] says." Curtin confirmed that the Russian fleet would depart in August, and over the following months, more information about the grand duke and his entourage passed through diplomatic channels to American officials. In late August, rumor had it that Catacazy was preparing his mansion in Washington for a royal visit; the impressive team of upholsterers, gilders, paperhangers, and painters seemed proof positive that Alexis would indeed come to America.[1]

Once the visit of the grand duke seemed a certainty, the next question was what his itinerary would entail. Although the first reports in the United States listed the eastern seaboard and the area west of the Rockies, that plan was far from certain and had been changed a number of times. As early as February 1871, Minister Catacazy had suggested a list of stops that included New York, Hartford, Bridgeport, Washington, Boston, Cambridge, Niagara Falls, Cleveland, Detroit, Chicago, Cincinnati, St. Louis, and a western leg through the Rocky Mountains as far as San Francisco. By July, the list of stops had been altered to include a buffalo hunt and a trip to Charleston, but no longer included San Francisco. Savannah was also considered as a possible stop. In fact, the itinerary continued to change over the next months, so that regional newspapers and local officials were constantly speculating about the likelihood of a royal visit to their cities. As late as January 1872, the grand duke's guardian, Admiral Constantin Possiet, advised against going to Charleston and Savannah since the railroads were still in such terrible condition after the war.[2]

This uncertainty and confusion did not dissuade some individuals from moving forward with special plans for the grand duke. Albert Bierstadt, the famous painter of American western landscapes, had heard about both the upcoming trip and the young Russian's desire to see a buffalo hunt, so he contacted General William Tecumseh Sherman to suggest such an event and encouraged the general himself to accompany the special visitor. Bierstadt also wrote Secretary of War William Belknap, as well as General Philip Sheridan, who had just organized a hunt for James Gordon Bennett, the well-known publisher and editor of the *New York Herald*. The artist then volunteered his services for the grand duke's reception in New York and served on several committees there, including the general reception committee.[3] There would be no national committee of welcome. Outside of the buffalo hunt, which was a group effort on the part of the federal government and certain motivated individuals, the grand duke's reception in each city was a local affair, organized and executed by local officials and citizens.

Planning for the grand duke's reception was one thing, but paying for it all was another, and there seems to have been some concern among the general public about who would foot the bill for the royal traveler and his accommodations. This issue would receive much discussion and some heated debate in many cities where citizens questioned the idea of a republican nation using municipal funds to host the representative of an absolute monarchy. When the legislature in Jackson, Mississippi reportedly passed a resolution to invite the grand duke, the *Hinds County Gazette* declared that the cost of a reception for Alexis should be borne by the members of the legislature who wanted him to come, not by the "empty pockets of the tax-payers." These debates over financial obligations often significantly delayed the planning of the grand duke's reception, and ultimately, the bulk of the expense was borne by the wealthiest citizens of each city, who underwrote ball and reception costs and donated the use of fine carriages and horses.[4] Fortunately, the grand duke traveled with a generous purse, allowing him to pay for his own hotel accommodations and to give an impressive number of gifts.

Some initial reception events, such as the reception of the Russian sailors, fell under the federal government's purview. According to one source, the federal government had an embarrassing track record on this count. The *New York Herald* complained that when Admiral David Farragut had visited Russia in 1867 he had spent fifteen thousand dollars of his own money to reciprocate the hospitality offered to the American officers and to sustain "the dignity of the United States," an amount for which he was never reimbursed. Underscoring that the visit of the Russian fleet was the first opportunity for the United States to show the same kindness to the Russian government and its naval officers, the *Herald* noted that there appeared to be no discussion of provisions for that purpose, and added, "Surely the authorities at Washington cannot possibly expect that the Vice Admiral or the Commandant of the Navy Yard will defray the expenses necessary to be incurred out of their comparatively wretched pay."[5]

There were also issues of protocol to consider. In one of the many tense conversations between Catacazy and Fish, Catacazy observed that the habit in Russia and in Europe was for an officer to be appointed as a representative of the government to receive and attend the grand duke. Catacazy suggested that the same honor be accorded Alexis. Catacazy also noted that, when the Prince of Wales came to visit in 1860, he was received and stayed at the White House. Fish replied that the Prince of Wales was the heir to the throne and, since the grand duke was not, he could not be treated in the same manner. Fish similarly rejected Catacazy's suggestion of an appointed officer. In fact, a similar issue of protocol had arisen the year before when Prince Arthur of England, the son of Queen Victoria, had visited the United States. President Ulysses Grant did not understand why he should be expected to pay respect to a child, particularly one who was not heir to the throne, and there had been much debate and discussion about how the prince should be received. Eventually, a compromise had been reached whereby Grant and Fish received Prince Arthur on their own terms at the White House and the Grants attended the ball for the prince only after the prince had greeted them outside their carriage. Given this wrangling over the reception of Prince Arthur, it should have come as no surprise to anyone that President Grant would be no more inclined to pay homage to the Grand Duke Alexis than to any other royal child. Fish summed it up rather succinctly: "while we have adopted many European conventionalities, we have not adopted all, & especially not those which are mere deference to birth, or rank."[6]

⸻ ◆ ⸻

Alexander II had several reasons to send his son on a long journey in 1871. The grand duke's love affair with Alexandra Zhukovskaya was certainly one reason. Zhukovskaya was a member of the nobility, the daughter of a famous poet, but an unsuitable choice for a grand duke who was expected to marry into another royal family. The tsar hoped that an extended period away from home would squelch his son's problematic romance. But the trip also had a larger significance; it was a good-will tour designed to strengthen and secure good relations between the United States and Russia. Despite their dissimilar historical development and political systems, for much of the nineteenth century the United States and Russia were on fairly good terms and shared certain commonalities that served to reinforce that sense of friendship. During the Civil War, Russia had supported the North; now that the United States was reunited, Alexander understood the need for a newly defined relationship.

This relationship seemed constantly in danger. First, there were the persistent claims of Captain Benjamin Perkins, a merchant marine who declared that Russian agents had initiated and then defaulted on contracts with him for powder and guns during the Crimean War. The case dragged on for years, and in 1867 his descendants tried to extract their losses from the U.S. payment for Alaska. This tension was only made worse by the bad behavior of the Russian ambassador, Constantin Catacazy, whom American officials described as odious and dishonest. His insulting tirades toward Secretary of State Fish and President Grant, and his refusal to respect the rules of diplomatic protocol and confidentiality, resulted in a request for his removal only months before the grand duke's expected arrival. So serious was the matter that Alexis's visit was almost cancelled. Once the grand duke had arrived, there were still complications. In many cities, officials questioned the wisdom of spending precious treasury dollars on Alexis's reception while, in other places, German and Polish Americans opposed Alexis's visit on political grounds. In New York, there was even a rumored assassination plot by Polish nationals, a threat taken so seriously that government officials hired Pinkerton's Detective Agency to investigate and provide bodyguards for the remainder of the trip.

Despite these challenges, the visit of the tsar's son to America was hailed a great success by everyone involved. Alexis was hosted and toasted wherever he appeared, the honored guest at dinners, balls, and special theater performances. His visit also coincided with several key events in American history. He toured Chicago within weeks of the Great Fire and hunted buffalo with Custer and Buffalo Bill Cody, only a few years before the final decimation of the great herds. In New Orleans, he was present when the Krewe of Rex parade first rolled through the city streets on Mardi Gras day. He visited New York as the first tower of the Brooklyn Bridge began to rise above the East River and the political ring of Boss Tweed began to fall. He admired the enormous underground caverns of Mammoth Cave and experienced the majestic wonder of Niagara Falls. In addition to his famous hunting guides, Alexis met other well-known Americans during his travels: Samuel Morse, the father of the telegraph;

Henry Wadsworth Longfellow, the poet; Cyrus Field, the main figure behind the transatlantic cable; Horace Greeley, the famous newspaperman and proponent of western expansion; Joseph Pulitzer, the newspaper publisher; and General George Meade, the hero of Gettysburg. Oliver Wendell Holmes wrote and read a poem for the grand duke, and Mathew Brady photographed him, as did Brady's chief rival, Jeremiah Gurney. He received many gifts during his travels and bestowed even more, and the public came out in droves to see him along rail lines, at train depots, and at events in the cities, waving handkerchiefs and climbing on rooftops and lampposts to get a better view. The press followed his every move and reported on what he wore, drank, and ate, how he danced and with whom, while businesses used his name in their advertising and offered new products with a Russian flavor. He was one of America's first celebrities, and his being a member of the Russian royal family made him all the more interesting and exotic. Not surprisingly, the success of Alexis's trip was viewed by many as a barometer of Russian-American relations.

The visit of Grand Duke Alexis in the winter of 1871–72 can be seen as a critical juncture in this narrative of Russian-American diplomacy. It was a chance to smooth over the rough spots and remind both countries of past and continued support and friendship. The visit was ripe with opportunity, and the fact that the guest of honor was the tsar's son made the stakes higher and the potential payoff bigger. Exchanging pleasantries with naval squadrons was one thing, but being charged with the care and entertainment of a royal child was another. Alexander's choice to send his son to the United States also indicated to many that the goal of the visit must be an important one. Consequently, the American press was deep in speculation. It was widely rumored that the visit was intended to find the young duke a bride. The *Brooklyn Daily Eagle* speculated that, "the politic Czar having shown so strong a disposition to cultivate good feeling with the United States, may regard a matrimonial alliance between a member of his family and some fair daughter of America a good way to secure the good will of the American people." The most prevalent rumor, however, was that Alexis was coming to cement a defensive and offensive alliance between the two nations, though the failure of the grand duke to visit Washington a second time led most people to dismiss that idea.[7]

The story of the grand duke's trip is more than just a tale of forbidden love, political intrigue, and colorful characters. It occurred at a fascinating and dynamic period in history. The year 1871 began with the Prussian victory in Paris, the collapse of the French Second Empire, and the declaration of a unified Germany. It was the year that Orville Wright, Stephen Crane, Marcel Proust, and the Russian "mad monk" Grigorii Rasputin were born. Mormon leader Brigham Young was arrested for polygamy, while the outlaw Jesse James remained at large. The journalist Henry Stanley set off on his famous expedition to Africa to find the missing Scottish missionary David Livingstone, and the doomed *Polaris* expedition set out to explore the Arctic. In 1871, P. T. Barnum established his "Grand Travelling Museum, Menagerie, Caravan and Hippodrome," a big touring circus with human and animal performers, and Heinrich Schliemann obtained a permit to excavate the ruins of Troy. The National Rifle Association was incorporated in New York City, and the Ku Klux Klan trials began in Federal District Court in South Carolina. In the world of art, James Whistler created his famous *Arrangement in Grey and Black: The Artist's Mother,* and Vasilii Vereshchagin painted his poignant battle scene, *The Apotheosis of War.* Lewis Carroll published *Through the Looking-Glass,* and Charles Darwin's *The Descent of Man* appeared, as well. In Fort Wayne, Indiana, Americans saw the first professional baseball game.

The year 1872 would be equally memorable. The city of Boston was ravaged by fire and smallpox, and Mount Vesuvius, the same volcano that had destroyed Pompeii in the first century, erupted again, the eighth major eruption of the nineteenth century. Roald Amundsen, the discoverer of the South Pole, was born, as was future president Calvin Coolidge, artist Piet Mondrian, ballet director Sergei Diaghilev, and the last Russian empress, Alexandra. The Metropolitan Museum of Art opened its doors in New York City, Arbor Day was celebrated for the first time in Nebraska, and President Grant and Congress created Yellowstone National Park. In Louisiana, Pinckney Benton Stewart Pinchback became the first black governor to take office in the United States, while Victoria Woodhull became the first woman to run for president of the United States and Susan B. Anthony was arrested and fined one hundred dollars for voting in that election. Claude Monet painted *Impression, Sunrise,* from which the term "Impressionism" was coined by a decidedly unimpressed art critic. Mark Twain published *Roughing It,* and one of Leo Tolstoy's neighbors threw herself under a train, inspiring the denouement of his spectacular novel *Anna Karenina*.

More narrowly, the grand duke's visit coincided with significant developments and events in the late nineteenth century, both in the United States and Russia. Alexis's grand tour coincided with a period of recovery and change in America, on the cusp of its Gilded Age. While the South bridled under the conditions of Reconstruction, the North also struggled to recover from the effects of the long and bloody war. At the same time, America was experiencing revolutions in communications and transportation, along with the rise of big cities and the problems of urbanization. The growth of big businesses and the increasing separation between economic classes strained the social fabric, as well. On the international scene, the United States was embroiled in conflict over the possible annexation of Santo Domingo and engaged in a battle of wills with England over the *Alabama* Claims, unsettled disputes from the Civil War that charged England with failure to enforce British neutrality. Though both situations were resolved peacefully, the possibility of war had seemed real at various points. Russia also faced a series of challenges at the end of the nineteenth century. In the decade before Alexis's visit, his father, Alexander II, had enacted a series of wide-ranging legal and administrative reforms, including the abolition of serfdom in 1861. Despite these reforms—which many considered too little, too late—the monarchy was plagued by an emerging revolutionary movement that continued to grow more radical and violent. It was, in fact, Tsar Alexander II who would become the focus of the revolutionaries' anger; in 1881, ten years after Alexis's visit, Alexander was assassinated, the victim of a terrorist's bomb. The international landscape was equally dangerous for Russia. The last decades of the nineteenth century saw the birth of new alliances and new rivalries for all the powers of Europe. In particular, Russia faced a Polish uprising, the specter of a newly unified Germany, and a hostile and often violent relationship with the Ottoman Empire. To assert itself in Europe and elsewhere, in 1870 Russia had renounced the Black Sea clause that prohibited Russian war ships in that body of water. The renunciation caused alarm in Europe and America, the greatest concern being a possible war between England and Russia. While the rumors that Alexander was seeking an alliance with the United States were probably untrue, the tsar certainly recognized that the Russian-American friendship was one worth retaining.[8]

Alexis was not the first foreigner of prominence to visit the United States in the nineteenth century, nor was he the only one to garner the attention of the American media and public. Charles Dickens visited twice, in 1842 and again in 1867–68, and while the first visit had been marred by Dickens's own disappointment with America and the bitter relationship that developed between him and the American press, he was warmly and enthusiastically welcomed during both visits as "The Literary Guest of the Nation." In 1851–52, the Hungarian revolutionary Louis Kossuth toured a number of cities over a three-month period, coming to America directly from his confinement in a Turkish prison where he had been locked away for his revolutionary activity in Europe. Kossuth began in New York and continued through several other major cities, traveling as far west as St. Louis and as far south as Louisville. When the Prince of Wales visited in 1860, he also toured many of America's major cities and was enthusiastically received with enormous crowds and balls, banquets, and special performances.[9]

Perhaps the foreign visit that offers the greatest opportunity for comparison, however, is that of the Marquis de Lafayette in 1824–25. Lafayette had participated in the American Revolution, moved by his belief in the ideas of freedom and liberty. Subsequently, he would serve as one of the founding fathers of the French Revolution, as well, but it was his role in America's war of independence that earned him a place in American history and popular culture. When Lafayette returned for a lengthy visit nearly fifty years later, he was enthusiastically welcomed as the honored guest at many balls, dinners, and parades. New biographies of the revolutionary hero appeared in the United States, as did souvenir items bearing his image. Yet even amid this frenzy of sentimental affection there were complaints about excessive idolatry and behavior inconsistent with republican values. Some observers even argued that those in big cities, particularly in the East, were more prone to the inappropriate displays.[10]

The visit of Lafayette created an opportunity for Americans to engage in a bit of critical self-examination; it served as a lens through which to discuss the success (or lack thereof) of the new republic and the idea of America's mission to spread republican values elsewhere. Already by the 1820s, some Americans worried that the country was drifting away from the core values on which the nation had been built, succumbing instead to the powerful pull of factionalism, sectionalism, and extreme individualism. Lafayette was a reminder of America's struggle and a symbol of the revolution, liberty, and unity. His presence seemed to temporarily bolster nationalism and cohesiveness as Americans engaged in public celebrations of one of the last living heroes of that era. This revival of republican values was reassuring for those at home, but could also be seen as a message to the monarchs of Europe about the success of a free and democratic society.[11]

The American tour of Grand Duke Alexis nearly fifty years later shares some characteristics with the celebrated visit of the French revolutionary. Alexis was also the honored guest at a variety of public gatherings, some of which included people of various walks of life, and he was also the center of press attention in many cities. His image and name were used for promotion and profit. Alexis's visit certainly raised concerns about appropriate behavior and the meaning of republican values, and the ways in which American behavior would be interpreted abroad. But the similarities largely end there. While Americans in 1824–25 worried about increasing divisiveness and searched for reassuring feelings of unity in the public celebrations over Lafayette, the soul searching of Americans in 1871–72 was of a different sort. These Americans were also searching for signs of unity, but in the form of reunification after a bloody and psychologically devastating civil war. The hosts of Lafayette feared factionalism and sectionalism; the hosts of Alexis had survived it. Their angst over how to host a grand duke and what all of it meant for the American national identity had a raw edge, the lingering wound of the previous decade. In this sense, the visits of Lafayette and Alexis are like bookends on the shelf of nineteenth-century American history, the one occurring at the beginning of a period of dangerous division, the other occurring at the end. Though both visits encouraged self-examination and a reassessment of republican values, the catalyst and the result of that examination would be different.

Moreover, while Americans in the 1820s could view Lafayette as a symbol of their own revolution, the central event of American history to that point, Alexis did not have that distinction. He was the son of the tsar, a grand duke, but not the heir to the throne. He represented his father, and it was well understood that his visit served a diplomatic purpose, but he was no hero and had no place in the American story. American fascination with him necessarily arose from different origins, particularly an infatuation with royalty and celebrity. Consequently, though there was no real discussion about whether Lafayette was worthy of public celebration, there were many debates about whether Alexis should be the center of such attention.

The visit of Alexis was unique in other ways. The grand duke was the first Russian of any prominence and the first member of the Romanov dynasty to visit the United States. Moreover, the widely held and often repeated belief that Russia had demonstrated friendship and support in America's darkest hour gave the visit even greater weight and importance. Private citizens and government officials at all levels repeatedly noted this friendship in their welcome speeches and highlighted the similarities between the two countries and their leaders, both of whom had taken the bold step of dismantling an economic system that was dependent on human bondage. This perception that Russia and America shared a special bond imbued the royal visit with a larger significance, and there was a sense among American officials that the success of Alexis's tour could determine the course of the Russian-American relationship. Among the general public, it seems fair to assume that most people cared little about the political significance of the visit and more about the opportunity to catch a glimpse of this celebrity, attend a fancy ball, or make a quick buck. Quite simply, the visit of a handsome, young Russian duke was exciting and fun, a memorable event that provided an excuse for celebratory public gatherings, voyeuristic curiosity, and corny humor.

But in addition to bad puns about the grand duke "Russian" off and poems that rhymed "Alexis" with "Texas," the Russian royal visit was significant in other ways. As Alexis made his way through the United States, each city claimed to have given him the best reception, the most elegant ball, the tastiest dinner, the most interesting city tours, and the prettiest dancing partners. However, while Americans were wondering what Alexis thought of them, deconstructing his every smile and yawn, and making wild speculations about his mood and impressions, they were also revealing a great deal about themselves. The discussions and comments in newspapers, state legislatures, city councils, and even private letters illustrate that Americans in the early 1870s were still wrestling with questions of national identity and regional tensions, and the visit of Grand Duke Alexis offered the perfect mirror in which to reflect these issues. At the same time, the Russian tour illuminated questions and developments that were just emerging on the national stage.

At the time of Alexis's arrival, the United States was experiencing the effects of the Industrial Revolution and was on the cusp of an era that would be characterized by a population boom and the dramatic growth of big cities. Though much of the grand duke's time in the United States was consumed with ceremonial balls and dinners, there were also educational and trade dimensions. As he traveled from city to city, officials showed Alexis local businesses, industrial facilities, and schools, usually as a scheduled part of the tour, but often enough, it was Alexis himself who inquired about these things and asked to learn more about American society and industry. In the spirit of municipal boosterism, local politicians and businessmen welcomed the chance to show off their city's most impressive features and, in some instances, held hope for future trade with Russia. Along these lines, Alexis toured the naval facilities in New York, Philadelphia, Annapolis, and Charlestown, and stopped at the Smith and Wesson factory in Springfield, Massachusetts. In Buffalo and Milwaukee, he visited grain elevators, in Cleveland he saw the Bessemer Steel Works, and in Chicago he viewed the inner workings of a pork-packing factory. In Memphis he inquired about the cotton industry and toured a state-of-the-art penal facility. This atmosphere of competition often brought to the surface old rivalries between cities, battling for cultural, economic, or political superiority. Lingering tensions between North and South bubbled to the surface, as well, articulated most clearly by southern leaders who seemed eager to prove that they too could host royalty in the appropriate manner and style.

The Russian royal visit also provided the opportunity for citizens to discuss and debate issues on the local and national level. In contemplating how a foreign guest, a member of a royal family no less, would view and interpret American politics and life, Americans were forced to look at themselves through new eyes, and what they saw was not always the best image. In some cases, this self-reflection led individuals to push local agendas or criticize local politics; in other cases, it highlighted problems on the national level, including the decline of the buffalo herds, the persistence of racism, the emerging political and cultural power of ethnic minorities, and corruption in national politics. Alexis's visit invoked comparisons between American politicians and the American political system with the autocratic government of Russia. The comparisons were not always favorable. In more than one city, President Grant was called a tyrant and local political leaders were judged worthy of exile to Siberia.

The appearance of the tsar's son similarly prompted many Americans to contemplate questions of national identity. In many places, there were lengthy and heated discussions about the use of public funds to host a member of a royal family, and many people lamented the fawning over the grand duke. Many noted the irony of a republican nation falling over itself to impress the representative of an old-world monarchy. Others, however, were happy to receive him, and there were many stories of pressing, eager crowds and competition for ball and banquet tickets. In the midst of these debates there was also the recognition that the visit of the tsar's son was being observed by other nations, as well. While some countries mocked America's effusive displays of welcome, they also understood its role in the Russian-American relationship. Finally, the grand duke's visit highlighted characteristics of late-nineteenth-century America that might not have been apparent at the time—for example, the growth of commercialism, the rise of a cult of celebrity, and the persistence of a secondary role for women in society. In several cities, young women were handpicked as dinner or traveling companions for the grand duke and his entourage. When women were not being displayed as ornaments or dancing partners, however, they were of little use to reception planners. A woman in Milwaukee, for example, questioned why women had been excluded from two separate banquets in that city.[12] At a time when the suffragist movement appeared regularly in the news and Victoria Woodhull attempted a run for the presidency, this was a timely question.

The Russian visit also has been remembered and misremembered in a variety of ways. There have been several museum exhibits commemorating the visit, and the Peabody Hotel in Memphis once recreated the eleven-course dinner given there for the grand duke in 1872. A tiny town in Nebraska for ten years held an annual event at the buffalo-hunt campsite called the Grand Duke Alexis Rendezvous that featured "living historians" portraying the characters of Alexis, Custer, Cody, and Philip Sheridan. In New Orleans, there is a Mardi Gras social club called the Krewe of Alexis, and for years an old, family bakery sold a special "Russian Cake" each year that was said to have originated with the grand duke's visit. On the other hand, Alexis's central place in the popular history of Mardi Gras, and the misperceptions about his visit there, demonstrate the ways that myths and popular culture can distort the writing of history. Mardi Gras legend has it that the traditional colors of Mardi Gras—purple, green, and gold—might have been selected in response to the Russian royal visit and that the theme song of the oldest club, Rex, may have been chosen to playfully mock the grand duke, who was rumored to have fallen in love with a traveling British burlesque performer whose show included the song. Though challenged in a variety of sources, the romantic legend that Alexis inspired the formation of the Krewe of Rex, its colors, and its theme song persists and appears in travel guides and newspaper articles every year during carnival season.

The most lasting result of Alexis's grand tour of the United States, however, was its role in stimulating American public interest in Russia. As the first Russian celebrity to travel through the nation, Alexis drew crowds wherever he went, and the detailed press coverage of his every move meant that average Americans, not just those in positions of power, could hope to catch a glimpse of him and learn about what he wore and with whom he danced in each city. The press satisfied and stimulated this curiosity about Russia with biographies of the royal family and lengthy essays on Russian geography, history, climate, and the national traits of her people. Meanwhile, some of the illustrated papers of the day, such as *Harper's Weekly* and *Frank Leslie's Illustrated,* printed detailed engravings of Russian political figures and scenes of Russian life. Although Russian-American diplomatic relations would cool considerably over the next decades, the American public's interest in Russian literature, art, music, and ballet would grow and continue long into the next century, overcoming the restrictions of politics and opposing ideologies. Considering the intense struggle over ideology and spheres of influence that would develop between these two nations in the twentieth century, the visit of Grand Duke Alexis in 1871–72 is a unique moment in the history of the Russian-American relationship when, for the most part, in public and official circles there was a conscious choice to focus on shared interests and mutual support instead of diplomatic conflict and potential differences. As a consequence, Alexis's visit would be fondly remembered by all those who participated in it and continues to be celebrated over a century later.

———————◆———————

Although most members of the Romanov family were faithful diary keepers, Alexis seems not to have developed this habit or, possibly, his diaries have been lost or destroyed. There are two extant diaries by Alexis, neither of which covers the period during which he traveled to the United States. Periodic rumors claiming the discovery of such a diary have so far proved false. Consequently, we have very little information about Alexis's views on America or his American travels with the exception of one brief letter he wrote to his mother. Luckily, there are other sources, including the notes kept by his tutor, guardian, and travel companion, Admiral Constantin Possiet. These notes include not only the details of the trip and observations about America, but also comments on the grand duke's mood and the admiral's fear that his charge would attempt to rendezvous with his forbidden love somewhere along their route. Finally, the grand duke's daily activities, where he slept and what he ate, were described in American and Canadian, and to a lesser extent, Russian newspapers. These sources, along with the surviving menus, invitations, and train schedules, proved invaluable in reconstructing his detailed movements in and between cities.

For the ease of the American reader, I have chosen to use the most common English spelling for the names of Alexis, Possiet, Catacazy, and several others who are mentioned repeatedly in the text. The same holds true for the names of Russia's leaders, such as Catherine the Great and Nicholas II, who are well known in the West. For some of Alexis's other family members, friends, and lovers, I have chosen to use the modern transliterated versions of the Russian names. I have also chosen to use the word "Indian" throughout the text. Although this word has fallen out of favor, it was the term used in the nineteenth century to describe the first settlers of North America and the term that appears in all the primary sources. Finally, I am using the term "buffalo" instead of "bison." Although the animal that resides in North America is actually the bison, the word "buffalo" was, and is, commonly used, and Alexis's famous hunt is always referred to as the "buffalo hunt." For that reason, I have chosen to use the popular, if technically incorrect, name to describe those large, woolly animals that Alexis, Custer, and Buffalo Bill hunted on the plains.

1

BORN IN THE SHADOW OF AN IMPERIAL CROWN

I wonder who he's walking with and flirting on the deck;
Oh give me just one chance at her, I'll break her little neck;

. . .

Alas! the day the news arrived this gallant duke would come;
'Twere better far for us poor girls he had remained at home.

. . .

They say he's handsome, graceful, too, and loves the ladies flair.
I'd give my new piano for a handful of his hair.

—*Detroit Free Press,* November 17, 1871

ALEXIS ALEXANDROVICH ROMANOV was a member of the Romanov dynasty, which had ruled Russia since 1613 and had produced such leaders as Peter the Great (who reigned 1689–1725) and, through marriage, Catherine the Great (1762–96). Alexis's grandfather was Nicholas I (1825–55), the grandson of Catherine the Great, who ruled Russia with a conservative program rooted in the principles of orthodoxy, autocracy, and nationality. His father was Alexander II (1855–81), the tsar who would reform Russia, liberate her serfs, and then die at the hands of terrorists. His brother would become Alexander III (1881–94), a reactionary monarch who, after the assassination of his father, made his primary goals the repression of revolutionary groups and the preservation of order. Alexis's other siblings all married into the preeminent royal families of Europe, including those of Great Britain, the German states, and Greece. His nephew, Nicholas II (1894–1917), would be the last tsar of Russia, murdered with his family by the Bolsheviks in the summer of 1918.

Alexis was born in St. Petersburg on the morning of January 14, 1850, in the Winter Palace, the traditional family home of the imperial family since the

1700s, now known as the Hermitage. Alexis was the fifth child to be born to Maria Alexandrovna and the Tsarevich Alexander Nikolaevich, the future Alexander II. As the fourth son, Alexis was never expected to be in line for the throne, but his birth was nonetheless cause for celebration. Alexis's imminent arrival was also a cause for concern, however. Only months earlier, on June 16, the royal couple had lost their first child, eight-year-old Alexandra, to scarlet fever. The parents took their daughter's death hard, and Maria Alexandrovna, in particular, already pregnant with Alexis, had suffered terribly. Her doctor and family worried about how grief had undermined her health and weakened her at a time when she needed her strength. Soon after Alexandra's death the family faced another loss, when Tsarevich Alexander's favorite uncle, Grand Duke Mikhail Pavlovich, died in September 1850. When Maria Alexandrovna went into labor, then, the family was still deep in mourning and anxious about the well-being of the weakened and still grieving mother. These concerns only intensified when the baby arrived: Alexis was very weak, and it appeared that he might not survive. For more than an hour, family and friends worried about the fate of the baby until finally the danger passed and the tiny grand duke rallied. Everyone heaved a sigh of relief when the tsar appeared with his new son in his arms.[1]

The grand duke's birth triggered a series of celebrations and proclamations. As was tradition, the imperial family held a mass in the large cathedral of the Winter Palace, and Tsar Nicholas I, the proud grandfather, issued a manifesto which was to be distributed throughout the empire announcing the royal arrival. In Moscow, cathedral bells throughout the city pealed in celebration, as did those of the centuries-old Ivan the Great Bell Tower in the Kremlin. The tsar also ordered an annual stipend of fifty thousand rubles to be released from the treasury for the maintenance of the new grand duke, and the baby's father bestowed generous gifts on the members of the household staff and sent three thousand rubles each to the governor general of Moscow and St. Petersburg for the care of the poor. Three weeks later, the tsar and many other relatives and high officials gathered in the cathedral of the Winter Palace for the christening ceremony of the newest grand duke, initiated by the echoing booms of the cannons at the Peter and Paul Fortress. Later in the afternoon, the marble hall of the Winter Palace was the setting of an elaborate luncheon that included vocal and instrumental music, and toasts to the health of the newborn. That evening, the city of St. Petersburg glowed with illumination.

The celebratory atmosphere was sustained by the birth of another grand duke one month later. When Grand Duke Constantin Nikolaevich and his wife had their first son and named him Nicholas, after his grandfather, the tsar ordered that two icons should be prepared in honor of his new grandsons, one of St. Alexis and one of St. Nicholas, both to be adorned in silver and gold in the traditional fashion.[2]

As a child, Alexis spent most of his time in the care of women, tended by nannies and governesses, usually from England and France. Alexis and his brothers also had Russian tutors to teach them their prayers and the fundamentals of reading and writing. During most of the year, the children occupied their own section of the Winter Palace, though they visited their parents daily, and in the summer, the family moved to the spectacular baroque Catherine Palace in Tsarskoe Selo. Literally "tsar's village," Tsarskoe Selo had been the royal family's country residence and a popular summer retreat for the upper nobility since the previous century. Here the young boys played outdoors, hunted small birds, gathered mushrooms, and rode horses. One of their favorite outdoor games was skittles, a lawn game similar to bowling, but they also learned to play croquet, and when the weather kept them inside, they played chess and card games. In the evenings, the children usually spent time with their mother. The young grand dukes did have male influences as well. A male instructor taught the boys how to stand at attention, march, and hold a gun, accompanied the children on their outdoor excursions, and frequently participated in their games. When Tsar Nicholas and his wife were in Tsarskoe Selo, they occupied the nearby Alexander Palace, which allowed the tsar to visit his grandsons often, taking them on walks through the palace grounds.[3]

Alexis was a bit sickly as a toddler, but by the time he reached the age of four or five his health seemed to improve. Early photos of him show a boy with a sweet face, light hair, and large eyes. From the time he was very small, Alexis exhibited a guilelessness and a preference for honesty and transparency, characteristics that, while admirable, interfered with his familial duties in early adulthood. One contemporary recalled that, while visiting the new empress in July 1855, shortly after Nicholas I had died, she was pleased to see the four little grand dukes, Nicholas, Alexander, Vladimir, and five-year-old Alexis. When the empress asked the boys for an account of their lessons, Alexis honestly admitted that he had not done well. His mother looked upon him sternly, expressing her disappointment, and the small boy lowered his head and his eyes filled with tears.[4]

Between the ages of seven and nine, many things changed for Alexis. At the age of seven, he moved from the care of female nannies and governesses to male teachers and joined his older brothers in a more demanding curriculum. His daily lessons now included a wide range of subjects: French, German, English, and Russian; history and geography; mathematics; penmanship and drawing; horseback riding and gymnastics; religious studies; and military instruction. The boys' daily schedule also incorporated visits to their parents. Alexis's life changed in one other significant way; it was during this period that Constantin Nikolaevich Possiet became the grand duke's guardian. Possiet was descended from a French noble family who had come to Russia during the time of Peter the Great. In 1858, Possiet assumed the position of governor to Alexis, though in reality, his duties went far beyond what we might interpret from his title. One of his primary responsibilities was to select teachers for the grand duke and to establish a program of instruction, meeting with the teachers on a monthly basis to give them plans and lessons. Possiet was also charged, however, with the much more difficult job of instilling his pupil with the discipline and conduct expected of a grand duke. This would prove to be the most challenging part of his job.[5]

Alexis was an average but rather lazy student, and throughout the early years of his tutelage Possiet repeatedly complained to the boy's parents about his underperformance. In September 1861, when Alexis was eleven years old, his father wrote him that, while he was glad to hear that Possiet was generally happy with his conduct, he would like Alexis to show more diligence in his studies. Several months later, the tsar scolded Alexis for giving Possiet problems and noted how much this news saddened him and his wife. Alexis's behavior and study habits were an ongoing topic of correspondence, however. In the fall of 1864, when Alexis was nearing the age of fifteen, his father stressed that they wanted to see continual, not occasional, diligence and reminded him of the promise he had made, presumably a promise to work harder and more seriously. It was a promise that would come up again and again. In June 1866, Alexander reminded Alexis of the promise and yet, later that summer, Possiet wrote in his diary that Alexis was lazy and that he had caught the sixteen-year-old smoking in the water closet. Despite his title and privileged upbringing,

Alexis was like any other teenager; when scolded for bad behavior, Possiet reported that he asked forgiveness but never seemed resolute about changing his ways. We should not judge Alexis too harshly, however. Sources from his father's childhood indicate that Tsar Alexander II was also frequently in trouble with his tutors and parents for laziness and poor performance in his studies.[6]

One significant portion of Alexis's education and upbringing, of course, was his military training. It was traditional among the nobility and imperial family to register newborn males for positions in elite military units; consequently, on the day of his birth, Alexis became chief of the Imperial Guards Moscow Regiment and a member of the Preobrazhensky and Egersky guards regiments. Alexis was also assigned to the navy, the only one of Alexander II's sons to be designated for a naval career at birth. Even in early childhood Alexis began to learn some of the fundamental skills of a military life such as marching, standing at attention, and holding a gun. By the age of seven, some type of military instruction became part of the boy's daily curriculum and, in the summer of 1860, when Alexis was only ten, he began his naval training on one of the imperial yachts, the *Shtandart*. Two year later, Possiet arranged Alexis's schedule so that he dedicated more time to naval training and less time to traditional lessons; art and music were relegated to free time only. In fact, the young grand duke began to spend more and more time on the sea. Initially, Possiet and his pupil stayed relatively close to home, venturing out to the Aland Islands in the Gulf of Finland and to the Gulf of Bothnia. But after a year or so, they began to travel greater distances, to the Gulf of Riga and the Baltic Sea, visiting Revel (Tallinn, Estonia) and Libau (Liepaja, Latvia) where Alexis saw a small home once occupied by Peter the Great (during his journey to Western Europe). During these travels, Alexis wrote many letters to his parents, describing his impressions. In the summer and early fall of 1867, for example, the grand duke sent telegrams to his mother from Malta, Marseilles, Salonique, Cadiz, Odessa, and Kiev. Alexis also spent several days in Constantinople and met the sultan and the patriarch of the Orthodox Church there. In 1868, Alexis traveled along the Volga to Uglich, Rybinsk, Astrakhan, and other cities, the Caspian Sea and Baku, and encountered many of the diverse nationalities in his father's empire, including Chechens, Tatars, Jews, and the Ingush.[7]

These trips were not without peril. Once, while sailing on Lake Onega, a large lake to the east of St. Petersburg, Alexis saved a young noble and his sister after their boat had capsized. For this, Alexis received a medal for courage from his father which he proudly wore during ceremonial events. The American press made much of this story during the grand duke's visit several years later as proof of his courage.[8] This was not Alexis's only brush with danger. In 1868, while serving as the head officer of the watch on the frigate *Alexander Nevsky,* the young grand duke had a harrowing experience at sea. The grand duke had been to Piraeus to participate in the festivities surrounding the marriage of his first cousin Grand Duchess Olga Konstantinovna and the Greek King George I. After sailing through the Mediterranean Sea, the Atlantic Ocean, and the North Sea, the frigate headed back toward Kronstadt; but on the night of September 25, it encountered fog and heavy rain. Bad weather and navigational errors resulted in disaster. The frigate ran aground on the isthmus between the Danish towns of Harboore and Thyboron, and in the ensuing attempts to get to shore two officers and four sailors drowned. By morning, the weather had cleared and the remaining men were able to safely reach the shore. Throughout this ordeal, Alexis refused to abandon the ship until Possiet expressly ordered him to do so. Years later, the grand duke's uncle would recall that Alexis frequently retold the tale of that frightening night, slamming his fist on the table with dramatic affect at the denouement.[9]

Not everyone recalled the event with fondness, however. A naval court in St. Petersburg conducted an investigation in early 1869 and found Admiral Possiet guilty of mismanagement and neglect and recommended a public reprimand. Two other officers received short sentences in jail. According to the correspondent for the *London Daily News,* the whole trial was a farce and the two officers were simply scapegoats for the real culprit, Possiet. The admiral, however, had a strong advocate on his side in the person of Grand Duke Alexis who, along with Tsar Alexander, ensured that he got off lightly.[10]

As Alexis made his way from childhood to adulthood, his immediate family experienced a decade of challenges, hardships, and devastating losses. In 1860, Alexis's eldest brother, Nicholas, the heir to the throne, fell from a horse while riding at Tsarskoe Selo and seriously injured his back. Over the next few years, his injury continued to give him pain, and in November 1863 one of the royal tutors noted that Nicholas could barely walk. Nonetheless, in April 1864, it was decided to send Nicholas on a trip to various cities in Europe, possibly for curative reasons since initially his illness was believed to be rheumatism. By the end of that year, however, his condition had worsened and he was in terrible pain, despite assorted treatments and consultations with various doctors. Throughout his illness, Nicholas continued to correspond with his brothers—for example, writing to Alexis from Florence, wishing him a happy birthday and complaining that he was under lock and key, one day better, one day worse. However, the tsarevich's illness continued to intensify, the pain in his back accompanied by headaches, forgetfulness, and vomiting. He died in Nice on April 12; the autopsy determined he had suffered from meningitis.[11] The royal family was devastated.

The death of the tsarevich raised another problem for the royal family. Nicholas had been engaged to marry Princess Dagmar of Denmark, and there is some indication that, on his death bed, he expressed a desire for his brother, Alexander, to marry his fiancée. This was problematic since at the time Alexander was in love with Maria Meshcherskaya, a maid at the court of his mother, the empress. The affair with Meshcherskaya was so intense that Alexander had apparently been prepared to renounce his right to the throne in order to marry her. It was a difficult pill to swallow, but in the face of his brother's death and his new role as heir to the throne, Alexander accepted his responsibility and married Dagmar, who took the Russian name Maria Fedorovna. For Alexis, his brother's marriage brought him not only a sister-in-law, but a dear friend. Alexis and "Minni," as Maria Fedorovana was called by family, remained fast friends to the end, and Minni was one of his strongest defenders in subsequent years when his reputation was less than sterling.[12]

Even as the tsar and his family suffered through these personal tragedies, the wheels of government continued to turn. When Alexander II inherited the throne in 1855, Russia was embroiled in the Crimean War, a conflict that made it glaringly obvious that Russia's military needed reform. The rank-and-file soldiers of the army were serfs, drafted into service despite often being in poor health, untrained, and usually illiterate. Thus, Russia's loss in the Crimean War could be seen as a reflection of her failing social and economic system. In March 1856, Alexander called together representatives of the nobility in Moscow and declared that it was better to abolish serfdom from above than to wait until the serfs liberated themselves from below. Over the next five years, provincial noble committees and a central editing commission worked out the details of Russia's most ambitious reform ever. Finally, in 1861, Alexander officially abolished the institution of serfdom, the system upon which the country's agriculturally based economy had relied for centuries. In fact, the emancipation of the serfs was not the only major reform undertaken during Alexander's reign. The tsar also enacted various educational reforms, introduced more generous policies toward Russia's ethnic minorities, created institutions of self-government at both the district and provincial level in the countryside, and established the judiciary as an independent branch of the government. Finally, Alexander attempted to modernize the Russian Army, its training, maintenance, and equipment. While most of these reforms had their shortcomings, they were, nonetheless, rather remarkable given the conservatism that had predominated under Alexander's father.

In many areas, however, traditional conservatism still reigned supreme. Such was the case with Russia's relationship to the Polish part of her empire. Toward the end of the eighteenth century, Russia, Prussia, and Austria had partitioned Poland three times until she no longer existed as an independent nation. In doing so, Russia had absorbed several hundred thousand square miles of territory, gaining upwards of five million new subjects, most of whom retained their ethnic, religious, and cultural identity and continued to agitate for greater freedom and even independence. In 1830, Polish nationalists had rebelled against their foreign oppressors. Though the Russian military ultimately won out, it was not easy and the Poles were made to pay a high price for their insubordination. The Russian government replaced the Polish constitution with the Organic Statute of 1832 that made Poland an indivisible part of the Russian Empire, confiscated the estates of insurgents, closed Polish institutions of higher learning, and secularized the lands of the Catholic Church. Under Alexander II, the Poles had regained some of their earlier privileges, but in 1863, they rose up again. Though the Poles had no standing army, it still took Russian forces over a year to suppress this outburst of Polish nationalism, with the result that Poland lost what autonomy it recently had attained under Alexander, and a process of Russification was initiated, featuring the required use of the Russian language in Polish schools.

In the midst of these imperial challenges, the Russian government faced another problem, one that would affect the tsar and his family much more directly. Since the early 1800s, Russia had witnessed the growth of an enlightened and educated intelligentsia that in a variety of ways challenged traditional ideas about Russian society and autocracy. This intelligentsia changed with every generation: it grew more distant from its noble roots as its composition became more diverse, and, as a consequence, it became more radical and less inclined to believe that Russia's problems could be fixed from within the system. By the

1860s some of these radical intellectuals could be rightfully called revolution-aries, and by 1880, one of these groups in particular, the People's Will, would set its sights on eliminating the lynchpin of the entire autocratic system, the tsar himself. There had already been one attempt on the tsar's life: in 1866, an emotionally unbalanced student, Dmitry Karakozov, attempted to assassinate the emperor. Though the would-be assassin was not clearly affiliated with any particular group, this threat led the Russian government to retreat from some of its liberal policies and return to censorship and restrictions on university life and curriculum. Neither the failure of Karakozov's attempt nor the ensu-ing crackdown on revolutionary groups halted the growth of the revolutionary movement; however, in 1881, Alexander would not be as lucky as he had been fifteen years earlier. In March of that year, the People's Will would successfully explode several bombs under and near the tsar's carriage, killing him and several others.

Alexis turned twenty years old in 1870, and the event was marked with a special coming-of-age ceremony. In 1797, Paul I had introduced a Law of Succes-sion to ensure a smooth line of succession and, among other things, the law set the age of majority for the tsarevich at the age of sixteen. Subsequently, when Nicholas I's son, the future Alexander II, had been the first to reach majority under the new law, Nicholas had introduced a new ceremony in which the heir took the oath of majority. From that point forward, all grand dukes took the oath, though the age of majority for non-heirs was set at twenty. On January 2, 1870, at one o'clock, the ceremony to establish Alexis's majority took place in the Winter Palace in the presence of an assembly of the elite of Russian officialdom. Alexis took an oath of loyalty to the crown and to Russia and swore to uphold his country's laws; then he affixed his signature to the oath, which was taken away for placement in the state archive. The ceremony concluded with a 301-gun salute by the cannons in the Peter and Paul Fortress, accompanied by the pealing of cathedral bells throughout the city. Now that Alexis was considered an adult, he was entitled to an annual stipend; by royal decree, Alexis was to receive 142,857 rubles and fourteen kopecks a year in silver. Alexis's majority was also the occasion for gift-giving. The tsar gave monetary gifts to a variety of teachers, tutors, and doctors, presumably all people that the tsar must have felt had contributed to Alexis's education and development. Though Alexis was now officially an adult, Possiet remained with him as a guardian, someone to help him adjust to independence and to teach him financial responsibility.[13]

Alexis reached another important milestone around the time he turned twenty—he fell in love. The object of his affection was Alexandra Zhukovskaya, the daughter of the famous poet Vasilii Zhukovskii who had served the royal family for over two decades as a Russian instructor to the wife of Nicholas I and chief tutor and educational supervisor to the future tsar, Alexander II. After retirement in 1841, Zhukovskii had moved to Europe where he married a German woman and fathered two children, Alexandra and Paul. Zhukovskii died in 1852, when Alexandra was only ten, but the children were well provided for, taken in by the tsar's extended family and raised in Russia. When she turned sixteen, Alexandra became an attendant to Alexis's mother, Empress Maria Alexandrovna. It seems that Alexis would have met Alexandra during this period, when she was a blossoming teenage girl and he was still a little boy; but if he did meet her, it must have only been in passing or he was too young to notice her. However, in November 1864, when Alexis was nearly fifteen, Alexandra did capture his attention; Alexis wrote in his diary that month that he had met Zhukovskaya "with whom I immediately became acquainted." Several days later, he wrote of dancing with her at a ball.[14]

Over the next few years, Alexis and Alexandra encountered one another on a regular basis. Alexis mentioned Alexandra in several diary entries in 1865, noting that he was getting to know her better and he liked her very much. She impressed him as "smart, happy and natural, although not especially beautiful." By December of that year, Alexis's diary entries reveal the beginning of a close friendship. Alexis wrote that he had gone ice skating with his brother Alexander, Maria Meshcherskaya, and Zhukovskaya, and while he and Zhukovskaya had skated together they had had a very interesting conversation. Alexandra had asked him if he had ever been in love before, and he had promised to tell her immediately when he did fall in love with someone. He concluded his entry, "I will need to keep my word; what to do!" He also noted that Alexandra would now be living in the Winter Palace; this new arrangement made her very happy, for it had long been her wish, and Alexis expressed his own joy at this as well. In 1866, Alexis wrote that he saw Alexandra often at lunches, dinners, and other social events. Sometimes she went ice skating with him and a group of other young friends. In May, when Alexis left for one of his ocean journeys, Alexandra gave him a small cross to wear. Their relationship at this point was still platonic, however, for Alexis noted that Alexandra was in love with someone named Bariatinskii.[15]

Friendship grew into romance sometime over the next few years. Alexis and Alexandra met frequently at gatherings at the Anichkov Palace, the residence of Alexis's brother and heir to the throne, Alexander Alexandrovich. There they participated in family gatherings and private theater performances of various sorts and soon fell in love. According to Alexis himself, by the winter and spring of 1869, the two had established a close bond that allowed them to share their deepest thoughts and feelings. During his travels along the Volga with Alexander and Minni in the summer of 1869, Alexis kept a journal, a gift from Alexandra, in which she asked him to write his thoughts and feelings for her to read later. Alexis happily agreed, declaring that it would make him happy to do something every day for his "dear little wife." The entries from this journal are intensely emotional and romantic, the very picture of passionate, young love. On July 13, Alexis wrote that, after reading her most recent letter, he was overcome by such strong emotions that he felt he might go mad, adding that his separation from her was terrible and made him sick, not knowing if he would ever see her again in his life. Several days later, Alexis wrote about a ball he attended in one of the Volga towns and how it could not compare to the balls in St. Petersburg when he danced the mazurka with her.[16]

The Volga trip took Alexis, Alexander, and Minni through a number of towns along the river, including Simbirsk, Samara, Khvalynsk, Volsk, Saratov, and Tsaritsyn (Volgograd). In many towns, they were welcomed with the traditional salt and bread, and invited to tour schools, hospitals, and churches; there were also balls and other festivities. Occasionally, the steamship would pull to the shore to allow the travelers to stroll or hunt birds. While on board, they read, had long conversations, wrote letters or in their journals, and drank tea. On one occasion, Alexis described a somber afternoon when he and Minni reminisced about his deceased brother, Nicholas; Minni grew teary-eyed at the memory of her former fiancé. In happier moments, Alexis sang to Minni's accompaniment on the fortepiano. Alexis was known to have a beautiful voice and enjoyed singing. Though Alexis described many pleasant evenings with Alexander and Minni, he mostly complained of the hot weather, boredom, loneliness, and difficulty getting to sleep. Frequently, Alexis and Minni talked about Zhukovskaya and how nice it would be if she were with them. Alexis missed Zhukovskaya terribly, and so he enjoyed writing in his journal because during this one time each day he was free to think about her without interruption. It was almost as if they were together again.[17]

By 1870, then, Alexis was deeply involved in the affair with Zhukovskaya, and it is widely held that the two secured a secret, unauthorized marriage. Despite her noble family background and close ties to the Russian royal family, Zhukovskaya herself was not of royal blood and, consequently, was not a suitable bride for the tsar's son—thus the need for a secret marriage. Though impossible to substantiate, there has been a persistent story that says the lovers went to Italy that year and were married in an Orthodox Church there. Lack of money and Alexis's service obligations forced them to return home, where the marriage was annulled and the priest who married them was deprived of his office. Despite the lack of documentation on this event, Alexis's descendants claim that the two did indeed marry and contemporary newspaper accounts consistently repeated the story of the runaway marriage.[18] Whatever the truth may be, it is absolutely clear that Alexis's parents were worried and distraught about the unacceptable relationship, resulting in a great deal of stress within the family. Meanwhile, Alexis, unlike his brother Alexander, could not accept that familial and imperial obligations trumped his own personal desires. Though there were reports across Europe and the United States that Alexis would marry a member of a royal European house, Princess Thyra of Denmark or one of the princesses of Prussia, the grand duke himself never considered such a possibility.[19]

It is ironic that Alexis's love affair with Zhukovskaya should have caused such problems within his family. There are numerous examples, several from this very period, of members of the royal family engaging in affairs and morganatic marriages, and Alexis certainly would have known about these scandalous relationships and the consequences of violating family and social expectations. His uncle, Grand Duke Nikolai Nikolaevich, had a very public affair with a Russian ballerina, Ekaterina Chislova, and fathered five children with her, installing his mistress and their children in a residence very near his own. A widely reported story holds that, as soon as a burning candle appeared in the favorite's window, a servant would come to tell Nikolai that he was needed because there was a fire somewhere in the city, and he would rush to his mistress's side. His wife, Grand Duchess Alexandra Petrovna, thought the situation so untenable that she complained to the tsar, who was not at all sympathetic. One of Alexis's other uncles, Constantin Nikolaevich, was also involved with a ballerina, Anna Kuznetsova. These were not the only violations of family and social expectations. Alexis's cousin, Nikolai, Fourth Duke of Leuchtenberg, had a morganatic marriage with Nadezhda Akinfieva, for which he lost his rank and was exiled. Nikolai's mother, and Alexis's favorite aunt, Grand Duchess Maria Nikolaevna, married first to Maximilien, Duke of Leuchtenberg, then wed again after her husband's death in a morganatic union with Count Grigorii Stroganov. There were also compromising liaisons in Alexis's immediate family. His brother Alexander had been prepared to renounce the throne in order to marry Maria Meshcherskaya, and dynastic chaos was only prevented by Alexander's recognition of duty to his family and country. Alexis had seen how these relationships had all played out, and yet these observations did nothing to dissuade him from heading down a similarly destructive path.[20]

Perhaps the greatest irony, however, was the affair taking place in Alexis's own home. During roughly the same time that Alexis was falling in love with Zhukovskaya, his father was involved with a new mistress, Ekaterina Dolgorukaya, who would eventually bear him several children. Thus, at the exact same moment that Alexander was sending Alexis to America, the tsar was also expecting his first child (born May 1872) with his new mistress and installing her and his second family in the third floor of the Winter Palace, under the same roof as his wife, who was by this time sick with tuberculosis. Eventually, after his wife's death, the tsar would marry Dolgorukaya. Despite these examples, and his own personal indiscretion, Tsar Alexander made it clear that he would never accept his son's relationship with Zhukovskaya, and in an effort to break his son's ties to this unsuitable woman, he decided to send Alexis on a trip to the United States. Alexander's decision came a little too late, however; it was already apparent by the time Alexis departed that Zhukovskaya was carrying his child.[21]

So, while the American people and the American press were fixated on the grand duke's every move and mood, the young Russian was desperately sad and longing for a woman he could never marry and a child he would never raise. According to one memoirist, he carried a miniature of her in a locket. His American hosts, by and large, knew nothing of the family drama that consumed the grand duke's thoughts and, to a large degree, dictated the terms of his journey. Alexis once wrote to his brother that, although he tried to always display a calm exterior, often he was struck by moments of incredible sadness; he concluded, "Every man is an actor, but Grand Dukes must be the best and most adept actors."[22] Grand Duke Alexis gave a masterful performance. At official levels, the young Russian appeared to be satisfied with his reception as the son of Tsar Alexander II and, as far as the American public was concerned, Alexis was having a splendid time, drinking, dancing, and eyeing the pretty girls.

2

GOD BLESS THE EMPIRE
THAT LOVES THE GREAT UNION

'Tis not to thy title Americans bow,
Nor yet to the coronet bright that ye wear—

. . .

But 'tis for the sake of thy father—our friend—
Whose love gave us strength thro' a perilous past,
And whose unselfish sympathy hastened the end
Which gave to the union true freedom at last.
   —*Chicago Times,* November 22, 1871

I N THE SECOND HALF of the nineteenth century, Russia and the United
States had a significantly different relationship from the one that future
generations would come to know. During this pivotal period in American
and Russian history, the two great nations were on very good terms. Situated
on opposite sides of the globe, they were an unlikely pair in many ways—one
a conservative monarchy, the other a young republic—yet over the course of
a century the relationship had developed from hesitant and uncertain beginnings to a mature and complex friendship that both countries sought to protect
and expand. Repeated encounters in trade, diplomacy, and technological matters had brought the two countries closer, while events on the international
scene—war, trade disputes, and the shifting power balance in Europe—often
pushed them together as well. Nonetheless, the Russian-American bond was
frequently tested by those same events and encounters and, occasionally, the
much-revered friendship seemed to be fraying.[1]

Following the abolition of serfdom and slavery, both Russia and the United
States were experiencing social transformations and trying to redefine them-

selves and their relationships with other nations. As the United States recovered from a brutal civil war, tensions continued between North and South, and new problems emerged with the birth of the Ku Klux Klan. On the international scene, the United States was at odds with Britain over the *Alabama* claims and embroiled in conflict over the possible annexation of Santo Domingo. Though both situations were resolved without violence, many had feared war. Meanwhile, Russia faced its own challenges of domestic reform and the growth of an increasingly radical, revolutionary-minded intelligentsia. Russia was also threatened on the international front, confronted with the birth of new European alliances and rivalries. In particular, Russia faced a Polish uprising, the ominous emergence of a newly unified Germany, and a contentious relationship with the Ottoman Empire. While the rumors that Alexander was seeking an alliance with the United States were probably untrue, the tsar certainly viewed the Russian-American friendship as one worth retaining, and the visit of Grand Duke Alexis in 1871–72 was clearly part of that effort.

———◆———

Russia and the United States already had a surprisingly long and active relationship by the time the grand duke set foot on American soil. This marriage of convenience must be understood in a broader diplomatic context. Since the end of the eighteenth century, Russian-American relations were both a reaction to and a facet of other relationships, particularly those between Great Britain and Russia, and Great Britain and the United States. The constant, if sometimes simmering, tension between these pairs over maritime power, fishing rights, and territorial expansion repeatedly drove Russia and the United States into one another's arms. Though separated by an ocean and the great land mass of Western Europe, Russia and the United States found common interests more than once at the expense of and in opposition to that imperial powerhouse of the nineteenth century, Great Britain.

The first diplomatic contact between Russia and America was actually a decision to avoid contact. When the American Revolution began, Catherine the Great (reigned 1762–96) had no desire to get involved in this faraway conflict, but she issued a Declaration of Armed Neutrality in March 1780, which effectively aided the colonies by declaring the right of neutral ships to enter American ports. The declaration also encouraged leaders in the American colonies to give Russia a closer look, and ultimately resulted in a formal mission to Russia. In 1781, Francis Dana, accompanied by a fourteen-year-old John Quincy Adams, traveled to St. Petersburg. Though the complexities of the war and Catherine's hope of convincing Britain to accept her mediation of the conflict prevented Dana from being received in any official capacity, he did meet with important Russian and foreign diplomats and tried to alleviate concerns that an independent United States would be harmful to Russian commercial interests, specifically its trade in naval stores. Dana's efforts at persuading Russia to assist the colonies were a failure, however, and it would be twenty years before the United States could establish an official representative at St. Petersburg.[2]

There were other contacts during Catherine's reign as well. In 1788, the famous American seaman John Paul Jones secured an appointment in the Russian Navy and served in the Black Sea under Prince Grigorii Potemkin, a talented soldier and leader, and one of Catherine's favorites. Jones's period of service, however, did not go well. He did not speak Russian, did not get along well with the British officers in the Russian Navy, and in the spring of 1789 he was accused of raping a twelve-year-old girl. Whether or not the accusation was true, Catherine took the opportunity to get rid of Jones; he was given leave, made his way as far as Paris, and died there three years later. Despite this rather disastrous episode, Russian-American ties continued to grow. At the end of the eighteenth century, at least four hundred commercial ships from Boston, New York, Philadelphia, and other American ports brought goods to Russia, and by 1800, "most New England houses and ships were put together with Russian nails, and it would be a rare vessel that did not have sails, tackle and anchors of Russian origin." However, more formal commercial relations were hindered by the lack of an official diplomatic relationship.[3]

Russia and the United States finally established full diplomatic relations in 1809. Alexander I, the liberal grandson of Catherine the Great, had become tsar in 1801, and he and his small circle of liberal friends were more receptive to establishing a diplomatic friendship with the United States. There were practical diplomatic reasons, as well. When President Thomas Jefferson proposed the idea of an official minister in 1807, both the United States and Russia had become increasingly isolated as France proved its superiority on land and Great Britain dominated the seas. In June 1809, the U.S. Senate approved the nomination of John Quincy Adams as minister to Russia, while Alexander had selected Andrei Dashkov as the first Russian minister to the United States. This new diplomatic bond was strengthened when, in 1813, the tsar offered to mediate an end to the war between the United States and Britain. Britain refused, and so it was not until the Treaty of Ghent in early 1815 that the war ended, but the Russian offer of assistance impressed the American government as a sign of good will.[4]

In the following year, however, a series of small complications threatened the developing friendship. In November 1815, in an episode oddly reminiscent of the John Paul Jones affair, the Russian consul-general in Philadelphia, Nikolai Kozlov, was accused of raping a twelve-year-old girl. A Pennsylvania court denied Kozlov's claim of diplomatic immunity and decided that crimes by foreign diplomats fell within the purview of federal courts. Meanwhile, the outgoing consul-general, Dashkov, continued to argue in favor of diplomatic immunity and demanded that Kozlov be cleared of all charges, and when these demands fell on deaf ears, he declared that he was ceasing all communication with the U.S. government. In retaliation, the Russian government in St. Petersburg declared the American *chargé d'affaires* there, Levett Harris, to be persona non grata, though he was permitted to carry out his official duties. The crisis was settled in late 1816. Alexander I and his cabinet were eager to maintain good relations and came to accept the argument that diplomats were answerable to the laws of the country where they resided at the time of the offense.[5]

In the 1820s and 1830s, the principal Russian-American interaction was trade. Though there was no official commercial treaty between the two countries, an impressive number of American ships traveled to Kronstadt and St. Petersburg with a variety of valuable goods, including sugar from the West Indies. In 1829, Nicholas I sought to modernize the Russian Navy and sent a mission to the United States to visit various shipyards and naval facilities. The visit led to the purchase of one steam corvette, but anti-Russian sentiment in Washington after the Russian government's suppression of the 1830–31 Polish uprising nearly wrecked the deal and interfered with an expansion of trade that might otherwise have followed.[6] The two countries finally signed a commercial treaty in 1832, by which time many Americans had lost interest in the Polish cause.[7]

In 1838, Nicholas I sent another mission to the United States to tour shipyards and port facilities, resulting in the purchase of one steam frigate which was delivered to Kronstadt in 1841. Russia also looked to the United States for help in railroad construction. In 1841, a group of Russian railroad proponents persuaded Nicholas to create a special committee to consider ideas for a Moscow–

St. Petersburg rail line; subsequently, the tsar approved a proposal to bring an American railroad expert, George Washington Whistler, to oversee construction. Similarly, the Russian government brought in American locomotive builders to set up a factory and train locals in the art, including Joseph Harrison Jr. of Philadelphia. These men all lived in Russia for several years, and Whistler even brought his family, which included his son James, the future painter.[8]

The Crimean War, which broke out in 1853 between Russia and an alliance of the British, French, and Ottoman empires, posed a serious challenge to Russian-American relations. Though the theater of war was far away and not an area of interest for the United States, there was much about the conflict that proved relevant. On the one hand, American officials saw Russia as a friend and Britain as a constant irritant; on the other, British trade was too profitable to cast aside easily. Soon, however, American ambiguity shifted in favor of Russia. In the summer of 1854, the United States offered to mediate the conflict between Russia and Britain, but the effort came to nothing. Russia and the United States did, however, sign a maritime neutrality agreement that was so friendly that it "bordered on a quasi-alliance." This did not stop the British from actively recruiting in the United States, a practice that angered Russian officials, who viewed it as a violation of the American position of neutrality. In fact, several British recruiters were arrested and put on trial, and the British minister to the United States, John F. Crampton, was dismissed over the matter. Many Russians would have welcomed a fallout between the United States and Great Britain. Constantin Catacazy, who was serving as secretary to the Russian legation in the United States, advocated encouraging American merchant vessels to set sail for Russia, hoping that if they were stopped by the British it might push America into the war.[9]

The American government had no intention of getting drawn into the Crimean War, but it did take the opportunity to study the military tactics being used. In the summer of 1854, the War Department sent a team of military observers to St. Petersburg, where they stayed for six weeks, touring military installations and learning about the Russian Army, as they waited for permission to head south. Ultimately, the American mission never made it to the Russian front, refused under the official claim that other groups had been denied the same request, so they were forced to observe the war from the British side. A considerable number of private citizens traveled from the United States to the Crimea, as well. Thirty-five American doctors from various places traveled to the region to offer medical aid, some out of sympathy for Russia, others for adventure, experience, or money. Pure profit was the motive for many other Americans. Though the United States remained neutral, a number of individuals took the opportunity to sell guns, powder, coal, and cotton to Russia and, in some cases, to its enemies as well.[10]

The Crimean War concluded in March 1856 with the Treaty of Paris. Tsar Nicholas I had died in 1855, and his son, the more liberal Alexander II, took the opportunity to remove Russia from a war that had exposed many of its weaknesses, particularly the poor physical condition of its peasant conscripts. Russia's attitude towards the United States, however, remained positive, and the person who deserves the most credit for this is the Russian minister, Eduard de Stoeckl. Serving as head of the Russian legation in the United States between 1854 and 1868, Stoeckl was personally popular, having married an American woman, and was active in the social activities of the capital. He also made sure to report all examples of American friendliness and sympathy to his government. At the same time, the period between the end of the Crimean War in 1856 and the beginning of the Civil War in 1861 was one of the most active periods in Russian-American trade relations, with the continuation of old business deals and the development of many new contracts. In 1857, for example, about 45 percent of Russia's cotton imports came from the United States, and that figure rose to 80 percent in the following year. Russia also imported American sugar, rice, and logwood. Military trade flourished as well. In the late 1850s, the William H. Webb Shipyards began building warships for the Russian Navy, and Samuel Colt, who had already been selling guns to Russia, secured a lucrative business deal to supply machinery and designs for Colt-style revolvers to be manufactured there.[11]

The next decade would prove to be a more challenging time for bilateral relations as both countries confronted reform and the opposition it aroused. In early 1861, civil war erupted in the United States over the issue of slavery at the same moment that Alexander II declared an end to the centuries-old practice of serfdom in Russia. American newspapers praised the tsar for this liberal reform, and for decades politicians and the press would refer to the serf emancipation in discussions about Russian-American relations. It would be a constant theme in the speeches welcoming Grand Duke Alexis a decade later. Once America had emancipated its own slaves, the two nations perceived a new special bond. Russian Minister Stoeckl placed great value on this mutual understanding of the importance of emancipation, and believed that this shared experience facilitated positive feelings.[12]

Sadly, America's path to emancipation was more difficult. While liberal Russians rejoiced at the news of American emancipation, the violence of the American process saddened them. Russian officials, concerned about the fate of the Russian-American friendship, were even more dismayed by the Civil War. Russia needed a strong ally in its ongoing rivalry with Great Britain and in reestablishing itself as a European power after the disastrous Crimean War. By 1862, the Russian minister of foreign affairs, Alexander Gorchakov, and others in St. Petersburg were frustrated with the American Civil War and worried that a permanent split in the American Union might occur. Consequently, Gorchakov pledged Russia's support for the Union, a declaration that was widely circulated in Washington and published in all the major northern newspapers.[13] This pledge did not, however, mean that Russia would intervene in the Civil War. The Russian government refused to join mediation attempts by France and, to a lesser extent, Britain, until the time came when North and South expressed a willingness to negotiate. The possibility of any Russian mediation effectively ended, however, with the internal distraction of the Polish revolt of 1863. Despite decades of foreign rule, the Poles of the Russian Empire had retained a strong sense of national identity and Polish nationalists still held out hope for independence. In January 1863, this desire for autonomy manifested itself in a sudden and violent uprising. The Russian government, however, was not interested in an independent Poland and suppressed the rebellion. International reaction varied. Though there was some sympathy for the Poles in the United States, especially at the beginning of the rebellion, American support waned as British and French support for the rebels grew.[14]

It was at this complex moment that Alexander II decided to send a squadron of the Baltic fleet to the United States. Though historians have disagreed about Russia's motives, it is widely believed that Russia wanted to prevent its best warships from being trapped in Baltic ports in the event of a general European war over the Polish issue. Certainly, many newspapers in the fall of 1863 recognized the diplomatic and military advantages to Russia's visit, both for Russia and the United States. Russia also may have simply wanted to demonstrate its growing naval capability. In any event, when some three thousand Russian sailors and officers arrived in the United States in September 1863, they enjoyed a hearty welcome, and over the next two months they attended numerous dinners, receptions, balls, and parades in New York, Philadelphia, Baltimore, and Washington. A separate group of ships from the Pacific squadron visited the West Coast, docking in San Francisco. These sailors were fewer in number, but their visit was longer, about ten months. Whatever the primary motive may have been, for many Americans, then and later, the arrival of the Russian fleet was a sign of friendship and a show of support for the North, and one that may have discouraged Britain and France from recognizing the Confederate government.[15]

One other point of Russian-American contact during the Civil War years deserves mention—the project to build a telegraph line connecting the two continents. In 1865, Western Union sent four men to Kamchatka in the far eastern region of the Russian Empire to explore the possibility of building a Pacific telegraphic cable. One of these men was George Kennan, the uncle of the later political advisor of the same name who became well known during the Cold War era as the "father of containment." The men made their way up the Kamchatka Peninsula with the help of native guides to explore the route for the proposed cable, and according to Kennan's memoir of the expedition, the terrain was difficult and uncharted, and the men suffered greatly from the intense conditions. Ultimately, the expedition was a failure; in 1866, when an Atlantic cable was successfully completed, the project was suspended.[16]

Russians and Americans continued to feel connected by other shared experiences, as well. In April 1865, when President Abraham Lincoln was assassinated by John Wilkes Booth, Russia expressed great sympathy for America's loss in both official and unofficial circles, and throughout Russia pictures of Lincoln were displayed next to those of Grand Duke Nicholas, the tsar's eldest and recently deceased son. Not long after Lincoln's assassination, Alexander II had his own brush with death. In April 1866, a suicidal and disturbed student named Dmitri Karakazov fired a shot at the tsar near one of the royal gardens in St. Petersburg. Though the attempt was unsuccessful, such an attack so soon after the American president's murder resonated in both nations. In response, Congress approved a joint resolution to congratulate Alexander on his narrow escape and the new president, Andrew Johnson, selected Gustavus Vasa Fox, assistant secretary to the navy, to deliver it. The mission had another purpose as well—to thank Russia for its continuing support and to broadcast this friendship quite publicly by stopping in France and Britain on the way. Fox and the naval officers were received and welcomed in St. Petersburg, Moscow, and several cities along the Volga, celebrated with dinners and receptions. They were, for the moment, minor celebrities, and had their photographs taken many times, and their images were in great demand.[17]

The year 1867 was an active one in Russian-American relations. In the late summer, a pleasure ship called the *Quaker City* dropped anchor in the Black Sea, and for the first time a large number of American tourists had the opportunity to see Russia and its people. Their experiences, moreover, were shared with a large audience back home through the pen of the *Quaker City*'s most famous passenger, Mark Twain. *Innocents Abroad,* which appeared two years later, would contain his impressions of Russia and his account of the tourists' reception by Alexander II at the tsar's Livadia Palace near Yalta. Twain observed, "Any man could see that there was an intention here to show that Russia's friendship for America was so genuine as to render even her private citizens objects worthy of kindly intentions."[18] At virtually the same time, another group of Americans had arrived in Russia; in August 1867, Admiral David Farragut and a naval squadron of four ships put in at the Kronstadt naval base, where they were met by the governor of the fortress, Admiral Lessovski, the same Lessovski who had visited the United States with the Russian fleet during the Civil War. In St. Petersburg, Farragut dined with Lessovski and his family in the cottage once occupied by Peter the Great, and paid a call to Cassius Clay and the other members of the American delegation in the Russian capital. Farragut also met Grand Duke Constantin Nikolaevich, the brother of the tsar and the head of the Russian Navy, who toured Farragut's ship, the *Franklin,* and exhibited great interest in everything about the American steamer. All together, Farragut and the squadron spent three weeks in Russia.[19]

The biggest Russo-American event of 1867, however, was the purchase of Alaska, or Russian America, as it was also called, by the United States. The idea to transfer this territory long predated the actual sale. Rumors about a possible sale had begun as early as the Crimean War, and a year after that war ended, Grand Duke Constantin officially proposed shedding the Alaskan burden, arguing that Russia's focus should be on strengthening its center. Serious conversations took place between Russian and American officials, but the turmoil of the early 1860s put any such discussions on hold. In the end, however, American expansionism, Russia's desire to concentrate resources elsewhere, and a shared desire to block British interests brought the two nations to the bargaining table. On March 30, 1867, U.S. secretary of state William Seward and Russian minister Eduard de Stoeckl signed the treaty obliging the United

States to pay $7.2 million for Alaska. The official transfer of the territory took place in Sitka on October 18, 1867.[20]

The Alaska purchase and the negotiations surrounding it were complicated by a particularly thorny matter called the Perkins claim. In June 1855, Captain Benjamin Perkins, a merchant mariner from Worcester, Massachusetts, met a man who claimed to be an agent and courier of the Russian government tasked with procuring armaments and powder. Over the next few months, Perkins met with various men acting as agents of the Russian government, including Russian Minister Eduard de Stoeckl, and secured what he believed to be legitimate agreements to provide these materials to the Russian government. In the meantime, Perkins spent a great deal of money acquiring the materials necessary to fulfill the orders. Soon, however, it became apparent that Russia was no longer interested in pursuing these arrangements or obtaining the discussed war materials. Left in the lurch, Perkins began to try to recover his declared losses through legal means. When he died in 1862, his claim was picked up by his wife and daughter, who made several appeals to the American and Russian governments. None of these produced any real results, but in 1867, Anna Perkins, destitute and hounded by debts, once again appealed to Congress for help. This time, however, she had a hook—since the United States was in negotiations with Russia for the purchase of Alaska, Mrs. Perkins and her attorneys asked that Congress withhold the amount of $385,231.31 plus interest from the payment to Russia, at least until her claim was evaluated once more.[21]

This bold proposition raised opinions on both sides. Between July and December 1867, several politicians presented petitions supporting Mrs. Perkins's request and the Committee on Foreign Affairs actually considered an amendment that would withhold a portion from the $7,200,000 purchase price. As the amendment was being voted upon, however, Stoeckl intervened, proposing that the amendment be withdrawn in return for his assurances that the claim would be given proper investigation and consideration. In fact, it would seem, Stoeckl gave out more than promises, and some of the bribes he distributed may have been to those who had supported the Perkins claim.[22]

Stoeckl's efforts were not in vain—the appropriation for Alaska went through as planned, and nothing was withheld for the Perkins claimants. Nevertheless, interest in the Perkins claim persisted and, when Stoeckl retired and was replaced by a new Russian minister, the case took an entirely new direction. The new Russian minister was Constantin Catacazy, a diplomat with a scandalous personal life and a strong personality that frequently seemed to rub people the wrong way. He arrived in the United States in late summer of 1869 and quickly developed a reputation as a difficult and dishonest man. By the fall of 1870, Secretary of State Hamilton Fish was writing in his diary, "It is a pity that one can never trust Catacazy or believe a word he says."[23] The Russian government had instructed Catacazy to investigate the Perkins claim, and he did so with relish. More than once, Catacazy wrote Fish that the claim was not deemed credible by the Russian government because of its "essentially fraudulent character," and he condemned the "entire worthlessness of the so-called claims."[24]

Less than a year after Catacazy's appointment to the United States, in early March 1870, the *Washington Morning Chronicle* published a letter purported to be written by Catacazy, referring to the "fictitious pretensions of the widow Perkins" and suggesting that Perkins had entrapped the Russian agents.[25] Shortly after, another document appeared, an unsigned dispatch addressed to the tsar that referred to the claim as an "iniquitous fraud" and its supporters as would-be plunderers of the imperial government. The document also attacked the reputation of Hamilton Fish, calling him a "very weak and vacillating man." Perkins's attorney asserted that the document had been written by Catacazy.[26]

Catacazy's involvement in the Perkins claim was not his only misstep with the U.S. government, however. The Russian minister had also been suspected of interfering in the resolution of the *Alabama* claims, a protracted and heated dispute between the United States and Great Britain that at various points seemed beyond resolution. During the American Civil War, the Confederacy had focused on disrupting Union trade routes, but once its ports were blockaded, the South needed help from abroad. Though Great Britain was officially neutral, many British merchants continued to do business with the Confederacy, selling ships to the Confederate government. The most notorious example was the *Alabama,* an ironclad built in Liverpool in 1862. For two years the warship terrorized the seas, confiscating goods and burning ships headed to or from the North. Subsequently, the United States accused Britain of failing to enforce its own laws of neutrality and demanded reparations. The matter was submitted to an international tribunal, but so tense were the negotiations that American newspapers proclaimed the possibility of war. In early 1871, rumors mushroomed that Catacazy was attempting to derail the settlement of the *Alabama* claims. Catacazy denied any meddling, but Fish believed he was guilty of the charge and there were others who shared his conviction. Catacazy's alleged shenanigans did not pay off; in the resulting Washington Treaty, concluded in 1872, Britain agreed to pay $15,500,000 in damages.[27]

Finally, Catacazy also had committed the unpardonable sin of having a scandalous relationship with a beautiful woman, then bringing her to Washington as his wife and expecting the other wives of the capital to accept her as one of their own. Catacazy had been the secretary of the Russian legation in Rio de Janeiro and, while there, he fell in love with, and wooed away, the wife of the Italian minister from Naples. When he became secretary to the Russian legation in the United States in 1851, he brought this woman to Washington as his mistress. A decade and a half later, when he returned to the United States as Russian minister, she accompanied him as his wife, and her appearance in this role set teacups rattling. If Madame Catacazy's checkered past were not enough of an obstacle to her acceptance by the other Washington wives, her renowned beauty was apparently the last nail in the coffin. According to a variety of sources, Madame Catacazy was a rare beauty with milky skin and golden hair, and it was her "singular superiority ... of personal attractions" that had done in her husband. The American press was convinced that this "tea-party intrigue" was a significant factor in the Catacazy imbroglio, and other sources hint at this as well. The removal of the Russian minister also meant the removal of his wife and, one paper declared it, "the triumph of Mrs. Fish and her following of the plain but proper Washington matrons, to whom the presence and power of the foreign diplomatic beauty has long been an unbearable affront." The *Cincinnati Daily Enquirer* sarcastically observed that Catacazy's successor, General Alexander Gorlov, was considered entirely acceptable to the American government—"Doubtless his wife is old and ugly."[28]

By June 1871, Secretary of State Fish and President Grant could take no more of Catacazy, and the U.S. Cabinet requested that the Russian government recall the troublesome diplomat. The expulsion would not be so easy, however. Preparations had already begun for Grand Duke Alexis to visit the United States in the fall of 1871, and the Russian government made it clear that such a visit could not occur if there was no Russian representative present. Though Grant and Fish were eager to be rid of Catacazy, they were persuaded by the American minister in St. Petersburg, Andrew Curtin, to compromise, and Catacazy was permitted to stay until the end of the grand duke's visit. He would be allowed to travel with Alexis and fulfill his official duties, but he would be persona non grata in official Washington circles. This uneasy resolution solved the matter for the purposes of the Russian visit, but the conflict remained an object of scrutiny and speculation, and there were many who criticized Grant and Fish for their failure to better navigate the scandal, and many others who worried about the future of the Russian-American friendship. When Alexis politely refused the invitation to visit Washington a second time before departing the United States, many attributed his response to the tension caused by the Catacazy affair.[29]

There was one other contentious issue on the international scene on the eve of Alexis's visit that placed the Russian-American relationship in a different light. In 1870, Russia repudiated the Black Sea clause of the Treaty of Paris that had concluded the Crimean War in 1856 and had prohibited Russia from keeping war vessels in the Black Sea and from maintaining naval vessels on its coasts. Never happy about these restrictions, Russia waited for the chance to push for revision, and that opportunity came in the fall of 1870 when France and Prussia went to war. At that propitious moment, Prince Gorchakov issued a circular to the signatory powers of the treaty stating that Russia could no longer be bound by the objectionable Black Sea terms. Britain, in particular, bristled at Gorchakov's announcement; in the words of British foreign secretary Earl Granville, the problem with Russia's stance was that it was "not a request to those Governments for the consideration of the case, but an announcement to them that it has emancipated itself, or holds itself emancipated, from any stipulations of the treaty." British fears about Russian encroachment into India and Afghanistan only intensified the matter. For a brief period, war between Russia and Britain seemed possible and a split in the British Cabinet over the issue threatened the stability of that government.[30]

The United States, of course, had no dog in this fight, but that did not prevent American officials from forming an opinion. While publicly the U.S. government declared its intent to always remain neutral in the event of a European war, privately there were many who sympathized with the Russian cause. In December 1870, Andrew Curtin wrote to Hamilton Fish, "Apart from the manner in which the Imperial Government abrogated the obnoxious article of the Treaty of Paris, there are sufficient reasons for all that is demanded by Russia, aside from a degradation a great and powerful nation could no longer suffer."[31] With so many challenges to the Russian-American relationship and so much activity on the international scene, it should come as no surprise that the visit of Grand Duke Alexis was viewed by both governments as a barometer of the decades-old friendship and imbued with great meaning and importance.

3

WHERE EVERY MAN IS A SOVEREIGN

Most noble Prince Alexis!
Our people of both sexes,
From Michigan to Texas,
Extend a welcome hand;
Your stay began to vex us,
To worry and perplex us,
And we pray the winds, Alexis,
To guide you safe to land.

—*The Grand Duke Alexis: His Grand Reception, the Magnificent Ball, Gorgeous Scenes, How He Dances, Looks, Walks and Talks* (1871)

I**N 1871, NEW YORK CITY** was not yet known as the "Big Apple" or "the city that never sleeps," but it was well on its way to earning those familiar monikers. What began as a small Dutch settlement in 1625 had developed into the most important urban center of North America by the mid-1700s, and by the time of the Revolutionary War, New York and its port were so central to the survival of the colonies that it necessarily became the focus of British attention. During the Revolutionary War, New York served as Britain's military headquarters and the jumping-off point for raids against the other colonies' coastlines. At the end of the war, despite the hardships suffered at the hands of the British, New York bounced back quickly, reestablishing traditional lines of trade and becoming the new nation's largest and richest city. The opening of the Erie Canal in the fall of 1825 secured New York's position of commercial dominance, particularly over nearby Philadelphia, and in subsequent decades New York also became the artistic and cultural capital of the country, a gathering place for writers, artists, and musicians, and home to many impressive theaters and opera houses. By the time Alexis visited New York, it was a growing city of nearly one million people, as large as Philadelphia and Boston combined, and had come to be seen as the archetype of the modern city. Many of the businesses, buildings, and other features that would come to represent New York City—Tiffany's, Wall Street, Central Park—were already in place, and the spectacular Gothic towers of the Brooklyn Bridge were also under construction. By the fall of 1871, the caisson and foundation stones of the tower on the New York side were just being put in place, but the base of the Brooklyn tower had been completed and was already visible above the East River at high tide by at least thirty feet. Some of New York's seamier aspects were also well known—brothels and tenements crowded with poor immigrants. Despite its darker elements, New York had already developed the reputation of a city of dreams and possibilities. A contemporary guidebook declared that New York City's "vast public works, its magnificent buildings, its leagues of roaring thoroughfares, and its colossal commerce … afford the most imposing monument the world has ever seen of the speed with which a youthful people may stride to opulence and power."[1] It was the ideal place for a celebrity tour to begin.

The excitement over the Russian royal visit came at a propitious moment for the American public. In 1871, the daily papers seemed to be filled with distressing stories of potential epidemics and civil strife. There was, for example, the threat of cholera, already appearing in American cities and carefully monitored by port officials in New York and elsewhere. First appearing in the United States in 1832, cholera had ravaged a number of cities in subsequent decades, including Chicago, St. Louis, New York, and New Orleans. Though the mystery of cholera's transmission had been solved by John Snow in 1854 during the London epidemic near the Broad Street pump, this disease, which had killed hundreds of thousands across the globe since 1800, still appeared from time to time in devastating outbreaks. In mid-November 1871, at the very moment that Alexis was expected to arrive, there were reports that a German steamer had arrived with cholera on board and over three dozen men had already died. The American press noted the irony of this unwelcome visitor. The *Charleston Daily Courier* remarked, "In the excitement of watching for our royal visitor, the Grand Duke, we had completely forgotten this ghastly guest, whom a month or two ago we were looking out for.... this dreary visitor has knocked at our gaily decked doors first." The *Philadelphia Press* similarly declared, "Between Prince and Pestilence all classes in New York will soon have a guest and a sensation."[2]

Cholera was not the only disease plaguing America's cities. Smallpox was a threat, as well. During the Civil War, smallpox had raged through the United States, especially in the South—even Abraham Lincoln had had it. Alexis's visit occurred in the middle of a series of outbreaks—between 1869 and 1873, smallpox killed over 1,000 people in New York, nearly 2,000 in Philadelphia, some 1,500 in Baltimore, more than 1,200 in Cincinnati, and over 600 in Washington, D.C. Other cities suffered equally high losses. Several weeks before the grand duke's arrival, a special correspondent for the *Philadelphia Inquirer* reported that smallpox had appeared again in New York City, Brooklyn, and Philadelphia, causing "fearful havoc among all classes ... spreading so rapidly that it will be necessary to provide immediately additional hospital accommodations for those who are so unfortunate as to be the victims of this pestilence." Other cities also carefully monitored the spread of the disease.[3]

Finally, yellow fever was also a threat, particularly in seaport and inland commercial cities of the South, such as Charleston and New Orleans.[4] In 1793, approximately 5,000 people had perished of yellow fever in Philadelphia, and Americans were terrified of another outbreak, particularly since the disease's spread was not yet understood. Yellow fever was by far the most dreaded disease in North America for well over a century, so much so that groups of armed citizens were known to stop trains suspected of carrying the disease from entering their towns, destroying tracks and bridges ahead of them. These fears were not entirely unwarranted—in 1878, the lower Mississippi Valley was struck, resulting in an estimated 20,000 deaths. As late as 1897, one federal official described yellow fever as the only disease "whose shadow ever crosses our path, and is always a source of dread, a constant source of expense, and at once a danger to our people and an onerous burden upon commerce."[5]

In the West and Midwest, it was not the spread of disease that terrified locals, but rather the spread of Mormonism. On December 4, 1871, President Grant declared in his message to the country that in Utah there still remained "a remnant of barbarism repugnant to civilization, to decency and to the laws of the United States." For four decades, the federal government actively waged a war of power and policy in an effort to convince the Mormons to abandon polygamy and adhere to the laws of the land. In fact, the government was still seeking the individuals responsible for the Mountain Meadows Massacre of 1857 in southern Utah, which had resulted in over a hundred deaths. Though by 1871, the appalling acts of violence by and against the Mormon community were no longer the most immediate concern, many people were distressed by the growing numbers of Mormons and especially by the practice of polygamy. Newspapers around the country doggedly followed the Mormon issue and the trial of Brigham Young in Salt Lake City for "lewd and lascivious cohabitation."[6]

Finally, in the South there were persistent racial tensions and increasing violence as the Ku Klux Klan appeared on the scene to threaten and intimidate emancipated slaves and their sympathizers. Founded in Pulaski, Tennessee, in 1866, the Klan quickly evolved from a group of like-minded ex-Confederates focused on amusement and mild forms of intimidation to a counterrevolutionary organization rooted in ideas of white supremacy that sought to undermine the Reconstruction agenda of Radical Republicans and their allies through extralegal means and violence. In 1870 and 1871, the U.S. Congress responded with the Enforcement Acts, measures designed to combat the intimidation methods of the Klan and protect the political and civil rights of newly freed blacks. Nonetheless, in late 1871 the dailies were filled with stories of Klan atrocities and the arrests of hundreds of Klan members.[7] Not surprisingly, many Americans were all too happy to concentrate on lighter and less distressing events. As one columnist in the *Herald* put it, Alexis's arrival would be a pleasant distraction and give New Yorkers "a healthy stimulant after the unwholesome political excitement of the past three months." The *Herald* was referring to the Tammany Hall imbroglio in New York, of course, but the same could be said for the other national concerns, as well.[8]

———————◆———————

As news of the grand duke's visit became public, the New York press seized the story, reporting in April 1871 that Alexis would arrive in early summer to begin a tour that would take him from the Eastern Seaboard, through the western states, and all the way to San Francisco. In response to this exciting news, a group of distinguished citizens formed an executive committee to oversee the arrangements and reception. By June, the committee actively began work on the grand duke's program, though it was now clear that the visitor would not be departing his homeland until August.[9]

The executive and reception committees in New York included many of the most prominent citizens of the city, and as the *Times* observed, a "simple perusal of the names would give full assurance that . . . there should not be anything niggardly in New York's ovation to the representative of the Majesty of the great Empire of Russia." And the list of names was long indeed—the reception committee alone consisted of 185 men, and the various committees for the ball at the naval yard included 71 men.[10] Many of the names remain well known even now. William H. Aspinwall was a successful merchant and credited with the successful construction of both the Pacific Mail Steamship Company and the Panama Railroad. John Jacob Astor was the heir to a great fortune earned in the fur trade, money that he put to good philanthropic use supporting the formation of the New York Cancer Hospital, the Children's Aid Society, and the Metropolitan Museum of Art. William H. Vanderbilt was the son of the famous railroad magnate, "Commodore" Cornelius Vanderbilt, and after becoming his father's chief lieutenant, he oversaw their New York Central & Hudson River Railroad. He also played a major role in the construction of the Grand Central train station. Several important newspaper men were also involved. James Bennett Jr. was the one-time intrepid reporter for and eventual proprietor of the *New York Herald,* as well as commodore of the New York Yacht Club. Horace Greeley was a newspaper editor and founder of the *New York Tribune* who embraced liberal causes such as abolition, women's rights, vegetarianism, and poverty relief. A promoter of the western movement, as well, Greeley became famous for popularizing the phrase, "Go west, young man, go west." Only months after the grand duke's visit, Greeley would be nominated as the Liberal Republican Party candidate for the presidency, a race he was not destined to win.[11]

Inventors and explorers were also represented in the reception committees. Cyrus W. Field was a self-made businessman and the central figure in the establishment of the transatlantic cable in 1866. Samuel Morse was, of course, the inventor of the telegraph, but he was also one of the founding members of the Academy of Design. Morse was so active in seeing to the grand duke's needs and attending the various functions throughout the royal visit that he missed a major telegraph convention in Rome. General John C. Frémont, known as the "Pathfinder of the Rocky Mountains," worked in the government office of topographical engineers exploring the upper Mississippi Valley, the Rocky Mountains, and the Sierra Nevada, and later served in the Union Army as a rather independent and controversial military leader during the Civil War. Henry Ward Beecher was the famous preacher and reformer, not to mention the brother of Harriet Beecher Stowe, author of *Uncle Tom's Cabin*. A dynamic and dramatic orator, Beecher supported a number of liberal platforms and was one of the few religious men to support Darwin's theory of evolution. Several of these men were also founding members of the American Society for the Prevention of Cruelty to Animals, brought into existence only five years earlier by Henry Bergh.[12] This impressive roster of hosts only added to the anticipation and high expectations for the coming festivities.

Over the course of the summer and early fall of 1871, excitement mounted in New York City about the grand duke's visit. The various committees had drawn up an extensive program that included a naval welcome in New York harbor and a busy schedule of meetings and festivities in the city. The orchestra of Louis Jullien, the famous musician, would be entertaining Alexis throughout his stay in the city, and Jullien had composed some new music in honor of the occasion. Such an elaborate schedule of reception events would cost a pretty penny, and this expense was to be borne by private citizens. A number of the city's large hotels offered to pay for the expenses of the military bands in the procession as they had done during the visit of the Prince of Wales, and the Astor House took the lead in presenting the reception committee with a generous check.[13]

As the reception committee worked busily at their task, the general public grew increasingly excited about the arrival of the imperial guests. On September 16, the *New York Times* reported that "fashionable circles are on the *qui vive* for the coming of the young Russian Grand Duke." The press made much of the anticipation of the fairer sex. The ladies of New York were said to be particularly excited, and there was a brisk business in exquisite dresses of silk, satin, and velvet, to be worn by "courtly dames and scheming mammas, who hope to catch the possible heir to an Empire." It was particularly the idea of a royal bachelor that would likely "flutter the doves of the American world." One woman, the papers claimed, intended to outdo all the others by having her coiffure illuminated by gas jets, the reservoir of which would be concealed "amid a wilderness of false braids, puffs, curls, and a French twist." Many young men anticipated the festivities with equal interest, but for a very different reason—the presence of the handsome young Russian would certainly bring together all the young beauties of the city.[14]

In the midst of all this enthusiasm, however, there were some snags. The political scandal surrounding New York's chief city officials created a thorny problem for the reception planners. The "Tweed Ring" that included State Senator William Tweed, Governor John Hoffman, Mayor Abraham Hall, and Parks Department president Peter Sweeney had recently been exposed and was under investigation for siphoning off millions of dollars from the city and state treasury. Under normal circumstances, such officials would most certainly have been included in the reception activities, but in the current situation, organizers wondered if these political embarrassments should be invited. This difficulty did not go unnoticed by the reading public. One "Old New Yorker" wrote to the *Times* asking that the city's citizens be spared the "mortification" of seeing this important foreign guest entrusted to the discredited officials and their "disreputable gang of political followers." The author suggested that perhaps the undesirable hosts could be kept away with a bribe equal to that which they would have stolen to pay for the necessary accoutrements for the festivities. Papers outside of New York noted the problem as well. The *Philadelphia Bulletin* supported the idea of excluding the scandalized city officers, since it would have been "an unpardonable insult" to have placed Alexis in their care, especially since in Russia men convicted of crimes such as those attributed to Hall and his colleagues "usually find their way to Siberia, where they operate with pickaxes and shovels." Similarly, the *Cleveland Daily Leader* conjectured that Alexis's itinerary in the United States had been altered because the tsar was apprehensive that "too long intimacy with a city which fostered a Connolly and a Tweed may work injury to the morals of his own son and heir." Thus, "Old New Yorker" was correct to assume that all eyes were watching to see how reception officials would handle this complicated maneuver. By late October, however, the matter seemed to settle itself. Mayor Hall announced that he would not receive Alexis in his official capacity, and Tweed remained disengaged from the reception preparations.[15]

In addition to concerns about New York's political scandal, there were other considerations about who should be invited. Tickets for the ball at the Academy of Music, for example, would not be available to the general public but rather the committee would distribute them to "none but persons who they, after due inquiry, find to be thoroughly respectable." In particular, the committee wanted to prevent the appearance of "shoddy aspirants for good society, Ring politicians and corner liquor-store millionaires." If tickets appeared in disreputable hands, the original ticket holders would be called to account. This would be but the first instance in which Alexis's visit highlighted the social and economic stratification of American society. Several Philadelphia newspapers mocked this exclusivity and classism; for example, the *Public Ledger* observed that, though the ball tickets were only ten dollars each, "money is no use unless the applicant can give satisfactory assurances to character, &c.," while the *Inquirer* coyly asked, "Gentlemen, let us know your requirements at once. . . . What number of grandfathers is requisite for admission?"[16]

Not everyone appreciated the efforts of the reception committee. There were some disgruntled citizens who scoffed at all the fuss over this "young Duck of Muscovy." George Templeton Strong, a conservative, wealthy New York lawyer wrote that, although he had been given a ticket for the welcome reception, he did not plan to use it, nor worry himself about the young Russian. Strong emphasized, "We are all sovereigns in America, and Alexis is a mere princeling." Strong was not the only one to note this problem. The *New York Times* observed that many people were beginning to sneer at the reception committee and its extravagant plans; after all, Alexis was visiting "a land where there are no subjects, where every man is a sovereign in his own right." But, despite America's foundation in democracy, "The approach of a son of the most mighty potentate on the earth has certainly stirred the sluggish blood of the Gothamites with a vigor that even the revelations of Tammany frauds failed to do."[17]

Complaints also arose about the reception committee's disregard for the rights of regular subscribers to the Academy of Music. These subscribers had paid 125 dollars for a theater box for twenty performances, a price that was high enough, one ticket-holder observed, "but was paid most cheerfully for the privilege of hearing Miss Nillson." Now those same subscribers were being told that in order to attend the special performance by Miss Nillson for the grand duke they would have to pay ten dollars extra. The Academy of Music received numerous complaints about this arrangement, but the management countered that, while regular guests may have become accustomed to Monday-night performances as part of their subscription, they were not guaranteed to be part of their prepaid package. But, to smooth ruffled feathers, manager Max Strakosch promised to tack on an extra performance at the end of the season. This compromise was not satisfactory to everyone, however, and some believed that Strakosch was only trying to exploit the grand duke's visit to make a few extra bucks. In fact, some subscribers threatened to file an injunction to restrain the sale of their seats to the general public, but were persuaded to withdraw the application.[18]

The impending arrival of the grand duke also fanned the flames of long-standing rivalries between New York and other cities, particularly Philadelphia and Brooklyn. At a time when American cities were growing by leaps and bounds, competition could be fierce. Philadelphia and New York had competed for the title of preeminent eastern city long before the royal tour, but the arrival of the grand duke intensified the rivalry. In June 1871, for example, the *New York Sun* quipped that Philadelphia always tried to rival or outdo New York, and though she was still far behind in many ways, she was catching up in one way, the growth of her public debt. Once the preparations for the grand duke's visit to New York had begun, Philadelphia newspapers struck back, taking swipes at New Yorkers for their snobbery. One Philadelphia paper declared that, while the New York reception was nice, "like most New York displays . . . there was nothing particularly novel about it," while another paper regretted that Alexis would be monopolized by the "moneyed aristocracy of New York—the poorest of all aristocracies," and that the reception ball would be restricted to those "whose purses are the reason of their presence." The *Philadelphia Bulletin* lamented that Alexis would be subjected to the "unpleasant displays of toadyism" in that "misgoverned metropolis" of New York, emphasizing that in Philadelphia he would be received with "American simplicity."[19] The use of the word "toadyism" was intended to sting. Referring to a shameless flatterer, "toady" was a contraction of "toad-eater," a term that recalled a charlatan's assistant, who would eat a toad, presumed to be poisonous, so that his employer could show off his skill at expelling the poison with some concoction that he would then sell to his awestruck audience. The term would be used often during the grand duke's visit to describe those who went too far in their appreciation of the young Russian.

The dispute between New York and Brooklyn exposed a deeper animosity. Brooklyn had chaffed under New York's dominance since the early part of the nineteenth century. In the 1830s, New York had tried to stop Brooklyn from achieving city status, and since at least the 1860s there had been a growing and vocal group who favored the idea of merging all the entities located around New York's harbor into one large city. In January 1898 those advocates would succeed, but even then, when the merger was a *fait accompli,* there were those in Brooklyn who felt themselves victims of an imperial expansion they had been unable to stop. Alexis's visit in 1871 and the arrangements surrounding it highlighted this tension. The *Brooklyn Eagle* made the same remarks as other papers about Alexis being subjected to "the noble company of flunkies and snobs" in New York, but there was more. The *Eagle* bristled at the assumption by New York organizers that the Brooklyn militia would happily participate in the welcome parade, stating that Brooklyn was tired of being "a mere tail to the New York kite." The paper added that the Russian visit offered an opportunity to challenge this status: "if Brooklyn is ever to be anything more than a provincial town . . . the time is ripe for taking that higher rank."[20]

While some New Yorkers may have been troubled by the negative press that resulted from such rivalries, the most serious concern facing the reception planners and U.S. government officials was the rumor that Polish exiles in New York were plotting to kill the grand duke. In the 1840s, many Poles had fled Europe, and by 1860 there were about 25,000 Poles in the United States. By 1870, that number had grown to about 50,000 with over 2,000 living in New York City alone. The Polish community had many reasons to be disdainful of the fuss surrounding the visit of the Russian duke. Alexis was a member of the dynasty that had participated in the partition of Poland and then subsequently crushed two attempts at regaining independence, the most recent in 1863. During that uprising, a group in New York had formed a Polish Central Committee, and though it had done nothing to actively assist its struggling brethren, Russian officials in the United States had watched the group closely.[21] Under such circumstances, and given the persistence even abroad of Polish nationalism, it should have come as no surprise to anyone that Polish nationals might take offense at the enthusiastic welcome of the tsar's son. Some Poles took offense at the suggestion that they would resort to such tactics. As the *New York Times* reported, "There seems to be throughout the City among the entire Polish population, young and old, the utmost indignation in consequence of the despicable intentions attributed to them, which they assert positively are without the slightest shadow of foundation . . . however much they may despise the rule of the Czar." Colonel Jullien Allen, a man identified by the *Herald* as "one of the prominent Polish exiles," echoed this assurance, adding that "the Poles are too brave a people to attempt cowardly assassination or even unmanly action by even rudeness."[22]

Indignation aside, several officials believed there was a genuine conspiracy afoot. In September 1871, Russian minister Catacazy wrote U.S. secretary of state Fish that he had received several letters from a man claiming to have information about a plot against Alexis. Catacazy interviewed the man, a Mr. Krzeminsky, who gave the names and addresses of several individuals who had formed a committee to kill the grand duke. This committee had contacted an international society and arranged for the travel of a hired assassin. In response, Catacazy hired Pinkerton's Detective Agency. After a week of investigation, Pinkerton's confirmed that the names and addresses provided by Krzeminsky were accurate and that some of the men named were indeed dangerous or of questionable character. Pinkerton's could not confirm an actual assassination plot, but did recommend that the individuals named be closely watched. Meanwhile, Catacazy had informed Fish of this threat and asked him to notify the district attorney for the Southern District of New York to investigate the supposed plot. On October 3, Fish wrote Catacazy that the information had been transmitted and that he should feel free to get in touch with the district attorney to convey any names or information of further use. Two weeks later, the *New York Tribune* reported that a secret meeting of the prominent Poles of New York and surrounding areas had met and "steps were taken to avert a danger said to threaten the Grand Duke Alexis on his arrival in New York."[23]

Whatever the truth, the threat of an assassination plot was serious enough to warrant the assignment of two detectives who stayed with Alexis constantly in New York and Washington. Moreover, the press subsequently wondered if any of the mishaps later in Alexis's trip, such as the derailment of a passenger train only hours before the ducal train was due to pass on the same track, had any connection to the Polish plot. Some papers resorted to gallows humor as well. The *Cleveland Daily Leader* reported that, at Brady's gallery in New York, Alexis had signed his name, "G. D. Alexis," adding, however, that if any "unfortunate Polander" had written the same thing, "there would have been a Coroner's inquest." The *Cincinnati Daily Enquirer* wondered if the rumor about the Polish plot had been invented by relatives of the Pinkerton's detectives to create a lucrative opportunity for the men.[24]

———— ✦ ————

Departing from Kronstadt in August 1871, the Russian fleet consisted of three vessels, the corvette *Bogatyr,* the clipper *Abreck,* and the frigate *Svetlana.* Alexis would be aboard the *Svetlana,* a wooden boat with an iron frame built in 1858 in Bordeaux. Together the three ships contained over seventy-five men, including several chaplains, and each ship had its own engineers and doctor, in addition to the officers and midshipmen. The most important men on board, however, were Admiral Constantin Possiet and the grand duke himself, holding the title of officer of the first watch. While some of the officers would travel with Alexis throughout his time in North America, most of them would stay with their ships. The fleet made several stops in Europe before taking to the open seas, dropping anchor in Copenhagen, Denmark; Plymouth and Falmouth, England; Marseilles, France; and Madeira, Portugal, where Admiral Possiet reported to the emperor that Alexis had bought a generous supply of strong wine, which he drank without moderation.[25]

The grand duke may have been attempting to drown his sorrows. In September 1871, writing from Falmouth, he asked his mother to forgive him for the stress he was causing her, but begged that she understand his plight. Zhukovskaya was about to give birth to his child and could possibly even die, but he was far away, unable to help her. Alexis declared, "This is too terrible; it is too much suffering for one man." Admiral Possiet witnessed Alexis's anguish and worried about his emotional state. In a draft letter to the tsar, Possiet described Alexis's intense despair, a subject he and Alexis had discussed often during their long journey across the Atlantic. Possiet tried to make the young duke understand the tsar's position and accept that a future with Zhukovskaya was impossible. Possiet reported that during these conversations Alexis was very sad and had sometimes wept. These talks, however, did not soothe the grand duke's aching heart. In November, as his ship approached New York, Alexis wrote his parents, apologizing again for all the grief he had caused them. He begged that both they and God would forgive him but also stressed how utterly miserable and alone he felt. Alexis clearly believed he had been abandoned by friends as well; he expressed disgust with the court gossip and with the reality that friendship could so quickly turn to contempt.[26]

These letters only convinced Alexander that Alexis had to be kept away from Zhukovskaya at all costs. This conviction was reaffirmed by Possiet's observations. Possiet recorded that Alexis's dedication to Zhukovskaya remained strong and that he was still determined to marry her at some point. Alexis had apparently told Possiet, "I can sail a year, two, three and five years, but after this, all the same, I must fulfill that which my conscience demands." Alexis sent his siblings sad, beseeching letters, as well, and they responded with sympathy, but also with warnings that their parents' minds were made up on the matter.

On September 17, Alexis's younger brother Vladimir wrote, "Many times I have talked with Mama about you. . . . her will is resolute, unbending, and the same is true of Papa." Yet, this resolve on the part of his parents did not mean that they were insensitive to his pain. Vladimir assured Alexis that, as much as he was suffering through this ongoing battle with their parents, "believe me, Mama is suffering twice as much. . . . I have never seen her so sad, even after the death of Niksi [Nikolai]." The empress was on the verge of tears each time they spoke of Alexis.[27]

As the date for Alexis's arrival approached and his frigate still did not appear, doubts arose anew, despite assurances from Russian and U.S. officials about the fleet's progress. Almost daily in late October, the *New York Times* reported that Alexis was expected momentarily but thick fog made it unlikely that the Russian squadron would attempt an approach, even if it were nearby. Meanwhile, the U.S. fleet remained on alert, anchored inside the bar at Sandy Hook, while the executive and reception committees also waited anxiously, their offices abuzz with last-minute details. There was considerable concern that the fleet's delay might interfere with the city's reception plans; if Alexis arrived within five days of the pending city elections, the National Guard would not be permitted to participate in the parade, due to an old law written to prevent intimidation at the polls by any armed force. The executive committee decided that, if the Russians arrived near election day, then they would spend one night in New York, then go to Washington, and the military parade would take place upon their return.[28] As the days passed, there were several false alarms, each generating a new frenzy of excitement.

Eventually, however, anticipation gave way to anxiety and concern for the safety of the grand duke and the other Russians. On November 5, the *New York Times* declared that the anxious elite of New York were conjuring up visions of "shipwreck and death by flood and fire." Other papers published poems about the young man's continuing absence: "Oh! Where is Duke Alexis now, tell me where is he? Is he roaming still upon the dark, the dark and treacherous sea! . . . If the Empress of the Russias knew how troubled he is now, Wouldn't she tear out old Neptune's eyes for raising such a row!" In fact, the Russian imperial family was worried. In late October, Catacazy received a telegram from Tsar Alexander asking that he be cabled as soon as his son arrived. Several weeks later, in early November, the U.S. minister to Russia, Andrew Curtin, telegraphed the London office of the New York Associated Press that the Russian government had received no word from Alexis since he left Madeira and so there were great concerns about his fate.[29]

The ever-fickle public also became weary of waiting. By early November, all of the preparations were complete for the grand duke's reception in New York, and the city's newspapers expressed the public's impatience with columns entitled, "Why Don't He Come?" The *New York Times* reported that the public's interest waned with each passing day, especially "the bright eyes of the New-York belles [which] have become dim and weary watching for his arrival." One magazine joked about yachts filled with beautiful ladies sailing out every day in the hope of meeting the Russian squadron: "We have heard of people fighting for a prince, beggaring themselves for a prince, and dying for a prince; but this is the first time we ever heard of people getting sea-sick for one." Another paper mocked the Russian squadron's slow pace, observing that, if Russia hoped to get the better of Turkey in the Black Sea, "she should overhaul her navy and introduce into that service something faster than a canal boat." Meanwhile, as the weeks of waiting dragged on, a Cincinnati paper took direct aim at "the snobs and toadies of New York." In a mocking tone that recognized an irony already being discussed around the country, the paper reported, "the flunkies are quite impatient.... they are ready and anxious to do homage to a scion of despotism, and will vie with each other in their humiliation before the august majesty of a boy of no better blood than the son of a mechanic or farmer."[30]

Finally, on the evening of November 11, a Russian ship appeared on the horizon. It was the corvette, *Abreck,* part of the grand duke's fleet, at sea for thirty-two days. After the requisite exchange of gun salutes and the presentation of colors, Vice-Admiral Stephen Clegg Rowan boarded the *Abreck* briefly to extend an invitation to Captain Lieutenant Frederick Schantz and his chief officer Nikolai Valetzki to dine aboard the *U.S. Congress* the next day. Lunch took place the following day in the early afternoon and included the Russian minister Catacazy as well as W. H. Aspinwall who, upon hearing a rumor that the grand duke's ship had arrived, had gone directly to Catacazy at the Clarendon and offered the use of his yacht, the *Day Dream,* if he could accompany the minister on his mission. Only a few days later, a second Russian corvette arrived, the *Bogatyr,* under the command of Captain Lieutenant Dmitri Sharov, and it too received a hearty welcome from the *Congress* and from its sister ship. In subsequent days, officers from both fleets dined with Catacazy at the Clarendon, encouraging rumors that one of the Russian sailors was, in fact, the grand duke incognito. Consequently, more than a few people were soaked in the rain waiting on the street outside the hotel for the disguised Romanov to appear.[31]

The long-awaited arrival of the *Abreck* and the *Bogatyr* also brought the first reliable news about the ocean voyage of the fleet and the possible whereabouts of the young grand duke. Captain Schantz of the *Abreck* reported that the fleet had arrived at Madeira on October 6 and, after only four days, had departed on the tenth en masse. Three days later, however, Admiral Possiet of the flagship *Svetlana* signaled that the ships should just plan to rendezvous in New York, presumably believing that the much slower *Abreck* would not be able to keep up. That was the last time the *Abreck* had seen the *Svetlana*. The *Abreck* then continued to travel west by sail and steam, delayed slightly by the breakdown of two boilers. When they arrived in New York, the men were shocked to discover that they were the first to arrive. The captain of the *Bogatyr* provided more information. His corvette had remained with the *Svetlana* for several more weeks before losing sight of her in severe weather on November 6. By Captain Sharov's estimation, that was about 820 miles from New York. Though both corvettes bore visible signs of the rough weather they had encountered, their captains expressed confidence that the *Svetlana* and its precious cargo would soon arrive safely.[32]

Finally, on November 19, the long wait ended with the appearance of the *Svetlana* off the coast of New York. There an American fleet under the command of Vice-Admiral Rowan was on hand to greet the special visitors with a display of Russian colors, and the two fleets, according to protocol, exchanged a series of gun salutes, a gesture of greeting and honor between the two admirals. Naval etiquette, however, did not permit a special gun salute or any other display for the *Svetlana*'s most important crew member, Grand Duke Alexis. As a lieutenant in the Russian Navy, Alexis could be welcomed with a grand reception only once he disembarked and reached dry land.[33] After the initial naval exchanges with the American ships, the Russian consul-general of New York, Vladimir Bodisco, along with Catacazy and the secretaries of the Russian legation, boarded the *Svetlana* to greet the grand duke. On shore, the New York reception committee prepared for the grand display scheduled for the following day.

Unfortunately, things did not go as planned for the excited hosts. November 20 was a gloomy day with drenching rains, which caused a bit of confusion about whether the reception would go forward as planned. Despite the bad weather, at ten in the morning several members of the reception committee stood at the gangways of the *Mary Powell* at the Vestry Street pier. Known as the "Queen of the Hudson," the *Mary Powell* was a fixture on the Hudson and known for her fine service and attentive crew.[34] While Jullien's orchestra and members of the Seventy-first Regiment band played on the deck, reception committee members checked tickets and admitted those approved to board the steamer that would carry the grand duke into the city.

Notably absent, however, were the members of the executive committee, who were apparently following an earlier decision to postpone the reception in the event of poor weather. After about an hour of confusion, and some frantic scrambling, a quorum of the executive committee was assembled, and they proposed delaying the reception until the following day, when they hoped the weather would be better, or until after the Russian guests returned from Washington, D.C. By this time, Catacazy and the Russian legation had arrived and were entrusted with the task of delivering the executive committee's message to the grand duke. Traveling on the *Northerner,* the Russian diplomats were followed by the *Mary Powell* and its excited passengers ready to lead the special guest into the bay.[35]

Once again, however, the committee's plans were foiled. For several months, the committee had planned an elaborate escort of military crafts and private yachts. When the moment arrived, however, nothing went as planned. Before the *Mary Powell* could reach the grand duke's ship, the Russian fleet guided itself into the bay, to the great chagrin of all those on board the American steamer, and what followed was a brief period of awkward uncertainty and agonizing inactivity as the Americans watched the Russian crew go through its paces and waited to respond appropriately. At last, members of the executive committee boarded the *Svetlana,* returning after about thirty minutes to announce that the grand duke would not come ashore until noon the following day, Tuesday, if the weather cooperated. Though this change of plans was a disappointment, the day was not a total loss for the guests on board the *Mary Powell,* who still enjoyed a sumptuous lunch as the band played and they steamed up the North River back to dock.[36]

Meanwhile, crowds of hopeful spectators all along the designated parade route stood in the pouring rain. George Templeton Strong, despite his expressed disgust for American toadyism, braved the weather, crowds, and thickets of umbrellas, "hoping vainly for a beatific vision of His Imperial Highness—such snobs we be." As the crowds became drenched and increasingly unhappy, some apparently resorted to alcohol to combat the boredom and the chill, a reliance on "artificial invigoration" that undoubtedly contributed to the many mistaken cries of "There he is!" By the time the American and Russian ships did arrive at the Battery, the crowd was rather unruly and nearly throttled three Russian sailors who committed the sin of not being the grand duke. A large and expectant crowd also lingered outside the Clarendon all day until Catacazy and the secretary of the Russian legation arrived and made it known that the grand duke would be sleeping aboard his ship yet another night.[37]

Finally, on Tuesday, November 21, Mother Nature smiled on the city of New York and the Grand Duke Alexis was able to go ashore and enjoy the reception as planned. At ten in the morning, carriages began to convey passengers to the *Mary Powell* until approximately 360 guests were on board, including the executive committee and the Russian legation. The *Mary Powell* approached the *Svetlana* and, after a few formalities, Alexis finally went aboard the American steamer. Once aboard, General John A. Dix, Civil War general and former minister to France, addressed the grand duke, citing the "long and uninterrupted" friendship of Russia and the United States and suggesting that, although America was a young nation, it might very well offer something of interest to the representative of a much older country. Alexis offered his thanks in English and expressed his desire to explore New York at length upon his return from Washington. The guests of the *Mary Powell* were then introduced to the grand duke and allowed to shake his hand, after which he lunched and finally set foot on American soil at about half past one in the afternoon.[38]

Once the grand duke had landed in New York, the reception program proceeded more or less as planned. The crisp, clear weather set the stage for a magnificent parade. The rain and disappointment of the previous day did not discourage many spectators from reappearing for a second try, so that Broadway was crammed with people from the Battery to Union Square. Homes and businesses along the route were bedecked with flags and banners, and eager onlookers sprouted from every door, balcony, window, and rooftop. Journalist Mary Clemmer Ames observed one man dangling from the spire of a church, "keeping humane mortals below in a perpetual fright lest he should drop upon the pavement and smash his foolish head." Ames admitted that she had come in from the countryside specifically to see the grand duke and, while others denied having made a special trip, she was "not ashamed to own it." Street peddlers and bootblacks were out in full force, as well, eager to make a few dollars from the waiting festive crowd. One sold chestnuts, another sold packets of candy that contained a small portrait meant to represent the grand duke, and a third made money with a dancing bear. As the parade began, the marching troops sustained the festive atmosphere with "the flashing of the bayonets in the warm sunlight, the stirring strains of the regimental bands, and the fluttering of gay banners in the breeze."[39]

The grand duke, escorted by Catacazy, General Dix, and Aspinwall, rode in a handsome carriage lined with maroon silk that was pulled by four fine black horses, secured with gold-mounted harnesses, while the others followed behind in separate carriages. The procession moved up Broadway, joined by more military bands along the way, accompanied by the pealing of the bells of Trinity Church, whose Gothic revival tower and spire were the highest point in the city. Nearby, city officials used the occasion to highlight the spectacular new Equitable Life Insurance Building and its ornamented entrance. The marble statue over the entrance, designed by John Quincy Adams Ward, an American sculptor of great renown, was entitled *The Protector* and consisted of a "genius of Life Insurance with spear and shield protecting a widow and her child." Installed in the fall of 1871, the statue remained wrapped in canvas until the grand duke's carriage reached the proper spot, at which time it was unveiled for the first time.[40]

The parade took Alexis and his party past other impressive sights that day as well. Further down Broadway, City Hall stood in all its splendor, its French Renaissance facade bedecked in bunting and evergreen for the occasion. Alexis also passed Grace Church, another Gothic revival masterpiece at Tenth and Broadway. It too rustled with Russian and American flags, and an arch declaring "Welcome Alexis!" spanned the street in front of the church. All along the parade route, the human menagerie cheered and waved, bouquets of flowers sailed through the air, and as far as the eye could see a "sea of handkerchiefs fluttered from delicate fingers." The entire parade from the Battery to the Clarendon was one long ovation, and Alexis bowed graciously and seemed pleased with the warm reception he received from the people of New York. It was a spectacular event and, according to one contemporary, "a picture that will live forever in the memories of the fortunate many who witnessed it."[41]

Such large concentrations of people were bound to produce problems, however. The crowd was particularly thick at Union Square and Fourth Avenue (now Park Avenue) near the grandstand and, although there were hundreds of policemen on hand, the situation grew dangerous as officers tried to clear the way for the procession and push the waiting spectators back onto the sidewalk. The throng was so dense and people pressed so tightly against one other that some struggled to breathe and began to panic. Men pushed and shouted, mothers cried out frantically for lost children, and the scene was such, according to the *Times,* as "might well be compared to some of those which have made Dante immortal." In other places, it was the behavior, not the size, of the crowd that posed the problem. Near Canal Street a group of ruffians grew rowdy once the procession had passed, moving up Broadway, knocking over women and children and "frightening thousands of country sight-seers out of their wits with their drunken shouts and yells."[42] All of this was unseen and unknown to Alexis, however, as he made his way to the Clarendon, where the executive committee and a number of ladies were waiting.

Opened in 1851, the Clarendon was a handsome five-story structure on Eighteenth Street facing Fourth Avenue, with accommodations for over 140 guests and an excellent dining room. In 1854, it had hosted a meeting of Cyrus Field, Peter Cooper, and a group of investors to raise money for the establishment of an underwater transatlantic telegraph cable. Situated within steps of Union Square and all the top theaters, exhibition halls, and social clubs, the Clarendon had earned a reputation as one of the finest establishments of its kind in New York and, perhaps, in the world. In fact, the Clarendon had become the favorite hostelry of celebrities and foreign ministers, and was known as "the headquarters of British aristocracy when visiting New York." Alexis was housed in a separate but adjoining wing of the Clarendon that consisted of three rooms richly decorated with frescoes, gilt-work, curtains of rich fabrics, beautiful statuary and art, and furniture of exceptional style and quality. The Clarendon had also added some decorations specifically for its Russian guests: the coat of arms of the Romanovs and paintings of the Emperor Nicholas and other members of the royal family.[43]

At the hotel, Alexis quickly passed through his rooms and appeared on the balcony, where he raised his hat and bowed to the cheering crowd below. At the same time, the mounted police and various military units and bands that had marched in the parade appeared on the horizon, calling forth another round of cheers. The soldiers saluted as they passed, displaying a discipline and precision that brought honor to their officers and admiration from all who watched, including the grand duke, who showed his appreciation with bows and salutes. When the last of the soldiers had passed, the spectators swarmed around the hotel, calling for Alexis again and again. The Russians stepped out onto the balcony three times, bowing and waving to the noisy throng, then departed for a brief service at the Russian Church on Second Avenue near Fifty-first Street.[44]

The Russian chapel was an attractive, yet modest, four-story brownstone with a simple facade and a small interior that necessarily limited the number of people who could accompany the royal visitors. These restrictions of space and protocol, however, allowed for a more intimate religious ceremony. At about five o'clock, the Russian party reached the church, where Reverend Father Nicholas Bjerring greeted them. Bjerring was a Catholic professor in Baltimore who had gone to St. Petersburg, embraced the Russian Orthodox faith, became a priest, and returned to America to preside over the newly founded Orthodox chapel in New York. Bjerring blessed Alexis, gave the benediction with the cross and welcomed the special guests, emphasizing the link between Orthodox Christians around the world and those in Russia. He wished the grand duke health and happiness, and then concluded with a brief service and a prayer, after which the Russian party returned to the Clarendon for a small private dinner with Catacazy and some of his friends.[45]

That evening, the Ninth Regiment band serenaded the grand duke at his hotel. As early as seven o'clock, excited celebrity-seekers had begun to gather at the Clarendon, and within a few hours the crowd was several thousand strong. Alexis, now in civilian dress, stood on the balcony and enjoyed the music as an excited crowd looked on. When the performance abruptly ended due to rain, he invited the band's leader, James Fisk, up to his quarters to thank him. Fisk was the infamous and colorful financier who only a few years earlier had helped to wrest control of the Erie Railroad from Cornelius Vanderbilt. Fisk had made his reputation as a fearless and aggressive speculator, and his and his business associates' shenanigans had resulted in the financial crisis called Black Friday in September 1869. A man for whom money was no object, Fisk had purchased the colonelcy of the Ninth Regiment, which allowed him to be part of the grand duke's reception. Alexis thanked Fisk and complemented New York's treatment of him thus far; Fisk responded that he would gladly do more and offered Alexis the use of everything he owned in the American continent. A reporter from the *Cleveland Daily Leader* sarcastically suggested that Alexis accept the offer and make the most of "Fisk's judges" on the Supreme Court of New York.[46]

As New Yorkers watched the grand duke's grand entrance, the rest of the country watched New York, and there was considerable anxiety about just how far some Americans would go in their adulation of Russia's royal son. Newspapers across the country bemoaned the disgusting toadyism on display and noted, "The occasional visits to the country of Princes, Grand Dukes and other sprigs of royalty ... serve to give American snobbery a chance to air itself." Most of the snide comments were aimed at New York elites, described as "delicate creatures ... who like lilies of the valley toil not." The *Washington Daily Morning Chronicle,* for example, sniped, "As we read the dispatch announcing the arrival of the Duke Alexis in New York, we came near saying, 'The long agony is over.' But yet it is not over. It is just begun. ... the palpitations of the heart of Toadydom were never more intense than at this minute." The *Weekly Arizona Miner* was likewise certain that the visit of the grand duke had put "the whole snobocracy of the United States upon the verge of insanity," particularly the women of New York and Boston, who were "cultivating their sweetest smiles and preparing to make fools of themselves generally." In many cities, it was reported that windows along designated parade routes were being rented for a hefty price, and there were even rumors that some individuals had paid Minister Catacazy for the privilege of an introduction to the grand duke. The *Pittsburgh Gazette* cringed at the embarrassing scenes in New York as people stood in the rain and cold to catch a fleeting glimpse of Alexis, or hovered near the kitchen where his food was prepared to smell the dishes he would eat; at least, the paper concluded, it could feel thankful that New York was not a representative American city.[47]

On Wednesday, November 22, Alexis and a few members of his entourage, along with Catacazy and members of the Russian legation, left New York bound for Washington. Departing the hotel at about eleven o'clock a.m. the procession of carriages made its way down Broadway and Canal Street to the Desbrosses Street landing, where the ferry *New Brunswick* was waiting to take them to the Jersey City train station. The special train provided by the New-Jersey Railroad and Transportation Company contained a kitchen, dining room, and a sitting room for reading or sleeping, all done up in magnificent style with the finest accessories. Anxious onlookers thronged the depot, but the train managed to depart on time, at half past eleven, after Alexis made a brief appearance on the rear platform, much to the delight of the cheering crowd.[48] The train passed through Newark, where Alexis stepped out on the platform and waved to an adoring crowd, and in Philadelphia, where it made a brief, virtually unnoticed stop; from there, it continued through Baltimore.

The people of Baltimore needed a distraction in the fall of 1871 from the daily reports on the arrest, investigation, and trial of Mrs. Elizabeth Wharton, an alleged murderer and possible serial killer. The sensational case was front-page news for months, even more so in late November as the trial was about to begin. Though Wharton was ultimately acquitted, at the time of the grand duke's visit, the gruesome story still gripped the public's attention. Nonetheless, the appearance of a handsome Russian prince was sufficient enticement to lure the people of Baltimore away from the Wharton spectacle and out to the train station. When Alexis's train reached Baltimore at about six o'clock in the evening, the duke rewarded their hearty cheers with a brief appearance on the platform before the train resumed its route to the nation's capital.[49]

The grand duke's train puffed into Washington at half past seven in the evening. The Russian guests made a smooth and quiet transition to their carriages, despite being greeted by some four hundred to five hundred people at the depot. The carriage containing the grand duke and Minister Catacazy proceeded directly to the minister's home on I Street, near Fourteenth, where a special reception awaited, as well as another eager group of spectators. After welcoming Alexis to his home, Catacazy then departed to make arrangements with Hamilton Fish for the official visit with the president the following day. Fish reminded Catacazy that, although he was persona non grata, he would be allowed to perform his official duties in introducing the grand duke to the president; but it was also understood that, under the circumstances, the reception of the grand duke would be brief, formal, and free of social embellishments. That night, following the reception at Catacazy's home, Alexis retired to the Arlington House, a fine hotel at Vermont Avenue that had been built only a few years earlier, near the White House. There, the grand duke and his retinue occupied the north wing, known as the Johnson House, a separate section of the hotel that contained eighteen rooms, including several elegant parlors and a large dining room.[50]

On Thursday, November 23, Grand Duke Alexis finally met with President Ulysses Grant in the Executive Mansion. A large crowd had gathered outside on the north portico, though only members of the press were admitted to the entrance hall. Members of the Cabinet and their wives who had been invited to attend the meeting began to arrive shortly after noon, including Secretary of the Interior Columbus Delano (and his wife), Attorney General Amos Akerman (and his wife), Secretary of the Treasury George Boutwell, and Secretary of the Navy George Robeson, as well as a number of other political and military figures. At one o'clock, the Russian visitors arrived, displaying full-dress uniform, and proceeded through the entrance hall to the Blue Room, where the American party waited. As agreed, the ceremony was short and there were no formal speeches, but despite the brevity and unspoken tension, the meeting created an impressive picture. There, under a sparkling crystal chandelier, Minister Catacazy presented the son of Tsar Alexander II to the president of the United States. Alexis cut a dashing figure in a blue uniform with gold epaulets and a light blue sash. The two men shook hands, and Alexis expressed his pleasure at meeting the head of the country with whom Russia had such good relations; Grant responded with his hope that Alexis would have a good journey through the United States. The president then introduced the members of his Cabinet, who also shook hands and exchanged greetings with the members of the Russian party.[51]

When the Russian and American officials were done with these formalities, the men all moved to the Red Room, where the Washington wives waited to be introduced. The Red Room had a long tradition of serving the interests of the ladies of the White House, and though Mrs. Grant had yet to refurbish it, the room was every bit as splendid as the Blue Room, with rich red accents, red upholstered furniture, and a magnificent marble fireplace. On one wall hung a Gilbert Stuart portrait of George Washington, the first piece of art purchased for the White House in 1800. Under the somber gaze of the first president, Alexis and his entourage met the administration's better half. The grand duke spoke briefly with Mrs. Grant, but the time spent in the Red Parlor was very short, and soon the Russian party boarded their open carriage and drove off toward the minister's home, where they spent much of the remaining day and evening. Mrs. Grant later wrote in her memoir that "we ladies were greatly disappointed" by the brevity and stiffness of the grand duke's visit. While she claimed not to remember the details of the Catacazy imbroglio, Mrs. Grant did recall that it had made the grand duke's reception awkward since, "in order to entertain the handsome young Duke, the offending Minister had also to be received, and their presence together at this time was very embarrassing." The sad result was that Alexis was received in an official capacity only, with no social entertainment, and the ladies of Washington were deprived of an evening of dancing with the dashing young Russian.[52]

Despite the brief visit, Alexis had made a favorable impression. Hamilton Fish recorded in his diary that the grand duke was "very affable, speaks English fluently, as does also Admiral Possiet." His remarks about Catacazy were not so kind, however: "Catacazy is limping, walking with a cane (I think) for the purpose of exciting sympathy & inducing questions to him to enable him to be in conversation with some persons at the reception." Fish worried that the tensions with Catacazy might jeopardize the success of the grand duke's visit. During conversation at the Executive Mansion, Alexis had expressed doubts about traveling to San Francisco, and Fish worried that this was a response to the American government's recent request for Catacazy's removal. Fears that the Russian-American friendship had been damaged by the Catacazy scandal increased when Alexis politely declined repeated invitations to return for a second visit to Washington.[53]

In fact, the secretary of state had reason to be concerned. In letters to Catacazy and to the tsar, Admiral Possiet confessed that even before arriving in the United States he had been opposed to a second trip to Washington, but then, after the "inhospitable welcome that Alexis received from the President," he was definitely against it. In fact, Possiet was repeatedly approached with the request for a second visit, even in the last leg of the trip. There were even discussions about whether it would be acceptable for the invitation to Washington to come from Congress itself, but since the circumstances that had caused Possiet to refuse the first time had not changed, he had to decline this offer as well.[54]

———◆———

Elsewhere in the United States, Alexis's visit created a venue for conversations about the successes and failures of the American governmental system. Members of the press used the royal visit as an opportunity to take shots at President Ulysses Grant and to draw comparisons between Russia and the United States, many of them unflattering. Many of the harshest comments about Grant came from southern newspapers, a trend that would be seen throughout the grand duke's time in America. The *Memphis Daily Appeal,* for example, called Grant the "American autocrat" who had deprived "states, communities, and individuals of hereditary freedom," and added, "Russia all things considered, is freer than the Southern States." The *Appeal* suggested that since the American form of government seemed to be moving toward "imperial instead of republican . . . we will want a proper ruler, and when an emperor is to be chosen why not take Alexis?" The *Charleston Daily Courier* similarly declared that, "the Republic, so far as the commonwealths of the South are concerned, has imitated and followed the politics and acts of the Czar, and . . . emulated his system of government." The *Atlanta Daily Constitution* took the comparison even further and used biting sarcasm to drive the point home. The paper published a mock letter purportedly sent by Alexander II to Grant, "the High and Mighty King, His Majesty, Useless the First." The letter recalled how America's founding fathers had created a country based on "that pestiferous dogma" of self-government, a system proved flawed by the American Civil War. The letter also compared the North's handling of the South to the way Russia had handled Poland, and congratulated Grant on his recognition that "the bayonet is the only fit instrument to despatch the business of government."[55]

Not all criticism came from the South, however. The *Boston Courier* wondered how Alexis would assess American society and government: "one cannot feel sure that a Grand Duke of Russia, where the great and able ruler is all in all and the people are only so many pawns, will fairly comprehend the precisely reversed order of things in this country." The *Courier* was particularly concerned about the grand duke's impression of President Grant: "It is not the slovenliness of his attire, nor the want of polish in his manners that especially vex us, though we should be glad to see improvement in these matters. . . . But a tinge of nature's nobility, a lurking show of greatness, either of mind or character, would console us infinitely." Moreover, the paper added, while Grant may have been a good enough military man, as president he was weak and too susceptible to "the office-seekers, the bearers of incense and of gift-offerings."[56]

———————◆———————

The day after his meeting with Grant, Alexis went to Annapolis for a tour of the Naval Academy, a stop that he had requested only two days before as he passed through Baltimore. The Russian party, accompanied by a group of naval officers, arrived amidst a cold, steady rain at the depot in Annapolis at about ten in the morning. At the Naval Academy, a battalion of marines in full dress welcomed the visitors, accompanied by the Russian national hymn and a twenty-one-gun salute fired from a battery of howitzers. Without stopping, the carriages proceeded to the quarters of the superintendent, Commodore John L. Worden, where the Russian party met more naval officers, as well as the wife and daughter of the commodore. These introductions were followed by a military drill and parade, a tour of the gunship *Santee,* and an inspection of the various facilities of the academy. After another booming gun salute, the Russian guests returned to the superintendent's quarters, where Governor and Mrs. Bowie and a number of young women, many of them officers' wives, waited to meet the grand duke. After brief pleasantries, the group moved to the adjoining quarters where a light, yet elegant, variety of foods awaited them. Commodore Worden and Alexis exchanged toasts, as did Secretary Robeson and Admiral Poisset, but it was Catacazy's words that drew the greatest applause. In a toast that would have special meaning for some of those present, the Russian minister lifted his glass to the most powerful members of the American government, "their *fairnesses* the women of America." At the conclusion of the toasts, the Russians departed, arriving back in New York late in the evening.[57]

Saturday, November 25, brought cold but bright weather for the grand duke's tour of the harbor fortifications. The steamer *Antelope,* anchored at the Thirty-third Street pier of the East River, sported Russian and American flags for the trip, and the band of the First United States Artillery was on board to offer musical entertainment. A significant number of invited guests were there as well, including senior members of the military and members of the New York reception committee. Once the steamer weighed anchor, the ladies and gentlemen mingled with the grand duke until the first stop, at Hallett's Point. Here operations were under way to remove the dangerous reef at the strait between Astoria, Queens, and Ward's Island known as Hell Gate, a narrow tidal strait that had caused hundreds of ships to run aground and many others to sink. Under the guidance of General John Newton, a system of underground tunnels was being built with the intention of exploding the treacherous rocks from below the water. The ducal party and guests proceeded to the entry point of these tunnels, where Alexis climbed down the ladders and descended into the shaft under the river to inspect the caisson as well as the operations and labor of the miners. The shaft was wet, and the roar of the river above was deafening, and more than a few ladies regretted that they had chosen to follow the handsome Russian underground. Upon emerging from the tunnels, Alexis witnessed the operations first-hand when a blast was detonated, throwing a column of water high into the air and jostling the steamer and all on board.[58]

Leaving Hallett's Point, the grand duke stood on deck in his great coat, smoking and chatting, and observing the various buildings and fortifications on both sides of the river as the *Antelope* steamed along towards Governor's Island. All along the way the royal party was welcomed with artillery salutes. An active army post since the eighteenth century situated on 172 acres in New York Harbor, Governor's Island was to be the site of what would be the first of many balls for the grand duke in the United States. A special room had been set up for dancing, with a beautifully polished floor and decorations of American and Russian flags. As the bands of the First Artillery and Governor's Island played, the grand duke danced away the afternoon, changing partners frequently to take a turn with all the young ladies present, though it was noted that he seemed to return repeatedly to Miss Sullivan, the niece of General McDowell. At five o'clock, the ball came to an end and the grand duke and his party were taken back to the Clarendon, where Alexis dined with a small group of invited guests.[59]

On Sunday morning, November 26, Alexis attended mass at the little Orthodox Chapel on Second Avenue. The *New York Herald* joked that Alexis probably needed the fortification of his soul against the coming week of events, a busy schedule that would undoubtedly "give him a chance to air all the Christian virtues, particularly resignation." The solemnity of his pursuit was lost, however, on the throngs of people who lined his path to the chapel and reminded him that he was, in their eyes, a spectacle. Following the service, Alexis returned to the Clarendon and spent a quiet day visiting with Aspinwall and other members of the reception committee. He also received Boston mayor William Gaston and a committee from the Board of Aldermen, there to invite the grand duke to visit their city, a proposal that he accepted. In the evening, Alexis and General Alexander Gorlov went for a quiet walk outdoors, free from pomp and the prying eyes of "lion seekers."[60]

On Monday, November 27, after breakfast, Alexis and several others, including the artist Albert Bierstadt, went by carriage to Mathew Brady's photographic gallery at the corner of Broadway and Tenth streets. Brady was America's most famous photographer, known for his portraits and photographs of the Civil War. During an era in which photographic techniques had developed to make portraiture cheaper and easier, studios actively sought to stimulate a public demand for photos, and more than anyone else, Mathew Brady created an enormous public market for portraits, especially those of celebrities, a collection for which he became famous. One popular manifestation of the public's hunger for celebrity portraiture was the *carte de visite,* a small calling card that displayed a photograph of the visitor. These photo cards became enormously popular in the 1860s, and people collected them and organized them into albums, much like later generations would collect baseball cards. By the time the grand duke arrived, it was expected that celebrities would stop at the best galleries in a city to have their picture made. The Prince of Wales had been impressed with the photographer's reputation and visited Brady's gallery in 1860; now, it was Alexis's turn. After inscribing his name in the guest book, Alexis had his portrait done in four poses, wearing civilian dress. Afterwards, he wandered around the gallery, admiring the other portraits such as those of Madame Catacazy and of his own parents, the emperor and empress. After navigating its way through the rather dense gathering that had assembled outside the building, the party drove back to the Clarendon, where the grand duke changed into his naval uniform and departed for his visit to the navy yard.[61]

The royal guest arrived about one-thirty in the afternoon, greeted by military officers and members of the reception committee. After an artillery salute and music by the Navy Yard Band and the First Artillery Band from Fort Hamilton, the grand duke was taken to a reception room for introductions, followed by a sumptuous feast. After the meal, Alexis took one turn around the dance floor and then exited for the primary purpose of his visit, an inspection of the yard and its work. The grand duke expressed particular interest in the workshop and the processes for repairing and launching ships. The tour of the yard was brief, however; the ducal party departed the navy yard at half past three to prepare for an evening at the theater.[62]

That evening, Alexis attended a performance of *Faust* at the Academy of Music, starring Miss Christina Nilsson, a blue-eyed, blonde soprano known as the Second Swedish Nightingale. The affair was a grand one, and well attended. On Saturday, some fifteen hundred tickets were sold, an unprecedented number, and by Monday a few clever speculators tried to turn a profit by scalping the coveted passes. The Academy of Music was thoroughly decorated for the evening, as was the proscenium box occupied by the grand duke, and the ladies who attended were dressed in their finest splendor. The performance itself was spectacular, so much so that the *New York Times* declared that "perhaps 'Faust' has never been better sung in New-York than on this occasion." With the exception of a few indignant subscribers deprived of their normal seats, the evening was a stunning success.[63]

————————✦————————

Even as Alexis enjoyed the various activities, however, he still felt homesick and despondent. Sometime after his arrival in New York, Alexis received a telegram from his father ordering him to continue to Asia before returning home. This was undoubtedly devastating news for the heartsick and lonely young man. His siblings back in Russia knew of their parents' decision and deeply regretted it. His younger brother, Sergei, assured Alexis in December 1871 that "we all think of you often and become so sad that we will still not see you for a long time." Alexis's older brother, the Tsarevich Alexander, echoed this sentiment and promised that the decision to keep Alexis away from home had not been an easy one: "You cannot imagine how much Mama misses you and how difficult it was for her to decide on the continuation of your voyage." Alexis made it obvious in his letters that he thought that everyone had forgotten him, but his brother Alexander insisted that such was not the case. "Dear Alexei, that is not just," Alexander wrote, "we think and talk of you constantly. . . . After Saturday lunches, at hunts, at the theater, everywhere, we miss you terribly and we constantly reminisce about you wherever we happen to be."[64]

Other friends and relatives got involved in this family drama, as well. One family friend, A. A. Tolstaya, urged Alexis to think of his mother and recognize that his choices affected everyone, not only himself. Alexis also received a long, stern letter from Ioann Rozhdestvenskii, another family friend. Rozhdestvenskii said that he had warned Alexis three years earlier about getting involved with Zhukovskaya, but understood how the naïve eighteen-year-old had fallen under the influence of an older woman, who was "fully mature with attractive qualities and feminine wiles." Rozhdestvenskii blamed Zhukovskaya for ensnaring the passionate young man and enticing him onto a "slippery road of unrestraint." He advised Alexis to forget about the idea of marriage and the hope that his child could ever be accepted by his family and by society: "you will not be able to look at him without blushing nor place him next to other children who were born after marriage." Nor would giving the child a legal name change this reality. Rozhdestvenskii counseled Alexis to follow the example of the prodigal son, change his ways, and place himself at the mercy of his father.[65]

Alexis's brother Vladimir intervened more directly. First, he encouraged Alexis to forget about a life with Zhukovskaya, and then he contacted Zhukovskaya herself. Vladimir explained to her that his many lengthy conversations with his parents had done nothing to sway them from their absolute rejection of the idea of marriage. He called upon their long friendship and her deep love for his brother, and begged her, "if you indeed love my brother... don't destroy him, but willingly, sincerely, give him up." Alexis was infuriated by this intrusion and lashed out at his brother only four days after arriving in New York City: "I am not surprised that you have fallen completely under their influence; it could happen to people of an even stronger character... but did you really think that all the things you fabricated about poor A.V., all her intrigues and cleverness that she supposedly used, all this trash would make my love waiver...?" The grand duke scolded Vladimir for writing such a letter to Zhukovskaya only days before she gave birth and concluded, "It's surprising to me how you can ask about my life... you, who are too smart to know that I could never act otherwise and would do anything to save her."[66]

The turmoil over Alexis's relationship with Zhukovskaya persisted throughout his trip to the United States and threatened to tear the tsar's family apart. Alexis was unrelenting in his commitment to Zhukovskaya and blamed his parents for his utter misery. The correspondence between father and son has a certain timelessness, and invokes the kinds of emotions that often erupt between parents and children over issues of love and youthful indiscretion. In December 1871, the tsar wrote to Alexis that he was distressed by his last letter from New York: "you are trying to justify your shameful behavior with sophism, which shows that you still do not acknowledge all its vileness." The tsar tried to assure his son that he and the empress loved him and were not trying to make him miserable, but rather, were trying to save him from an unhappy life.[67]

———————— ◆ ————————

On Tuesday, November 28, the day after the performance at the Academy of Music, the grand duke was witness to a display of a different sort—a review of the Metropolitan Fire Brigade in Tompkins Square. Despite the cold weather, a sizeable crowd milled about the square several hours before his anticipated arrival. A little after one in the afternoon, Alexis and his suite, accompanied by Catacazy, Aspinwall, Board of Fire Commissioners president William Hitchman, and a number of others arrived to the sounds of a cheering crowd and the Russian national anthem. Alexis, dressed in blue pantaloons, white hat, and brown overcoat, then walked around the square examining the fire engines before ascending a platform to view the parade of the fire brigade. The Russian party then returned to the Clarendon, where one of the fire commissioners proposed that Alexis test the efficiency of the fire department. The New York Fire Department already possessed the standard features of a fire station with which we are familiar today—uniforms that could be easily put on, the fireman's pole, and so forth—but only days before, a system of telegraph calls and signals had been implemented to facilitate a quicker response time. Alexis and several commissioners walked to the fire-alarm box on the corner of Seventeenth Street and Fourth Avenue, about a half a block from the hotel, and telegraphed, "Fire in Union Square." Before Alexis could reach the hotel balcony, the sounds of galloping horses and swiftly rolling wheels could be heard, and in moments several engines and ladder companies arrived in the square. Within three minutes of the initial alarm, two streams of water were directed at the nearby Everett House, and within five minutes ladders had been raised to the hotel windows and fireman were already on the adjoining rooftops.[68] The grand duke was suitably impressed.

Later that evening, the Brooklyn Navy Yard hosted a ball for the Russian guests. The reception committee had taken every precaution to assure the success of this splendid affair, selecting the naval store building as the venue for the ball and ordering that only the carriages of those bearing the proper tickets would be admitted through the entry point at York Street. The guest list for this event was somewhat broader, or perhaps, more political, than that of the other festivities. The committee limited the tickets to twelve hundred, but invited President Grant and the Cabinet and their accompanying ladies, distinguished officers of the U.S. Army and Navy, and a number of private citizens. The ballroom was on the third floor and had been decorated with the requisite Russian and American flags and nearly 100,000 yards of bunting, as well as with highly polished sword bayonets and pictures and models of military vessels. Perhaps the most notable of these was the model of the USS *Miantonomah,* which had visited Russia in 1866 with Assistant Secretary of the Navy Gustavus Vasa Fox, and the USS *Wampanoag,* which had accompanied Admiral Farragut and his squadron in 1867. All of the brilliantly lit candle chandeliers increased the chance of fire, but extra fire hoses had been concealed behind the curtains as a precaution.[69]

When the grand duke finally appeared at ten that evening, he was welcomed into the Navy Yard by an impressive presentation, including a battalion of marines in new uniforms with burnished arms. As he entered the building and made his way to the ballroom, the other guests cheered, having already waited two hours for the event to begin. Now, with the arrival of the young Russian, the ball could officially commence. The first dance of the evening was led off by Alexis and Miss Braine, daughter of the chairman of the committee of arrangements, and the dancing and socializing continued until well after midnight. When the many guests proceeded to gather their belongings and leave, however, they discovered that the coats and cloaks had been ticketed and stored in a haphazard manner, and some guests waited for hours in an attempt to locate their things. Eventually, many people simply gave up and returned home, and for days afterwards the *Brooklyn Eagle* was filled with ads for lost cloaks, overcoats, gloves, and hats that had been left behind or mistakenly taken at the Brooklyn ball. Nonetheless, the ball was considered a great success and a memorable occasion, even for those who lost their coats in the frenzy of the evening.[70]

The next day, Alexis failed to attend the planned breakfast at Jerome Park, apparently still recovering from his late night in Brooklyn. By late morning, however, he had sufficiently rested and emerged from his quarters at the Clarendon for a brief shopping tour of the city with Catacazy and Count Olsufiev. His first stop was Savony's photographic gallery on Broadway, where he reviewed the portraits on display and had his own portrait done in several poses. Alexis also stopped at Stewart and Tiffany's jewelry store, where he purchased several bronze statues as well as a few small pieces of jewelry. A little later, Alexis set out with Catacazy, Aspinwall, and other members of the reception committee for a tour of Central Park. The grand duke admired the beauty of the park, although the cold weather made it a little difficult to enjoy such an open-air activity. Consequently, the remainder of the afternoon was spent indoors, relaxing at the Clarendon.[71]

While Alexis spent the afternoon quietly resting, the rest of the city was abuzz with anticipation of the ball that evening at the Academy of Music. The reception committee had limited the number of tickets to twenty-five hundred, and each member of the committee had a certain number of tickets for which he was responsible to the treasurer. Tickets were ten dollars each for one gentleman and one lady. Despite this careful planning, that evening a number of well-dressed individuals besieged committee members in hopes of acquiring tickets to the ball, which were simply not to be had. Many of these individuals then set off in search of speculators selling tickets at some of the other local hotels and, according to the *New York Times,* many tickets, in fact, were sold at a nice profit. At the Fifth Avenue Hotel, one speculator offered a box at the Academy of Music that night for three hundred dollars, the same box that the reception committee had sold for fifty dollars. The *Times* did not know if the overpriced box had found any takers. As a precaution, the committee had appointed someone to check tickets to the ball and to specifically be on the lookout for tickets with the names of well-known citizens on them.[72] Moreover, a large police force was on hand to direct carriages and control the crowd.[73]

The ball was set to begin at nine o'clock, though a number of eager carriages arrived thirty minutes before and had to wait in the cold. About one hundred persons entered when the outer doors finally opened, but the room remained rather quiet and subdued since the committee had decided not to begin the music or dancing until Alexis's arrival. The parquet of the Academy was floored over to create a larger area for dancing, and the stage was hung with light-colored silk tapestry. One wall featured a moonlit garden scene, while other walls were hung with striped silk and gold fringe; garlands of flowers streamed from the ceiling and a fountain with changing-colored lights illuminated part of the room. Other decorations included Russian and American coats of arms, representations of Lincoln and Alexander II holding their respective emancipation proclamations, and portraits of the grand duke's parents.[74]

By ten o'clock, it was growing bitterly cold outside and the special entrance erected on Fourteenth Street, decorated with lace curtains, did nothing to protect anyone from the wind. Consequently, when Alexis arrived at half past ten, Bierstadt quickly hustled him inside and led him to a private box, a stealthy entrance that went largely unnoticed by most of those present until the band struck up. As the dancing began, all eyes remained fixed on the handsome Russian duke, even those of the dancing couples. Finally, Alexis, dressed in a naval frock coat with open lapels and two stars on his breast, joined the dancing with Mrs. Hoffman, wife of Governor John Hoffman, on his arm. The band played a selection of music from Offenbach's opera *Les Brigands,* in addition to pieces suitable for other dances, such as lancers, waltzes, quadrilles, galops, and polkas. One newspaper noted that, though the floor was exceptionally crowded, it was the tendency of some dancers to follow the grand duke that made it difficult to move about properly.[75]

After Alexis had worked up an appetite, it was time for the banquet at Nilsson Hall. The hall was brightly lit and decorated that evening with flowers, plants, Russian and American flags, and statues of George Washington made of chocolate. After dinner, Alexis danced several quadrilles with some of the most prominent ladies there, including Samuel Morse's daughter and William Aspinwall's wife. The grand duke left at a late hour, and the other guests dispersed soon after. When the evening was over, the *New York Herald* praised the festivities, noting with humor that, due to the Tammany Hall embarrassment, "the great magnates of the municipality who toasted Albert of Wales and Tommy of Japan in years gone by were conspicuously absent."[76]

Thursday, November 30, was Thanksgiving Day, and so there was no major activity planned for the grand duke. In the morning, Alexis attended a Thanksgiving service at the Orthodox Chapel, accompanied by Admiral Possiet and several members of the Russian legation, and in the afternoon he relaxed in his hotel quarters and conversed with a few friends. Later that day, William Aspinwall held a dinner for the grand duke at his home at the corner of University Place and Tenth Street which included the traditional fare of roast turkey, pumpkin pie, and plum pudding. There Alexis also had the pleasure of viewing Aspinwall's growing art collection, which included a number of paintings by the old European masters. In the evening Alexis and a few others, both Russians and Americans, went out to Bryant's Opera House. Built in 1870 by Daniel Bryant, this performance hall was the home of Bryant's Minstrels, a blackface troupe that specialized in "minstrelsy, and to that particular form of light sketchy representation belonging thereto." It was also the original venue of the song "Dixie," written by Daniel D. Emmett sometime in the late 1850s and popularized in theaters in New York and New Orleans. By the time of the grand duke's visit, "Dixie" was so popular that it was included as the final number in every performance of Bryant's Minstrels.[77]

On Friday, Alexis and his suite were taken on a tour of West Point. Though it was a very cold day, the weather was beautiful, perfect for an excursion up the Hudson River, and the *Mary Powell* was dressed in brightly colored banners and streamers. At the Thirty-fourth Street wharf, Alexis, Catacazy, and Aspinwall, as well as a number of Russians from the grand duke's suite and from the Russian legation, boarded the steamer to the strains of a Russian hymn played by Jullien's thirty-piece band. All of the Russians wore handsome uniforms and warm great coats ornamented with shoulder straps displaying the imperial crown. Once on board, Alexis exchanged greetings with a number of people and then moved to the saloon, where he joined the Aspinwall party and engaged in casual and easy conversation, "with no stiffness nor formality, nor social ice." The grand duke moved freely about the steamer, smoking and conversing with other passengers, "neither neglected nor bored, but . . . made to feel that he was master of the situation." Occasionally, he went on the upper deck to enjoy the cold breeze and admire the scenery, which he declared some of the most beautiful he had ever seen. At noon, a light lunch of coffee and sandwiches was served below deck and Alexis partook eagerly.[78]

After lunch, the *Mary Powell* pulled up to Knox's Battery, where she received a twenty-one-gun salute and all the guests disembarked and headed toward the parade ground. Alexis arrived in an elegant barouche, escorted by a cavalry company, and was driven in a circle around the parade ground, and then introduced to the superintendent, General Thomas H. Ruger. In the distance, the drums of the approaching cadets could already be heard. Soon the cadets arrived and stood at attention for the grand duke's inspection, after which they marched around the parade ground several times and then to their barracks. Alexis then toured the public offices, hospitals, barracks, museum, and library, returning to the *Mary Powell* at about half past two. As the steamer set out for New York once again, dinner was served, with scrumptious foods covering two elegantly decorated tables. Dinner was followed by dancing, and for several hours the guests waltzed to the melodic strains of Jullien's band. Eventually, someone suggested a Virginia reel, a step entirely unfamiliar to the young Russian. According to one account, Alexis enjoyed this dance immensely and "went up the middle and down again with infinite zest," but when he tried to pass under an arch of hands, his "majestic proportions were too much, and the arch broke amidst peals of laughter." In the evening, Alexis once again visited the Academy of Music and listened to the opera *Mignon,* sharing Governor Hoffman's box with Albert Bierstadt.[79]

On December 2, Alexis attended a special ceremony at the Academy of Design on the corner of Twenty-third Street and Fourth Avenue. At a few minutes past ten o'clock Alexis and his party were met by Professor Samuel Morse, Albert Bierstadt, William Page, and several other artists for the presentation of a painting intended as a gift to his father, the tsar. The large canvas was done by Page, a New York artist known particularly for his portraits, and portrayed Admiral David Farragut on the SS *Hartford* entering Mobile Bay during the Civil War. In September 1869, a committee of individuals had decided to purchase the painting as a gift for Tsar Alexander, and then subscriptions had been taken from around the country at one hundred dollars each. In the end, almost one hundred donors, including notable figures such as Hamilton Fish, William Tweed, and John Jacob Astor, had subscribed. The painting was to be accompanied by an elaborate parchment scroll thanking Russia for its sympathy during the Civil War and for the hospitality shown to Farragut and his men during their visit to the empire in 1867. Beneath this message, the scroll was signed by the subscribers. Once the organizers found out that Alexis would be coming to the United States, they decided to present the painting to him to take back to his father. Now, General John A. Dix presented the painting to Alexis with a short address about the continuing good relationship between their two countries, and the grand duke responded with a brief reply of thanks. Soon after, he departed for the Clarendon and the remainder of the day was spent in quiet leisure. At some point that afternoon, Alexis visited Brady's photographic studio again, a fact that became known to many of the ladies of New York. According to the *New York Times,* it was estimated that over three thousand ladies visited Brady's that day, many of whom purchased photographs of the handsome young Romanov.[80]

After almost two weeks in New York, Alexis must have been tired of the endless activity, but there remained yet one more event in his honor. On the evening of December 2, the New York Yacht Club welcomed the grand duke with a splendid dinner at Delmonico's, New York's most famous eating establishment. Founded in 1837, Delmonico's specialized in serving the finest in local produce and the best of European sweets and pastries, and soon established itself as the premier place for wealthy New Yorkers to dine. The restaurant's reputation grew under the stewardship of Lorenzo Delmonico, so much so that when Lorenzo went bankrupt in 1851 after a bad investment and put the restaurant up for auction, not only did the New York business community refuse to bid on it, but his customers actually loaned him the money to keep it open. Delmonico's became the site of the most prestigious and elegant dinner parties in New York and the regular hot spot for celebrities and politicians. One writer noted, "A social history of the upper classes in New York during the last quarter of the nineteenth century could have been compiled without leaving the reservation desk of Delmonico's Fourteenth Street restaurant." Such a restaurant was the logical choice to wine and dine a grand duke.[81]

At seven o'clock in the evening, Alexis and his suite arrived at Delmonico's, where they were joined by the leaders of the yacht club and other invited guests in the main parlor of the restaurant. Among those distinguished guests was Gustavus Vasa Fox, who would subsequently host a lunch for the grand duke in Lowell. All of the Russian party were dressed in naval uniforms, but Alexis was particularly dashing, his breast glittering with medals. Commodore James Bennett Jr. welcomed Alexis and the other guests, and after a bit of pleasant conversation, led them into the dining hall, where they were presented with a magnificent scene. The members of the yacht club were all finely dressed as required by the club for such special events, and the hall was beautifully decorated with streamers, flags, and coats of arms of each nation, as well as a "magnificent piece of confectionary" made to resemble the grand duke. The centerpieces on the tables were models of yachts and various cups won by members of the yacht club, including the trophy cup won by the *America* in 1851, henceforth known as the "America's Cup." Jullien's orchestra played in the background. The dinner included the standard toast to both countries' leaders, as well as an invitation to Alexis to accept an honorary membership in the club. Thanking the yacht club for its generosity and complimenting its excellence, Alexis added, "I am a man of the sea myself, and can appreciate the enthusiasm with which you enter into all that regards yachting." Though other princes, dukes, and kings would be made honorary members—the Prince of Wales in 1861, King Edward VII in 1901, King Olav of Norway in 1958—Alexis would be the only Russian granted this honor.[82]

On Alexis's final morning in New York, he went to the Orthodox Chapel again and, in the afternoon, he and his staff drove to the photo gallery of Mathew Brady's biggest rival, Jeremiah Gurney, on the corner of Sixteenth and Fifth Avenue. Like Brady, Gurney was known for his portraits of famous individuals, including Charles Dickens, Samuel Morse, Mark Twain, and opera singer Euphrosyne Parepa-Rosa. After being photographed as a group, the Russians returned to the Clarendon and spent the remainder of the day there until it was time to meet their train for Philadelphia.[83] There were rumors that Alexis had requested an interview with the women suffragists and that Catacazy had arranged a meeting with Victoria Woodhull at her home on Thirty-eighth

Street near Fifth Avenue. Sadly, there is no evidence that this meeting ever took place—a pity, since Woodhull's bid for the American presidency on the immediate horizon would have undoubtedly given the grand duke and notorious feminist much to discuss.[84] Moreover, a meeting with Woodhull would have provided an interesting contrast to the media's representation of American women as shallow, frivolous, husband-hunters.

When all was said and done, the grand duke's reception in New York was a good beginning to his visit to the United States. Alexis seemed to have enjoyed himself and sent a telegram to that effect to the reception committee in the days after his departure.[85] For many New Yorkers the royal visit was a boon. Just as there had been those who made the most of the Marquis de Lafayette's visit, now New York businesses took advantage of Alexis's arrival to make a quick buck, as well, either by capitalizing on the social events associated with the visit, selling Alexis-themed items, or simply using Alexis's name in their ads. By the 1850s there were some 2,300 weekly and some 200 daily newspapers in the United States, a development that contributed to the growth of advertising in a modern sense. Previously, advertisements had been more about announcing the availability of goods, but by the time of the grand duke's arrival, advertising had its modern goal of luring customers in with clever language and enticing promises. Alexis's visit was the perfect hook for advertising in the fall and winter of 1871–72. For example, one business in New York offered "Alexis ties and cravats, Alexis collars, Alexis hats, gloves, canes, and perfumes," while a cobbler on Broadway displayed in his window the "Grand Duke of Russia's double decked shoes." The wine merchant and grocer, Bouche Fils & Company, advertised that they had for sale the very same wine used at the reception of the grand duke, "Napoleon's Cabinet Champagne." Knox's Great Hat Emporium attempted to persuade customers that after Alexis had attended religious services he had asked to be taken to their store. Claiming that Alexis had seen Knox's hats in Russia on American tourists and wanted to select some for himself, the ad declared that he had purchased fifteen hats and tried to persuade Knox to return to Russia with him. In fact, Knox's had been one of the earliest businesses in New York to recognize the potential of celebrity endorsement and advertising with the current topics of the day.[86]

There were some significant problems to be sorted out after the grand duke's departure, however. There were reports, for example, that Louis Jullien, the famous musician, had run off with the money he had received from the reception committee, failing to pay the members of his orchestra before he fled. The defrauded musicians held "an indignation meeting," asking the reception committee to pay them and threatening to ask the grand duke for payment if they were not gratified. The reception committee claimed to owe them nothing, having contracted with Jullien, not the individual musicians. There was also a problem with the payment to William Page for the painting he made of Farragut. According to one report, Page never received full payment for the painting from the reception committee and, when he attempted to address the situation, he was told that there was no more money to be had; in fact, members of the committee were going to have to spend money out of their own pockets to ship the painting to the emperor. Finally, there were reports that Brooklyn Navy Yard authorities had miscalculated in their financing of the ball, using up the monthly appropriation they received from the federal government that was intended to pay for all of the navy yard's expenses. Consequently, two hundred laborers had been laid off from the Brooklyn Navy Yard after the ball until the books could be balanced. The *Brooklyn Eagle* declared this to be just one example of the mismanagement of the current administration, while the *Ottawa Citizen* wryly noted, "the Grand Duke will dance while the laborers pay the piper."[87] Despite these problems, members of the New York elite believed the Russian visit had gone spectacularly.

Little did New York know, but it had set the example against which all other cities would compare themselves and their own receptions for the grand duke. For the next two and a half months, city officials across America would compete with one another, girls would vie to dance with the handsome young Russian, and each city would declare that Alexis liked it best and considered its women the most beautiful. The press would follow his every move, often with front-page stories, and extol his virtues and attributes. Alexis was reported to be an accomplished musician, especially on the piano, a first-class skater, "passionately fond of flowers," a good artist in drawing and painting, and skilled with a rifle and sword. He was also very brave and preferred brunettes. With few exceptions, Alexis was described as tall, handsome, and intelligent looking, with a pleasant and easygoing nature. People of all walks of life took an interest in the Russian visitor, attending balls or parades, or simply standing along the rails as his train passed by.[88] America had been swept up in Alexis mania.

4

LEAVING HIS RUSSIAN STEPPES BEHIND

> There's a Muscovite youth named Alexis,
> Who an officer first of the deck is,
> And he came here to see
> What this country might be,
> Ere our land to his own he annexes.
>
> —*Saturday Evening Post,* December 30, 1871

W HEN ALEXIS left New York, he traveled to several other cities in the Northeast, beginning with Philadelphia. Though Philadelphia was not originally on the grand duke's itinerary, local newspapers had begun to print stories about his visit to the United States some six months before his expected arrival, and as the date of the event approached, Philadelphia city officials began to discuss the possibility of inviting him. While many approved of the idea, there was considerable disagreement over the financial obligations such an endeavor might entail. One city councilman proposed that the reception should not exceed twenty-five hundred dollars, while others demanded that the arrangements for Alexis be done at no expense to the city.[1] As the dispute dragged on, the local press began to weigh in on the matter. The *Inquirer* enthusiastically promoted the idea of a reception, citing Russia's friendship during the Civil War, but reminded readers that the city should give Alexis "a hearty, spontaneous welcome, not forgetting our own dignity, nor bow too low because it is a prince that comes our way." The friendship should elicit the respect, not the title.[2]

The city government's inability to agree on the proper reaction to the appearance of Russian royalty finally prompted a group of "influential and public-spirited citizens" to take the lead. With the support of Mayor Daniel Fox, these men met on November 22 at a local wine and liquor store where they discussed the possibility of a parade, a ball, and a banquet, and decided to send out an announcement to merchants inviting their participation. The following day, a larger, public meeting was held at the mayor's office with Governor James Pollock and a number of other prominent gentlemen in attendance. The assembled party selected Mayor Fox as chair of the general reception committee, and chose an official arrangements committee of fifteen persons, with General George Meade, the hero of Gettysburg, as the chair. Fox also assembled various subcommittees to be in charge of the floor of the ballroom, subscription of tickets, music and dancing, printing cards and souvenirs, and refreshments. With these preliminary steps in place, General Meade sent a letter to the Russian minister Catacazy asking for a meeting with Alexis in New York.[3]

The men who had taken it upon themselves to invite and plan the reception of the grand duke were among the upper crust of Philadelphia society: prominent attorneys, politicians, businessmen, philanthropists, and newspapermen.[4] General George Meade was perhaps the most famous of the men involved, a military engineer who had fought in the Mexican-American War, and had served as commander of the Army of the Potomac, with which he had his famous victory over Robert E. Lee at Gettysburg.[5] Several others—Joseph Fell, John Edgar Thomson, Matthew Baird, and Joseph Harrison—were involved in the railroad business. Baird was the owner of the Baldwin Locomotive Works and a prominent philanthropist, contributing to such worthy organizations as the Academy of Fine Arts and the Northern Home for Friendless Children, an orphanage founded to care for the children of soldiers. Harrison had been involved in railroad development in Russia in the 1840s when his firm had been hired by the Russian government to construct locomotives and railcars for a four-hundred-mile line being built between St. Petersburg and Moscow. Despite various difficulties, Harrison's firm successfully completed the project, which included the construction of a cast-iron bridge over the Neva River. It was the largest and most expensive bridge in the world at the time. So pleased was Tsar Nicholas I with Harrison's performance that when the bridge opened in 1850 he awarded the American engineer the ribbon of the Order of St. Ann.[6]

John Rice was also a household name in Philadelphia, though not always a popular one. One of the most active and well-known builders in Philadelphia, Rice could take credit for construction of the Continental Hotel and many of the city center's banking and market houses. He was also president of the Public

Buildings Commission, the organization that had authorized the erection of a vast, ornate, new City Hall (which still stands at the intersection of Market and Broad streets). This decision was unpopular with many Philadelphians even before construction began; many were already concerned about the ever-escalating cost of the project and the commission's unchecked ability to milk the public. In November 1871, the *Philadelphia Bulletin* took to task the Public Buildings Commission's successive and questionable "raids upon the public treasury," calling for "Mr. Rice's Building Ring" to be held accountable for its expenditures. Rice's participation in the grand duke's reception plans gave the press more ammunition. The *Bulletin,* for example, expressed approval—tongue in cheek—that the grand duke would be guided about the city by "such a noble type of the Philadelphia gentleman of culture, refinement and genius as the President of the Building Commission." Alexis would no doubt learn much from Rice about "the tricks of the voting on the site, the stealing of the tickets of his opponents, and the purchase of the Legislature of 1871." One barb added, "It is understood that Mr. Rice was kept off the Ball Committee because he wanted to roof over one of his excavations at Penn Square for the purpose, and tax the city for the bill."[7]

By the end of November, the committees entrusted with various details of the grand duke's visit, now bloated with dozens of members, were busy making plans. In particular, the reception committee and the committee on the ball gave considerable attention to the question of who would be admitted to the ball and how that exclusivity would be accomplished. Ultimately, the committee members decided to limit the ball to one thousand attendees and to sell subscriptions to the "Grand Duke Alexis Reception Fund" that would entitle the subscriber to tickets to all the various events. Fifty dollars would buy tickets for a couple to attend the breakfast and ball, with coupons for two reserved seats in the balcony of the Academy of Music on the evening of the ball. Though the Philadelphia press had ribbed New York planners for their elitism, Philadelphia hosts were no better, debating how to sell tickets "so that none but those of good repute could obtain them." In subsequent days, members of the subcommittee on subscriptions and tickets screened applicants at their individual businesses throughout the city, "thus guaranteeing against indiscriminate admission." By early December, ticket sales were booming and the ball preparations were in their final stages. The *Inquirer* commented that the ball would be "on a grand scale, and will doubtless eclipse anything of the kind ever attempted," and added, "If Philadelphia had as much time to prepare as New York had the affair would fully equal theirs. As it is it will not be far behind."[8]

Meanwhile, the citizens of Philadelphia anticipated the duke's arrival with enthusiasm. While some regretted that the royal visit would be so brief, the *Philadelphia Inquirer* predicted that the festivities would be grander than those arranged for the Prince of Wales several years earlier. Others predicted that the visit of the young Russian would have an impact in the fashion world. The *Public Ledger* reported that the "Alexis cut of hair" was now in fashion, as was fur trim on coats, boots, gloves, and hats of all types. An "Alexis ginger ale" was now being sold in the city as well. The *Bulletin* published an entire column of puns about the coming visitor. One joke, for example, remarked that, "The supper-room of the Academy will present abundance, and the ball floor a-bear-dance."[9] Local businesses also took advantage of the excitement. One company claimed that, upon his arrival in America, Alexis had immediately requested Kitchen Crystal Soap; he and his suite all used it, "it being a penal offense to use any other in Russia."[10]

Late in the evening of December 3, somewhere around eleven o'clock, the train carrying the grand duke and his suite chugged into the train station in Philadelphia, puffing steam into the cold night air. Mayor Fox, General Meade, Admiral Turner, and John Rice met the grand duke and his retinue with ten coaches loaned by private citizens and escorted them to the Continental Hotel, where a squad of thirty police officers stood by to keep order. Despite the late hour and the dropping temperature, a sizable crowd huddled outside the Continental, but their patience and perseverance came to nothing; when the Russian guests arrived, they were promptly whisked by a private stairway to their apartments, where the grand duke had a bite to eat, smoked a cigarette, and retired. The rooms for Alexis and his entourage contained elegant carved furniture, upholstered in blue velvet, with portraits of the Russian imperial family on the walls and a large yellow flag with the Russian double-headed eagle over a large mirror in the parlor. Outside the hotel, the Russian flag flew in honor of the royal guest.[11]

Located at the corner of Chestnut and Ninth, the Continental from its inception had been surrounded by scandal and controversy. In the mid-1850s, John Rice proposed the construction of a grand hotel that would bring prestige to Philadelphia and, to that end, he and a group of other men formed a company with the intent of selling shares to fund the project. The company, however, faced immediate opposition. But despite accusations of "bogus subscribers" and fears that the hotel would be too large, creating a fire hazard and street congestion, construction began in 1857, and when the hotel was completed in 1860, the end result was magnificent. Constructed of Nova Scotia stone and pressed brick, the hotel stood six stories high, and the five hundred sleeping rooms had first-class furnishings and gas lights.[12]

The morning after Alexis's arrival in Philadelphia, a rather large crowd milled about the Continental Hotel, but the police made certain that no one ascended to the grand duke's apartments on the second floor except those few who had permission. A little before ten o'clock, Governor John Geary was presented to the grand duke, and shortly after, the entire party left the hotel, bound for Girard College. Alexis rode in an open barouche, with two footmen, drawn by four bay horses in gold-mounted harnesses, accompanied by Meade, Geary, and Catacazy. Before making it to this first destination, however, the procession nearly encountered disaster. At the intersection of Eighteenth and Coates, the carriage containing ex-governor Pollock and surgeon general of the navy, Dr. Jonathan Foltz, lost a wheel, causing the horses to panic. Luckily, no one was injured thanks to the help of an unknown bystander who prevented the horses from bolting. A few days later, when Alexis was preparing to leave Philadelphia, he gave the mayor twenty-five dollars to reward this unknown hero, could he be identified. Not surprisingly, the promise of reward money unearthed a number of "heroes." Though the *Inquirer* reported on December 6 that the individual who had seized control of the frightened horses was Charles Wolbert, five other men had laid claim to the reward money as well. Eventually, a witness confirmed that Wolbert was the right man, but Wolbert asked the mayor to give the reward money to the Northern Home for Friendless Children as a Christmas present.[13]

Once the cavalcade of carriages could roll again, the party continued its progress to Girard College, an institution that owed its existence to Stephen Girard, the richest man in the city at the time of his death in 1831, who had left two million dollars for the establishment of a college to educate free orphan white boys. The college opened in 1848, and by the end of the century Girard College was educating an average of 1,500 boys at any given time.[14] That brisk December morning, Alexis was greeted by a cheering crowd and 150 cadets, fully armed and equipped. The college band played the "Russian Hymn," and the president of the college, William H. Allen, and other directors welcomed the visitor and led the party to the chapel, where over 500 pupils and other college administrators waited for a glimpse of the Russian guests. Alexis then took a brief tour of the school and climbed back into his carriage for the next portion of the city tour. Leaving Girard College, the party proceeded west on Girard Avenue across the Schuylkill River to Fairmount Park and George's Hill, so named for the family that had donated the land to the city three years earlier.[15]

The next stop was Belmont Mansion and its newly built pavilion, where workers had been hard at work all morning, hanging decorations and arranging flowers for the grand duke's breakfast. The mansion dated back to the Revolutionary Era and in subsequent decades became the center of hospitality for American dignitaries and distinguished visitors. George Washington, for example, had been a frequent visitor, as had the Marquis de Lafayette. Eventually, the property became part of Fairmount Park in 1867.[16] The pavilion hall was built in a Pompeian style with walls made almost entirely of windows, its outside panes stained orange so that they glittered in the sun "like gilded bronze." Great effort had gone into the decorations for the grand duke's breakfast. The most memorable of the flower arrangements was one made to look like an enormous Russian crown, topped by a double-headed eagle made of white roses, one beak holding an American flag and the other holding a Russian flag. Outside, a large canvas gallery had been erected between the hall and the mansion, decorated with colored bunting and American and Russian flags. The menu included Russian caviar, broiled English mutton chops, pheasant, potatoes, salad, olives, fruit, puddings and jellies, coffee, and a variety of wines, champagnes, cigarettes, and cigars. The lunch began at eleven o'clock, but two hours later only half of the planned meal had been served and time was running out, so General Meade stood and apologetically requested that the imperial party and the others involved in the procession prepare to leave and continue the day's events. Before they adjourned, however, Meade raised his glass to the emperor of Russia and to the president of the United States, and also toasted to the health of the grand duke. Alexis reciprocated with his wish for the prosperity of Philadelphia, adding, "I beg you to accept me as your best friend."[17]

Baldwin Locomotive Works, at Broad and Hamilton streets, was the grand duke's next destination. Founded in 1831, the factory had become one of the largest, if not the largest, in the United States, employing 2,500 men and making eight locomotives each week. Proprietors Matthew Baird, Charles T. Parry, and Edward. H. Williams conducted the tour, lingering for some time at the boiler, machine shops, and other places that showcased their industry. Alexis "examined with great interest" the narrow-gauge locomotives under construction and "expressed himself as greatly pleased with the machinery and surprised at the extent of the works." Alexis was particularly interested in viewing the passenger and service engines, which burned anthracite coal, of which there were large quantities in the Donbass region of the Russian Empire. The tour concluded with an effusive welcome from the factory's many workers.[18]

As Alexis toured the locomotive factory, a large crowd loitered outside Independence Hall, accompanied by a large police force already stringing ropes from the building's main door to the curb to provide a safe aisle for the guests to reach the hall. In addition to the crush of regular citizens, several organized groups had arranged themselves outside the building to hail the royal visitor. The cadets from the Soldiers' Orphans' Institute, affiliated with the Northern Home for Friendless Children, were there in uniform, alongside members of the Matthew Baird Cornet Band. When the grand duke finally arrived, there was a cacophony of cheers and cornet music and the crowd swelled in its enthusiasm to witness the spectacle. Inside Independence Hall, Alexis viewed various relics of the Revolution, the Liberty Bell, and portraits of famous American statesmen; outside, faces pressed against the windows to watch his every move and expression.[19]

From Independence Hall, the procession made its way through streets lined with spectators to the Philadelphia Navy Yard, a historic site founded in 1762 that saw the birthplace of both the Continental Navy and the Marines.[20] Inside the navy yard, the various buildings had been decorated with bunting and flags, and about twenty-five naval officers waited to greet the grand duke near the office of the commandant, George Foster Emmons. A member of the Wilkes Exploring Expedition in 1838–42 that discovered Antarctica, Emmons was a veteran of the Mexican-American and Civil wars, and had been the commander of the USS *Ossipee,* which had been charged with transporting American commissioners to Sitka for the official transfer of Russian America to the United States on October 18, 1867.[21] Now, Emmons was once again at the center of a significant meeting of Russians and Americans.

After a formal welcome and several national airs performed by the Marine Band, a squad of marines led the party to view the naval works. The first stop was the upper shiphouse and a survey of the vessel that was currently on the sticks, followed by a stop at the smaller shiphouse and the lower wharf, where Alexis received a twenty-one-gun salute. At this point in the tour, a steam tug arrived to take the party to League Island to view the ironclads, but due to time constraints, this part of the tour was cancelled, so the party retraced its steps back to the commandant's office, boarded carriages, and returned to the Continental. There the grand duke remained indoors, taking dinner at six o'clock and resting before the ball.[22]

The Academy of Music was beautiful enough to impress even a royal visitor. Modeled on La Scala Opera House in Milan, which was famous for its spectacular acoustics, the Academy of Music opened in 1857 and became the principal auditorium of Philadelphia and the venue for lectures and performances of all types; in the fall of 1870, both Susan B. Anthony and Senator Charles Sumner of Massachusetts had lectured there.[23] In preparation for the ducal ball, the whole of Broad Street in front of the academy was covered with an awning, decorated and festooned with carpet and the Russian colors, and brightly lit with enormous calcium lights. The central box inside the hall that had been reserved for the grand duke was filled with exotic plants, draped in the flags of the two countries, and decorated with portraits of his relatives. The stage had been transformed into a "vision of fairy land," and several large chandeliers had been brought in specially for the event. The mirrored walls added to the dazzling effects of the lights, while two fountains gurgled with ten gallons of perfume for scenting handkerchiefs. The dancing began with a waltz at nine o'clock and continued until the arrival of the Russian party shortly after ten. When the handsome grand duke entered his box, the audience stood and the bands struck up the Russian anthem as the curtain rose to reveal the elaborate decorations on the stage. The crowd murmured its approval and erupted in applause, while Alexis bowed in appreciation. The music that night included selections by Kreutzer, Strauss, and others, and after nearly an hour of dancing, Alexis and his guests moved to the Green Room for the banquet. Ten married and ten single ladies were waiting there, invited by the committee to dine with the young Russian and his suite. Shortly after eating, the Russian party left and returned to the Continental, but the remainder of the guests continued dancing until dawn.[24]

The *Philadelphia Inquirer* noted that the Academy of Music never had looked so brilliant or had such an impressive assemblage. Philadelphia's men were dressed in their finest, and "the belles of Philadelphia appear to have exerted themselves each to outdress the other." The paper described in some detail the toilettes of some of the most distinguished ladies, concluding, "the Goddess of Fashion never was represented before in this city by toilets so surprisingly rich and *distingue* or by subjects so truly endowed by nature with all the attributes that constitute a lovely, bewitching woman." The *Inquirer* concluded that the ball would "stand out in bold relief for the brilliancy of its surroundings, the noble motives which prompted it, the social, political, and military position of those present, the rank of the youthful but distinguished guest, and the friendly relations existing between the two nations so widely separated by time and space." The *Press* added that an affair such as the ball "does more for the refinement of the American people than a score of aesthetical lectures."[25]

Not everyone agreed that the ball in Philadelphia represented the height of refinement and taste, however. Alexander McClure—a lawyer, legislator, and newspaperman—declared that the ball for Alexis was "the crowning exhibition of this reign of shoddy" that had emerged after the end of the Civil War. This nouveau riche had acquired its wealth with great rapidity and, therefore, had no understanding of the protocols of society: "Entertainments became so lavish in expenditure and so gaudy in awkward decoration ... and at the theatres, churches and other public places a profusion of diamonds flashed from the hands and necks of women whose general demeanor indicated entire ignorance of the proper use of such decorations." While McClure admitted that the ducal ball was one of the most impressive social events that he could recall, with women of society who displayed the simplest and most restrained elegance, he noted that there were far more women "overladen with the most expensive laces and trimmings, and their heads, necks, waists, arms and fingers flashing the refulgence of a pitched together medley of diamonds and rubies."[26]

On Alexis's last morning in Philadelphia, December 5, he visited the fair that was being held for the benefit of the aged and infirm at the Methodist Episcopal Church. While some had mocked the idea of bringing a Russian prince to such a modest event, others thought it would give him a view of genuine American society and offer him a "temporary refuge from his persecutors." Bishop Matthew Simpson, former confidante of Abraham Lincoln, presented the grand duke with a knitted afghan, an elaborate example of needlework that was said to have taken an elderly lady of St. John's Church six years to make. The afghan remained on display for the remainder of the fair and was to be forwarded to Alexis at a later date. After the presentation of the unique gift, Alexis visited the tables, chatted with the young ladies, and made a number of small purchases, including small bouquets of flowers which he immediately gave to the ladies he encountered as he strolled through the fair. When he had seen everything,

Alexis departed for the Continental to breakfast and prepare for his departure from the city.[27]

The Russian guests left the hotel at about half past eleven and were on the train headed back to New York shortly after noon. As Alexis left, most citizens in Philadelphia heaved a sigh of satisfaction. The *Inquirer* said that the reception of Alexis far outshone the "tawdry show, vulgar toadyism and snobbish attempts at courtly ceremonies that characterized the reception of the Prince of Wales" some years earlier; "If the arrangements had a fault it was that they were too elaborate, too exciting upon our good-humored guest, and that they were cruel in their excess of courtesy rather than kind." One writer for the *Press* believed that more than any other event thus far the festivities in Philadelphia had shown the grand duke the largesse of American generosity and hospitality as well as the degree of refinement reached by the American people. Another journalist worried, however, that Alexis might have been put off by the poor appearance of the city, "the dirtiest and worst-paved city that he ever saw in his life." Despite the city's reported shortcomings, Alexis seemed appreciative of the treatment he received there; he left two hundred dollars for the staff at the Continental that had waited on him during his stay and promised the governor that he would return to Philadelphia for the Centennial Exhibition.[28]

The grand duke's visit to Philadelphia was not without conflict, however. Some complained about the kowtowing of the reception committee and the exclusivity of the various events. While the members of the committee meant well, the *Evening Bulletin* observed, some were overzealous and "unused to the ways of gentlemen," and others tended toward displays of toadyism.[29] Similarly, another paper complained that only a select few had been allowed near the honored guest, while the masses were "having their risibilities excited by the flunkeyism displayed by a few of the prime movers in the festivities, men of whom more good sense was expected." Regardless of a man's political or military successes, the paper said, Philadelphians were not forgiving of such snobbishness. The public was thus particularly hard on General Meade, whom they accused of placing himself at the center of all of the reception activities and behaving in a way most unbecoming of a decorated war veteran.[30] Interestingly, it was the elitism of certain events that bothered some members of the press, not the elaborate reception for a member of royalty.

A more serious accusation surfaced when the *Detroit Press* reported that a "colored gentleman" in Philadelphia had not been permitted to buy a ticket to the ball for the grand duke. The paper remarked, "This fellow ought to have learned long ago that equality of races only means the right of colored men to vote the Radical ticket."[31] The *New York Times* also reported on the incident, adding that the man, whose name was Thomas J. Dorsey, had addressed a letter to Alexis, complaining of this insult and criticizing the toadyism of Philadelphians. In the letter, Dorsey said that he attributed the discrimination to "the flunkey spirit in certain poor-souled republican Americans, who, while they are ever as ready to fawn upon the great, are also ever ready to insult the humble and friendless." Dorsey declared to Alexis, "I regard you a much better republican than those Americans who have, in my person, insulted a man on account of the accident of his complexion."[32]

Born a slave in 1810, Dorsey and his family had left Maryland for Philadelphia in the 1830s via the Underground Railroad. Despite little formal education, Dorsey had become a well-known caterer and set up a successful business on Locust Street. According to W. E. B. Du Bois, Dorsey outranked all the other caterers of his time and could boast that he had dined with men like Charles Sumner, William Lloyd Garrison, and Frederick Douglass in his Philadelphia home. His mastery of the "gastronomic art" had made him friends, important contacts, and a great deal of money. His exclusion from the grand duke's ball was indeed an insult. The *Times* observed, rather unkindly, that Dorsey should have sent his letter of complaint to the political pariah, soon-to-be ex-minister Catacazy, rather than Alexis: "A sensitive person would hesitate to make known the fact that he had failed in trying to force himself into a social gathering where he was not wanted, but, if he will do such a thing, he ought to tell it to a fellow sufferer who has experienced a similar rebuff."[33]

In fact, Dorsey was not the only African American to be excluded from the celebrations in Philadelphia. Thomas Chester Morris, the only black newspaper correspondent in the Civil War, was also reportedly excluded from the ball because of his race. Shortly after the end of the war, Morris had traveled to Russia, where Cassius Clay had introduced him at the Russian court, and he had dined with the royal family and attended the annual review of the imperial guard. These impressive credentials were apparently not enough to change how he was viewed in some circles.[34] These incidents were but the first during the royal visit to highlight the problem of racism in America.

The grand duke's brief stay in Philadelphia had another unexpected consequence—it encouraged chef James Wood Parkinson to mount a campaign to define and celebrate "American cuisine." One of the most influential American cooks of the nineteenth century, Parkinson had come from a culinary family and had been trained in the art by chefs from several European countries. By the 1840s, Parkinson had become famous as a restaurateur in his own right with a restaurant that was considered one of the finest in America, a rival to those in Vienna and Paris. By the time of Alexis's visit, Parkinson had retired from the business, but he still retained a great pride in America's culinary abilities. On July 31, 1874, a story in the *Philadelphia Press* roused that pride. According to the article, Alexis had insulted American cuisine in a book that he had written about his trip. The grand duke had reportedly said that, while traveling in the United States, he had frequently asked the proprietors of the many hotels he visited to bring him American dishes to taste, but they had shrugged their shoulders, declaring that there was no such thing as American cuisine and that all the best cooks in America were French. The *Press* called upon Parkinson to address this insult, and the retired confectioner and caterer responded with strong words and a call to arms.[35]

Parkinson wrote a lengthy essay, which the *Press* published, challenging the grand duke's impression that there was no "American cuisine." Parkinson explained, "It is only in the private houses of our well-to-do citizens, where there are American cooks who understand American viands, that any just idea can be formed of our real status in these arts." In fact, Parkinson stated, the grand duke had set himself up for disappointment: "Intelligent as the Duke Alexis showed himself as a traveler in pursuit of knowledge, it must be stated that the course pursued by the Prince of Wales party . . . was wiser," for those visitors had hired a famous American caterer to cook for them throughout their trip. Parkinson urged the organizers of the World Exposition in Philadelphia, due to be held in 1876, to plan a food pavilion where chefs from around the world could show off their nation's cuisine. Parkinson declared, "Let justice be done to our country in all these respects at the coming Centennial, and the Grand Duke Alexis will alter this chapter in his book, and publish to the world quite a different report."[36]

———————•———————

When Alexis concluded his visit to Philadelphia, he returned to New York for a day of rest and recovery (December 6) and then set off once again for Boston, stopping along the way in Bridgeport, Connecticut, and Springfield, Massachusetts. Bridgeport was one of the smallest cities he visited, with a population of only about nineteen thousand, but it housed several important munitions factories, an industry in which the young Russian had a vested interest. Connecticut governor Marshall Jewell had recognized the Russian's likely interest in the weapons factories and had extended an invitation, coupled with special arrangements by the president and directors of the New York & New Haven Railroad Company for a comfortable train to convey the visitor.[37]

At eleven o'clock in the morning, the grand duke's party arrived in Bridgeport, where a vast throng of about three thousand awaited his appearance. Mayor Epaphras Goodsell welcomed the Russians, as did Governor Jewell, with a speech that highlighted the unique possibilities of American society: "In showing you some of our manufacturing establishments, allow me to call your attention to the fact that ... our laboring and all other classes are more or less educated and intelligent, which brings everybody on an exact equality in the end." The result of this, Jewell added, was that men of the highest offices often had once worked as common laborers: "With few exceptions, the governing class of this generation is the laboring class of the last." Alexis offered a brief statement of gratitude, and the party prepared to leave, but the crowd was so dangerously thick that, when the train attempted to make its escape in the direction of the munitions factory, it had to move slowly and cautiously to avoid injuring anyone. Two children, in fact, were tangled in the press of the crowd and had to be passed overhead to safety. According to one newspaper account, their mothers hardly noticed, however, so focused were they on the departing train; one reporter drily noted, "Babies in Bridgeport are evidently more numerous than dukes, and can be better spared."[38]

Once the train had carefully inched its way out of the station, it traveled a short distance to the Union Metallic Cartridge Company, a munitions factory established in 1867 with a work force of about four hundred, many of them women, and a reported daily output of about 400,000 cartridges. Here Alexis was met by fellow Russian Alexander Gorlov, a small-arms expert who had served as colonel of artillery in Russia and, during the American Civil War, had been sent by the Russian government to study American rifles and metallic cartridges. Over the next decade, Gorlov was enormously influential in reshaping Russian small-arms systems, modifying American designs to meet Russian demands and arranging and supervising Russian orders for guns and cartridges in American factories. By the time the grand duke arrived in the Connecticut valley, Russia had been purchasing guns and ammunition from America for several years. Gorlov gave Alexis a tour of the Union Metallic Cartridge factory, showing him each step in the production process. During the tour, Alexis also met the superintendent of the factory, who presented the grand duke with several gifts—a sporting rifle in a rosewood case and a case containing model Russian cartridges in all stages of the manufacturing process. The various departments, and even some of the machines themselves, were decorated with bouquets of flowers for the occasion, and everyone, including the workers, was dressed formally, causing Alexis to marvel at the sight of the female machine operators in silk dresses and hair ribbons.[39]

Alexis marveled over something else as well. Still mulling over the meaning of Jewell's speech, he turned to the governor at one point during the tour and asked if these workers were what one would call "the common people" and if they really could aspire to hold office. Jewell assured Alexis that, while perhaps these very workers might not achieve high office, others of their class certainly could. Alexis pressed on, asking Jewell if he knew of any such cases, and the governor explained that he himself had once been a tanner, a realization that seemed to genuinely puzzle the young Russian.[40] This episode contrasts with the classism and elitism that prevailed in so many of the other events associated with the grand duke's American tour and was but one of several opportunities for Alexis to witness the various manifestations of democracy.

The visit to Bridgeport also included demonstrations of various cartridges and firearms, the coup de grâce being a display of the firepower of the Gatling gun by the designer himself. Invented in 1862 by Richard Gatling, the original model of the gun had a central axis with six barrels into which cartridges were fed by a hopper powered by a hand crank and could fire two hundred rounds a minute. Alexis seemed to enjoy these displays, but there was no time to linger since lunch was already prepared and waiting. Delmonico's had catered the meal, such an elegant and magnificent spread that many present declared that no better food had ever been served in Connecticut.[41]

After lunch, the grand duke and his entourage continued to Springfield, passing through New Haven and Hartford, where hopeful and excited locals clustered along the rails. Situated on the Connecticut River, Springfield was home to the famous Smith and Wesson factory. The royal party arrived late in the afternoon at about five o'clock. Mayor William Smith and several other city officials waited with carriages to take them to the pistol factory. Though no official parade had been planned, the city was well represented by citizens who cheered and waved as the procession made its way from the railyards toward the factory. Alexis was eager to tour this major facility since his country had just negotiated its first contract for revolvers with Smith and Wesson; in fact, the Smith and Wesson revolver would remain the Russian choice until 1895. There at the factory, Alexis met owners Horace Smith and Daniel Wesson who presented him with a special gift: a six-shooter pistol with a mother-of-pearl handle, gold inlay, and the coats of arms of Russia and America. Alexis was thrilled to receive the gift and would later use it during the buffalo hunt. Niceties completed, the men went on a quick tour of the factory, examining the various points of production. At the conclusion of the tour, Wesson had a surprise for Admiral Possiet: "a handsome silver-mounted revolver of the navy pattern."[42]

The party then made its way by carriage to the Massasoit House, a fine hotel near the railroad station which could boast of such guests as Abraham Lincoln, the Prince of Wales, Charles Dickens, Daniel Webster, and the Hungarian revolutionary and exile Louis Kossuth.[43] The grand duke and his party along with several dozen guests sat down to a short, but elegant, dinner. There, amidst glasses of champagne and the sweet perfume of fresh flowers, the men enjoyed a hearty meal and exchanged a series of toasts. A number of glasses were raised to the prosperity of Springfield and the health of the grand duke, followed by one particularly maladroit toast by the Russian minister. Never one known for his tact, Catacazy declared, "We have found here a city with remarkable facilities for preparing to kill people and we have also found a very fine city whose people know how to receive and entertain visitors very agreeably." There followed an awkward silence, broken only by "the cracking of almonds and a whispering around the table." Soon after this the Russian guests departed for the train depot, leaving the station at about seven o'clock for a week in Boston.[44]

———————◆———————

Though some sources indicated that Boston was already on the grand duke's itinerary, Boston city officials had wasted no time in extending an invitation to the young Russian visitor. In late September, long before Alexis made his appearance on America's shores, the Boston Common Council had discussed the possibility of a reception for Alexis, establishing a committee to see to the preparations and proposing to pay for the festivities from the "Incidental Expenses" account. In late November, a committee of city council members traveled to New York to propose a visit to Boston, and the grand duke accepted. The papers in Boston, meanwhile, had given ample coverage to the young Russian's progress, or lack thereof, across the ocean, and closely followed the reports from New York about how the royal guest was to be received there, poking fun at the nervous anticipation of that city's well-to-do. The *Boston Herald* joked that the fashionable people of New York were dismayed by the grand duke's absence, adding, "if he does not come soon their clothes will be out of style."[45]

Once Boston officials had received word that Alexis had accepted their invitation, they gathered with other prominent citizens to plan a worthy reception. The organizers included Boston's most influential men, such as George Hillard, former owner and chief editor of the *Courier* and the U.S. attorney for the District of Massachusetts; Eben Wright, a successful attorney; Enoch R. Mudge, a wealthy merchant engaged in cotton and wool manufacturing; and George Upton, a trustee of the Humane Society of Massachusetts. With such a list of participants, one reporter noted, "you may depend upon it that something stupendous is to happen." The program of events devised by this able group was declared by the same reporter to be "creditable to Boston, and likely as not make other cities—perhaps New-York, it is ventured—envious."[46] Meanwhile, Boston businessmen began to use the grand duke's name to attract customers. At Litchfield's dry dock at 232 Broad Street, citizens could view "The Monster Whale" for only twenty-five cents. This "leviathan of the deep" was discovered in Boston Harbor and towed onto Winthrop Beach by five local fishermen and was said to be seventy to eighty feet long, sixty feet in circumference, and with jaws that would open to about twenty-four feet. The dock owner, eager to make his money before the beast was taken away, used Alexis's name to draw more attention to his unusual display and repeatedly advertised, "The Grand Duke Is Coming to Boston to See the Big Whale."[47]

———————◆———————

On December 5, the reception committee announced the upcoming ball at the Boston Theatre and assembled a committee. The general ball committee was enormous, consisting of nearly 150 men divided into subcommittees to deal with invitations, music, refreshments, decorations, and floor management. The committee set the price of tickets at ten dollars for gentlemen and five dollars for ladies; tickets were printed, and rapidly sold. Meanwhile, the Board of Aldermen anticipated that the events in Boston would create an unusual demand for carriages, and so it sought to protect the public from unscrupulous hack drivers (hired carriage drivers) by setting specific rates for hacks leaving the ball according to the number of passengers and the destination within the city. The *Boston Herald* added to the city's anticipation of the big event with its detailed, and sometimes tongue-in-cheek, descriptions of the reception plans. In addition to a ball and city tour, the grand duke would also be honored with a "grand crush" that would allow Boston officials to show the city to best effect and would also offer the young Russian the chance "to compare the charms of Boston girls and dowagers with those of New York fawns and Philamedelfy gazelles."[48] Everyone would want to see the Russian sensation and be a part of this memorable event.

Alexis arrived in Boston on Thursday December 7 late in the evening. Despite freezing temperatures, people had been congregating at the depot for some time, and this "press of curious humanity" jostled and swayed in restless anticipation as a force of some thirty police officers tried to maintain order and restrict entry into the station building itself to a safe number. As the imperial train finally crept into the station with "aristocratic slowness," the crowd erupted into high-spirited shouts and gestures as a number of city officials boarded to meet the grand duke. After brief introductions, the complete party braved the deafening whoops of the crowd and climbed into coaches for the Revere House.[49]

Situated on Bowdoin Square, the Revere House hotel had been built in 1847 by a group of men from the Massachusetts Charitable Mechanic Association who named it for the first president of that organization, Paul Revere. It was a fine hotel that could boast of many distinguished guests, including the Prince of Wales. By the time of the grand duke's arrival on that cold December evening, Bowdoin Square was teeming with people, but the young Russian had been promised a quiet evening, so the crowd had to wait until the following day to ogle him. Alexis was able to sneak into the Revere unmolested, leaving those outside to admire his baggage as it was unloaded from his carriage. Inside the hotel, Alexis briefly met members of the invitation committee, and then the Russian party had a snack before retiring. A cluster of five rooms had been set aside for the grand duke and his suite, finely appointed apartments with rich upholstery, elegant draperies, and exquisite accessories, such as Chinese vases, Turkish rugs, exotic plants, and a set of Bohemian wine glasses specially manufactured for the occasion.[50]

Alexis's first full day in Boston, however, did not begin well. Officials at City Hall had expected the young Russian to arrive there at nine in the morning, but as the clock chimed the hour for the ninth time, there was no sign of him. Meanwhile, a thick crowd had formed outside the white granite facade, on the ground, in windows, and on rooftops. Inside, the lower corridors of the hall were bursting at the seams, as were the aldermen's rooms on the second floor, where most of the city aldermen and members of the Common Council waited. Unbeknownst to them, at that appointed hour the grand duke was still tucked away, oblivious to the swarm of citizens and the mounted police and cavalry who paced in the cold outside the Revere House. At last, Alexis rose and had a cup of coffee, emerging at nearly ten o'clock to face a throng of thousands and the strains of the Russian national hymn.[51]

Finally, shortly after ten o'clock, the imperial party arrived at City Hall. Several score of people who had maneuvered their way into a good viewing position in front of the hall found their plans foiled when they were unceremoniously moved aside so police could form a corridor between the gate and door of the building to create a safe path for the royal guest. Proceeding through the entrance hall of rich decorative wood and marble flooring, the ducal party was led directly to the office of Mayor William Gaston. After meeting a number of city officials and admiring a series of drawings that showed scenes of Boston in the previous century, Alexis, his entourage, and the reception committee went up School Street and through Beacon Street, both dense with curious onlookers, to the State House to meet the governor and other state officials. Erected in 1713, the State House was one of the oldest public buildings in the United States, the scene of the Boston Massacre in 1770. The Massachusetts Constitution had been planned there, and in 1835 the antislavery activist William Lloyd Garrison had escaped a mob by hiding within its walls. Three companies of cavalry stood at attention to receive Alexis at the State House and, upon his arrival, the sergeant-at-arms took the young Russian up the grand stairway to the Council Chamber where Governor William Claflin waited to receive him. After a brief address of welcome, Claflin introduced Alexis to a number of individuals who were there by special invitation, including several ex-governors and mayors from neighboring cities; then the original party, now joined by the mayor and governor, went downstairs to board their carriages for the ride to Harvard University.[52]

It was about noon when the imperial party set off for Cambridge. The procession made an impressive sight, its fine carriages accompanied by two bands and a military escort. People from all walks of life, the wealthy and the indigent, had gathered along the roads, each hungering for a glimpse of "the Pretty Prince."[53] The ride to Harvard took about an hour and would have been nothing to speak of had it not been for an incident involving one of the carriages. Somewhere along Columbus Avenue, the horses of the carriage containing Admiral Possiet became spooked and took off at a mad dash, and were only stopped when they encountered a heavily laden wagon in their path. Though no one was seriously hurt, Possiet and the other men in the carriage were quite thrashed about and shaken. For the second time in less than a week, the ducal party had barely escaped injury.[54]

Meanwhile, at Harvard, the faculty and students eagerly awaited their special guest. If the contemporary newspaper accounts are accurate, the students had, perhaps, gotten a bit carried away by their excitement, seeing the royal visit as an opportunity for pulling pranks. Someone had ordered dozens of hacks out to the college, though there were no genuine fares waiting for a ride. Someone else had ordered four hundred quarts of ice cream from Copeland's to be delivered to Massachusetts Hall, but, of course, when there was no one there to accept it, it had to be taken back to the city. A restaurateur on Tremont Street received an order to cater a grand dinner for over one hundred people at the university president's home, an order that the president had not placed. Finally, the pranksters had also painted the words "Café Pierre Noiree" over the entrance to Dane Hall, the law school building, a petty act of vandalism that nonetheless took two hours to erase.[55]

When the Russian party had arrived safely at Harvard, it was greeted by the faculty, a roaring crowd of students, and the president of the university, Charles William Eliot. After brief introductions, President Eliot conducted the grand duke on a tour of the various buildings, which included a stop at Holworthy Hall, a dormitory reserved for upperclassmen, where Alexis viewed a student's room and left his autograph and portrait just as the Prince of Wales had done eleven years earlier. The tour concluded at the library where John Sibley, the university librarian, showed the group Harvard's collection of Russian books: the *Codex Sinaiticus Bibliorum,* a gift from Alexander II, as well as some volumes that had been given to Harvard by the Imperial Academy of Sciences in St. Petersburg. When the university tour had ended, the members of Porcellian Club, a secret gentleman's society at Harvard, treated Alexis to a glass of wine and a cigar, before he continued on to a "cold collation" at the president's home with about forty other people, including Henry Wadsworth Longfellow.[56]

Leaving Cambridge, the royal party next went to Charlestown to tour the navy yard. Seventy-one years earlier, Secretary of the Navy Benjamin Stoddard had written to President John Adams that the old Boston Navy Yard, "besides being private property ... is so much surrounded by wooden houses as to be thought too dangerous a situation for building a valuable ship." Stoddard instead recommended the purchase of twenty-three acres in Charlestown for the purpose of creating a government dockyard.[57] Alexis and his suite were invited to watch the discharge of several torpedoes and to review the marines, and the presentation was capped off with a booming twenty-one-gun salute. The guests then proceeded to the commandant's home for a large reception. Some three hundred invitations had been distributed, and the gaiety and dancing went on for several hours until it was time for the grand duke to return to the Revere House to prepare for the next big event of the day, the ball at the Boston Theatre.[58]

The Boston Theatre was, in its day, one of the largest and finest opera houses in the country, and no expense had been spared on the details of its construction. Opened in 1854, the structure was equipped with an enormous domed auditorium supported by wire lathing instead of wooden laths, one of the first uses of this construction method. The theater could seat over three thousand spectators and featured a tremendous cut-glass chandelier which "had the appearance of a great glowing jewel." For a week, members of the decorating committee had been hard at work, and to good effect. On the night of the ball, the entry hall overflowed with a "floral magnificence whose profusion of color and fragrance was tropical in its suggestions." The *Herald* reported that over three thousand dollars had been spent on plants and flowers alone. The auditorium's interior was equally splendid, and the rear of the stage displayed a large painting of the Winter Palace with an equestrian statue of Nicholas I in the foreground. In front on the stage stood a balustrade enhanced with a line of gas jets that helped to light the stage, and eleven chandeliers were suspended from the ceiling, casting a warm glow over the room. Two musical groups were on hand to provide entertainment, a military band and an orchestra of fourteen violins and thirty-seven other instruments.[59]

In the hours before the ball was set to commence, a thick mélange of people had begun to gather on the street outside the theater, and despite the subfreezing temperature, it continued to grow larger and larger as the much-awaited time drew near. Patient but restless, the hopeful onlookers rubbed their hands together and shifted back and forth, their warm breath creating small wispy clouds in the frosty air. When the first guests began to arrive, there was hardly room for the horses to pass, but the large battalion of police, some one hundred strong, parted the human sea to make a path. Soon the strains of the orchestra and the palpable anticipation of the finely attired guests filled the ballroom, which rustled with shimmering fabrics and sparkled with jewels. One woman wore a dress of black lace trimmed with folds of satin, accessorized with a pearl necklace and diamond pendant; yet another glowed in green satin with a lace overskirt, low corsage, and emerald necklace. The end result was spectacular, "a study for any painter whose eye had been cultivated to the truest appreciation of the most tasteful embellishment of the 'human form divine.'"[60]

There was much excitement and there were many false alarms as the guests closely monitored the entrance for the arrival of the royal visitor. Finally, Alexis appeared and all eyes were on the handsome, broad-shouldered young Russian as he made his way to the balcony that had been specially set aside for him. Clad in a black dress suit, pearl shirt studs, white necktie, white kid gloves, and blue sash, the grand duke was a fine sight, one that would not be soon forgotten. Alexis listened to the Russian Hymn briefly and nodded to the applauding sea of faces before descending to the floor to lead off the dancing. According to one report, Alexis "made no concealment of his shortcomings," but followed the cues given by his partners, and "no fatal mistakes were made."[61] Louisa May Alcott, already a successful writer, was also at the ball and recorded her own description of Alexis and his dancing partners: "A fine sight, and the big blond boy the best of all. Would dance with the pretty girls, and leave the Boston dowagers and their diamonds in the lurch."[62]

The dancing continued late into evening long past the dinner hour, and one observer declared that, had the grand duke not made the first move, "the enchanted spectators would have sat supperless in the galleries or gazed askance from the edge of the floor, unmindful of the necessity of eating, until an assembly of starved skeletons alone was left." Luckily for all, sometime around midnight Alexis led the way to a separate room where a lavish dinner awaited the royal party and members of the committee. Once replenished, the grand duke returned to the dance floor, this time to promenade and observe the other dancers. Alexis departed at about two o'clock in the morning, and over the next hour the ballroom gradually emptied and the guests scattered for home through the raw and piercing wind, no doubt warmed by the memory of an unforgettable evening.[63]

The ball may have been a success on the face of it but was not without problems. The lavish decorations and sumptuous food apparently came at too high a cost. In the weeks that followed, a committee audited the expenses of the ball and reported that the receipts showed a shortfall of some 5,700 dollars. As one man noted with humor, "It is said that the ladies of Boston are crazy over him, but it appears from the failure of the ball that the men of Boston don't go very strong for Royalty."[64] Moreover, not everyone appreciated the omnipresence of the police at the ball. Several days after the grand duke's departure, the *Herald* received a letter that complained about the excessive number of police and their ungentlemanly demeanor, as well as their particular interest in guarding those areas where food was to be found. Using a stereotype that would still be familiar to modern readers, the anonymous letter writer stated, "It seems a noticeable fact, however, that wherever there are any refreshments there is where you find policemen." Finally, the ball also resulted in an extended lawsuit. At one point during the evening a bust on an upper balcony toppled, falling into the audience below and striking a guest named Elizabeth Kendall on the shoulder. Kendall then attempted to sue the city of Boston and several members of the committee of arrangements. The case went all the way to the Supreme Court of Massachusetts, where it was ultimately decided that Kendall could not prove that the city or committee members had been negligent.[65]

On Saturday, December 9, Alexis and his party left the Revere House at nine o'clock in the morning, bound for Lowell to visit Gustavus Vasa Fox. It was surely difficult for Alexis to rise so early after such a late evening, and the bitter cold of the morning likely compounded the duke's reluctance to leave his warm, cozy bed. But Alexis himself had requested this particular meeting, so he was not in the position to oversleep. Gustavus Vasa Fox had been assistant secretary of the navy (1861–66) and had gone to Russia in 1866 carrying a message from the American government congratulating Alexander II on escaping a recent assassination attempt. Fox had spent about seven weeks in Russia, traveling to St. Petersburg, Moscow, and a number of smaller cities, and had been welcomed, wined, and dined wherever he went. Now Fox was happy to return the hospitality.[66]

On the appointed day, the Middlesex Street station in Lowell was already crowded long before the special train arrived and, when it finally did, the roar of the excited spectators and the chiming of the church bells could be heard throughout the city. Fox and Mayor Edward Sherman met Alexis at the station, and then the entire party set forth in several carriages for a tour of a number of the city's textile mills. At the Middlesex Mills the grand duke admired beautiful shawls; at the Lowell Company Mills and Merrimack Mills he examined carpets, cotton calicoes, and the weaving process; and at the Lawrence Company he toured the hosiery and finishing department. Lastly, Alexis requested to see the boarding houses where the workers lived, inspecting the bedrooms, the kitchens, and the type of food they received. Genuinely impressed, the grand duke told Fox that he wished Russia had such facilities for workers.[67]

After spending the morning at the mills, it was time for lunch. Fox had been preparing for weeks, ordering supplies and inviting friends for the special occasion. The exterior of the house was immaculate, having received a fresh coat of paint for the occasion, and sported Russian and American flags, as well as a laurel wreath and ribbons that Fox had brought home as a souvenir of his own reception in St. Petersburg. A large throng cheered the grand duke as he arrived at the Fox residence and made his way inside, where Fox introduced Alexis to the assembled guests, a number of whom were female relatives of Fox and his wife. After these brief introductions, the remainder of the visit was free of formality, and Alexis and the other Russians could admire Fox's mementos from his trip to Russia, including diplomas of honorary citizenship in various Russian cities, as well as photographs and paintings of the Russian capital. Fox also showed the men an exquisite snuffbox featuring a portrait of Alexander II on ivory surrounded by diamonds and a malachite album that contained the visiting cards and autographs of the imperial family. The party then moved to the dining room, similarly decorated with portraits of the emperor and empress and photos from St. Petersburg. There, amid copious floral arrangements and tokens from Russia, the guests enjoyed a "choice and profuse repast" provided by a Boston caterer, after which the women retired to the parlor while the men moved to another room to smoke and talk. At about one o'clock, the friends parted and the imperial party returned by train to Boston to relax a bit and freshen up for the next item in the grand duke's busy schedule.[68]

At about four o'clock, Alexis and his suite arrived at the Boston Music Hall, which was bedecked in flowers and banners and already filled to capacity. One reporter joked that Alexis seemed "lost in contemplation of the beautiful sight before him . . . or . . . calculating how much time he should have to give up to his entertainment." The "Order of Exercises" featured eight choral pieces, including works by Mendelssohn and Rossini, accompanied by an organ and a full orchestra led by one of the country's most famous conductors, Theodore Thomas. But the pièce de résistance was an original song written by Oliver Wendell Holmes set to the tune of the Russian Hymn and sung by twelve hundred children. The schoolchildren all unfurled tiny American and Russian flags and waved them enthusiastically, creating "a pretty though somewhat bewildering effect," which the grand duke appeared to enjoy a great deal.[69] When the last song had been sung, Alexis applauded and then appeared ready to hurry off, but the schoolchildren clapped their hands and waved their handkerchiefs with such sincerity and enthusiasm that the duke had little choice but to pause and bow to his small admirers. Sadly, many of the adults in the hall subsequently tarnished the glow of the event with an embarrassing display. As soon as the grand duke had departed, members of the crowd inside the halls rushed for the royal balcony, ripping apart the bouquets of flowers in an effort to secure some relic of the royal presence. While these individuals would surely have blushed with indignity at being called thieves, the *Boston Courier* declared that it was, indeed, stealing.[70] So much for the claim that Bostonians were above embarrassing displays of celebrity worship.

That night, the evening of December 9, Alexis and his suite attended yet another formal affair, a private banquet at the Revere House. Two hundred of the leading citizens of Cambridge and Boston organized the banquet, agreeing to finance it themselves, supplemented by revenue from ticket sales. To that end, the organizers set ticket prices at twenty-five dollars each. The guest list was impressive and included many prominent politicians and businessmen, as well as luminaries such as Henry Wadsworth Longfellow and Oliver Wendell Holmes, while the hall itself was modestly decorated with flags, coats of arms, blue and white streamers, flowers, and urns of fresh fruit. The banquet began at eight o'clock, and the menu included a delectable assortment of dishes.[71]

Once everyone was sufficiently sated, Robert Winthrop stood and gave a long opening speech, welcoming Alexis with sentiments that would be repeated many times during the grand duke's excursion—enthusiasm for the Russian-American friendship and praise for Alexander as the liberator-tsar. Referring to the exceptionally cold weather the United States was experiencing at that time, Winthrop joked that either Alexis had brought the frigid temperatures with him or the American climate had decided to put on a show for the Russian guest. Indeed, Winthrop added, "the very elements seem to have bestirred themselves in sympathy with our earnest desires to make your Imperial Highness feel perfectly at home on American soil."[72] After a series of toasts and cheers, Alexis responded with praise and good wishes for the city of Boston.

The speeches did not end there, however. Next, Governor Claflin gave a speech, followed by Mayor Gaston, President Eliot of Harvard, Reverend Phillips Brooks, Gustavus Vasa Fox, Oliver Wendell Holmes, U.S. Attorney George Hillard, the poet Professor James Russell Lowell, and a number of others. Holmes read a poem that he had composed specifically for the grand duke's reception; the poem promised, "We can show him Auroras and pole-stars by night; There's a Muscovy sting in the ice-tempered air, And our firesides are warm and our maidens are fair." George Hillard made an awkward attempt at evocative political imagery, declaring, "It is better that the Russian eagle and the American eagle should employ their beaks in eating out of the same dish than in pecking out each other's eyes." Putting a more humorous twist on this image, Professor Lowell added, "I would say that I hope that our two eagles will never get into conflict, for in glancing at one of them I notice that our proud bird would be at a decided disadvantage, as the other has two heads." In another attempt at humor, Lowell added that, since the purchase of Alaska, "Our relations with Russia are now of the most intimate and cordial kind, for the Emperor has made us the *keeper of his seals!!!*"[73]

The ex-minister Catacazy spoke last, and once again his words were clumsy and inappropriate. Referring to his own recent troubles, he began by declaring that, were he to sculpt the goddess of diplomacy, he would portray her "in a dark cloak with a finger on her lips." Catacazy continued that he, more than anyone, should hold his finger to his lips as closely as possible, but that evening, he would instead place it over his heart in order to celebrate the friendship between Russia and America. The ex-minister concluded by wishing health to his counterpart, the American minister at St. Petersburg, a sentiment that was well received. Longfellow later wrote to a friend that several of the speeches that evening were "amazingly funny" and described the grand duke as an "amiable and handsome youth."[74]

On the following day, December 10, Alexis spent the morning indoors, breakfasting, reading the morning papers, and discussing the previous day's events over cigarettes. The afternoon proceeded in a similar fashion, the grand duke tucked away in his apartments at the Revere House, which was just as well since the temperature hovered around freezing all day long. By early evening, however, the young Russian was forced to rouse himself and prepare for the next reception event, another concert at the Boston Music Hall led by the great conductor Theodore Thomas.[75]

The concert was scheduled to begin at eight o'clock, but the hall was filled beyond seating capacity long before then, the side and rear aisles dense with those willing to stand rather than miss this spectacular event. The program that evening proved an excellent one. The Handel and Hayden society sang pieces by Haydn and Mendelssohn, and the orchestra performed a piece by Glinka. Though the audience seemed to enjoy the performance immensely, Alexis appeared distracted and eager to leave. The *Boston Herald* observed that he seemed to applaud "as if it was a matter of duty" and then left before the performance was over. Several reports indicated that the young Russian was battling a cold and under the care of a local physician. The grand duke's departure neither marred the event nor dampened the spirits of the audience, however. Only a short while after Alexis had abandoned his seat in the front balcony, a young man who had been standing in the aisle sauntered over and without any embarrassment occupied the vacated chair. Many in the audience clapped in amusement, to which the young man responded with a series of gentlemanly bows before resuming his seat for the conclusion of the concert.[76]

If Alexis was indeed under the weather it did not excuse him from the demands of his densely packed schedule. No sooner had the Russian party left the music hall and returned to the Revere House than they departed yet again, this time for the Observatory at Cambridge. Harvard had taken the first steps in establishing its observatory in 1839, and several years later, the appearance of an incredibly bright comet only intensified and cemented Harvard's determination on this front. Over the next several decades the Harvard Observatory was one of the leading astronomical establishments in the world, discovering, among other things, the eighth satellite of Saturn, and leading the way in photometry, the measurement of the brightness of stars. Since Alexis had been unable to worship in his own church that day, the *Boston Herald* suggested that it was appropriate that he could observe the heavens on the Sabbath.[77]

The events of Sunday concluded the official reception of the grand duke. If there had been any desire to fete the grand duke further, it was squelched by the news that Albert, the Prince of Wales, was terribly ill. As Alexis received this sad news, he requested that the remainder of his stay in Boston be free of public displays. On Monday, December 11, the grand duke took a carriage around the city with a few members of his suite, stopping near Faneuil Hall to shop. Alexis was simply too famous to blend in, however, and when he emerged from the hall, he was at once accosted by an adoring crowd. He then returned to the Revere, where he spent the afternoon quietly resting until evening. Dinner was a private affair, hosted by the grand duke himself in his suite. A number of prominent political figures were in attendance, as well as Gustavus Vasa Fox and several literary figures, including Longfellow and Holmes. The men enjoyed a pleasant evening of food and conversation, finally parting ways after nine o'clock.[78]

On the morning of Tuesday, December 12, Alexis visited several public schools in the city, beginning with the Rice primary school at the South End. There the Russian visitors toured the school, observing lessons in art, music, and reading. Alexis apparently took particular interest in the reading lesson that employed "Dr. Leigh's phonic system." Dr. Edwin Leigh was a physician and educator of some fame in 1871 who had developed a method to teach beginning reading in English that involved a specially designed phonetic alphabet that gave a unique symbol to each separate sound that a letter can make.[79] Alexis thought the system intriguing and inquired about the possibility of purchasing books and charts. The Russian party also briefly visited the Girls' Normal School, where Alexis listened in on classes in German, English literature, composition, and chemistry, after which some seven hundred pupils gathered in the auditorium to sing for the royal guest. That evening, the grand duke attended a special performance of Shakespeare's *Henry VIII* at the Globe Theatre, starring Miss Charlotte Cushman as Queen Catherine. Cushman was a tremendously successful actress, known especially for her ability to convincingly play male roles, what were known as "breeches performances."[80]

Alexis and his entourage also visited the rooms of the Massachusetts Historical Society, where Admiral Possiet presented the society with several oak leaves, the significance of which was not lost on those present. In 1838, when

George Sumner, a future member of the historical society and the younger brother of the well-known politician Charles Sumner, was traveling through Russia he gave Emperor Nicholas I an acorn gathered at the grave of George Washington at Mount Vernon. The emperor was touched by the humble yet symbolic gift and ordered the acorn planted at the royal summer residence at Peterhof near the cottage once occupied by Peter the Great. When Gustavus Vasa Fox visited Russia in 1866, he was shown the tree that had resulted from this acorn and now, five years later, when Alexis came to the United States, the gift was remembered yet again.[81]

Alexis also paid a visit to what was universally described in the Boston papers as "the big organ."[82] From its earliest days, the Board of Directors of the Boston Music Hall had planned to install a grand organ and, in fact, the proceeds of the very first concert in November 1852 had been set aside as the basis of an organ fund. Over the next five years, an organ committee established a subscription to enlist donors and the Music Hall Association agreed to contribute ten thousand dollars. The chairman of the organ committee then went to Europe, visiting organs and organ factories in England, Holland, France, Belgium, and Germany, finally negotiating a contract with Eberhard F. Walcker of Ludwigsberg. It took five years to build the $60,000 organ, which was twenty feet deep and forty-eight feet wide with eighty-nine registers, but after a five-month journey across the Atlantic and months of installation, the Boston Music Hall could boast the largest organ in the United States and the fifth largest in the world.[83]

The grand duke's last day in Boston was December 13, and he spent it in a quiet manner, relaxing in the hotel in the morning and then taking a stroll in the afternoon. Seemingly undisturbed by the freezing temperature and the many eyes that followed him, Alexis walked with a member of his entourage through a brisk snow wearing a brown overcoat, stove-pipe hat, and no gloves. The men were unmolested by the citizens of Boston, but not unobserved. A reporter from the *Boston Herald* shadowed the pair and reported on their walk the next day, noting that the grand duke had a "refined, intelligent, healthy and very English-looking face" and he bore himself like an average American but with far less self-importance than the typical American "aristocrat."[84]

Alexis departed Boston the following day after a modest breakfast and the cheers of a small crowd outside the Revere. The crowd was much larger, some four to five hundred strong, at the Lowell depot as the grand duke and his suite boarded their special five-car train on the Vermont Central Line. At nine o'clock, the train groaned to life and Alexis stood on the rear platform, bowing to the noisy throng. As the grand duke made his way to Canada, the *Boston Herald* declared that he had left "naught but pleasant recollections and warm affections in the breast of every Bostonian."[85]

———————◆———————

Alexis spent about a week in Canada visiting Montreal, Ottawa, and Toronto before returning to the United States by way of Niagara Falls. Discovered by Europeans in the seventeenth century, Niagara Falls had been first described by Father Louis Hennepin, a Belgian monk of the Franciscan order, who had encountered the impressive sight in December 1678 during an expedition with French explorer Robert de LaSalle. By the early nineteenth century, hotels had popped up on both the American and Canadian sides and Niagara had acquired its reputation as the ultimate honeymoon destination. By the 1840s, over forty thousand people a year arrived at the falls, and more facilities were built to meet the demand for food and accommodations. Entrepreneurs of all sorts saw the potential in this increasingly popular tourist attraction, and a variety of amusements and activities became part of the Niagara Falls experience, such as a ride aboard the *Maid of the Mist,* a steamer that would take visitors on a thrilling and wet ride to the base of the falls. Though its popularity meant a certain amount of tacky urban sprawl and the loss of its original charm as a breathtaking surprise hidden in the wilderness, it continued to draw visitors, so that by 1871, Niagara Falls was part of the standard tourist itinerary for well-to-do American travelers. Not everyone was awed by the enormous waterfall, however. When he visited in 1882, Oscar Wilde famously said, "Every American bride is taken there, and the sight of the stupendous waterfall must be one of the earliest, if not the keenest, disappointments in American married life."[86]

The grand duke's tour of the falls began in Barnett's Niagara Falls Museum. The museum's owner was Thomas Barnett, an Englishman who had moved to Canada and established a museum of natural curiosities which soon became a popular attraction, featured in the earliest guidebooks of the area. Barnett soon discovered, however, that with popularity came competition, primarily in the person of Saul Davis, owner of the Table Rock House, a one-stop tourist spot that combined a small hotel with a store, restaurant, and tours behind the falls. For about a decade Barnett and Davis attempted to ruin one another, one burning down his rival's staircase to the falls, the other obstructing the flow of tourists to his neighbor's business. At one point, the rivalry became so violent that one of Davis's men killed one of Barnett's guides in a scuffle. Ultimately, Davis would be the victor; when Barnett went broke in 1877, Davis bought his museum and operated it for another ten years. In December 1871, however, Barnett was still a contender, and his museum could boast an impressive and diverse collection, including live and stuffed animals, skeletons of exotic creatures, weapons and art from Asia and the South Pacific, and the yet-to-be identified mummy of Ramses I.[87]

It was here at Barnett's museum that the Russians donned oil-cloth outfits, laughing and talking in their native tongue as they navigated the awkward, but necessary, costumes. One reporter observed, "Any one who has ever seen a party of fisherman by the sea, fully rigged in their oil-skin suits for stormy weather, can imagine how royalty looked on the occasion in question." Once everyone had dressed, the party walked down the steps at the river bank and under the falls. The scene that greeted the royal spectator was truly sublime for, as impressive as the falls were in the summer months, they were even more so in winter. A silvery, icy sheen covered the banks of the river and the trees and rocks that bordered it, and as the water rushed over the upper edge to crash down into the freezing river below, it tossed huge chunks of ice about in the churning depths. After admiring this wonder of nature for some time, the party returned to Barnett's to shed their wet suits and view the curiosities in the museum.[88]

It was midafternoon when the Grand Duke Alexis and his party walked across the suspension bridge that led to the American side. Officially opened in 1855, the eight-hundred-foot-long bridge had been designed by engineer John Roebling, architect of the Brooklyn Bridge. It was made of two tiers, the upper one for trains and the lower one for carriages and pedestrians, and it afforded a spectacular view of the falls and the surrounding area. Stopping at intervals to take in the scenery, the imperial party crossed the bridge and then proceeded to the Spencer House, a four-story hotel only steps from the falls that advertised a dining room with "viands that delight the eye and palate, linen, china, and silver of unexceptional quality, servants ready without impertinence, and prompt without bribery." In preparation for the Russian guests, the proprietor had executed a quick renovation of the hotel, and for several days before the planned arrival, workmen were busy painting and repairing the building.

The rooms set aside for the grand duke and his entourage had been carefully outfitted and redecorated with new carpets, curtains, and richly upholstered furniture to suit the occasion of a royal occupant. All along the route between the bridge and the hotel, a line of excited onlookers cheered the arrival of the special visitor, and the halls of the hotel were filled, as well.[89]

At about five o'clock, Catacazy presented the board of trustees of the village of Niagara to Alexis, and the president of the board, Daniel J. Townsend, addressed the grand duke with words of welcome and the admission that, aside from the spectacle of Niagara Falls, they had little to offer the royal visitor except good wishes for a pleasant journey and a safe return. Alexis replied with thanks, adding that the lack of a formal reception was actually a relief, as he and others were tired and welcomed the chance to rest.[90]

On the following day, Alexis viewed the American side of the falls before departing by means of the Central Railroad for Buffalo, New York. The people of Buffalo, like those of so many other cities, had been monitoring the grand duke's movements as he made his way around the Northeast and headed to Canada. By early December, it became common knowledge that he would likely come to Buffalo. The proprietors of the Tifft House received word from Frank Thomson, manager of the grand duke's transportation, that the royal party intended to arrive in Buffalo on December 23 and would require four sitting rooms, seven bedrooms, a private dining room, and accommodations for eight servants. Even with a specific arrival date in hand, there was no rush to arrange a public reception. The *Buffalo Commercial Advertiser* noted that it was probably just as well since Alexis "must be heartily tired by this time of being made a spectacle."[91] Moreover, the *Advertiser* acknowledged, Buffalo simply was not equipped to host the royal traveler in grand style and to attempt to do so would likely make matters worse. Despite these views, it was necessary to make some minimal preparations, so members of the Buffalo Club held a meeting to form a committee of arrangements.[92] The reception would be organized and run primarily by private citizens, a choice that the *Advertiser* heartily endorsed: "To our thinking it is a greater compliment to invite a guest, distinguished howsoever he may be, to private courtesies, than to tender him the forced formalities of a municipal welcome."[93]

Alexis arrived in Buffalo at half past four in the afternoon on December 23, and there awaited a large, happy crowd. The weather in Buffalo was so much warmer than it had been recently that the city newspaper warned that, unless temperatures dropped again, wagons and carriages would have to take the place of sleighs. As had been promised, there were no speeches or elaborate presentations at the train station, and the Russians were immediately taken to the Tifft House, where another cluster of well-wishers had assembled. The Tifft House, a five-story building on Main Street, was the only hotel in Buffalo, and would continue to be the only one for several years after the grand duke's stay.[94]

That evening, a private reception was held at the Buffalo Club House on the corner of Delaware Avenue and Chippewa Street. The Buffalo Club was a social organization founded in 1867 by the leading professional and businessmen of the city, among them ex-president Millard Fillmore. The members of the club had done a spectacular job in preparing the house for a royal reception. The billiard room had been converted into a ballroom, its floors covered in white cloth, and its furniture removed to create the greatest possible space. Elegant oil paintings and Russian and American flags ornamented the walls, and the band of Albert Poppenberg, the well-known composer and musician, had been hired to supply musical background to the visual splendor. The grand duke arrived at nine o'clock, Fillmore delivered a welcome address, and the young Russian was introduced to the guests. Dancing began soon after and, over the next hour or so, Alexis participated in several quadrilles, stopping periodically for refreshments in the supper room, which also was beautifully decorated. Throughout the evening, he was the focus of all eyes, and "by his dignified, unassuming manner won his way to favor at once." At eleven o'clock, Alexis retired, but the party continued for another hour without him.[95]

Alexis spent Sunday, December 24, in a quiet fashion. In the morning, he strolled about the city undisturbed by pesky onlookers and, in the afternoon, he attended mass at the North Presbyterian Church. For this special Christmas service, five hundred children sang in the choir. Alexis and his party sat in pews reserved for them near the pulpit, and the church was particularly full that afternoon with curious members of the congregation. At the conclusion of the service, the Russians returned to the Tifft House for the remainder of the day. The following day was Christmas Day, and the grand duke had another restful day with few demands on his time. The weather was "mild as Spring," at least compared to what it had been in recent weeks, allowing for a pleasant morning stroll. In the afternoon Millard Fillmore and several other men from the Buffalo Club gathered Alexis from his hotel for a trip to Fort Porter. Colonel

Robert E. Johnston, commandant of the post, welcomed the royal visitors and took them on a tour of the grounds. The grand duke was then honored with a salute of guns before returning to the Tifft House for dinner.[96]

That evening, Alexis attended the opera at the Buffalo Academy of Music. Built in 1852, the academy had served as the city's premier performance theater for years, featuring such famous names as Charlotte Cushman and Lotta Crabtree. That night, the building was decorated with Russian and American flags and insignia, and unusually full for a Christmas performance. The opera was *Martha,* performed by the famous English soprano Euphrosyne Parepa-Rosa.[97] The performance of such a beloved celebrity would have drawn a large crowd under any circumstances, but the presence of the grand duke added considerable appeal to this particular performance and accounted for several hundred dollars more than usual in the receipts. Alexis and his party arrived at eight o'clock with little flourish and dressed very plainly. Several papers took the opportunity to critique the excesses of American upper classes, while commenting on the grand duke's modest attire. His simple style—no white tie, no flower in his button hole, no velvet collar on his coat or other "fashionable weaknesses"—was noteworthy, and he "looked and behaved himself like any ordinary young gentlemen . . . much to his credit." The opera *Martha* was familiar to Buffalo audiences, having been performed there many times, and this performance did not fail to please, though one wonders how much any of the patrons actually heard or saw of the performance. According to one report, though Parepa-Rosa made a very attractive Martha, "the singers sang at and the audience looked at Alexis." The grand duke, however, was watching the stage, and enjoyed Parepa-Rosa'a performance so much that on the following day he sent her a gold, turquoise, and diamond bracelet.[98]

The next morning, Tuesday, December 26, Grand Duke Alexis and his party left the Tifft House in three carriages for a visit to the Niagara grain elevator. The proprietor, Cyrus Clark, had arranged for a passage to be cut through the ice in the river to allow the schooner *Delaware,* which was loaded with oats, to be moved to the elevator. The grand duke then observed as the machinery took grain out of the *Delaware,* loaded trains of cars, one at either end of the elevator, and spouted the grain back into the ship, all at the same time. Clark also gave Alexis a tour of the building, which left him covered in dust, "looking more like a working miller than a scion of royalty." Alexis and his party were favorably impressed with the industrial machinery, and the grand duke left with a diagram of the elevator. The *Buffalo Commercial Advertiser* noted that this exhibition should have been of particular interest to Alexis since a group of citizens in Odessa had recently requested a diagram and plans of the Niagara elevator with the intention of erecting a similar structure. The Russian party left directly from the elevator for the next leg of their trip through the Midwest.[99]

THE GRAND DUKE'S RECEPTION.

COLUMBIA. "My long-lost ALEXIS! I am so glad you have come!"

The illustrated newspapers of the day published many engravings of various scenes, real and imagined, from Alexis's trip. *Harper's Weekly*, December 9, 1871.

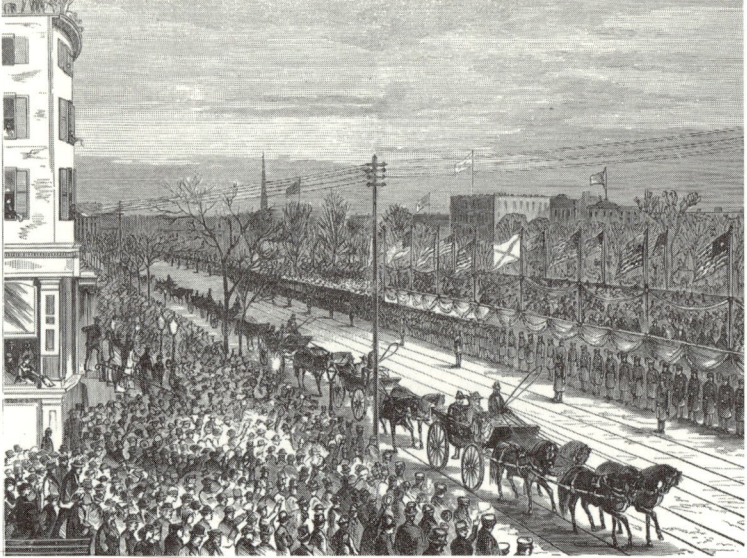

One Russian newspaper printed copies of illustrations from *Harper's Weekly*, such as this one of the parade for Alexis in New York. *Vsemirnaia Illiustratsia*, January 22, 1872.

Illustration of Alexis at the ball in Brooklyn, also taken from *Harper's Weekly* and printed in a Russian newspaper. *Vsemirnaia Illiustratsia*, January 22, 1872.

CHICAGO & NORTH-WESTERN RAILWAY,

MILWAUKEE DIVISION.

TIME TABLE		TENDERED TO
OF A		**HIS IMPERIAL HIGHNESS,**
Special Train		THE

Grand Duke Alexis

OF RUSSIA, AND SUITE,

Tuesday and Thursday, January 2d and 4th, 1872.

JAMES H. HOWE, General Manager.
ARTHUR A. HOBART, Supt.   JNO. C. GAULT, Gen'l Supt.

One of the many special train schedules printed during Alexis's time in
the United States.
Private collection of Jim Crain.

Alexis gave many gifts while in the United States, including
this diamond-encrusted stick pin to Buffalo Bill.
Courtesy Buffalo Bill Center of the West, Cody, Wyoming, USA.

Each ball given for the grand duke featured ornate and much-coveted invitations.
Private collection of Jim Crain.

Alexis at age forty-six. Reproduced from Iosif Starkovskii,
Aleksei Aleksandrovich, velikii kniaz' kratkii istoricheskii ocherk piatideciatiletiia,
1850–1900 (St. Petersburg, 1900)

5

"ROAMIN' OFF" TO THE MIDWEST

The trampled Pole, with burning soul,
Beholds the great ovation
To Russia's Bear, whose bite and growl
Have crushed his noble nation.

. . .

Forget the years of wrongs and tears
Poor Poland had to suffer,
Frown down all jeers, walk on your ears
To please this Russian duffer.

—*Chicago Republican,* December 16, 1871

A S ALEXIS COMPLETED the most northern leg of his tour, he headed for the cities of the Midwest—Cleveland, Detroit, Chicago, Milwaukee, and St. Louis—where his visits moved at a moderate pace, with fewer balls and receptions. His time in the Midwest, however, was far from uneventful. Midwestern city officials and businessmen were as eager as those in the East to show off their growing cities and industry, and they hoped to prove that Boston, New York, and Philadelphia were not the only places that had something to offer the foreign visitor. Newspapers in the Midwest emphasized that in their part of the country the grand duke would find an earnest and genuine welcome of real, down-to-earth Americans, not the flashy, snobbish toadyism of the East. The Midwest, however, was also the place where Alexis would encounter the most serious opposition to his visit, from German Americans who took offense at the idea of hosting a member of Russia's oppressive ruling family. These individuals, in many cases first-generation Americans, expressed outrage and disgust that their adopted brethren would so willingly and enthusiastically bow down to a member of one of the most oppressive monarchies in the world.

———•———

Alexis's first stop in the Midwest was Cleveland. Founded in 1796 as the capital of the tract of land called the Western Reserve, Cleveland grew steadily, facilitated by railroad construction and the completion of the Erie Canal in 1825. In subsequent decades, Cleveland changed dramatically as its population grew and diversified; by about 1860, 33 percent of Cleveland's population was German and 22 percent was Irish. The city's economy also grew, transformed by war and industrial growth, primarily in the iron and steel industry. By 1871, Cleveland was a bustling city of over ninety thousand residents, "regularly and beautifully laid out, ornamented with numerous shade-trees," with a myriad of social, civil, and religious institutions, and a home-grown aristocracy eager to show off the city's wealth.[1]

From the first news of the grand duke's American tour, city leaders in Cleveland hoped that the young Russian would make a stop in their city. Catacazy's telegram of February 1871 had mentioned Cleveland in the list of possible stops, and though no one was certain what his final itinerary would be, many in Cleveland remained optimistic. In early September, while Alexis was still in England, the *Plain Dealer* suggested, "As Cleveland lies directly in the young man's way, we presume he will have to pass through here." Nevertheless, once the Russians had landed in New York, Cleveland city officials decided not to leave the matter to chance. On November 28, the Cleveland City Council passed a resolution asking Mayor William Pelton to invite the Grand Duke Alexis to their city. Once Alexis had accepted the invitation, Mayor Pelton assembled an enormous committee of private citizens to see to the reception, eventually whittling this larger group down to ten men who would handle the details. Even before the reception plans were begun, however, some citizens expressed anxiety about the potential cost of hosting the young Russian. The *Leader* called these fears unnecessary and premature, but added that it would not be appropriate for the festivities to be a "tribute wrung from the tax list." Instead, it should be a "spontaneous offering" of the people, and the cost should be borne by Cleveland's wealthy citizens. The paper emphasized, however, that

Cleveland should not attempt to duplicate the extravagant reception and ball of New York.[2]

This fear of how Americans, and citizens of Cleveland, would behave in the presence of the royal visitor was echoed in other papers, as well, and once again, America's republican values were called into question. A journalist at the *Cincinnati Daily Enquirer* maintained, "it is well and proper that the representative of a foreign and friendly power should be kindly received … but this fawning and toadying and bowing the knee to a youthful sprig of Royalty is sickening and disgusting—a sad commentary upon our boasted republican ideas of equality." The *Plain Dealer* agreed, but warned that, the moment anyone honored him because he was royalty, then "republican dignity and independence [would be] thrust aside to our infinite shame."[3] One church leader in Cleveland delivered an address on the dangers of "toady snobocracy." Dismayed by the "ruling sham aristocracy of the large cities in the East" who had allowed "hospitality to degenerate into servility," he called upon the people of Cleveland to give Alexis a republican welcome "unpolluted by the meanness of ignorant upstarts." Of course, most often it was the wealthy class that was seen as committing the crime of toadyism. The Cleveland press accused the "bogus aristocracy" of America of disgracing the country, adding that "persons of this class are apt to flatter themselves that their vulgarity is hidden under their masks of ostentatious display or affected bearing."[4]

In fact, it was the wealthiest and most prominent citizens in the city who involved themselves with the grand duke's reception. James Bennett was a businessman, Civil War veteran, founder of the Republican Party in Cleveland, and city council member. John H. Devereux was an engineer and railroad manager who during the Civil War had supervised the Union rail lines; at the time of Alexis's visit, he was general manager of the Lake Shore & Michigan Southern Railroad. Devereux had several children, one of whom, Henry, was the model for the drummer boy in Archibald Willard's painting *The Spirit of '76*. Perhaps the man with the most interesting, if tragic, story was Amasa Stone Jr. In 1871, when Alexis visited Cleveland, Stone was one of the city's richest men, but his life was filled with tragedy. In 1866, his only son, Adelbert, a student at Yale College, drowned while swimming in the Connecticut River. Then, in 1876, a truss bridge on the Lake Shore Road railroad at Ashtabula collapsed, sending the train plummeting into the ravine below and killing ninety-two passengers.

An investigation followed and, though Stone was not blamed directly, it was widely believed that his alterations to the bridge design had led to the disaster. In subsequent years, Stone faced financial difficulties, and he committed suicide in 1883. Two years before his death, however, he donated $500,000 to Western Reserve University to found Adelbert College in memory of his son.[5]

As the reception committee made its preparations for the coming visitor, many businesses had their own plans to capitalize on the special occasion. McGinness, Ruffini & Company on Superior Street advertised that Alexis was coming to Cleveland solely for the purpose of purchasing a pair of their elegant fur gloves. Pearson & Willard declared, in a clumsier bid for customers, "Alexis is coming—so is Christmas, when everybody will have to buy oysters." Meanwhile, Benedict's on Superior Street advertised "Alexis caps," while William Days' on Public Square offered the "Alexis Curls, very latest, at ten dollars per pair." Finally, the grand duke's visit was expected to affect fashion, as well. The *Cleveland Daily Leader* reported that the latest style for earrings and pendants was a gold yacht or man-of-war with the name "Alexis" in black enamel on the stern.[6]

On Tuesday, December 26, the Russian party departed Buffalo, arriving in Cleveland in the early evening. The depot was packed with people, but policemen had secured an enclosed space for the reception, and so there were no difficulties as the grand duke descended the platform and Mayor Pelton gave a warm speech of welcome. However, Pelton's speech was the only part of the reception that could be described as warm. The winter of 1871–72 was a cold one in the Midwest, one of the coldest people could remember. That winter, one Cleveland resident wrote to his son, "This is the severest winter I have ever known in Cleveland, + I never saw so much snow here before—It is all over the country + causes much distress." Consequently, the speechmaking was kept to a minimum. Alexis thanked the mayor, and everyone proceeded to the waiting carriages, which were led by a police escort to the Kennard House through streets and sidewalks of thickly bundled onlookers.[7]

Opened in 1854 on the corner of St. Clair and Bank, the Kennard House was a five-story hotel with elegant furnishings. The lobby was stunning, designed in the Moorish style with columns, mirrored panels, and portraits of Spanish women, along with an ornate, colorful fountain copied from the Alhambra in Spain. The rooms designated for the Russian guests were located on the second floor and contained carved walnut furniture upholstered in crimson fabric, windows draped with lace curtains and heavy crimson damask, and rich velvet carpet on the floor. Outside the Kennard, a large group of people stood in the cold and watched as the grand duke's party entered the building and ascended to its temporary accommodations. As the band of the Cleveland Grays serenaded from below, Alexis stepped onto the balcony and looked down on the sea of upturned faces, white clouds of warm breath hovering about their heads in the cold night. Tipping his hat, Alexis then retreated into his suite for a quiet evening of dinner and rest.[8]

On Wednesday, Alexis and his party had requested that they remain undisturbed in the morning, and so the travel-weary grand duke was permitted to sleep in, rising at about nine o'clock to snack on coffee and bread, followed by a more complete breakfast at just before noon. The grand duke was undoubtedly relieved to remain indoors on such a frigid morning, the temperature hovering just above freezing, but the cold did not intimidate the most determined of Alexis's fans. The street outside the Kennard was thick with hopeful citizens, and there were many false alarms that morning as the crowd shuffled in the cold and waited for the young duke to appear. Finally, at a little after noon, the Russian party emerged and climbed into carriages to proceed to the Cleveland & Pittsburgh Railway station, where a special train waited to take them to Newburgh. At the station, the crowd was "uncomfortably large," temporarily impeding movement, but soon everyone was on board and the train crawled forward out of the station.[9]

At about half past one, the Russian visitors arrived in Newburgh at the temporary platform erected for this occasion at the iron and steel works. The Cleveland Rolling Mill Company had evolved from several older iron mills, and had expanded and reorganized in the 1850s and 1860s to include several blast furnaces and a Bessemer converter, only the second Bessemer steel works to be established in the United States. The Rolling Mill Company focused primarily on the rerolling of worn rails for the growing railroad industry. As Alexis and his party exited their train car, they faced a pleasant, if overwhelming, sight—both sides of the tracks were lined with people of all walks of life, "from the sooty laborer who had dropped his work to the young girl who had evidently spent hours in preparation for the grand occasion."[10]

The grand duke and his entourage toured the buildings of the factory, observing the huge air pumps and the furnaces used for melting iron, and proceeding to chairs on a special platform in the center of one of the buildings to witness the factory's use of the Bessemer process for purifying steel. From the furnace above, workers poured molten pig iron into one of the enormous retorts until it reached the proper amount, at which point the mouth of the retort was raised and air was forced through it to decarbonize and purify the metal, creating in the process a bright light that illuminated the whole building. The purified metal was then poured into a special receptacle and transferred into molds. The grand duke was riveted throughout the entire process, occasionally asking for further explanation at various stages. Having observed the decarbonization process, the party moved to the adjoining building to witness the operation of the giant trip hammer, a piece of machinery that compressed and shaped large lumps of steel taken directly from the furnace. Once the group had watched the hammer at work for several minutes, it was time for them to return to the city, having spent about an hour at the steel works.[11]

At the Euclid Street station back in Cleveland, the Russian guests boarded carriages to be taken to the next activity of the afternoon, a demonstration by the Mazeppa Hook and Ladder Company at Monumental Park in the center of the city. As the carriages drove around the square, a spectacular sight emerged—five steamers and hose carts, "polished into dazzling brightness," stood in line, accompanied by fine horses and firemen in full uniform and white gloves. Chief of the Fire Department James Hill, towering on horseback, saluted Alexis and then put his men through several drills, marching them past the carriages. By this point in the day, however, the temperature had dropped into the single digits, and so Hill chose not to use water in any of the drills and even abbreviated the demonstrations for the sake of the shivering onlookers. From Monumental Park, Alexis and his party proceeded to the Inventor's Exhibition, a large affair with some twelve hundred entries that included pianos, furniture, clocks, sewing machines, and a variety of engines. That evening, despite a statement by the royal party that they would not accept any hospitality from private citizens, Alexis attended a reception at the home of Amasa Stone.[12] The following morning, Alexis took a drive to see some of the oil refineries in the area, returning to the Kennard for a full meal before departing for Detroit.[13]

Many were disappointed by Alexis's brief appearance in public during his single day in Cleveland. But, as the *Cleveland Daily Leader* observed, "the weather was intensely cold all the afternoon and he would need to be more than mortal in order to enjoy the exposure of riding about the city in an open carriage." Not everyone was so forgiving. Some voiced a more serious complaint about the program, namely, that Cleveland's "bogus aristocracy ... principally made up of people unduly inflated by riches or position acquired by fortuitous circumstances" had monopolized the royal guest; consequently, the "hard-handed, warm hearted, honest sons of toil, who form the foundation of that prosperity, which created so much wonder in our visitors," were deprived of an opportunity to meet him. The offending event, of course, was the party at Stone's residence and, in the opinion of "A West Sider," it was "exceedingly attenuated" to call this an official reception, where only few officials were invited and "lackies stand at the door and want you to show your card before you enter." Another letter laid the blame squarely on the shoulders of Mayor William Pelton who, as one elected by the people, should have represented the people and withstood the pressure of "parties who seize public occasions to make themselves conspicuous." In succumbing to these influences, the mayor had "led the Russian bear into a trap, catered to the aristocracy, and deceived the people who ... elected him."[14] Once again, some Americans believed that the pretensions of a pseudo-aristocracy at home were far more damaging to republican values than the reception of an actual aristocrat from abroad.

As citizens in Cleveland debated the success of the grand duke's visit to their city, Alexis was on his way to Detroit for a very brief visit that included a city tour, several official meals, and a night at the opera. The most interesting and significant item on Alexis's Detroit itinerary, however, was a visit to the House of Corrections. Opened in 1861 to replace the overcrowded and poorly constructed county jail, the House of Corrections employed an enormously successful program through which the inmates engaged in the manufacture of chairs. So successful was this endeavor that the House of Corrections actually generated an average income of twenty thousand dollars a year that went into the city treasury. The grand duke's interest in this jail, and in other places he visited, may have come from Russia's ongoing project to reform its own prison system and, in recent months, the director of the Prison Committee at St. Petersburg had been inspecting penal institutions in a number of American cities.[15]

———◆———

The next stop on the grand duke's journey was Chicago, a city that faced unique challenges in hosting the famous traveler. Chicago had been among Catacazy's suggested list of stops in February 1871, but since that time much had changed.

Only weeks before Alexis's visit, on October 8, an enormous fire had broken out in the city. Allegedly begun by Mrs. O'Leary's cow, the Great Chicago Fire swept through the city and raged for two days, consuming two thousand acres, eighteen thousand buildings, and killing at least three hundred people. Another ninety thousand had been left homeless. It undoubtedly came as a surprise to many when Chicago was named as one of the grand duke's future stops in November. Undaunted by recent events, however, city officials viewed this as exciting news, and on December 19, the Chicago City Council voted to establish a committee to plan the grand duke's reception.[16] The fact that Chicago had been in flames only weeks earlier did not dissuade the enthusiastic supporters from this ambitious proposal. Quite to the contrary, city officials and local businessmen understood that there was much at stake. As one of America's fastest-growing cities, Chicago wanted to change the way it was perceived by the outside world. The political and social elite of the city saw the royal visit as an opportunity to demonstrate that Chicago was still a great city and could host royalty with the same grace, sophistication, and grandeur as the big cities of the East. While cities like New York, Boston, and Washington, D.C., set the bar for social and cultural sophistication, Chicago was known for its slaughterhouses and had the reputation as a "secondary city that preferred butchered hogs to Beethoven."[17]

Even before the Great Fire, Chicago had a reputation for crime and other negative symptoms of urban growth. As one of the first national media events, the fire had garnered attention all over the country, and even the world, and along with the stories of heroism and charity came stories of exploitive and mercenary behavior, as well as outright theft. Some argued that the fire had been a punishment from above and a much needed cleansing, and the negative press encouraged rival cities to view Chicago's devastation as an opportunity for advancement.[18] The *Missouri Democrat,* for example, promoted humanitarian aid for Chicago, but simultaneously noted that the "tide of travel and commercial intercourse" would not wait for that city's recovery and so St. Louis should do its best to attract these travelers by building superior hotel accommodations. The Milwaukee press had been more blunt. Though city officials were generous in sending fire assistance and financial aid during and after the fire, the *Daily Milwaukee News* suggested that the disaster was a punishment for the vanity and greed of a city with "so vast a population, wealth so enormous, greatness so gaudy and glaring, wickedness so consummate." In the following months, the *Milwaukee News,* in an all-too-common slur, featured headlines about "Chicago Hoggishness, Manners and Ingratitude" and the "Greed and Gratitude of a Hog."[19] Needless to say, such harsh assessments raised the stakes for Chicago city officials to host a successful visit for the grand duke.

In the days before Alexis's arrival, city officials and private citizens worked together to plan a program of events and to select committees to oversee various particulars of the reception. As to the question of how the reception would be financed, the mayor emphasized that the committee would pay all of the expenses out of their own pockets. Mayor Medill also suggested that, after the initial city tour, Alexis should be entrusted to General Sheridan for an introduction to "some of the lovely young ladies unconsumed by the fire." Local businesses also joined in the excitement. The Great Atlantic and Pacific store (subsequently known as A&P) advertised that customers could "see Alexis" at the store on West Washington Street, but the many customers who took the bait discovered that the grand duke could be viewed only in the form of a tinted lithograph that came with the purchase of tea.[20]

The men who volunteered to host the Russian guests were the city's leaders in business and politics. Jonathan Young Scammon, for example, was an attorney with a history in the railroad and banking industries, and one of the original founders of the Chicago Academy of Sciences and the Astronomical Society. William Coolbaugh was a banker and senator, and had served as president of the Union National Bank of Chicago in the 1860s, while Samuel McCrea was a director and vice-president of the Board of Trade. Cyrus McCormick was the famous inventor of the grain reaper and proprietor of the *Chicago Herald,* and Potter Palmer was a leading retail store owner and real estate developer, and the citizen who probably lost more property than any other in the fire. The reception committee also included judges, politicians, and newspapermen.[21]

Alexis and his cortege left Detroit for Chicago on the morning of December 30 accompanied by Henry Sargent, superintendent of the Michigan Central Railway. Along the route, Alexis was periodically called upon to step out of the rear car to wave to those who had gathered along the tracks though, according to the *Tribune,* he "would rather get a beating than be stared at by a crowd, no matter how much it admired him." At Calumet, the train was met by the first reception party, who boarded the imperial train and rode with the grand duke until they reached Chicago, where a good-sized crowd loitered around the Tremont House on Michigan Avenue, where Alexis would spend his nights.[22]

The Tremont House has a history that is worth a quick diversion. The first Tremont had been built in 1832 on the corner of Lake and Dearborn and had been a thriving establishment until fire destroyed it in 1839. Within a year, the Tremont had reopened in a new building on the same intersection, but it too succumbed to flames within a decade. A third Tremont had been erected on the site in 1850, the tallest brick building in Chicago at the time. It quickly developed a reputation as one of the finest hotels in America, and among other things, was the site of speeches by Abraham Lincoln and Stephen Douglas at the beginning of the U.S. Senate campaign of 1858. Lincoln also stayed there after he became president, as did Ulysses S. Grant. This third Tremont also met a fiery end in the Great Chicago Fire, as frantic residents rushed out into the streets through stairwells and over banisters. The owner of the hotel, John Burroughs Drake, also fled the burning hotel, carrying his money and silver with him. Before reaching home, however, Drake saw that the Michigan Avenue Hotel further down Congress Street was at that point still untouched by the fire. Surrounded by flames and having just lost his own hotel, Drake made a remarkable and bold decision—he located the owner of the Michigan Avenue Hotel and offered him one thousand dollars on the spot to purchase the hotel and its furniture. The owner eagerly agreed, sure that the building would perish within hours, and papers were quickly drawn up and signed. When the fire had run its course, the Michigan Avenue Hotel was one of the few downtown buildings standing, and Drake quickly renamed it the Tremont. This fourth Tremont was the hotel where Alexis stayed, and it would continue to operate under this name until the fifth Tremont opened in 1874.[23]

When Alexis arrived and entered the parlor of the Tremont, Mayor Medill greeted him with a short address of welcome, apologizing for Chicago's modest reception, but assuring him that the city's limited accommodations were not a reflection of its feelings. Though Chicago had been "reduced almost to a pioneer condition by a blast of flame," the spirit of the people was strong and Medill invited Alexis to visit again in 1876 when, he believed, Chicago would be hosting the National Centennial Jubilee. Alexis responded, "Permit me to predict that the energy which raised you to the height of your former prosperity still abides in your citizens and will help to make your future greater than your past." Alexis thanked the mayor, and after the Russian and American parties had greeted one another, the grand duke retired to his luxurious suites on the first and second floors.[24]

On his first morning in Chicago, Sunday, December 31, Alexis awoke to a "disagreeable and disgusting" winter day. Though he received several invitations to local churches, Alexis decided to stay in since there was no Greek Orthodox church in the city. Later, after coffee and hot rolls, the grand duke went out for a walk with two of the other Russians, attracting quite a following all along the streets through which he passed, seemingly unaware of the "faces of beauty … pressed against window panes." When the trio returned to the Tremont, they were met again by a sizable crowd through which, the *Times* reported, Alexis pushed his way, "almost impatiently, as if weary of being forever looked at." For the remainder of the day the grand duke ate, smoked, and relaxed indoors, safe from the snowy and rainy weather. This decision was a great disappointment to the Vienna Lady Orchestra, which had engaged the Globe Theatre for that night only, in anticipation of performing for the royal party.[25]

New Year's Day (Monday) brought better weather and, consequently, a large crowd assembled at the Tremont House, so that by midmorning the halls and corridors inside and the streets and sidewalks outside were virtually impassable. At half past ten, General Sheridan entered the grand duke's private apartments and Alexis, his entourage, and the reception committee soon boarded carriages for a city tour. All along the route, men and women lined the streets, waving and craning their necks to catch a glimpse of the young Russian. The *Chicago Evening Journal* joked that the grand duke's arrival had undoubtedly spoiled the plans of some men who usually spent New Year's Day engaged in the "annual and praiseworthy custom of taking multifarious drinks at the ladies' expense." The procession went down Michigan Avenue through the burnt district, where the Russians expressed "great sorrow at the loss of the city" and regret that they had not visited it before the disaster. Although it was New Year's Day, workmen were busy with reconstruction, and only stopped briefly to watch the procession go by.[26]

The grand duke's destination that morning was the University of Chicago. Established in 1857, the university was a Baptist institution that owed its existence in large part to the generosity of Senator Stephen A. Douglas, who had donated ten acres for its founding. This first University of Chicago would eventually succumb to its debts and cease instruction in 1886, subsequently being replaced by the current University of Chicago, the philanthropic legacy of John D. Rockefeller.[27] For Alexis's visit, President Dr. John C. Burroughs and the "ladies of the university" greeted the party, presented them with a variety of sweets and coffee, and introduced them to the faculty and other college officials. President Burroughs then guided them to the observatory that housed one of the world's largest telescopes with an eighteen-and-a-half-inch lens, the work of Alvan Clark and his sons, the famous astronomical instrument makers of Cambridge, Massachusetts. Though Alexis did not spend much time at the observatory, the *Times* reported that he was very impressed with the large telescope.[28]

From the university, the group proceeded to the Union Stock Yards. There they toured the stables where owner John B. Sherman kept his famous mammoth steers, one of which reportedly weighed thirty-five hundred pounds. Next, the party drove to tour Benjamin P. Hutchinson's pork-packing business, the leading pork packer in the area until Philip Armour moved to Chicago in 1875. As the Russians watched from the upper floor of the plant, the workmen below demonstrated the slaughtering and butchering of some three thousand hogs, a display that both impressed and repulsed Alexis, who admitted that he did not like the sight of blood. The party then returned to their carriages and set out for lunch at the Transit House, a six-story, three-hundred-room hotel owned by the Stock Yards Company. Following lunch, the tour continued to Dexter Park where the Prairie Shooting Club invited Alexis to join them in shooting pigeons. A young man handed Alexis a double-barreled breechloader and, when the trap opened, the grand duke fired and killed the bird with his first shot, to the great delight of his audience. The exercise was repeated many times, and in the end, Alexis hit ten out of seventeen pigeons. The party then boarded the carriages again. Along the route and in the parks, the streets were thick with men and women jockeying for a view of the exotic visitor.[29]

On Tuesday, January 2, Alexis's last morning in Chicago, he began his day with a more complete tour of the burnt areas of the city, beginning with the city's water works. Dedicated in 1867 and completed two years later, the Chicago Water Tower had been constructed to improve the city's water supply system. The whole party, including Alexis's entourage, Mayor Medill, General Sheridan, and other city luminaries, descended into the bowels of the waterworks that held the pumps and engines that supplied the city. The *Chicago Times* reported that Alexis was amazed by the well that fed the waterworks and its tunnel that connected to the lake. When the group emerged, the tour continued to the residence of Mahlon D. Ogden, located on Walton Street between North Clark and North Dearborn, the only home on the north side not consumed by the flames.[30] From Ogden's home, the procession weaved in and out of the city streets of the burnt district to drive home the magnitude of the destruction, past the ruins of St. James Episcopal Church to the Board of Trade Building, where a large crowd awaited the grand duke's arrival. Alexis met the members of the board, and the board's president addressed the general congregation, expressing regret that the Russian guests could not have seen the beautiful building they once occupied, now among the ruins of the city. The grand duke responded with a brief statement of thanks and the hope that Chicago would return to greatness. The group then returned to the Tremont to gather their bags and be on their way to the Milwaukee depot.[31]

After Alexis's visit to Chicago, the mayor and the other organizers expressed satisfaction with the outcome. Surprised at the overall size of the city and the extent of the damaged district, but pleased that large areas had been untouched by the flames, Alexis had predicted that with the aid of the city's railroad system the rebuilding would be quick, comparing it with Moscow's slow recovery after the Napoleonic invasion. While it had taken Moscow nearly ten years to rebuild, Chicago would surely do so in under four years, given its technological advantage. On his last night in Chicago, Alexis sent Mayor Medill a check for five thousand dollars, intended to assist the "unfortunate sufferers who were rendered destitute by the terrible calamity." The *Chicago Evening Journal* noted this generous donation, thanked the grand duke, and offered "the wishes of our citizens that he may kill 5,000 buffaloes on the plains this winter."[32]

———◆———

While in the Windy City, Alexis and his party made a brief excursion to Milwaukee, a well-established center for meatpacking and for the production of beer with over seventy thousand residents, many of them German. The Milwaukee press had brutally mocked other cities for toadyism and fawning over the grand duke but, like the papers in most major cities, it too had followed the young Russian's every move since the moment he stepped on American soil. On November 30, the *Sentinel* felt compelled to justify the attention being paid to the grand duke, noting the long friendship between Russia and America and the friendly reception of Gustavus Vasa Fox during his visit in 1866. The paper also took to task those who advocated giving the grand duke the cold shoulder "for fear some churls may call us 'toadies,'" and declared that those who would advocate that stance demonstrated an ignorance of history and a lack of good breeding.[33]

The first hint that Alexis would come to Milwaukee came through a widely publicized announcement in mid-December by Mayor Harrison Ludington. In response, a group of citizens met at the Chamber of Commerce to talk with the Common Council about inviting Alexis to Milwaukee, after which the council passed a number of resolutions to extend an official invitation to the grand duke and to establish a committee of arrangements. The *Sentinel* was optimistic about the developing plans, based on the "well-known energy and ability of the gentlemen who are taking the lead in this matter," and predicted that, if the program continued to mature along the lines in which it was conceived, then it would definitely reflect well on the city and her people. The arrangements committee of 27 created an unwieldy reception committee of 250 individuals, in addition to a number of subcommittees to deal with specific aspects of the program, such as music, carriages, flags, and decorations.[34]

Only a few days later, a small invitation committee that included the mayor and Jeremiah Curtin traveled to Niagara Falls. Curtin had studied Russian while in college and developed a love of Russian literature. The visit of the Russian fleet in late 1863 and early 1864 further stimulated his interest, and he befriended one of the officers, who gave him language lessons for several months. By the fall of that year, Curtin had obtained the position of secretary of the American legation in St. Petersburg, working there until the fall of 1869. According to his memoirs, Curtin deserves credit for convincing the Chamber of Commerce and City Council to invite the grand duke. At Niagara Falls, the committee read the formal invitation to Alexis, and Curtin spoke to the grand duke in Russian, citing a Russian proverb that said that a house should be judged not by the ornaments without, but by the hospitality within. Although Milwaukee could not offer "so sumptuous a reception as those given in the older and richer cities of the Atlantic coast," Curtin said, the city's welcome for the grand duke would be enthusiastic and sincere. Alexis accepted and proposed a short stay in early January.[35]

Meanwhile, back in Milwaukee, the reception committee haggled over the details of the program. One committee member suggested they not aim too high, observing that none of the other cities of the Midwest had tried to rival the "colossal scale" of the receptions in the big cities of the East, and neither should Milwaukee. Likewise, the *Sentinel* believed that, instead of spending too much time or effort on "a huge dance or a monster meal" to impress Alexis, Milwaukee should show the grand duke its factories and schools and other sites that could serve as examples of America's dedication to education, industry, and ingenuity. The *Sentinel* did, however, advocate a proper reception for Alexis to demonstrate that they were not "insensible to the graces that adorn civilized life."[36]

Planning the grand duke's reception and schedule was in the hands of Milwaukee's finest citizens. Harrison Ludington was not only heavily engaged in the lumber and mining businesses, but also owned a great deal of real estate, including one parcel that he leased to the Pabst Brewery for ten thousand dollars, a significant amount for the time. Angus Smith had become involved in the grain trade in the 1850s, before moving to Milwaukee and building the city's first grain elevator. In subsequent years, he built five more elevators, each larger than the last, eventually reaching the capacity of over one million bushels of grain. One of the most colorful figures involved in the grand duke's reception was Governor Lucius Fairchild, a "Forty-niner" who had spent six years searching for gold before returning home and becoming a lawyer. After losing an arm in the Civil War at Gettysburg, Fairchild went on to serve as Wisconsin secretary of state for two years, then as governor for three successive terms.[37]

There were some in Milwaukee, however, who opposed the grand duke's pending visit, particularly some of the city's German residents. The German population in Milwaukee had increased dramatically after the failed European revolutions of 1848, when these so-called "Forty-eighters" from German and Austrian lands arrived in huge numbers. At the peak of this wave in 1854, as many as sixteen thousand German immigrants arrived in Wisconsin in a period of three months, and many of these settled in Milwaukee. By 1870, five of Milwaukee's seven daily newspapers were in German and about one-third of the city's population was German in ethnicity. Among many, especially those of the "Forty-eighter" mindset, patriotism ran deep, as did a passionate belief in the necessity of liberal democracy. This strong tendency among many of the Milwaukee Germans led them to oppose the grand duke's visit.[38]

On Friday, December 15, a call of protest appeared in the *Daily Milwaukee News* encouraging a meeting the following day for all those who felt their "republican principles violated in consequence of the official invitation to a scion of the Russian despot." The purpose of the gathering was to voice their opposition and "preserve the honor of our city." The designated meeting place was the hall of the Freie Gemeinde, or Free Society, a social organization that also served as a means for the more liberal Forty-eighters to disseminate ideas about science, liberalism, and other topics. The call of protest had been initiated by a Czech immigrant, Isaac Neustadtl, and included twenty-six other signatures. The men who had signed their names to the call of protest were not the types to be easily dismissed. Peter Engelmann was the first principal of the German-English Academy in Milwaukee, the school that would ultimately give birth to the Milwaukee Public Museum. The museum's first director, Carl Doerflinger, was also one of the signers. August Greulich had served both in the state senate and the city's Common Council, and Leonard Schmidtner was a prominent architect in the city, the designer of many of Milwaukee's most impressive structures.[39]

The men who gathered at the Freie Gemeinde hall drafted a resolution that labeled Alexis as the "principal exponent of despotism" and declared it "unworthy of freemen to honor any individual for any other thing except his intrinsic worth." The Germans added that the "servile ovations tendered in the Eastern cities . . . raise the blush of shame to the cheeks of every republican." The resolution concluded, "we solemnly protest against his being invited here in the name of all citizens . . . [and] we expect our fellow citizens to refrain from any . . . servile and ridiculous honors." Moreover, any reception of "an auxiliary of despotism" would clearly show to the oppressed peoples of the world that "the sympathy often expressed in this country for their liberation is nothing but empty sound."[40]

Public reaction to the German opposition was mixed. The *Sentinel* had refused to publish the call of protest but reported on the meeting and suggested that any opponents of the grand duke's visit "can close the blinds so that their pure republicanism will not suffer detriment by having to look upon this icon of royalty." Suggesting that these men did not speak for all Germans in Milwaukee, the *Sentinel* reprinted an article from a Waupacca newspaper that accused the German opponents of being hypocrites, remarking that if Alexis were Prince Frederick William of Prussia "we venture to say that every Teutonic knee would be bent." Subsequently, the *Daily Milwaukee News* criticized the *Sentinel* for its abuse of the Germans. Emphasizing the respectable nature of the protestors, the *News* not only published the meeting announcement, but defended the right of "every citizen who uses respectful language, and whose character is good . . . to be heard."[41]

Conservative Germans had something to say about the protesters, as well. *Der Seebote* was a German-language newspaper in Milwaukee that had been founded as a response to the anticlerical, anti-Catholic views espoused by the Forty-eighters. In the ruckus over the visit of the grand duke, the conservative Catholic *Seebote* printed an article entitled, "Candidates for Siberia," which described how Alexis's mother was shocked at the cruel treatment of her son by the Germans in Milwaukee, particularly since she was herself a German by birth. The article listed the names of those who had signed the opposition document and said that these names had been inscribed in a black book of the St. Petersburg police so the protesters could be immediately arrested and shipped to Siberia should they ever set foot on Russian soil.[42] Despite this tongue-in-cheek threat, the German protestors were in no danger, but neither did their complaints prevent the grand duke's reception from going forward as planned.

On January 2, the weather was wet and cold, topping out at a mere thirty-four degrees, yet the depot was a hub of activity all day. By midafternoon, the crowd had grown to several thousand individuals until it filled every elevated spot near the depot that might offer a better view. Finally, at just before five o'clock, the agonizing wait was over and the crowd cheered excitedly as the ducal train crawled into the station. The transition from train to carriage was quick, and the procession of Russians and local officials moved through crowded streets to the Plankinton House, where the grand duke and his entourage entered through an arch decorated with American flags and a phrase of welcome written in Russian. The Plankinton sported colored bunting, flowering plants, cut flower arrangements, and portraits of Alexander II, Grant, Lincoln, and Washington, and the rooms designated for the Russian guests had been elegantly decorated as well. It was here, in this suite of rooms, that the governor and mayor briefly welcomed Alexis and then departed, leaving the Russians to rest and prepare for the banquet.[43]

The dinner that evening at the Plankinton was a lavish event, and the atmosphere was one of mutual admiration and affection. Various speeches and toasts underscored the friendly relationship between Russia and America, while others proposed that, despite their very different forms of government, the two nations shared a "spirit of liberality." Finally, one speaker declared that Russia and America were both young countries with bright futures, as opposed to England and France whom he characterized as decaying and distracted. Once the toasts had come to an end, the dinner began in earnest with an expansive spread that included wild game, Russian caviar, and an assortment of other dishes. The most impressive desserts were macaroon models of the Moscow Orphans' Home and the statue of Peter the Great in St. Petersburg.[44]

On January 3, the grand duke's second and only full day in Milwaukee, the program committee had planned a city tour with stops at significant sights in the city. The morning got off to a slow start, however, the result of a late evening and a cold morning. When Alexis finally appeared, the *Chicago Times* declared that the grand duke "looked as if the festivities of the previous evening had not agreed with him," with red eyes and his face "that peculiar color which indicates late hours and indigestion." If, in fact, the royal visitor was suffering from a hangover, the Milwaukee papers chose not to mention it. Accompanied by state and city officials, the Russian party rode through blinding snow, touring the Seventh Ward and its impressive residences, eventually arriving at the enormous grain elevator built by Angus Smith. There, Smith demonstrated how the grain went up one side and down the other by steam power, and though the grand duke seemed interested, he "did not evince a disposition to linger in the building any longer than politeness required." Alexis's next stop was the National Asylum for Disabled Soldiers. The group toured the several levels of the soldiers' home, visiting the injured soldiers, many of whom were missing arms or legs. The grand duke showed great interest in the operation of the home, and expressed particular amazement that the place could run so well without the presence of women. By the time the ducal party completed the tour, the snowstorm had subsided and so the return to the Plankinton House was quick and without incident.[45]

As Alexis rested within the confines of his rooms, others were preparing for the crown jewel of the reception program, the ball at the Newhall House. Located on Broadway and Michigan, the Newhall House was Milwaukee's other major hotel. It had opened in 1857 and, with six stories and three hundred rooms, it was intended to rival the best hotels in New York and Chicago. Unfortunately, the hotel was plagued with problems, namely an inability to turn a solid profit, and, more seriously, an unfortunate tendency to catch on fire, and by the time of Alexis's visit, the hotel had already survived several fires. Years after the grand duke's stay, this persistent problem would prove deadly when the Newhall's final owner, John Antisdel, decided that to combat his hotel's problematic reputation it would simply be best not to tell guests when the hotel was on fire, hoping that any situation could be resolved quickly and quietly. In January 1883, this criminally stupid policy led to a disastrous fire that claimed more than seventy lives and destroyed the hotel. The fire burned for at least two hours before the night watchman, reluctant to disobey orders, called the fire department. When the fire crews arrived some two minutes later they faced a scene of chaos and carnage as the raging blaze drove guests to jump from windows and land on the concrete below. Fireman began to rescue guests as quickly as possible, including the world-famous midget General Tom Thumb and his wife, but even with these heroic efforts, many guests were burned beyond recognition. Declared one of the worst disasters of the nineteenth century, the fire led to a widely publicized investigation. Though the owner was not charged with any crime, the tragedy did lead Milwaukee to develop building codes and a building inspection department. Fortunately, as the city prepared for its royal guest in January 1872, this grim end to the Newhall House was far in the future.[46]

Throughout the day on January 3, the final preparations for the ball were under way, as the manager oversaw the placement of the national colors and shields of the two nations, lush green plants, and bouquets of flowers. Music for the evening would be a special performance of the orchestra of the Milwaukee Musical Society, and Hans Balatka, the founder of the society, would be its conductor. The organizers had spared no expense and had distributed over eight hundred invitations.[47]

The invitation to the ball and reception had stated ten o'clock as the starting time, but guests began to gather hours earlier, until the halls of the Newhall House hummed with excitement and sparkled with the jewelry and finery of Milwaukee's wealthiest citizens. The ladies stood out in particular with the richest and most spectacular dresses, so that the *Sentinel,* diplomatically, declared it difficult to choose the best dressed. At nearly eleven o'clock, the grand duke and his party finally arrived and, as the band played the Russian national anthem, the special guests promenaded up and down the length of the hall. The dancing began soon after, and it was well after midnight before dinner was announced and the many dancers and spectators made their way to the parlors to eat. Many guests and too few seats, however, meant that the diners had to rotate through in turn, but the atmosphere was festive and no one seemed to mind.[48]

On the following day, January 4, Alexis and his party left Milwaukee in midmorning, accompanied to the depot by a large delegation of citizens. The *Milwaukee Sentinel* declared the visit a success and noted that the Russians had expressed great satisfaction with their treatment in the city. There were, however, concerns about the cost of this short, but expensive, visit. On January 6, the *Sentinel* asked, "Who Pays the Bill?—That is what some of the dear people desire to know in reference to the hotel bill of the Grand Duke and his party." The *Sentinel* assured its audience that the grand duke paid his own hotel bill in each city he visited. In the case of the Plankinton, the total amount had been six hundred dollars. Several days later, the reception committee met and when all the bills were settled a surplus of fifty dollars remained, which was promptly turned over to the Home for the Friendless.[49]

The grand duke's decision to visit Milwaukee had also fanned the flames of competition with her rivals. As the Russian party had approached Cleveland, the Milwaukee papers had mocked Cleveland's modest reception plans. After Alexis had come and gone from Milwaukee, the Cleveland press retaliated with stories about the lavish amounts spent on dresses for the ball there, and the *Plain Dealer* commented, "That will do for a rural village; but here in Cleveland we don't think a $1200 ball dress amounts to much. Dresses costing more than that are worn at many private receptions." Milwaukee believed it had shown the royal visitor a spectacle like none other; "Simple-hearted Milwaukee!" the *Cleveland Plain Dealer* condescended.[50] The harshest commentary came from Chicago. In a case of civic pride run amuck, the *Chicago Tribune* called the eager spectators at Milwaukee's Plankinton House "rural lion-hunters." Once Alexis had left Milwaukee, the *Chicago Times* wrote, "Milwaukee was insufferably dull.... The life of the little place seemed to have vanished with the grand duke," and the whole city seemed listless and lachrymose, with "no further object in living."[51] Milwaukee hurled its fair share of insults as well. In a long and scathing condemnation entitled "The Meanness of Chicago," the *Sentinel* declared that, although the fire had prevented Chicago from hosting Alexis in the proper manner, it had not taught its people humility. In fact, the *Sentinel* argued, "the flames of hell itself could not take the brag out of them." The *Daily Milwaukee News* noted that the grand duke must have been "considerably surprised ... and somewhat disgusted ... at receiving some forty or more letters begging for money." The paper declared that this was characteristic of Chicagoans, known for their greed and "hoggishness," and concluded that Alexis must have been eager to leave "that detestable place."[52]

When Alexis left Milwaukee he passed through Chicago once more, stopping for less than twenty-four hours, before continuing on to St. Louis. Traveling on the Chicago, Alton & St. Louis Railroad, the imperial train departed for St. Louis on Friday, January 5, at a little before nine in the morning. Chugging through the countryside, some members of the imperial party played cards and smoked as they admired the scenery while others, such as Alexis and Admiral Possiet, wrote in notebooks or took advantage of the rhythmic sway of the train to doze. The route took them through a number of cities, and at each of these stations crowds of spectators had gathered. At Godfrey, the young women of the Monticello Seminary waved their handkerchiefs and sang "My Country 'Tis of Thee." The royal train did not stop at Springfield because, according to the *Democrat,* the "dignified Senators" did not invite Alexis to stop. Despite this decision at the official level, the general populace was eager to welcome the grand duke, and some five thousand people gathered at the depot as the train slowly rolled through town and Alexis waved to the cheering throngs. Indeed, so large was the crowd that a shed upon which a numbers of boys had perched to catch sight of the royal guest collapsed, leaving one boy with a broken leg. In the midst of that thick crowd were members of the legislature. The *Chicago Times* gently mocked the capital's politicians who, despite their steely resolve to avoid an unseemly display of kowtowing, had shown up in such numbers that both houses had adjourned early. Apparently, "the discipline of neither branch of the general assembly was strong enough to keep members in their seats." Continuing to more "hospitable regions," the imperial party steamed on to St. Louis.[53]

Initially a settlement for French fur traders in the 1760s, St. Louis had been incorporated in 1822 and, within a decade of incorporation, had become a boomtown, facilitated by the growth of the steamboat industry along the Mississippi River and the country's westward expansion. Between 1840 and 1860, the population of St. Louis increased dramatically with the influx of immigrants, primarily from Ireland and the German states. By 1870, the city had a population of over 300,000 and was in the midst of a golden age, spurred on by its advantageous location in the center of the nation and with ready access to water and rail transportation.[54]

The first conversations about the grand duke's visit to St. Louis began in mid-December after the *Missouri Democrat* announced the exciting event and urged the governor to come down from Jefferson City to deliver a welcome speech to the royal guest, stressing that St. Louis could not afford to be outdone by other cities. Several days later, the paper reported with frustration that the St. Louis City Council had made no moves to plan a reception for Alexis, adding, "if the City Council is so overwhelmed with a sense of its constitutional restrictions that it dare not act, let it so report, and a committee of citizens will take the subject in hand."[55]

Even as the *Missouri Democrat* criticized city officials for failing to take the initiative in planning a reception, however, the creaky wheels of bureaucracy were, in fact, beginning to turn. On December 16, the City Council met to discuss various ideas for receiving the grand duke and his traveling party. Once again, as had occurred in New York and Milwaukee, European transplants were hostile to the entire idea. Several aldermen of German background opposed the reception, and though their complaints failed to stop the city from receiving the royal visitor, they did result in an agreement that the festivities would not be charged to the city treasury. Subsequently, Mayor John Brown appointed and announced a reception committee and a floor committee. The *Missouri Democrat* agreed with the decision; while city authorities owed Alexis some sort of reception and show of respect, private citizens should pay for it. After all, the *Democrat* observed, "The fathers and mothers will want to gaze upon him, and the daughters will want to dance the lancers with him; and when this triangular anxiety can be satisfactorily appeased at the trifling cost of $10, we don't see the use of making any fuss about it."[56]

As in the other cities on the grand duke's tour, the men who prepared to receive the Russian visitors were the social, political, and financial leaders of the city. Scottish-born businessman Joseph Brown had worked in the steamboat business, building gunboats for the U.S. Navy during the Civil War, later serving as a state senator, mayor of St. Louis for two terms, and president of the Missouri Pacific Railroad. The ball committee contained two very famous newspapermen—Stilson Hutchins and Joseph Pulitzer. Hutchins was, among other things, one of the founders of the *St. Louis Times* and its editor at the time of the royal visit, and later, founder of the *Washington Post*. Pulitzer was only twenty-four in the fall of 1871, but had already made a name for himself as a young and energetic state representative. In the years after the grand duke's visit, of course, Pulitzer would become famous as the owner of the *St. Louis Post-Dispatch* and the *New York World*.[57]

As the reception committee worked out the final details of the grand duke's program, excitement simmered throughout the city. On the day before Alexis's expected arrival, the office of the Chicago & Alton Railroad on Fourth Street displayed one of the special train timecards in its window, creating a "decided sensation." As in many other cities, local merchants also demonstrated the adaptability of advertising. The St. Louis Book and News Company advertised leather, ivory, and gilt fans, "just the thing for the Alexis ball," something that "every lady should possess." One merchant pulled out all the stops in appealing to potential customers; in an advertisement for "Pauviue" hair tonic, H. N. Barker and Company boasted that the grand duke's hair, which "the ladies say is perfectly lovely, being brushed in soft waves up from a broad forehead," would soon be made even more lovely by the application of their product, which could be acquired at their shop at Twelfth and Warren streets.[58]

Finally, on January 5, the ducal train steamed toward St. Louis and a delegation from that city boarded a train to meet the royal guests and conduct them by carriage to the Southern Hotel.[59] Built in 1865, the Southern Hotel on the corner of Fourth and Walnut streets was St. Louis's premier hotel for over a decade until an enormous fire destroyed it in April 1877. Soon after, the rebuilt Southern would be the scene of a grisly murder. The incident caused such a stir that the hotel had to change the number of the room in order to rent it again, and when the hotel was slated for destruction in 1933, souvenir hunters gutted the room in which the victim perished, stripping it of its door, window frame, and other trimmings.[60] All this gloom and doom, however, was far in the future when Alexis came to town, and in January 1872, everyone was focused on making the hotel look its best for its royal guest. Organizers had prepared a group of rooms in the northeast corner of the building, redecorated for the occasion with new frescoes and new furniture. In addition to its deluxe accommodations, the hotel also stocked an impressive selection of wines, ales, and brandies, and could boast of a fine dining-room menu.[61]

On the grand duke's first day in St. Louis, the weather was cold, only twenty-six degrees, and the flag at the Southern Hotel flapped in the "shivering breezes." Alexis had a leisurely morning, taking coffee at nine o'clock and going for a walk in the vicinity of the hotel, bundled up in a dark-brown overcoat. Meanwhile, Admiral Possiet, escorted by two members of the reception committee, visited the Mercantile Library. The men soon reconvened at the hotel for a late breakfast, or early lunch, while excited citizens congregated outside in anticipation of the formal reception to take place at noon until the corridors and halls of the Southern were filled with people. A diverse cross-section of St. Louis society, the crowd included women with babies, well dressed ladies, small boys, old men, "giddy girls and society belles . . . rich men and poor men, the learned and unlearned, the dirty and the clean." As they waited for the object of their excitement, members of the crowd gossiped about Alexis, his appearance and manners, and occasionally murmured and rustled when it was rumored that the grand duke was on his way.[62]

At last Alexis appeared, dressed in grey slacks and a double-breasted coat with a purple scarf. Mayor Brown welcomed the grand duke with the usual remarks about friendly relations between Russia and the United States, and thanked him for moving beyond the nation's capital to see more of the country. The mayor added that while St. Louis was a city still in its infancy, its citizens were happy to show him the public buildings, institutions, factories, and the "stupendous bridge across the Mississippi" then under construction. Alexis thanked his hosts and replied that he had come further west to see "the sources from which the wealth of your great country will be in the future mainly derived," and specifically repeated his desire to see the new bridge. His brief speech was met with loud cheers and applause.[63]

Following the speeches, Alexis was introduced to the assembled guests, dutifully grasping the hands thrust before him and applying "a hearty pressure with his immense Ducal digits." One woman was heard to declare that she would forever after keep her glove in a glass case. Soon after leaving this reception, Alexis received a delegation of Creek Indians on their way to Washington, the first Native Americans the Russians had encountered. Alexis met these unusual visitors with pleasure, and Admiral Possiet reportedly elicited laughs all around when he asked one Creek how they provided for the necessities of life and the man replied, "'same as civilized white men.'" In keeping with the attitudes of the time, the *Missouri Democrat* described the Creeks as "neatly dressed and . . . fair representatives of the better educated half-breeds."[64]

In the early afternoon, Alexis and his party boarded carriages for a ride around the city. The streets surrounding the hotel were lined with eager spectators, and the balconies and windows of the facing buildings were at maximum capacity. As the carriages trundled through the city streets, the grand duke and his party admired the storefronts and elegant private residences, inquiring politely about the public school system and the number of children enrolled. All along the route, people stopped to stare, point, and wave at the exceptional visitor. At one point, an estimated crowd of two thousand men, women, and children followed the carriages, falling behind only after several city blocks.[65]

Later that evening, Alexis and several members of his party accompanied the mayor and members of the reception committee to a performance of Lydia Thompson at the Olympic Theatre. Though not quite six years old, the Olympic had already become one of the most fashionable gathering places in the city. For days before the performance, the theater had advertised in the *Missouri Democrat* the grand duke's likely attendance, the typeface increasing in size as the evening drew nearer, and it was widely reported that the Russian party had requested that Ms. Thompson perform *Bluebeard,* which included the song "If Ever I Cease to Love." Managers Charles Pope and Charles Spalding went to great lengths to decorate the interior of the theater and to secure the band from the St. Louis Arsenal. On the night of the big event, the theater was full, many seats having been reserved in advance, and everyone seemed to enjoy the performance, especially Alexis who, rumor had it, had been captivated by Ms. Thompson. This story grew in scope when Alexis subsequently asked a member of the reception committee to deliver a gift to Thompson, an exquisite gold-and-amethyst bracelet set with diamonds valued at five thousand dollars. The American press went wild over the story and reported it widely, unaware that these speculations would give birth to a legend in a city further south on the Mississippi.[66]

Sunday, January 7, dawned cold and white, with large flakes falling well into the morning until there was an accumulation of some six to eight inches. Since there was no Orthodox church in St. Louis, Alexis could enjoy the warmth of his room on this cold morning, drinking coffee and reviewing the local paper. As noon approached, he set out for a brief stroll along the snow-covered sidewalks, returning to receive visits from a number of military men, officers from the arsenal band that had serenaded him the previous evening. Over wine and cigars, the men engaged in military talk for more than an hour until Alexis and his men were collected in a horse-drawn sleigh for another tour of the city.[67]

The sleigh ride took the visitors through snowy streets and went well until the corner of Twelfth and Pine, where a group of boys who had been throwing snowballs at passersby all afternoon discovered a unique target. With cries of "There's the Juke!" and "Give it to the son of a Czar!" they released a barrage of snowballs aimed at the royal bull's eye. The grand duke ducked but was not quick enough, and "feigned a smile while the cold snow sifted down his neck." When the story of this assault on Alexis got out, the *Philadelphia Inquirer* smirked that St. Louis had the proud honor of giving the grand duke "a touch of our pure Democracy, unrestrained by the presence of Imperialism." Alexis probably wished he had gone instead with Admiral Possiet and Count Bodisco, who were enjoying a pleasant discussion of technological matters at the home of James Eads. When both parties had returned to the hotel, dinner was served to the tune of lively conversation, particularly the topic of the upcoming buffalo hunt.[68]

Monday, January 8, was the date set for the grand ball, and all day soldiers from the arsenal and volunteers from the hotel worked to transform the dining room of the Southern into a ballroom. As the hours passed, the parlors and halls of the Southern grew dense with curious onlookers, ladies and men of all ages and social standing. One paper reported with sarcasm that none of these had come to see Alexis, of course; more likely, they had coincidentally just dropped by to see a friend, yet "a bevy of fashionable girls evidently found their friend at the foot of the stairs at the ladies' entrance, for they remained there two long hours." Meanwhile, a number of prominent officials, among them Cassius Clay, arrived to collect the grand duke, and struggling against "a black mass of humanity" around the hotel entrance, the combined party quickly ducked into their carriages and headed for the Merchants' Exchange and the office of James Eads at the Illinois and St. Louis Bridge Company.[69]

A talented engineer who had made a name for himself building ironclad gunboats during the Civil War, Eads was one of only a handful of engineers engaged in advanced bridge design and construction at the time of the Russian visit. Of particular importance were his innovations in the use of caissons to sink bridge foundations and his experience with the "caisson sickness" suffered by some of his men. This puzzling illness would ultimately kill fifteen men working on the St. Louis bridge and cripple a number of others; these deaths and injuries would serve to enlighten John Roebling as he coped with the same problem during the construction of the Brooklyn Bridge. At Eads's office, Alexis and the other Russians expressed great interest in his design for a steam-powered gun carriage for heavy-siege guns and monitor turrets, but the real centerpiece of Eads's work at the moment was, of course, the St. Louis bridge, already under construction for several years. Alexis was impressed with the plans for the bridge, and when he and the others proceeded to the actual structure, the grand duke was full of questions as he climbed over the abutments and then rode out into the river to investigate the middle and eastern piers. When his curiosity had been sated, Alexis and the others returned to their hotel to rest until the ball later that evening.[70]

Early in the evening, crowds began to gather outside the Southern, gawking at those lucky individuals with tickets who alighted one after another from the parade of carriages. At ten dollars for gentleman and five dollars for ladies, ticket prices were too steep for many, including Henry Wicker, who wrote to his family, "I know one man in St. Louis who won't attend."[71] At nine o'clock the arsenal band took its place at the head of the main stairway and began to play, opening with a Russian march and continuing to play throughout the evening. Over the next hour or so, the glittering guests promenaded in the halls, and in the opinion of the *Missouri Democrat,* "the youth, and beauty, and elegance of St. Louis society was fully represented." The room rustled with dresses of satin, silk, velvet, embroidery, and lace, in shades of pink, salmon, cream, and brown, accented with diamonds and other jewels, and topped by special coiffures, ornamented with flowers and ostrich plumes. The decorations for the ball were equally impressive. As in other cities, the organizers here had used flags, bunting, flowers, and greenery, but the St. Louis hosts had added something more—cages of chirping canaries. At the base of the staircase that led from the hotel lobby to the dining room had been placed two twelve-pound cannons.[72]

Finally, shortly after ten o'clock, the grand duke and his entourage arrived, escorted by members of the reception committee into the ballroom, while the sounds of a Russian march thumped in the background. Alexis was simple, but elegant, in a dress suit with white gloves and a white tie. As the orchestra played the Russian Hymn, committee members presented dozens of ladies and gentlemen to the grand duke, after which the dancing began with a plain quadrille. According to the *Missouri Democrat,* the grand duke danced with enthusiasm, yet in a dignified manner, and seemed most comfortable when dancing the lancers; in other American dances he moved just the least bit awkwardly, "his tall, straight frame unable to gracefully execute the unfamiliar steps." One of Alexis's dancing partners that evening was Miss Sally Britton, who years later would recall her good fortune in her memoir, describing Alexis as "quite the handsomest man I had ever seen: more than six feet in height, of superb physique, very blonde, he was indeed an Adonis." The festivities went on long into the early morning hours and, according to the *Democrat,* the grand duke practically had to be dragged away.[73]

On the day after the ball, everyone seemed to be moving a little slowly, guests and hotel employees alike. The grand duke took his coffee late, then went for a walk through the business district with a member of his entourage. According to a reporter from the *Missouri Democrat* who presumably followed the Russians on their walk, the two men discussed the previous evening's festivities as they strolled, comparing their observations about American society and American women. Alexis purportedly complained that he wanted to choose his own company in conversations, and especially in dance, and believed that he should be able to dance with the same lady more than once if he so desired. The *Missouri Democrat* later declared it was an "erroneous and ridiculous impression" that the committee had selected all of the grand duke's dancing partners. That evening Alexis and several of the other Russians went to the Olympic Theatre, quietly and without any pomp and circumstance. Though they tried to remain invisible, a number of people noticed them and, when they departed, the audience applauded.[74]

On Tuesday, January 10, Alexis was "permitted the privilege of a private citizen," mingling amongst the guests in the Southern's parlors without formality. The grand duke and one of his companions also took a drive around the city and strolled in the vicinity of the hotel, picking their way through the slushy puddles of melting snow. In the evening, Alexis attended an elite soiree sponsored by a social club called the Home Circle. The organizers used the same room in the Southern in which the ball had been held and had arranged for the decorations to remain in place. Alexis arrived at about half past ten in simple dress attire and circulated freely within the large and fashionable crowd, free from the plans and preferences of committee members. He danced with a number of ladies and chatted amiably with the gentlemen, and appeared to enjoy himself immensely. It was subsequently reported that Alexis was a bit shocked by the independence of American women, however. Apparently, at least three young ladies refused the grand duke's request for a dance; each displayed a full dance card and, presumably, did not see fit to break an American heart to try and win a Russian one.[75]

Wednesday, January 11, was the grand duke's last day in St. Louis, and the crowds were still as interested as they had been upon his arrival. People gathered at the Southern at an early hour, and as the hotel porters loaded the grand duke's baggage into wagons, each piece was "wonderingly scrutinized." Though the *Missouri Democrat* mocked these curious oglers, it then went on to describe in detail the unique size and shape of the royal trunks and bags. While the grand duke's bags were being admired, the man himself slipped away for a shopping expedition. Visiting a number of shops on Fourth and Fifth streets, Alexis placed clothing orders that he intended to collect on his way back across the country after the buffalo hunt, and he purchased gifts for the Indians he expected to meet in the coming days.[76]

Alexis returned to the hotel shortly after eleven o'clock to find a cavalcade of carriages waiting out front along with an impatient crowd. After changing his clothes, the grand duke reappeared to a roar of applause and joined Mayor Brown and members of the reception committee, who escorted the Russian visitors to the train depot on Biddle Street. Along the way, Alexis told the mayor that he had enjoyed his time in St. Louis and had begun to plan a return trip, already scheduling several personal appointments for that time. The depot was thick with people, making it difficult for the royal party to board its train, but the train managed to depart on time, bound for Kansas City and the buffalo hunt.[77]

As Alexis departed, the *Missouri Democrat* boasted that his reception in St. Louis had been well executed and that he had made a number of friends due to his "frank, open, manly and modest bearing." Not everyone shared this view, however. One woman complained, "There has been immense excitement here over the Duke.... I did not see him and was rather disgusted with the people making such a fuss over him." Perhaps hers was a case of sour grapes, however, for her husband, who did meet the grand duke on his second visit to St. Louis, declared him a handsome, good fellow, not at all a snob, and "as fine a looking man physically as you see in ten thousand." Moreover, the husband added, "I don't find fault with people for running after him for it is an event of a lifetime to see a party of distinguished men travel through this country in such royal style."[78]

6

SO HAPPY TO BE HUNTING AGAIN

Alexis killed a Bison! Oh! Happy buffalo!
By royal hands and royal ball from this dull world to go.
How envied, then, should be your fate;
For history will record the date
When this young fledgling potentate
Your shaggy head laid low.

—*Memphis Daily Appeal,* January 26, 1872

O NE OF THE MOST memorable events of the grand duke's tour was his great buffalo hunt on the western plains with William "Buffalo Bill" Cody and Lieutenant Colonel George Armstrong Custer. The American public, already captivated by the "Wild West," with its open grassy plains, herds of elk and buffalo, and villages of Indians, found the combination of a Russian duke and a group of military and popular heroes irresistible. Moreover, in 1869, the Union Pacific and Central Pacific railroads had met in Promontory, Utah, completing the transcontinental railroad, and Alexis and his companions would be some of the early beneficiaries of this revolution in transportation. The buffalo hunt received more press coverage than any other part of Alexis's trip and has continued to fascinate Americans over a century and a half later. It is probably the best-known episode of the grand duke's trip, particularly for those interested in Buffalo Bill, Custer, and the Old West, as well as the ephemera associated with those people and places.

The popular interest in the buffalo hunt, then and now, however, has made it very difficult to figure out what actually happened. Several first-hand accounts and at least a dozen other versions of the hunt story have emerged over the years, creating inconsistencies and outright inaccuracies. Even the versions recounted by Buffalo Bill Cody diverge slightly from one another as the great showman embellished his stories with each retelling. Even worse, others have relayed the event as though they were present when, in fact, they were not. Finally, many of these various accounts "borrow" so heavily from one another that the same phrases and mistakes appear in multiple places.[1] The most reliable account seems to be that of a journalist from the *New York Herald* who traveled with the hunting party and reported each day's events back to his readers. Using his account, supplemented by the few other first-hand reports, it is possible to reconstruct what happened during those few days on the plains when Russian royalty pursued American buffalo.

The idea of a buffalo hunt for the tsar's son had long been in the works. In early July 1871, the artist Albert Bierstadt contacted Lieutenant General William T. Sherman with the idea, claiming to have heard that Alexis was interested in hunting buffalo. Bierstadt inquired, "As his visit partakes of a somewhat national character, would it not be [illegible] to give him one on a grand scale, with Indians included, as a rare piece of American hospitality?" Bierstadt also suggested that the Indians might demonstrate their dancing and hunting skills for the Russians. Although Sherman liked the idea, real planning did not begin until the fall when Secretary of War William Belknap indicated that army funds would be made available to underwrite the expense of the hunt; this message was then conveyed to General Philip Sheridan, commander of the Department of the Missouri. By late November, Sheridan had responded that, while there were plenty of buffalo in the area, a hunt at that time of year would require Alexis to "undergo the inclemency of the weather at this season on the plains." But, if the grand duke was willing, Sheridan could arrange it.[2]

In the meantime, Sheridan also pursued Bierstadt's idea regarding Indian entertainment. Through channels within the Department of the Interior and the Office of Indian Affairs, Sheridan requested that Spotted Tail, chief of the Brule band of the Lakota Sioux tribe, and a band of his warriors participate in the hunt. Spotted Tail played an important role in the relationship between the American government and the Sioux. Since the 1850s, he had advocated peaceful coexistence with the whites, while simultaneously struggling to retain hunting rights and other traditional freedoms for the Brule.[3]

By early December, Sheridan received word from the subagent to the Brule, Todd Randall, that Spotted Tail and several hundred of his people had agreed to join the campsite. The Brule would receive ten thousand rations of coffee, sugar, and flour, and one thousand rations of tobacco for their trouble. More than one newspaperman saw these provisions as a bribe to ensure that the Brule, in the parlance of the day, would conduct themselves "like white men." One reporter observed, "This perhaps may be considered a questionable way to secure a foreign guest from scalping or murder while in the United States, but when it is known that the Indians are armed and outnumber our soldiers almost ten to one it will be admitted that Sheridan's . . . policy is about the only safe one to pursue."[4]

In subsequent years, Buffalo Bill would claim that he had been tasked with contacting Spotted Tail. In a lively account of the meeting, Cody described riding through the winter and sleeping on the ground, ever on the lookout for an attack. Emphasizing the dangerous nature of his assignment, Cody declared that, while Spotted Tail was friendly, some of his young warriors were hostile and quick to react. Upon finding Spotted Tail's camp, Cody waited until night to ride in, covering his head and shoulders with a blanket to conceal his true identity. Once at the chief's lodge, he explained the purpose of his visit, using the Sioux agent Todd Randall as an interpreter. Spotted Tail agreed to participate in the royal hunt and offered Cody food and accommodation for the night. The chief also applauded Cody's decision to sneak into camp, telling him that some of the Sioux warriors disliked him and might have given him trouble had they met him outside the village.[5]

All of these plans went forward without any assurance that Alexis would participate in the hunt. In fact, several messages between American and Russian representatives indicate that, as late as mid-December, a royal buffalo hunt seemed unlikely. On December 20, Secretary of State Hamilton Fish wrote Secretary of War William Belknap that he had been informed by the Russians that, "as the time for the departure of his Imperial Highness the Grand Duke Alexis has been fixed by His Majesty the Emperor and his route arranged accordingly, it is not in the power of the Grand Duke to dispose of the time which such a hunt as is proposed by Lieutenant Sheridan would require." While many sources claim that the grand duke was invited to a buffalo hunt while visiting the White House in late November, a more concrete invitation seems to have occurred only in late December, when General Sherman traveled to Chicago and met with Alexis to persuade him to change his travel plans to include an adventure out west. On January 3, Sheridan happily telegraphed Townsend that Alexis had "withdrawn his declination."[6]

Now that the grand duke had committed to the hunt, Sheridan began to hammer out the details. Once again contacting the War Department and the Office of Indian Affairs, Sheridan requested assistance and assurances regarding the appearance of Spotted Tail and his people, and reiterated his promise of rations. This time, Sheridan could offer a specific time frame, January 12 to January 20. As Sheridan worked to ensure that everyone and everything would be in place for the hunt, officials of the Union Pacific railroad communicated with one another about the schedule of the grand duke's train, both for its right of way on the tracks and for the printing of the special timecards.[7]

The coup de grâce of Sheridan's plan was his inclusion of Lieutenant Colonel George Armstrong Custer, whom he invited in early January. In early 1872, Custer had just turned thirty-two years old, but his name was already well known across the country and beyond. Despite graduating at the bottom of his class at West Point, Custer had earned a reputation during the Civil War for bravery and fearless leadership and became the youngest man ever promoted to major general. After the Civil War, Custer had reverted to his prewar, regular army rank of captain, but in 1867 he received a promotion to the rank of lieutenant colonel in the Seventh U.S. Cavalry. In this new rank, Custer had engaged in battles with the Cheyenne and Lakota Sioux, perpetuating his image as the dashing young hero on horseback.[8]

Final preparations for the hunt began on January 8, when Captain James Eagan and First Lieutenant Joshua L. Fowler, along with some five dozen men from the Second U.S. Cavalry of the North Platte Station, traveled to Red Willow Creek to establish a campsite. First Lieutenant Edward M. Hayes, regimental quartermaster of the Fifth U.S. Cavalry, was also on hand to serve as quartermaster for the hunt. Eagan's party brought extra horses, thirty tents for the soldiers and servants, three wagons of supplies for the hunting party, and twenty-five wagonloads of goods for the Brule. Other supplies were sent to Camp Alexis, as well, including some sixteen hundred pounds of beef to feed the men from the Second Cavalry who would escort the hunting party. A group of horses was also stationed at Medicine Creek, roughly halfway between North Platte and Red Willow Creek, where Sheridan had decided the party would stop for lunch on the way to the campsite.[9]

Departing St. Louis around noon on January 11, the imperial train traveled twelve hours on the St. Louis, Kansas City & Northern Railway, reaching Kansas City at about midnight. Here the train transferred to the Kansas City, St. Joseph

& Council Bluffs Railroad and continued through the night, switching rail lines once more (to the Union Pacific Railroad Company) and bypassing a number of small towns. Unbeknownst to Alexis, he offended some locals in Leavenworth as he sped through town sometime around two in the morning, making any royal sighting impossible for those who waited hopefully in the dark. The *Leavenworth Daily Commonwealth* professed to be nonplussed, explaining, "blessed are they who expect nothing as they will never be disappointed." In the end, however, the people of Leavenworth were not so forgiving of the royal snub; as Alexis passed through again at the end of the hunt, the *Daily Commercial* declared, "We cast an old shoe after the first sprig of royalty that ever invaded Kansas."[10]

The imperial party appeared in Omaha late in the morning on January 12, welcomed at the Union Pacific depot by several thousand people, including several classes of schoolchildren. Local officials were there, as well, including Omaha ex-mayor Ezra Millard and the territorial governor, Alvin Saunders. Though Alexis would not be spending the night in town, a room at the Grand Central Hotel had been made available for him to freshen up and rest. In fact, he could not have spent much time resting since his very brief stay in Omaha (less than five hours) included a visit to the governor's mansion, a dinner, and a general public reception that allowed citizens to shake the grand duke's hand. In addition to the festivities in the city, Alexis received New Year's greetings from abroad, where his family and friends were celebrating Russian New Year.[11]

Despite the brevity of the grand duke's stay, there was one unsavory bit of business. The *Omaha Tribune* told the embarrassing tale of a woman who, at the end of the dinner, demanded to know where the grand duke had sat and on which plates he had eaten. The perplexed young waiter told her, and she promptly occupied the grand duke's chair and took his plates, delightfully eating bits of cake that he had left behind, sharing them with several ladies who had joined her. The *Tribune* categorized the episode succinctly: "Americans have often proved the fact that in whatever they undertake, they can beat the world. And there is a case of disgusting toadyism that stands alone, without a parallel in the history of any other nation."[12]

Shortly after three in the afternoon, the ducal party departed Omaha, now accompanied by a number of American military officers, as well as S. H. H. Clark, superintendent of the Union Pacific Railroad, and J. J. Dickey, superintendent of the Western Pacific Telegraph Company. Dinner was served on board the train, but the movable feast proved festive and enjoyable nonetheless, and the members of the party only retired to bed after midnight.[13]

Early on the morning of January 13, at about six o'clock, the grand duke's special train pulled into North Platte, where it was met by members of the Second Cavalry and Buffalo Bill Cody, attired in one of his famous decorative buckskin suits. According to the reporter of the *New York Herald,* the three or four hundred "rustic inhabitants who form the settlement" were also there, but unlike the cheers and excitement of their eastern counterparts, these residents of the western plains quietly removed their hats and displayed only "reverential curiosity." The party had breakfasted on the train, so when Alexis and the others alighted at the depot, it was primarily for the purpose of introductions. Sheridan introduced Cody to the grand duke, and the two men exchanged a few pleasantries about the hope and promise of a successful and enjoyable hunt. One member of the duke's party asked Cody if he always dressed in such a manner, and Cody responded that he had gotten this particular suit specially for the occasion, and that the locals in North Platte had already teased him considerably about putting on airs, a comment that drew laughter from everyone within earshot.[14] In fact, Cody had a penchant for embroidered shirts and embellished coats, and many of his show costumes were quite ornate.

At about quarter past eight, Sheridan gave the sign to depart for the campsite, with Cody in the lead as the designated guide for the hunt. Alexis and the other Russians climbed into ambulances, horse-drawn wagons that could accommodate several people and could handle the rough terrain of the countryside, while the other Americans intermingled with the Russians and regaled them with tales of life on the plains. The cavalrymen rode on horseback. By several accounts, a shortage of horses led Cody to offer his own beloved horse, Buckskin Joe, to train manager Frank Thomson. In the words of Cody's sister, Buckskin Joe was "buckskin in color, and rather a sorry-looking animal, but he was known all over the frontier as the greatest long-distance and best buffalo-horse living." Later, Cody reportedly allowed the grand duke to ride Buckskin Joe during the hunt.[15]

The route to the camp on Red Willow Creek was already familiar to some members of the party. Custer and the Seventh Cavalry had ridden the area in 1867 while scouting for hostile Indians as part of General Winfield Scott Hancock's Kansas campaign, pioneering a trail between Fort Hays, Kansas, and

Fort McPherson, Nebraska. Soon after, the route began to appear on military and surveying maps, and the trail became even better established by the "Millionaires' Hunt" of September 1871. That hunt party had consisted of a group of wealthy businessman: James Gordon Bennett Jr., owner of the *New York Herald;* Henry E. Davies, a prominent New York attorney; Leonard Jerome, a well-known New York financier and the grandfather of Winston Churchill; and Carroll Livingston, a member of the New York Stock Exchange and collateral descendant of Chancellor Livingston, who had administered the oath of office when George Washington took the presidency. For over a week, the men had a grand adventure hunting buffalo, elk, rabbits, wild turkey, and wild duck under the guidance of Sheridan and Cody. Davies went on to commemorate the hunt in a short book, *Ten Days on the Plains.*[16]

The hunting party that set out from North Platte the morning of January 13, 1872, was a large one, around 125 people, including the Russian party, the American officers, soldiers from the Second Cavalry, the members of the Band of the Second Cavalry, and others like train manager Frank Thomson, Buffalo Bill, the unidentified journalist from the *New York Herald,* and the telegraph operator J. J. Dickey. Though Alexis had traveled to the United States with over 75 men, only a few Russians accompanied him on his adventure out west. Among those were Admiral Possiet; Consul General at New York Vladimir Bodisco; the grand duke's physician, Dr. Vladimir Kudrin; Secretary to the Russian legation Lieutenant Shirkov; William Machin; Lieutenant Karl Tudeer; Alexander Olsufiev; and Count Pavel A. Shuvalov. At some point, the Omaha photographer Edric Eaton had joined the group, as well.[17]

The sky threatened snow even as the men left North Platte, and in less than an hour flakes began to fall. According to the *Herald* reporter, though no man uttered a word, "all anticipations of a few days' sport were mingled with despair." Luck was on their side, however, and the clouds soon broke to reveal a brilliant sun that shone the rest of the day. At Medicine Creek, the party stopped for a quick lunch of sandwiches and champagne and, after a change of horses, continued to Camp Alexis. For hours, the men rode through rolling prairies and vast, open spaces punctuated by copses of trees and prairie-dog mounds, arriving at their destination just before dark. As the men came over the horizon, they cheered at the sight of a "splendid military camp" and the band of the Second Cavalry struck up the Russian national hymn. Above the tents and campfires an American flag fluttered in the brisk January breeze.[18]

The campsite that would house the grand duke during his two-day adventure on the plains was situated on a low grassy plateau with a rising terrain and ridgeline off in the distance that looked south toward Red Willow Creek, a tributary of the Republican River in southwestern Nebraska. The area encompassed several acres and was mostly flat, but had been leveled out where necessary to create a place suitable for the erection of a large number of tents. The tents were set up in the traditional military format—"officers on one end, enlisted tents in parallel line running perpendicular to the officers' line, and the wagons parked well off to the north." The campsite would ultimately include two hospital tents outfitted with floors and stoves to be used as dining tents and ten wall tents to house the special guests. Several of the wall tents had floors, as well. Nonetheless, these were not luxurious accommodations. The one extant photograph of the grand duke's quarters shows a tent about nine feet by nine feet, with walls just under four feet high. The roof of this wall tent at its highest point would have been about eight and a half feet. Inside, the photograph reveals a stove and some crates, but little else.[19]

At Camp Alexis, members of the hunting party dismounted and gathered to warm themselves around one of the roaring campfires. They soon discovered, however, that some of their number were missing, including Lieutenant Shirkov and Custer. About the time that Sheridan was preparing to send out a search party, Custer came over the hill, followed by the others. Their ambulance had broken down some five miles back, forcing them to cover the last stretch on foot through the snow. Once the entire party had reassembled, it was time for dinner. Inside the large dining tents decorated with flags, the hungry men ate several courses of local game, including a prairie chicken shot by Custer. There was also, of course, a selection of choice wines. After dinner, some of the party sang songs and others told stories around the blazing campfire. The party retired early, tired after a long day of travel and eager to be well rested for the much-awaited hunt the next day.[20]

The next day was January 14, Alexis's twenty-second birthday. In New York, the Russian fleet celebrated his birthday, and Minister Catacazy held a dinner for the officers of the fleet at the Clarendon Hotel. Alexis, however, felt the distance from home particularly keenly on that day and later wrote his mother, "My birthday occurred during a hunt in a camp and no one knew about it, that is, of the Americans." One account of the hunt, however, described a celebration of Alexis's birthday with champagne over breakfast; perhaps the lovesick young

Russian exaggerated his sadness to elicit greater sympathy from his parents. In any event, the grand duke's birthday, celebrated or not, was also the day that the young Russian would get his first shot at an American buffalo. After breakfast, Cody left the campsite to scout out the nearest herd, and sometime before ten o'clock he returned to report that a herd was grazing some fifteen miles away. The men all mounted their horses and headed out, except for Sheridan, who was indisposed and remained behind. The first day of actual hunting was cold, with snow on the ground as much as eighteen inches deep in some places, but the sky was clear, "an unbroken field of blue." Edric Eaton's photograph of the first day of the hunt shows Alexis in a jacket and trousers of heavy cloth and topped off by a Cossack-style hat. Custer, attired in an astrakhan hat and fringed buckskin suit, the very one he would wear four years later at Little Bighorn, was given the task of guiding Alexis in the hunt.[21]

It had been agreed by all that Alexis should get the first kill of the hunt, but how that first kill occurred is difficult to tease out of the wildly divergent, and even intentionally farcical, accounts. According to the *New York Herald,* when the hunting party reached the buffalo herd, Custer charged through the animals, scattering them and selecting one large bull for Alexis. He gave Alexis the signal, and the grand duke rode up to the bull and fired his revolver, most likely the Smith and Wesson he had received as a gift earlier in his trip. The wounded animal was then finished off with a rifle shot and everyone cheered. Alexis then severed the tail of the "wild horned monster" as a trophy.[22] Buffalo Bill's version is much more colorful. Cody takes credit for helping Alexis make the first kill and portrays Alexis and his trusty revolver as far less capable. According to Cody, he allowed Alexis to ride Buckskin Joe, and told him that "all he would have to do was to sit on the horse's back and fire away." Yet even with this supposed advantage, the young Russian failed to take down a buffalo, firing six shots from his revolver to no effect. It was only when Cody handed Alexis his own beloved rifle named after the legendary Renaissance femme fatale Lucretia Borgia that Alexis successfully killed his first buffalo. The grand duke was elated; he threw down the rifle, waved his hat, and began talking excitedly in Russian to members of his suite. Cody remarked that the grand duke's reaction was a surprise to everyone: "Old Buckskin Joe was standing behind the horse that I was riding, apparently quite as much astonished as I was at this singular conduct of a man he had accepted in good faith as a buffalo hunter." The first kill was followed by an impromptu celebration of champagne.[23]

Other accounts of Alexis's first attempt at buffalo hunting were less flattering and even insulting. One article pointedly noted that Alexis's first kill was an "aged veteran." J. J. Dickey, the telegraph operator who had accompanied the hunting party, later recalled that he had always suspected that "Cody, to help the duke out, shot the animal from the opposite side." The *Cleveland Daily Leader* saw much to be mocked in the grand duke's buffalo hunt, as well. First, it joked that "there is great rivalry among the buffaloes for the honor of the first shot from the illustrious Grand Duke." Several days later, the *Leader* reported that Alexis first mistook mules for buffalos and killed several before he could be stopped. Then, seeing that the grand duke needed help, the others chased down a buffalo and tied it up, at which point the young Russian calmly and coolly "approached the spot where the wild beast was confined by ropes and lariats of raw hide," and shot it, harpooned it, and finished it off with a club. Cody later addressed these exaggerations in his memoir, stating, "It was reported in a great many of the newspapers that I shot the first buffalo for Alexis, while in some it was stated that I held the buffalo while His Royal Highness killed it. But the way I have related the affair is the correct version."[24]

Once the grand duke had killed his first buffalo, several members of the party decided to return to camp while others went off to continue hunting. Though the *Herald* made no mention of it, Cody later recalled that as the group returned to camp they encountered a small herd of buffalo. As the herd crossed their path some thirty feet away, Alexis shot into the crowd and a cow fell dead. The grand duke was clearly as surprised as everyone else by his lucky shot. When the ambulance arrived soon after, corks once again flew in celebration of Alexis's kill, and Cody stated, "I was in hope that he would kill five or six more before we reached camp, especially if a basket of champagne was to be opened every time he dropped one." There is no clear agreement on how many buffalo the party killed that first day. According to the *New York Herald,* only four were killed. Cody said that several of the hides and heads were preserved for the grand duke to take home as souvenirs, and photographs of the hunting party do show several buffalo tails.[25]

The party continued hunting late into the afternoon on that first day before returning to the camp for dinner. According to Cody, one of the main items on the menu was buffalo. Although no description has been left of the actual menu that evening, a description of the dinner served at the "Millionaires' Hunt" of early fall 1871 can give an idea of what the entrees likely would have been—buffalo tail soup, stewed rabbit, filet of buffalo with mushrooms, ragout of prairie dog, roasted elk, antelope, black-tailed deer, wild turkey, broiled teal, mallard, antelope chops, buffalo calf steaks, sweet potatoes, mashed potatoes, green peas, tapioca pudding, champagne, claret, whiskey, brandy, ale, and coffee.[26] It is safe to assume that the grand duke ate at least as well.

The next morning the hunting party that set out was substantially larger. The previous evening Spotted Tail had arrived and encamped nearby with between four and six hundred of his people, including sub-chiefs named Black Hat, Whistler, War Bonnet, and Two Lance. The weather was once again cold and clear, and during the day the men occasionally encountered deep snow as they pursued buffalo. The hunt began in a rugged canyon, and Sheridan, who had joined the party, guided Alexis to a herd and offered him first kill of the day. The grand duke pursued a mother and her bull calf over dangerous and rough terrain with enthusiasm and impressive horsemanship, taking both animals down. At this point, Alexis and his suite were treated to "a scene that few white men, who have lived many years upon the Plains, have ever witnessed," as Spotted Tail and his men charged a herd of buffalo, taking down a number of them with bow and arrow alone until the plateau was strewn with the bodies of the huge beasts. Alexis was fascinated by this display, and wished to examine one of the buffalo more closely to better appreciate the power of the arrow. One of the young warriors, perhaps eighteen years old, showed the grand duke that he had killed one buffalo with an arrow that had gone completely through the animal. When he had located the arrow, he asked Custer to present it as a gift to Alexis, who gladly accepted it as yet another trophy from his memorable hunt. The men had champagne and lunch in the field, and eventually made their way over frozen ground and snow drifts back to camp, observing but not pursuing herds of buffalo along the way. They arrived at camp as it was becoming dark, and since no loaded firearms were allowed in camp, the men all discharged their weapons in the air as the tents appeared on the horizon, prompting an echo of cheers from those inside.[27] After an exciting day and many miles on horseback, the hunting party enjoyed another sumptuous dinner.

Dinner was followed by a "war dance" or "grand powwow" performed by the Brule warriors, ornamented with blankets, buffalo robes, and trinkets, their faces colored with red and yellow paint. Buffalo Bill's sister, who was not present at the event, later published a book that recounted her brother's escapades. Relying on her brother's stories, she described the dance in words that are unsettling to modern ears, but would have seemed perfectly fine to her contemporaries: "The outlandish contortions and grimaces of the Indians, their leaps and crouchings, their fiendish yells and whoops, made up a barbaric jangle of picture and sound not soon to be forgotten. To the European visitors the scene was picturesque rather than ghastly, but it was not a pleasing spectacle to the old Indian fighters looking on … [who saw] … too many suggestions of bloodshed and massacre in the past, and of bloodshed and massacre yet to come." After the dance, Spotted Tail, with his wife and daughter, and some of the other chiefs, were invited to the imperial tent, where they were treated to a variety of luxuries, including champagne.[28]

The most frequently recounted tale about the grand duke's interaction with the Brule describes how he and Custer flirted with Spotted Tail's daughter. According to the journalist from the *New York Herald,* "Miss Spotted Tail" was a comely sixteen-year-old whose fair appearance during the war dance attracted the attention of both the Americans and Russians, many of whom found her more interesting than "the sanguinary stories of the warriors who were shouting and stamping in the circle." Throughout the dance, men sent small gifts of candy and trinkets her way, hoping to receive some sign of favor, but the young maiden exhibited the "coyness characteristic of her sex." Finally, one young officer of the Second Cavalry, perceiving himself in the lead for her affections, quickly made for his tent and retrieved a pair of earrings as a gift for her, at which point Custer came forward and, taking advantage of his ability to speak the "Indian sign language," asked the young lady if he could have the honor of placing the earrings in her ears. She agreed, but to some of his romantic rivals it seemed that he took longer than necessary in the task, putting the second earring in without changing position, so that he had to put his arms around her neck. In the end, Custer also kissed the young lady. As this story was repeated in various places, Alexis was also credited with carrying on a mild flirtation with Spotted Tail's daughter, embellishing upon the popular rumor that the grand duke had an appreciative eye for the fair sex.[29]

As the second day at Camp Alexis drew to a close, the members of the hunting party could praise themselves for another fruitful day of hunting although, once again, the accounts differ on just how successful. The *Herald* reported that Alexis killed two buffalo, Spotted Tail and his men eight, Sheridan and the others forty-four, for a grand total of fifty-six buffalo. Cody later recalled that Alexis killed eight buffalo in all during the hunt at Camp Alexis and declared the young Russian "really accomplished" in the saddle. Cody estimated that over the two day period the entire group had killed several hundred buffalo. The various displays by Spotted Tail and his men had also been a success. Before the men parted ways, Alexis generously distributed gifts to the Brule, red and green blankets and a large bag of silver dollars. On the morning of their departure, Eaton took a number of photographs, including portraits of Spotted Tail, Buffalo Bill, and Custer at the request of the grand duke.[30]

It is safe to say that the buffalo hunt was the grand duke's favorite part of his tour. Writing from St. Louis in late January, Alexis told his brother Vladimir that, although he had already written their father about the hunt, "I must tell you, that I was so happy to be hunting again and had such emotions that it is now even humorous to recall." He continued, "If you could have been there with me, you would have felt the same way." Alexis hoped he would get to hunt bears during his trip on the Mississippi River. Alexis sent Vladimir a photograph of himself with Custer, calling him "one of the most notable buffalo hunters" in the party.[31]

When the two days of buffalo hunting were over, the party set out for North Platte, leaving the members of the Second Cavalry to break camp. Returning to the train station at North Platte, the hunting party stopped again at Medicine Creek to eat and change horses, and the remainder of the ride was uneventful, except for a few broken springs and a tipped wagon. Alexis rode in an ambulance with Sheridan and Cody, and arrived ahead of all the others. Apparently, that early arrival had a story behind it. In his memoir, Buffalo Bill later explained that, on the way back to North Platte, Sheridan had regaled Alexis with tales of Cody's time as a stagecoach driver, eventually giving Cody the reins and telling him to shake them up a bit. Cody cracked the whip and the horses sped forward, easily pulling their light load over the hilly terrain. Cody recounted that the horses "fairly flew over the ground," and he had difficulty holding them, especially since there was no brake on the wagon. Meanwhile, Sheridan and Alexis were jostled all about, barely able to keep themselves inside the ambulance. When the wagon finally stopped, Alexis claimed to have enjoyed the ride, but requested that they move at a slower pace for the remainder of the trip. Once the entire party had reached the North Platte station, the men had dinner and recounted the events of the hunt over bottles of champagne. It was during this last evening together that Alexis gave Cody the fur overcoat that he had worn on the hunt as a special gift.[32]

The imperial party stayed at the North Platte station only a few hours, leaving for Denver via Cheyenne later the same day. In Cheyenne, they paused briefly to allow the territorial governor of Colorado, Edward McCook, ex-governor John Evans, and several other officials of the territorial government to board the train. After about thirty minutes, the train departed only to be delayed once again, this time by a much more serious matter. An imperfectly secured rail shifted and threw two cars from the tracks: Sheridan's car came off the track completely and rolled over, landing on its side, while the grand duke's car suffered only a partial derailment. Though the passengers of both cars were shaken and frightened, a more serious disaster was avoided only by the quick thinking of one of the occupants who managed to pull the bell rope and alert the engine to stop the train. The grand duke's car was easily righted on the track, but Sheridan's car had taken a more serious tumble and would take several hours to fix. Sheridan thus insisted that Alexis and the rest of the train continue on, and so they did.[33]

The grand duke's train arrived in Denver on the evening of January 17 after about nineteen hours of travel. A large and enthusiastic crowd awaited the imperial guest in Denver and followed him a distance of at least a half-mile from the depot to his hotel, the American House. Completed in 1868, the American House was deemed the first modern hotel of the West, a simple, three-story brick building located on the corner of Sixteenth and Blake streets. Its unadorned exterior was misleading, however, for inside the hotel revealed a "broad, graceful stairway with the carved, spindle bannisters . . . carpeted in a rich wine red, walnut furniture, silk upholstery on divans . . . plush curtains and plush bottomed chairs." The sleeping rooms were outfitted with soft feather mattresses and bathtubs that would be filled by the staff on request. The hotel also featured a beautiful and spacious dining room with exceptional cuisine, and a cellar stocked with the best wines, champagnes, and liquors. For the grand duke's visit, the hotel's manager, Henry Smith, had set aside and refurnished thirteen rooms on the second floor, which included a special private dining room, and the duke himself would be settled in parlor number twenty-five, reputed to be the best in the house.[34]

Alexis rose late on January 18, no doubt exhausted after a long day of travel, and finished breakfast only around noon. Fortunately, the reception plans for the day were low-key, consisting of a tour of the area's interesting sights and a meeting with members of the territorial legislature, then in session. In the early afternoon, Governor McCook and the legislators called upon the grand duke at the American House for introductions and light conversation. Two of the legislators were Mexican, which was of particular interest to Alexis, who inquired about their role as representatives of their people. Next, Alexis and his party were taken on a tour of Denver. It was a brisk but clear day, affording the party the full opportunity to appreciate the area's stunning scenery. After pausing to view Pike's Peak, the tour continued to the west side of Denver, making a short stop at the brewery of the Denver Ale Company, where Alexis "refreshed himself with a draught or two of some of the choicest productions of the establishment." The party next proceeded to the Holly Water Works, where the Russians examined the powerful machinery that pumped water into the city.[35]

The crowning event of the grand duke's stay in Denver was a ball held at the American House arranged by the Pioneer's Club, an organization composed of early settlers of the Rocky Mountain Territory and Colorado. The ball was smaller than some of those Alexis had attended in other parts of the country, with only about four hundred people, and the decorations and the costumes were modest by comparison, but everyone seemed to enjoy themselves, and it was reported in the papers that the grand duke participated in almost every dance of the evening. J. J. Dickey, the Western Union man who had accompanied the hunting party, also attended the ball in Denver and recalled, "that night we all danced, had the finest of refreshments, and a royal good time."[36]

On the following day, January 19, Alexis, Sheridan, and the others accepted an invitation from the Colorado Central Railroad Company to visit the mines of Clear Creek Canyon. The special narrow-gauge train left about noon and made its way to Golden City, where the party was wined and dined at the Golden Hotel. After this pleasant diversion of about two hours, the trip to the mines resumed in carriages for some eight to ten miles. Dickey recalled that "besides the wonderful scenery we were treated to a splendid lunch beneath the shade of an overhanging rock." At their destination, the party toured several mines, and Sheridan amused everyone by singing some old army songs, with everyone eventually joining in the chorus. It was a very cold day, but the beauty of the natural surroundings more than compensated, and everyone on board expressed pleasure with the day's activities. Periodically the carriages stopped to allow Alexis to appreciate the scenery and, according to the *Herald* reporter, "Several of the peaks which crown the lofty cliffs were properly christened and will hereafter be known as 'Peak Alexis' and 'Sheridan's Peak.'" The party returned to Denver about five o'clock and departed for St. Louis at about ten that evening.[37] Before returning to charms of city life, however, Alexis would participate in yet another impromptu buffalo hunt.

During the short visit to Denver, Custer had heard that there was a large herd of buffalo near Kit Carson, Colorado, and it was decided to arrange another hunt for the grand duke and his companions. Chalkley Beeson, a cattleman and violin player from Kit Carson who had been hired to play at the ducal ball, had been bragging to his friends in Denver about the scores of buffalo he regularly saw at home. When Custer caught wind of these stories, he approached Sheridan, who quickly made arrangements with the Kansas Pacific Railroad for horses and wagons to be waiting for the train near Kit Carson. Chalkley Beeson was enlisted as a guide. When the grand duke's train arrived at Kit Carson on January 20, the Americans and Russians in the party climbed onto horses and into ambulances. It appeared that the whole town had come out to see the grand duke, but since time was of the essence, no time could be wasted on "idle ceremonies," and the party immediately set off for the hunting grounds and camp that had already been prepared.[38]

This quickly organized hunt has also inspired several retellings of uncertain reliability. Miguel Antonio Otero's father had been selected as the head of the reception committee at Kit Carson and was part owner of Otero, Sellar & Company, the store that had been commissioned to provide many of the necessary provisions. The younger Otero claimed to have been one of the wagon riders on the Kit Carson hunt, entrusted with delivering a gallon keg of whiskey to Sheridan. Unbeknownst to Otero, the driver of the wagon and another man with him had been drinking the whiskey during the entire ride. When Sheridan discovered that much of his whiskey had been consumed, he rushed out of his tent, "looking hotter than a boiled owl." Otero remarked, "In all my life I never heard one man bestow on another such curses as the General used on the driver."[39]

Chalkley Beeson reported a similar tongue-lashing in his account. According to Beeson, at one point he, Sheridan, and a few others had walked to the top of a hill to observe the hunting party, only to see a group on horseback firing with abandon and driving a pack of buffalo directly toward them. With bullets falling all around them, Beeson and the others began to run, but Sheridan, who had short legs, decided to throw himself face down on the ground instead. When the riders stopped and Sheridan got to his feet, he expressed his rage in no uncertain terms. Beeson recalled, "There was only one man in the army who could equal him when it came to a certain kind of expletive, and that was Custer himself. I don't know what kind of language Pa Romanoff used to [sic] Alexis when he got mad, but that slip of royalty got a cussing from Phil Sheridan that day that I bet he will never forget. He didn't spare anybody in the bunch, not even Custer and the grand duke, and he included all their kinsfolk, direct and collateral."[40]

The hunting party stayed at Kit Carson for two days (January 20–21) and succeeded in killing many buffalo, perhaps as many as forty. According to the journalist from the *Herald,* the hunt in Colorado was far more exciting and vigorous, for unlike the "sluggard animals of Nebraska," the buffalo of Colorado "were disposed to make a desperate effort for escape … were fleet-footed, and dashed across the level territory at a speed worthy of an express locomotive." Alexis once again proved himself a skilled sportsman, even in the face of a charging bull, and took down five buffalo on his own. The *Herald* reporter humorously noted, "The Colorado buffaloes will be among the few denizens of the United States to whom the visit of the Grand Duke Alexis will be a subject of sincere regret." In fact, the killing continued even after the visiting party was on board the train headed to Kansas. Between Kit Carson and Topeka, the men saw many buffalo herds and, shooting from the moving train, managed to kill quite a few; Alexis reportedly killed at least six.[41]

———◆———

Even as Alexis caroused with the likes of Buffalo Bill and Custer, however, his heart remained heavy. In a letter to his mother, he thanked her and the other members of his family for the gifts they had sent, and described his homesickness during the recent holiday: "You can imagine how sad I was to greet the New Year alone, among strangers, for the first time in my life without all of you." The lonely young man asked, "How many more New Years will I have to greet without you?" Alexis continued, "Yes, it is difficult to be alone, difficult to be among strangers, always alone in your sorrow and smiling when you are crying inside." He asked his mother to forgive him for always returning to the subject of Zhukovskaya, but he felt he could not do otherwise, "because these are the thoughts in my mind." Moreover, Alexis found his official duties exhausting. He declared to his mother, "I will be glad when we finish our journey because I am terribly tired of all the ceremonies and celebrations and it makes me sad to play this role for so long, especially when this is not really what is on my mind." By late January, Alexis's anger toward his brother Vladimir had cooled somewhat, and he apologized for the harshness of his previous letter, explaining that he had been overwhelmed by so many bitter feelings and thoughts that he had unfairly lashed out. He assured Vladimir that he would faithfully and honestly serve both their father and their brother to the best of his ability, and would even happily give his life for them, but stressed that his honor was more valuable than his life. As Alexis had told Possiet and other members of his family, he had a responsibility to Zhukovskaya and believed he had to follow his heart and his own sense of honor. He asked Vladimir to look after his son if something should happen to him and to send "you know who" 25,000 rubles. Still terribly sad, Alexis also told his brother that he loved him and begged Vladimir not to forget him.[42]

———— ◆ ————

When the buffalo hunt was over, Alexis and his party headed east again, stopping briefly in Topeka and Jefferson City before a short stay in St. Louis. In Jefferson City, the grand duke witnessed American democracy in action for the first time, observing the conduct of business in both the House and the Senate. According to the *Missouri Democrat,* the young Russian seemed to grow bored after the first few minutes, whispering to Admiral Possiet and fidgeting in an agitated manner: "He crossed and recrossed his legs, pulled his side whiskers out to their utmost capacity, and stroked his hair," shifting a black silk hat from hand to hand. The grand duke may have been bored, but the spectators in the hall were not. All eyes stayed on the intriguing young man from the moment he entered until the moment he left, the ladies delighting in his good looks and the men commenting approvingly on his athletic build. From Jefferson City, the Russian party proceeded to St. Louis, but this second stay in that city was more relaxed and informal than the previous visit several weeks earlier. There were no official dinners and receptions, and the Russians were allowed to recuperate from their big adventure out west. Much of their time in St. Louis was spent indoors as Alexis caught up on his correspondence, a wise choice since the weather was exceeding cold. The *Missouri Democrat* complained, "No wrappings served to keep the cold out, and no locks, nor doors, nor windows restrained it."[43]

Though Alexis hid from the cold during most of his second visit to St. Louis, he did engage in several activities of note. Curious about the adaptability of the soil in Missouri for growing grapes, the grand duke invited Charles Haven, the manager of the Park of Fruits Association, to meet him at the Southern Hotel. After a fruitful discussion of grape cultivation, Alexis promised to send cuttings from vines on the Black Sea coast, and Haven promised in return that he would plant the cuttings on a plot of ground that would be called Mount Alexis.[44] Alexis and Custer also spent a great deal of time together, strolling around the city and having their picture taken by John A. Scholten, the leading photographer of St. Louis. Scholten photographed Alexis and Custer in the costume of buffalo hunters, several of Custer alone, and at least two with both men. Meanwhile, Admiral Possiet spent this time making arrangements for the final leg of their journey through the South and their transportation on the Mississippi River aboard the *Great Republic*.[45]

———— ◆ ————

As Alexis departed St. Louis for the last leg of his American tour, he would have been surprised to know that his visit had contributed to two early movements that continue to be important today—the animal rights and conservation movements. The widely publicized buffalo hunt, for example, provided the opportunity for some Americans to debate and denigrate the appearance of the now-famous American Society for the Prevention of Cruelty to Animals (ASPCA). Founder Henry Bergh had become a very public, and in some cases reviled, figure in the years after the ASPCA's founding in 1866, for both his views in general and his repeated attempts to stop hunting activities in various places. In January 1872, for example, Bergh made several attempts to halt a pigeon shoot in Jerome Park in New York City. Criticizing Bergh for "fighting windmills," the *New York Herald* declared that amusements such as pigeon shooting, fishing, or "careering over the prairie behind the buffalo herds, in the company of General Sheridan and the Grand Duke Alexis," were "sinless and harmless" amusements. Indeed, the *Herald* reporter who accompanied the members of the Alexis hunting party took repeated jabs at Bergh in his reports. On the first hunt in Nebraska, he noted that all involved had a "glorious time, lacking only the presence of Mr. Bergh to give it the highest flavor of enjoyment," while at Kit Carson several days later, he reported that Alexis, Custer, and Sheridan, "far away from the jurisdiction of the tender-hearted Bergh, poured a shower of bullets into the ranks and flanks" of a herd of buffalo. Other papers had used the visit of Alexis to attack Bergh as well. The *Philadelphia Inquirer,* for example, delighted in reporting that Alexis had successfully participated in a pigeon shoot in Chicago, "without any regard for the feelings of Mr. Bergh."[46]

For other Americans, however, the grand duke's adventure out West raised heightened awareness of the decimation of the buffalo herds. The first attempt to prevent the destruction of the herds occurred before Alexis's arrival, on March 13, 1871, when Representative R. C. McCormick of Arizona introduced Bill No. 157 into the lower house of Congress. Though that bill was unsuccessful, the public conversation about the buffalo herds continued into 1872. In January 1872, the *Cleveland Daily Leader* described a recent appeal to Congress by Civil War General William B. Hazen for governmental intervention in the wasteful slaughter of American buffalo. The *Leader* noted that many people, including soldiers of the U.S. Army, were guilty of this "buffalo murder . . . this reckless waste of animal life" and specifically mentioned the grand duke's recreational hunt, as well. The completion of the Pacific Railroad had made it possible for anyone with the necessary cash to acquire a ticket and travel out west to hunt the buffalo, many of whom were not even consumed by their killers, but left to feed the wolves and the crows. As a consequence, the plains were "whitened . . . by the skeletons of wantonly killed buffaloes" as the species slid closer to extinction. In February, two senators—Henry Wilson of Massachusetts and Cornelius Cole from California—presented yet another bill to protect the buffalo and other wild animals of the plains, and in April 1872, McCormick raised the issue again. The bill went nowhere, however, nor did another bill submitted by McCormick two years later. At this point, the conversation in Washington included the question of how the decimation of the buffalo affected the Native American population. Apparently, some had argued that killing the buffalo would subdue the Indians by depriving them of food, but many others believed that starving them was more likely to provoke a declaration of war.[47]

In the spring and summer of 1872, on the heels of the Grand Duke Alexis hunt, the *New York Times* printed several stories related to "the evils of buffalo hunting" and "buffalo slaughter."[48] That same year, W. E. Webb published *Buffalo*

Land, a book that bemoaned the fate of the buffalo as the railroads brought more and more people west to hunt them and advocated a game law to protect the endangered animals. Two years later, a few months after McCormick had raised the issue again, the *Times* reprinted a story from a Denver paper that described the likely extinction of the buffalo, adding that, "if the bison were a wild and savage animal, if to kill one required any especial skill or bravery or nerve, there might be some justification for the enormous slaughter ... but the fact is that the bison is an exceedingly mild-dispositioned animal." By the 1880s, the plight of the buffalo had captured the attention of the famous western artist Albert Bierstadt, the very man who had helped organize the grand duke's famous buffalo hunt. In his 1888 painting *The Last of the Buffalo,* Bierstadt presented two groups on the brink of extinction in one vivid scene—a Native American man on horseback, his arm drawn back as he prepares to kill a buffalo calf. Finally, in 1902, Congress granted an appropriation for the purchase of twenty buffalo to be kept in Yellowstone National Park, but it was too late; the great buffalo herds had disappeared twenty years earlier.[49]

7

THIS YOUNG DUCK OF MUSCOVY

Alexis! O Alexis!
It seems so very queer.
How you can so perplex us
With your yellow beard and hair!
So set the girls on fire,
So make the men perspire,
A. Romanoff, Esquire,
You handsome polar bear!

　　　　—*New Orleans Times,* February 14, 1872

A FTER TOURING the great American cities of the East, the rapidly expanding cities of the Midwest, and the frontier towns of the West, there remained one region of the country for Alexis to visit before departing the United States. The South had been ravaged by the Civil War, but many cities were still eager to see him and determined to host him in style. While the rest of the country had wrestled with the appropriateness of a republican nation hosting a member of royalty, in the South that question had yet another dimension. Several members of the American press noted the irony of southerners fawning over the son of an abolitionist. The *Cincinnati Commercial* asked, "Is it not sad that people who have been robbed, so to speak, of their slaves should treat a member of a family of Abolitionists with distinguished consideration?"[1] The *New Orleans Times* was, perhaps, even more cynical and resentful about the glorification of Russia's emancipation of its serfs and America's abolition of slavery. To the first instance, the *Times* stated that "Russia never cackled over that egg; emancipation was adopted there as a mere political measure." As for America's own emancipation, it had come about, as "strictly a war measure, and ... it would have been foregone in the interests of peace at any early period of the war." The *Times* bitterly concluded, "though the serfs were emancipated by his father, Russia was not idiotic enough to make them either rulers or gods.... We have done both with ours." Even Alexis was surprised by the invitations from southern cities, confessing to his mother that he thought it a bit odd, given the fact that Russia "had continually been for the North, that is, against the Southern states."[2] But in this case it seems that southerners were willing to lay aside old animosities for the privilege of hosting a celebrity, even one with such complicated associations.

As the grand duke made his way through the South, he met rehabilitated Confederates, freed slaves, and the newly created King of Carnival. His visit coincided with a difficult period, when the physical reconstruction of the South was still ongoing and Reconstruction politics were still intertwined with violence and corruption. Alexis's visit also served to magnify lingering regional conflicts. Less than a decade after the end of the Civil War, many southern elites felt the need to demonstrate their region's equality with, or superiority to, the North. Over time, these hopes would become part of a powerful social myth about the ability of the South to regenerate itself, and the words "New South" came to symbolize that transition from one kind of society to another. The "New South" myth was intended to create a new conception of the region, a definition of the South of which southerners could be proud. This idea of a "New South" would restore the prestige and power of the region without sacrificing the much-revered memory of the "Old South." In the difficult era of Reconstruction, the visit of Grand Duke Alexis, then, was important to southern cities as it gave them a chance to criticize their northern brethren and show that, even after defeat, they were progressive, economically thriving, culturally sophisticated, and worthy of respect.[3]

Numerous southern newspaper reports testify to this sense of competition with the North. While many American cities condemned the fawning of elites in the Northeast, especially in New York, the complaints found in southern newspapers revealed the lingering anger and resentment of the southern states toward the northern states. Even before the grand duke had set sail, the *Richmond Whig* commented that no people in the world loved princes, kings, and emperors as much as "the Democratic people of the United States," predicting that "there is not a Yankee woman who would not readily embrace him." Once Alexis had arrived, the *New Orleans Republican* disapproved of the way in which the grand duke was being feted by "half the wise people and all the fools at the North," and criticized the "flunkyism" of those who "think they cannot go to breakfast unless dressed in furs and blazing in diamonds." The *Republican* likewise mocked the entertainments that the young Russian had endured in the North, including "fancy fairs, obese matrons, visits to hospitals, and spread eagleism generally." Similarly, the *New Orleans Times* noted that, while it was no surprise that northerners saw Russia as their natural ally, it was "one of the consolations of the South for their defeat in that struggle, that her people are not expected or inclined to participate in this snobbery to the semi-civilized Muscovite."[4]

In Memphis, the papers also expressed this utter disgust with the North: "The accidental Grand Duke is simply the son of a man whom we know nothing of.... His reception in the North should not be an example to us. And as we do not propose to let shoddyism and toadyism shape our rules of society in the South, it would be best for us to stand aloof as a body collectively, and let those who propose to ape the North and its kind do it individually." The Charleston press was equally sharp in its criticism of the extravagant expressions of fealty being shown to the grand duke, especially in New York, where "this is even more noticeable than at any other portion of the United States." The *Courier* noted that "for a people that profess to despise the claim of a superiority of blood to indulge in such extravagant ablutions" was simply ridiculous, and the bad behavior cut across gender—"if the men were foolish, the women were, or appeared to be, actually demented." While these articles criticized toadyism in and of itself, these correspondents clearly thought that the people of the North were more prone to it than others. Taking a different approach, however, the *Savannah Advertiser* believed that the South could upstage the North. Early in the grand duke's visit, when his exact itinerary was unknown and it was hinted that he might visit Savannah, the *Advertiser* challenged, "As the weather is too cold at the North for any out door amusements, we could show the young man some of our national sports ... and make him wish he had come direct to Savannah instead of visiting those stupid places, New York and Washington."[5]

Although some southern newspapers professed to care little for royalty and even less for the opinions of those in the North, it is clear that many in the South winced at how that region was being portrayed by papers around the country, especially in the North. This may have been particularly true in New Orleans, which was having such a difficult time during Reconstruction. The city's papers frequently reported on what newspapers elsewhere said about the South in general, and New Orleans in particular. In December 1871, the *New Orleans Times* declared that "several leading Northern papers" had recently reported on "the decay of New Orleans," attributing it to misadministration, among other things. This prompted one reader to complain to the *Times* about excessive taxes on businesses and ask, "Is it any wonder that the decay of New Orleans should be a frequent theme with the correspondents of Western and Northern newspapers?" A month later, the *Times* noted that papers in the North had been commenting on the "present disorganized state of public affairs in Louisiana ... attributing them, in the main, to climatic influences." The *Times* acknowledged the horrible state of affairs in Louisiana, but insisted that the "Radical party and its failure to govern the people properly" had placed Louisiana in this situation and made it the laughing-stock of the country. Other New Orleans papers recognized the problems, as well. The *Republican* concluded that Alexis should not visit New Orleans, to avoid "the comparison ... between the progress visible in the North and the stagnation apparent in the South."[6] These debates were pointless, however, for Admiral Possiet had already determined that the final leg of the grand duke's American tour would be through several southern cities, beginning with Louisville, Kentucky.

Founded in 1778, Louisville was located on the Ohio River at the point where the river crossed a limestone ledge, forming the Falls of the Ohio. Louisville's identity became tied to the river and the steamboat industry, and the city evolved from a frontier village to a thriving commercial center in the early nineteenth century. During this period of growth, the population of the city quintupled and came to include thousands of German and Irish immigrants. In the period after the Civil War, Louisville also became more industrial, producing cement, leather, furniture, and whiskey, and its railway connections multiplied as well, facilitating the trade of these industrial goods. By 1871, Louisville was a city of over 100,000 with a solid, growing economy and many of the conveniences of a modern city.[7]

The people of Louisville were certainly aware that the grand duke would soon be traveling through the United States, but the city's major papers gave the trip scant attention. Even as the handsome Russian spent his first days on

American soil, the subject of great fascination and admiration on the East Coast, the Louisville press showed little interest in the Russian travelers, declaring that the girls of its city were not at all excited about the grand duke's visit. The *Courier Journal* did, however, ask in October, "Are we to permit our imperial young friend ... to visit these Western shores without an invitation to visit Louisville?" Perhaps it was this question that encouraged a group of leading citizens to send an invitation to Alexis on Saturday, January 20, suggesting a ball and a trip to Mammoth Cave. For several days, the citizens of Louisville were on pins and needles, waiting to hear whether the Russians could fit another city into their itinerary. Finally, on January 25, Custer telegraphed the grand duke's acceptance, as well as a request for some quiet time before and after the proposed reception and ball. With this confirmation in hand, the leading men of Louisville set about creating the necessary committees to oversee the exciting event.[8]

The men involved in inviting Alexis and planning his reception were, as elsewhere, the social and business leaders of the city. General William Preston, chair of the overall reception committee, was a lawyer, veteran of the Mexican War and the Civil War, ex-minister to Spain and Mexico, and a former congressman. Isaac Caldwell, a very talented and respected lawyer who later served as president of the University of Louisville, chaired the arrangements committee. Other committee members included John Baxter, a businessman who served on the Common Council and the Board of Alderman, and ultimately became mayor in 1870. David Yandell was a surgeon and medical professor at the University of Louisville known for promoting high standards for students and continuing education for doctors, a platform he continued as president of the American Medical Association.[9]

The most fascinating man involved in the reception plans was M. Lewis Clark Jr. The "M" stood for "Meriwether," and he was, in fact, the grandson of the famous explorer William Clark of the legendary Lewis and Clark expedition. He was also an important figure in the birth of the Louisville horse racing industry. Shortly after the grand duke's visit in 1872, a group of horse breeders in Louisville interested in reviving the horse racing business in the area approached M. Lewis Clark Jr. for help. Clark was also the grandson of one of the founders and the first president of the Oakland Race Course, and he was wealthy and had important social connections through his mother's family, the Churchills. After studying the racetracks of England and France, Clark filed articles of incorporation in 1874 for the Louisville Jockey Club and persuaded over three hundred other men to subscribe to his racetrack with the promise that the city of Louisville would become known for its horse racing. The track that would become known as Churchill Downs, later famous for the Kentucky Derby, opened in May 1875. By 1894, however, the track was losing money and the stockholders decided to sell it. Clark then traveled through the South as a judge at racetracks, but over time his health began to deteriorate, and in 1899 he committed suicide at the Gaston Hotel in Memphis.[10]

The plans for the grand duke's reception were reminiscent of those in other cities, complete with a formal reception, ball, and banquet and accommodations at the city's finest hotel, the Galt House. Colonel Jilson P. John, the proprietor and manager of the hotel, was in charge of the arrangements, and his reputation as a host and manager served as a guarantee to locals that the affair would be what it should be, "magnificent in every particular and honorable to Louisville and Kentucky, so distinguished for hospitality." By January 26, arrangements for the grand duke's visit were well under way. For the ball, two thousand invitations had been sent out, with tickets available at ten dollars each. Among those invited were the officials of neighboring cities and the governors of adjoining states, as well as General Philip Sheridan and Jefferson Davis. To facilitate the reception plans, local railroads had all agreed to offer seats at half price for anyone wanting to travel to Louisville during the grand duke's visit. There were also plans for the Russians to attend the city's opera, creating a frenzy for tickets.[11]

Louisville felt particular pressure to put on a good show. Several of the city's newspapers stressed its reputation, and that of Kentucky generally, for splendid hospitality, and the word "chivalry" was repeatedly used. There were also other good reasons to give Alexis a worthy reception. The *Courier Journal* reminded readers that Kentucky had furnished two ministers to Russia, Charles S. Todd and Cassius Clay, both of whom had been treated well in St. Petersburg. A proper reception of the tsar's son was the least that could be done in return. Moreover, an impressive reception of the grand duke would undoubtedly enhance America's reputation among the nations of Europe: "It is not only pleasant, but useful and valuable to be thought well of abroad, and the courtesies and hospitality we show to strangers may be some day remembered to the advantage of some of us traveling in distant lands." Finally, one newspaper declared that Alexis already had a special affection for Kentucky, a consequence of the parallel between his "pioneer ancestor and Kentucky's first settler, for Peter the Great was the 'Boone' of Russia."[12]

The day before Alexis was due to arrive, all Louisville was in a "fashionable flutter." The imminent appearance of the young aristocrat was the all-consuming topic of conversation, and a boost to the luxury economy, as well. Women spent thousands of dollars on silks, satins, lace, and embroidery, and local dress makers worked day and night to complete their orders in time for the ball. The press suggested that some ladies would be wearing upwards of fifteen thousand dollars in dress and jewels. The men of Louisville also indulged in new purchases, acquiring coats, vests, and gloves, but on a much more conservative scale. Though the *Daily Ledger* wholly approved of the city's decision to host Alexis, it also found much humor in the feverish excitement and frenzy of spending. Though the fathers and husbands of Louisville were exasperated by the profligate spending of their daughters and wives, "the beautiful angels smile so bewitchingly, as they sow their money like it were flower seeds, that husband and father repress their grief and soothe their lacerated feelings with the reflection that the Grand Duke only comes once in a lifetime."[13]

At last, on January 31, the big day arrived. The city was bustling with people from all sections of Louisville and neighboring states, and the hotels were booked to capacity. Private citizens had volunteered some twenty-five carriages, which were waiting at the depot at Fourteenth and Main to meet the imperial train, and the immediate area around the depot was thick with people; faces peered from every window, ladies waved handkerchiefs, and little boys climbed telegraph poles. Several hundred people had climbed up on the roof of the depot, and every available surface was covered with human beings. When Alexis finally arrived at quarter past three he was escorted by General Preston from the train to a carriage, and the procession made its way to the Galt House. One woman who was fortunate enough to have secured a view from a second-story window remarked that Alexis was "decidedly better looking than his pictures."[14]

The Galt House was actually the second of four hotels in Louisville to have that name. The first Galt House, which had once housed Charles Dickens, burned in 1865 and was replaced by a second version, completed in 1869. This second Galt House was designed in the Italian Renaissance style as almost an exact replica of Michelangelo's Roman Palazzo Farnese, and featured a spectacular entrance hall with a circular medallion depicting General Grant and General Lee shaking hands, surrounded by the words, "United We Stand—Divided We Fall." Alexis and his suite were ushered through this entrance hall and up to their apartments, where they were given some time to refresh themselves.

The rest of the hotel and its environs, however, were alive with excitement, as the first floor filled with those eager to be a part of this memorable event. The hotel was brightly illuminated and glowed in the night like a fairy-tale castle, and throughout the rooms and halls stood arrangements of flowers and rare plants provided by a local florist. Alexis would be staying on the third floor in adjoining rooms facing Main Street, his entourage nearby. Another room had been designated as a private dining room for the guests.[15]

After what surely seemed like an eternity to the guests waiting below, the grand duke descended to greet his admiring fans. In the standard formal attire—black suit, white vest, tie and gloves, accented by gold buttons—Alexis made a striking sight. In the presence of the various committees and legislators assembled there, General Preston welcomed Alexis on behalf of the people of Louisville and Kentucky, noting the bond that existed between Russia and the United States and stressing that the outpouring of hospitality toward the grand duke was a "spontaneous offering of the people . . . in an unofficial way." These brief remarks were followed by a period of introductions and handshaking until the doors of the ballroom were thrown open and a forty-piece band struck up the Russian national hymn to signify the beginning of the ball.[16]

The ball and the banquet that followed were spectacular affairs. Despite the ticket prices, which were considered too expensive for some people, the rooms were packed with excited guests. Under the glow of the chandeliers, women of all ages danced and mingled in fine dresses and eye-catching jewels. The *Courier Journal* dedicated almost an entire column to descriptions of the ladies' gowns—blue brocades, silk embroidered and trimmed with lace, green crape trimmed with satin leaves and green moss flowers, pink silk edged with pink crepe and tea roses—but declared that it was impossible to do justice to the splendor of the fashions. The dances included the typical fare for a ball of the day—quadrilles, polkas, lancers, waltzes by Strauss—but also included a piece composed and arranged since the grand duke's arrival in the United States. Alexis danced with a number of ladies whom he was allowed to select himself and, according to one reporter, he danced well, a testimony to his excellent "terpsichorean education." As the dancing concluded, Alexis and his many hosts moved to the ladies' breakfast room, which had been converted into the banquet hall and decorated with American and Russian flags, banners, and flower arrangements. Here, too, there was little room to move and one woman declared that "she felt while going to the banquet that she was in a mob rushing to the supper room." For most guests, however, the crowd was no deterrent and the festivities continued late into the night. The following day the papers took special note of the young ladies with whom Alexis had danced and to whom he had paid special attention. The *Courier Journal* stated triumphantly, "It was almost a foregone conclusion that the comliness [*sic*] of our Kentucky beauties would be to his princeship a novel sensation, surpassing any previous experience."[17] Alexis may have enjoyed himself, but one detects his sense of boredom by this point in his trip; he wrote to his mother that the reception and ball were nice, "like usual."[18]

On the grand duke's second day in Louisville, he slept in, rising only at nine o'clock. After a leisurely breakfast later in the morning, Alexis opened his parlors to receive callers, whom he greeted with "such an easy grace and cordial frankness in his manner as makes all feel as if they were meeting an old friend of long acquaintance." Shortly after one o'clock, the party began to make preparations for a city tour while eager spectators gathered around the hotel. By the time the grand duke's party emerged, there was a crowd some two thousand strong, but the general party had no difficulty in boarding the carriages. Before long the visitors and their escorts were winding their way through the streets of Louisville and the fashionable resident district on Broadway, where many of the homes had been designed by Henry Whitestone, the architect of the Galt House. The Russian party also visited beautifully situated Cave Hill Cemetery, where many of the city's first families had been buried. The tour continued with a drive by the city's waterworks, located at Zorn Avenue and River Road. This water-pumping facility had opened in 1860, and its designers had wanted it to be pleasing to the eye in the hope that its attractive appearance would help locals accept the idea of a water company. The result was a spectacular structure that embodied the spirit of Greek architecture and resembled a palace ensconced in columns. From the waterworks, the procession made its way through busy streets to the Ohio River bridge, the longest iron bridge of its time.[19]

Leaving the bridge, the ducal party was taken to the locomotive works of the Louisville & Nashville Railroad, where they inspected the machinery and operations, and they also drove by the city hall, still under construction, with its impressive 195-foot clock tower. The grand duke and his entourage next proceeded to Third Street for lunch at the Kentucky Club, where the guests were met by displays of Russian and American flags and the heavenly aroma of the carefully prepared feast. Wine, port, sherry, and champagne flowed freely, and the atmosphere was cordial and relaxed. Wrapping up with coffee and cigars, the Russians returned to the Galt House to prepare for the final event of the day, a performance of *Cinderella* by the famous Worrell Sisters at the opera house.[20]

The Worrell Sisters—Sophie, Irene, and Jennie—were the daughters of a once-famous circus clown and had grown up on the stage, singing and dancing their way into the hearts of audiences in numerous American cities and countries as far away as Australia. In the 1860s, the sisters moved to New York and purchased a theater on Broadway, which they operated briefly without much success. Their popularity surged again, however, after Lydia Thompson's "British Blondes" made burlesque more popular in the United States. Mark Twain noted in January 1868 that, although he had not seen the Worrell Sisters himself, he had heard others talking about them: "the young men seem as if they are not going to get over the fascination those girls have inspired them with."[21] In 1872, the Worrell Sisters were still at the peak of their popularity and were fortunate enough to be part of the city's welcome for Alexis.

On the night of the grand duke's visit, the opera house glowed with "the bright costumes and still brighter faces of the beauties of Louisville and Kentucky," and as Alexis and his party entered they were met with applause and a standing ovation as they took their seats in the two lower proscenium boxes set aside for them. The performance began with a special ode of welcome dedicated to the grand duke, performed by J. W. Fuller and Parson Price, both of Louisville. The rhyming ode celebrated the genius and strength of will of Peter the Great, and to Alexis declared, "Son of that old heroic line, a welcome we extend, And to thy land a greeting warm, in friendship's name we send." There was much applause, and then the performance of *Cinderella* began. When the show ended, the grand duke and his party returned to the Galt House.[22]

Thursday, February 1, was another very cold day in Louisville, but Alexis and his party did not have the luxury of sleeping late since the train bound for Mammoth Cave left at nine o'clock. The guests all sat together on the train in pleasant conversation, and at each station they observed excited and welcoming crowds hoping to lay eyes on the young Russian. The train stopped only once, however, at Elizabethtown, where Alexis and several members of his party alighted to look at some dogs and horses belonging to Custer. At noon, the train reduced its speed and lunch was served. All in all, the trip was pleasant and without incident except for a stubborn cow that had to be frightened from the track.[23]

For this last leg of the trip, Alexis's own traveling party was accompanied by Custer and M. Lewis Clark and their wives. Libbie Custer claimed that she had been given the task of recruiting attractive young ladies to accompany the grand duke's party during these days, a request that would offend most modern-day sensibilities. Libbie had been told that "Kentucky must be patriotic in more ways than one and that the eloquent greetings and enthusiastic speeches from the delightful state must be followed up by phalanges of the very prettiest and most vivacious belles." According to Mrs. Custer, a few of these girls traveled on the train to Mammoth Cave and served as a distraction for the young Russian visitor; Mrs. Custer recalled, "I don't think that on our arrival that the grand duke knew whether he was in a cave or on top of a mountain."[24]

Mrs. Custer also made some observations about her Russian traveling companions. The Russians typically ate rolls and coffee, what Americans might consider breakfast, at noon, and so those traveling with them adopted this custom, as well. Libbie also noted that the Russian men had impressive stamina when it came to liquor, which she attributed to Russia's cold climate. "It is a real pleasure to sit next to them," she noted, "for, should American gentlemen take the amount of wine they do, the lady would be forced to listen to the idiotic mumbled silliness a man, politely tight, inflicts on her." As for the individual members of the grand duke's party, she described Admiral Possiet as "all sunshine and sweet simplicity," and Alexis as a magnificent singer, always joking with his suite and forever smoking a cigarette. She also recalled that despite Possiet's efforts to interest Alexis in the towns they passed, the young Russian was more interested in the pretty girls and other social pursuits.[25]

The group arrived in Cave City shortly after one o'clock, and left immediately by coach for Mammoth Cave, the world's longest underground labyrinth. The cave began to capture the public's attention after the War of 1812 when the current owner established a staff of slave guides and a tradition of guided tours. Subsequent owners expanded upon the cave's tourism potential by building support buildings and a hotel, and in 1839, the cave was used as an underground hospital for tuberculosis patients. By the end of the nineteenth century, Mammoth Cave had become a major tourist attraction, drawing such famous visitors as William Jennings Bryan; the emperor of Brazil, Dom Pedro; and Edwin Booth, Shakespearean actor and brother to Lincoln's assassin.[26]

Donning special "cave costumes," the grand duke's party descended into the depths of the cave in the midafternoon and remained underground some four and a half hours. Both the Russian and American visitors were impressed with the cave's various features and inquired about its formation and early explorers; some of the visitors also experimented with the acoustics of the cave, shouting and delighting at the echoes. The amateur spelunkers also had to navigate a narrow passage known as the "Fat Men's Misery," and several members of the Russian delegation came to understand the origin of the name as they squeezed through with great difficulty. Toward the end of the excursion, Alexis seemed to grow weary or perhaps found the impenetrable darkness a bit daunting, for at the Echo River the grand duke and about half the party turned back. Overall, Alexis seemed to enjoy the tour, but he also seemed a bit unnerved by the enormity of the cave at times—when one of the guides dropped a lit piece of paper to demonstrate the depths of one of the pits, everyone involuntarily took a step away from the edge, but Alexis shuddered and said, "Let us move on." Alexis did admit to his mother that there were places in the cave where it was difficult to pass even on all fours and that the women had an easier time squeezing through the cave than the men. He noted that they spent a long time underground and were terribly tired when it was all over. At the conclusion of the tour, the party partook of some refreshments and then took the coaches back to Cave City where the Russian party boarded their train for Memphis.[27]

Memphis was founded in 1819 and, until about 1840, it remained a "primitive and pestilential little mudhole striving to survive as a town." By 1850, however, Memphis had the largest inland cotton market in the world and, over the next decade, the city continued to grow dramatically. The Civil War was a devastating blow, of course, and in the early years of Reconstruction, Memphis suffered its share of violence, including a race riot in 1866 that killed and injured dozens of individuals. The city was also plagued by periodic epidemics, one relatively minor outbreak of yellow fever in 1867, a series of outbreaks of cholera, small-pox, and yellow fever in 1873, and another outbreak of yellow fever in 1878. These episodes were financially devastating, since any citizen with the ability to do so fled the city, crippling the city's commercial life and depleting the tax base. By the end of 1878, Memphis was bankrupt and, in January 1879, the state repealed the city's charter. Somehow, in the midst of all this postwar recovery and the threat of another epidemic, Memphis found the wherewithal to host a Russian grand duke.[28]

It is not clear if the grand duke would have visited Memphis had it not been for the initiative of city officials. On January 3, 1872, Mayor John Johnson telegraphed Alexis in Chicago, congratulating him on his safe arrival and inviting him to visit the city of Memphis. Admiral Possiet replied on Alexis's behalf that they were happy to accept the invitation, but were unable to name their precise arrival date. On January 6, the Board of Aldermen and the City Council passed a resolution authorizing the mayor to extend the hospitalities of Memphis to the grand duke during his stay there, and the mayor appointed a committee to oversee the reception plans. The committee consisted of some of the most prominent citizens of the city: R. A. Pinson, president of the Chamber of Commerce; I. M. Hill, former city councilman and founding member of the Memphis City Railroad Company; Napoleon Hill, one of the founders of Memphis's first public library and, later, president of the Cotton Exchange; J. W. Scales, former city recorder, and a number of other distinguished gentlemen. On January 9, the committee met at the Union and Planter's Bank on Madison Street and began to make concrete plans for the grand duke's reception and continued to meet over the next few weeks as the details fell into place.[29]

Not everyone was excited about Alexis's visit, however. The *Memphis Daily Appeal* expressed concerns about the impression Memphis would make on the visitors and the money that would be spent on the endeavor. Comparing the cotton mills at Riga in the Russian Empire to those of Memphis, the *Appeal* anticipated that the Russian party would be shocked by the barbarism of the cotton industry in the southern city; while the Russian mills employed many women and children, those in Memphis did nothing to help the poor, despite "two thousand women driven to prostitution for want of employment." The *Appeal* chastised, "This $100,000 proposed to be squandered, if invested in a cotton mill, would save many a poor girl, as much beloved as the fairest daughter of wealth, from a fate which innocent maidenhood starts back appalled." The paper suggested that it would be better "for these generous good papas, who pat their pretty daughters on downy cheeks, to tell them that they might better use the money wasted in dress for the royal ball in rearing an industrial home for hapless, helpless women." The paper further suggested that the mayor should "promulgate an edict against the whole scheme," and advise the citizens of Memphis to "exercise a little common sense, and not to waste their wealth in vain gew-gaws and trappings." Finally, the *Appeal* echoed the concerns raised in other cities about embarrassing displays of toadyism, observing that most citizens of the city knew nothing of courtly dress and manners and those who did were most susceptible to bootlicking. The paper feared that the people of Memphis would present themselves "as asses to Russian royalty in more aspects than one."[30]

One of the most poignant arguments against hosting the grand duke came from an unidentified Polish resident of Memphis. In a letter to the *Daily Appeal,* he expressed disgust with the lavish reception of the grand duke, declaring, "the American people really are, what they have been for years termed by the most influential and best newspapers of the country—shoddyites and codfish aristocracy." He emphasized that his country and his people had suffered greatly at the hands of the Russians and urged his fellow Americans not to "degrade themselves, or cringe, scrape and bow to a young man merely because he is accidentally a prince." Citing the distinguished record of the Poles who participated in the American Revolution, the author asked, "Has the Russian monarchy ever tendered such services to this country as did Kosciusko, Pulaski, and thousands of others of my countrymen?"[31] Once again, it was the voice of a recent immigrant that spoke most sharply on the question of national identity and the meaning of republicanism.

While some citizens may have squabbled over the cost or appropriateness of the grand duke's reception, many others displayed unabashed commercialism. Menken Brothers, for example, advertised "evening silks, rich laces, kid gloves in opera shades and new styles" for the Grand Duke Alexis ball. Another clothier, Waggener's, advertised that the grand duke was on his way to Memphis, which would necessitate new dress suits, all of which could be found in its inventory. Some enterprising citizens were thinking even bigger. The *Daily Appeal* reminded its readers in mid-January that Russia had a burgeoning cotton industry and so the Russian visit might have long-term commercial results.[32]

Excitement grew as the date of arrival drew near, and as the reception committee made the final arrangements for the grand duke's visit. Local newspapers seemed to shed their reservations and became more enthusiastic and supportive. The *Daily Appeal* announced, "It is but right that Memphis should put on the best appearance possible, so that she may be talked of with admiration and wonder in the courts of Europe," and proposed, "A ball that will enable the gallant young stranger to carry with him to his northern home a never-fading picture of the first Southern community of which he has been the guest." The February issue of *Southern Farm and Home* featured a likeness of the grand duke on its cover. In preparation for Alexis's arrival, the Peabody Hotel had prepared luxurious rooms for the Russian guests, decorated with rosewood furniture, Brussels carpets, large mirrors, marble tables, and bouquets of fragrant flowers. For the ball, a number of chandeliers had been installed in the great salon, along with "a gas device, with the words 'Welcome, Alexis,' in flaming characters." Only 250 tickets for the ball and banquet had been printed, so they were in great demand.[33]

Alexis arrived in Memphis in the early afternoon of Friday, February 2, 1872. The cold, grey drizzle did not frighten away the many eager onlookers who clustered along the railroad and the streets, excited and boisterous, and loud enough to "deafen the ears of a donkey." Such was the jovial mood and behavior of the crowds that the appearance of any distinguished-looking gentleman resulted in screams of "There he is!" followed by loud laughter. The welcoming committee, led by R. A. Pinson, a former colonel in the Confederate Army, met the grand duke's train shortly after one o'clock and proceeded aboard to greet the honored guest. After the necessary introductions and some pleasant small talk, the welcoming party and the ducal party left the train and boarded a carriage for the Peabody Hotel, a fine new facility. There the mayor gave Alexis a formal welcome and the grand duke retired to his room with the hope of resting a bit. The crowd outside, however, had a different idea, maintaining a steady roar until Alexis appeared on his balcony and tipped his hat a few times. Only then did the crowd disperse and leave the young duke to recover from his travels.[34]

After Alexis and his companions had a chance to rest, they proceeded to dinner at half past six to enjoy a feast of staggering proportions that included southern dishes like chicken gumbo and hominy. Following dinner, the grand duke and his party were the honored guests at a ball held at the Overton Hotel, a landmark of Memphis that during the Civil War had served as a hospital for Confederate soldiers and, after the capture of Memphis, for federal troops. Alexis made his grand entrance at half past nine and, for forty minutes, the grand duke then stood at the head of the ballroom, graciously shaking hands and greeting some two hundred couples as they were introduced to him. Another four hundred guests stood by and watched with envy. The *Memphis Daily Appeal* emphasized that the ladies, in particular, were in fine form that night:

"It is no exaggeration to say that the ball presented an array of loveliness, grace and elegance that could not be surpassed in the United States."[35]

The grand duke began the dancing by honoring the wife of Colonel Pinson, Mrs. Sina Duke Pinson, who was dressed in a gown of green silk. Mrs. Pinson, who later died in 1936, reminisced about the grand duke's visit and that first dance until the last years of her life. At midnight, the guests of the ball sat down for a small supper, complete with a Russian cottage made out of nougat and a fully rigged Russian ship of meringue. Dancing resumed after dinner, and though Alexis retired early, many others danced well into the early hours of the morning. On Saturday and Sunday, the grand duke relaxed in the company of his own entourage, rarely venturing outside except to take a short stroll late in the afternoon.[36]

On Monday, February 5, Alexis and his traveling companions toured the city. The carriages picked up the party at about two, and they continued to the cotton shed of Busby and Johnson, where Alexis learned about the process of storing cotton until it was sold, compressed, and ready to be shipped. The party then traveled to the commission house of Estes, Fizer, and Pinson, where they dismounted to examine the McGehee cotton bale, which had won awards at fairs all over the Mississippi Valley for its "silky fineness and extraordinary length of the staple." Following this, Alexis was taken to see a cotton press on his way to the county jail. The Russian visitors toured the penal facility with the architect, who answered questions and explained the building's special features. Completed in 1868, the building was a four-story brick structure and was especially notable for its "ingenious design to prevent escapes." The jail's design included a space filled with sand between the three-foot outer wall and the inner wall so that, "if an inmate removed brick to create an escape opening, he would encounter an endless deluge of sand.... And any movement of sand would activate an alarm system." Alexis seemed impressed by the facility in general, but expressed confusion at why the prisoners should be allowed to remain in idleness, while law-abiding citizens were required to work to support themselves.[37] That evening there was yet another ball at the Peabody, where Alexis danced the night away and left the other guests with happy memories of the evening.

Alexis met several other interesting men during his time in Memphis. One of these was a young black artist named Tom, a former slave who had seen a sketch of the ball at Catacazy's Washington residence and had made a copy that was so impressive that someone suggested that he give it to the grand duke as a gift. The scene portrayed Alexis handing his cigar to Madame Catacazy to light her cigarette as the rest of the party sat around the table having coffee and cigars. Alexis then conversed with the young artist, inquiring about his life as a slave; Tom stated that "the kindly relations that had ever subsisted between his old master, his father, mother and himself were in wise interrupted by their freedom, that he felt a high sense of gratitude for all that had been done for himself and for his race by the people of the South." Alexis responded in kind that he could understand the young man's feelings since "much the same subsisted between the Russian nobility and the serfs, who had been freed by his illustrious father."[38] One wonders if most Russian serfs would have agreed.

The grand duke also met Jefferson Davis, former president of the Confederacy. On their first encounter, Possiet and Davis talked for half an hour about the Civil War and politics in general and, two days later, the admiral visited Davis again. Possiet found Davis to be intelligent and kind, and of a generally noble appearance, and he declared it was difficult to imagine that this man had been at the head of the "wrong affairs."[39]

Alexis and his party left Memphis after breakfast on February 7. The *Great Republic,* the steamer that had been chartered for fifteen hundred dollars a day and significantly modified for the occasion, was trapped in ice above Columbus, and for days the Russian party had been unsure if they would travel to New Orleans by river or by rail. The *New Orleans Times* found an opportunity for humor in the predicament, declaring, "Republicans are all averse to royalty, consequently we are not surprised to hear of the steamboat Great Republic [sic] willfully permitting herself to be frozen up in the Mississippi in order to escape the duty of carrying the grand duke to New Orleans." The *Daily Appeal* used Alexis's travel woes as a plug for the necessity of a southern transcontinental railway: "He has surely done more than any living man to make the country comprehend the necessity for an ever open route to the Western ocean, and as surely fixed its initial point at Memphis." When Alexis and his entourage finally did depart, it was on the *James Howard,* a side-wheeler that, at 318 feet, was the largest inland steamboat ever built. A great crowd lined the bluff as Alexis and his party boarded the *James Howard* and headed south to their next destination.[40]

That next stop was New Orleans, a romantic and complex city near the mouth of the Mississippi River, plagued by floods, fever, and sticky, tropical heat since its establishment by French explorers in 1718. During its first century, the city's development and emerging character were determined by a variety of outside forces. As one historian has described it, New Orleans was "buffeted by the winds of geopolitical conflict almost as regularly as it was battered by the periodic hurricanes that blew in from the Gulf of Mexico." Over the course of the nineteenth century, New Orleans began to develop its own unique personality, a blend of French, Spanish, Creole, and American influences, among others. By 1872, the most recognizable features of New Orleans were in place—the French Quarter and Jackson Square, St. Louis Cathedral, Canal Street, the St. Charles streetcar, the Garden District, and the annual Mardi Gras celebration— and the city was becoming a destination for tourists.[41]

While New Orleans might seem like the perfect place to conclude the grand duke's tour of the United States, in many ways the city was even less prepared for a royal visit than Chicago had been. The years after the Civil War in Louisiana had seen an incredible amount of politically inspired violence, much of it intended to terrorize freed slaves. While all ex-Confederate states had suffered their share of violence, due to its racial makeup Louisiana experienced considerably more. Louisiana was one of three ex-Confederate states where black slaves had outnumbered free whites in the 1860 census, and so the enfranchisement of former slaves created numerous challenges to the state's traditional political and social life. Louisiana's military occupation, from 1862 to 1877, was also longer than that of any other ex-Confederate state. During this same period of time, Louisiana had five governors, all of whom faced challenges, threats, and the possibility of replacement or impeachment. In the summer of 1866, political and racial tensions had erupted into street violence that left at least 38 dead and 184 wounded.[42]

In mid-1871, things had begun to heat up again when opponents of Governor Henry Clay Warmoth launched a movement to overthrow him. The ensuing struggle included a rival Republican Convention, a rival legislature, plans to impeach Warmoth, and the threat of open clashes. By early January 1872, the situation had grown so tense and lawless that both sides, including New Orleans mayor Benjamin Flanders, begged the president to declare martial law. Grant refused, but federal troops were deployed from Jackson Barracks to prevent violence, patrolling for over a week in the city and remaining on alert for some time afterward.[43] Given the volatility of the political situation in New Orleans, Admiral Possiet's approval of this particular step is rather surprising.

From the time of his arrival in New York, the various newspapers in New Orleans had followed Alexis's travels closely, reporting almost daily about his latest adventures and future plans, including his intention to visit some of the southern states. Some New Orleanians clearly took these early announcements seriously, for on November 26, 1871, an editorial in the *New Orleans Republican* discussed the possibility of Alexis's visit and whether the South was equipped, or inclined, to fete him properly. It was only in mid-January 1872, however, that the first article appeared in the local press with some conviction about a visit to New Orleans. That article reported that the grand duke had been "captivated" by Lydia Thompson and hoped "to pay the performance of the company another visit in New Orleans." The following day, the *New Orleans Bee* reported that the grand duke would take the *Great Republic,* "unquestionably one of the finest steamers . . . [a] floating palace," down the Mississippi River to the Crescent City.[44] These articles seemed to confirm that New Orleans was now on the grand duke's itinerary, and the primary reason given by the press for this dip into the Deep South was the salacious icing on the cake. The reports in New Orleans and elsewhere that Cupid's arrow had struck the grand duke initiated a persistent rumor that would continue to be repeated for over a century and become an entrenched part of Mardi Gras lore—that Alexis had become infatuated by a burlesque performer and had followed her to New Orleans.

Once it seemed likely that Alexis would stop in New Orleans, some merchants saw a great advertising opportunity. In December 1871, Rice Brothers and Company placed the following advertisement in the *Daily Picayune:* "The entertainment at the Revere House, Boston, in honor of the Russian Grand Duke, is universally conceded to have been a magnificent affair. . . . it could scarcely have been . . . otherwise, every dish being cooked in a Charter Oak stove," which, of course, they just happened to sell in their store on Camp Street. As the grand duke's visit grew nearer, the number of such ads increased and grew more preposterous. One ad, for example, claimed that "the Grand Duke thinks his trip and trouble richly rewarded since he saw the Orient safety lamp, from 62 Camp and 15 Dauphine streets." Two others advertised the sale of "the Grand Duke Alexis kid gloves" and the "Alexis hat." Finally, one store made the following pitch: "It is not supposed that the Grand Duke does his own washing; but if he did it is certain he would do it with the Ringen washer, which is sold by Mr. Haller, the sole agent, at No. 49 Camp street."[45]

As in many other cities, merchants and store owners were quicker to jump on the Alexis bandwagon than city officials, the prospect of making money being a far greater motivator than the dread of spending it. The New Orleans City Council did not discuss the matter of a royal visit until January 26, when the *Daily Picayune* reported that members "had some talk about the reception of the Grand Duke Alexis, without reaching any conclusion." While the mayor proposed setting up a committee to consider some sort of reception, one council member "was against the city spending a dollar." Another complained that New Orleans could scarcely pay its own debts, much less afford spending city funds on the Russian visitor. He added that "he had heard of no taxpayer desiring any such reception."[46]

Three days later, the staff of the *Daily Picayune* weighed in on the question, underscoring "the generally expressed opinion that our city should not be lacking in a display of hospitality to the Grand Duke Alexis," though the reception should be "devoid of fictitious splendor." The local *Times* agreed that New Orleans could not be shown up by the other cities that had hosted the grand duke, reminding its readers of the city's maritime relations with Russia and the importance of maintaining those ties. Referring to the difficulties Louisiana still faced in the wake of the Civil War, the *Times* advised, "whatever trouble, political or financial, we labor under should be thrust aside in cases of such emergency." Nonetheless, the paper advocated a modest reception: "While our people are naturally and very properly averse to the gorgeous show displays, of which the Eastern cities are so prolific, a tasteful and probably much more acceptable programme can be arranged for the royal party."[47] Still, city officials seemed reluctant to commit to any plans. Though the grand duke was expected to visit soon, his steamer was trapped upriver in ice, leaving the exact date of his arrival still unknown, and with Mardi Gras only two weeks away, the city and its citizens had other plans to consider as well.

What happened next is still a matter of debate among popular chroniclers of Mardi Gras. On January 31, the *Times* reported that a group of respectable young men had taken it upon themselves to establish some order over the traditional carnival festivities. On February 1, the first announcements appeared in the papers that a self-proclaimed "King of Carnival" named Rex would be organizing the Mardi Gras festivities and, therefore, requested that "all parties desirous of taking part in the celebration . . . report to him immediately through their marshalls, stating character of display, probable number, and whether with or without music."[48]

It is unclear precisely what inspired the men who created Rex, or if the grand duke's visit was a catalyst in any way. Mardi Gras had been celebrated in some form in New Orleans since the early nineteenth century, and the first carnival organization, the Mistick Krewe of Comus, appeared in 1857, but the carnival celebration as a whole was not coordinated in any real way. Individuals and small bands of masked revelers wandered the streets to celebrate the last hurrah before Lent in what one newspaper called "a day of vagrant mummery," but there had been no effort to establish rules of order or to enlist the cooperation of local businesses or city authorities until that Mardi Gras of 1872. Moreover, the only parades had taken place at night. The *New Orleans Bee* described the lack of organization and decorum in the old carnival celebration in this way: "Maskers, rarely with any design and with but little sign of wit or humor, showing nothing but unmeaning grotesqueness, used to move through the streets, singly, in couples or in threes or fours, and the day light spectacle was simply an exhibition of the vulgarest buffoonery." If the *Bee*'s description is at all accurate, it is easy to understand why the volunteer organizers would have felt compelled to take action. The *Republican* noted that, beyond the obvious benefit to local citizens, the organization of Mardi Gras would make New Orleans more attractive to visitors as well. Estimating that some fifteen thousand people would travel to the city to witness carnival, each of them spending an average of fifty dollars, the *Republican* stressed the immediate and future reason for putting the best face on Mardi Gras. If each of these visitors went home and gave a glowing account of their time in New Orleans to family and friends, the number of visitors might be expected to double the next year. Tourism, then, may have played a role in Rex's creation as well.[49]

Whatever the inspiration, over the next few days Rex issued a series of edicts that asked for the cooperation of Mardi Gras revelers, the mayor, the superintendent of police, and various other officials, urging them to shut down schools, the post office, the Louisiana State Lottery office, and the customs office for the port of New Orleans. Rex also appealed to Governor Henry Clay Warmoth to "refrain from the exercise, or attempt to exercise, any gubernatorial privileges or duties" on Mardi Gras day, and "in order to better preserve the peace and maintain the dignity of the realm ... disperse that riotous body known as the Louisiana Legislature." Even the Congressional Investigating Committee, in New Orleans to scrutinize Louisiana politics, was asked to cease its investigation temporarily. Surprisingly, all governmental bodies agreed to these requests. A new tradition had been born—the organized, daytime Mardi Gras celebration—and though Alexis really had nothing to do with it, he would forever be linked to its creation and given credit in subsequent decades for serving as the inspiration for a new Mardi Gras organization, the Krewe of Rex, and its leader, Rex, the King of Carnival.[50]

While some citizens were focused on the upcoming Mardi Gras celebration, others continued to work on plans for the grand duke's visit, though ultimately, these two major events would intersect in a memorable way. With Alexis's arrival less than two weeks away, the City Council finally appointed the mayor, Benjamin Flanders, and the administrator of assessments, Hubert Bonzano, to make arrangements for the grand duke's reception. By February 8, the organizers at City Hall could report that accommodations for the Russian party had been arranged and a plan of entertainments completed. For Mardi Gras, a special platform was erected in front of City Hall where the grand duke and his party could watch the procession of the Mistick Krewe of Comus. City officials stressed, however, that these activities were done in the thriftiest fashion possible; the lumber used to construct the Mardi Gras platform, for example, would be carefully dismantled so it could be used again.[51]

There were also those who worried about the potential for elitism or classism of the sort that had been seen in other cities. The *Times* approved of the plans in general, but hoped that Mayor Flanders and Administrator Bonzano could for once "forego the orthodox list of the 'professionally prominent,' and choose gentlemen ... whose experience and innate refinement would prove a preventative to those violations of etiquette which are unhappily attributed to the American people." The *Times* suggested that, in addition to the public arrangements being made for the royal visitor, some private "institutions of a social character" might contribute as well, such as the Louisiana Jockey Club. Subsequently, a group of private citizens began organizing a ball for the grand duke, and Dan Rice extended an invitation for the royal party to attend a performance of his circus. Alexis also received an invitation from Lydia Thompson, who requested his presence at the Academy of Music, where her company would perform in the burlesque *Kenilworth,* an adaptation of Sir Walter Scott's novel by the same name.[52]

As the reception plans fell into place, city officials also had to consider the matter of tickets, both the number of tickets that would be issued for the Mardi Gras platforms and who would get those coveted bits of paper. Ultimately, organizers decided that two sets of tickets would be issued; only women and children would be eligible to receive tickets for the day, while the evening tickets would be available to men accompanied by one or more ladies. City officials recommended that hotel managers apply for tickets for their guests as early as possible, particularly since the number of visitors streaming into the city for the two coinciding events was enormous and the number of tickets limited. Beginning in mid-January, the *Atlanta Constitution* ran ads for an organized excursion from Atlanta to New Orleans for Mardi Gras and reported that many had already purchased tickets. The paper noted that Mardi Gras was "the grandest, most unique and most enjoyable festival to be witnessed in the United States," and made a point of adding that the Grand Duke Alexis of Russia would be there. Consequently, New Orleans city officials had good reason to expect large numbers of visitors. In fact, the *New Orleans Republican* would report on the day before Mardi Gras that "St. Charles and Canal streets, with their near approaches, were literally uncomfortably crowded," and the throngs continued to arrive with every boat and train.[53]

As excitement swelled over the grand duke's approach, so too did concerns about the ability of New Orleans officials to pull the whole thing off. In early 1872, the political climate in New Orleans was dicey and the public pulse was erratic, making the job of city officials more difficult and the outcome of the reception more uncertain. Moreover, several local papers remarked on the plight of the mayor and his associates, who were inexperienced in arranging a royal reception and had no precedent to rely upon. In many places, newspapers had used the Russian visit to poke fun at mayors, lieutenant governors, and governors for their lack of sophistication. In Kansas, the press had spread a story about Lieutenant Governor P. P. Elder that would haunt him until his dying day. Reporters claimed that, during the dinner at the Fifth Avenue Hotel in Topeka, Elder pointed to the Kansas motto printed on the menu, "Ad astra per aspera," and explained to the grand duke, "Them words is Latin." Though Elder vehemently denied the veracity of the story, the former Kansas official was still struggling to dispel the myth over thirty years later. In 1905, *Field and Farm* reported that Elder "has always chaffed under the accusation.... the old man to this day is bitter when it is mentioned." In New Orleans, the papers painted the mayor as an unsophisticated rube, declaring that he had set up his parlor as a practicing room for bows and genuflections, while busily studying the *Court Journal* and Chesterfield's book of etiquette.[54]

There was also one particularly significant voice of opposition. Valerii Sulakowski, a Pole who had commanded the First Polish Regiment in the Civil War, protested the proposed reception in a passionate plea, "in the name of Republicanism ... in the name of human rights." In a document published in New Orleans in anticipation of the royal visit, Sulakowski took his fellow Americans to task. Recalling his own move to the United States some twenty years earlier, he described how in coming to America he had found "a secure refuge from the vengeance of Russian despotism." Sulakowski urged his fellow Americans to show nothing but "scorn and hatred for the representative of the most odious and despicable despotism of the world." Assuming that Alexis would see his pronouncement, Sulakowski declared, "You have crossed oceans and continents to find on the banks of the Mississippi an exile, armed with American citizenship, who taps your felon shoulder and tells you, again and again: 'Monseigneur, you are a scoundrel,' and bids you bear back to Russia that eternal curse of immortal Poland."[55]

———————◆———————

Many Americans had conflicting notions about royalty. On the one hand, they were drawn to the sublime nature of royalty, its power and symbols, while at the same time they felt they should reject the political philosophy of monarchy and the subservience that went along with it. The best example of this bipolar attitude toward royalty can be found in the creation of the Krewe of Rex, the Mardi Gras organization founded on the eve of Alexis's visit to New Orleans. Its creators chose titles and symbols of royalty, including the titles "Rex" and "King of Carnival," as well as the use of proclamations published in local newspapers that mimicked royal edicts. This conscious use of such powerful titles and symbols suggests, most obviously, a desire to associate themselves with the notion of royalty and demonstrate, or emphasize, social superiority and the traditional predominance of white elites in New Orleans, a city still wrestling with racial tension after the Civil War. It also, perhaps, indicates an effort to mock the adulation that was being lavished upon the tsar's son. These competing desires represented an inner conflict among white elites in New Orleans who were both fascinated by the idea of royalty but, at the same time, repelled by the behavior it elicited, both at home and especially in the North.[56]

The same phenomenon can be found in Mobile, Alabama, and Memphis, Tennessee. Carnival-like celebrations had been staged in Mobile in some form for decades but, in 1872, citizens decided to organize the public festivities and created a royal overseer, Emperor (or King) Felix. In Memphis, where there had been no celebration of Mardi Gras, citizens created an entirely new festive tradition patterned on those in New Orleans and Mobile, including a "king of carnival" called Momus. Ironically, newspapers in these same cities would loudly decry the inconsistency of republican citizens fawning over royalty. For example, even as some of its own citizens were creating a carnival king, the *Memphis Daily Appeal* complained of the "disgusting adulation and unmanly worship of a foreign prince," asking, "How does this jingle with the spirit of the Declaration of Independence?" Despite the incongruity of celebrating democracy and royalty simultaneously, however, new elite societies with titled heads arose in all three of these major southern cities in the stressful period following the Civil War.[57]

While most cities do not have such vivid examples of social hypocrisy regarding royalty, Alexis's tour did prompt consideration of this juxtaposition around the country. As Americans contemplated the visit of the grand duke the question arose of how—if at all—a republican nation should host a member of royalty. In many cities, journalists and other observant citizens noted the irony of Americans, heirs of a revolution against monarchy, fawning over royalty. The *Hartford Daily Courant* declared that "it will not add much to our national reputation in Russia, if we forget ourselves and our position, and try to make this prince think that he has fallen among princes and the riches of royalty here." In McKenzie, Tennessee, the *Times* wrote, "are not we Americans making ourselves fools about this distinguished foreigner.... We profess to be a republican people, whilst he is one of the representatives of the most absolute monarchy in the world." Despite these concerns, in many cities people believed that it was appropriate and even necessary to welcome the young Russian in style. In Memphis, the *Appeal* asserted that it was "perfectly consistent with our republicanism and manhood that Alexis should be received with as much of honor as we are in the habit of bestowing on our own distinguished men," but toadyism and exclusivity should be avoided at all costs, and the reception of the grand duke should be an affair open to all. The *New Orleans Daily Republican* echoed this view, stating that "respect will therefore be paid, not to a young prince, but to the great and progressive Russian people." Ultimately, the *Philadelphia Inquirer* believed that all the hand-wringing was simply a manifestation of insecurity: "The nervous dread from which some 'freeborn Americans' suffer, lest they may compromise their dignity by undue civility to a noble guest … is every whit as sure a mark of low birth and breeding as the servility of the shoddy pretender."[58]

In fact, many Americans were sensitive to how the apparent contradiction would be perceived by others. Other countries did find humor in America's "servile adoration of royal personages." Newspapers from Toronto, London, Dublin, and Vienna all mocked America's obvious fascination with royalty. When the *London Standard* made fun of the inconsistency of a republican nation falling over itself to host a member of royalty, the *Cleveland Daily Leader* complained that "because we do things in good style, it does not follow that we are ready to abjure our political faith."[59] The *New York Tribune* noted that, when some citizens in Philadelphia had disapproved of taking Alexis to the simple Methodist Fair, they had revealed a bitter truth about Americans, "that we are the only nation under heaven ashamed of being ourselves in the eyes of strangers." Other nations welcomed their guests with ease and comfort, but Americans behaved self-consciously: "let a foreigner of note come among us, and while we display our ships and shops and schools … we betray a frantic haste to alter our manners, dress, and meals into what we conceive to be the usage of good society in Europe." The problem was that, having been laughed at by other nations for our ill breeding, Americans "slip into these grossly vulgar mistakes in trying to prove our good breeding."[60]

———————◆———————

As Americans anguished over questions of national identity and foreign commentary, Admiral Possiet continued to worry about Alexis's state of mind. In early February, he wrote that the trip was going well and that Alexis had been cordially welcomed with introductions, ceremonies, and receptions wherever he went. Nonetheless, there was some opposition to the grand duke's visit, a "hostile spirit" which was most active in New York, Milwaukee, and New Orleans though, thankfully, without any serious consequences. Possiet tried to protect Alexis from these negative aspects of the trip, whenever possible destroying newspaper articles that he deemed unsuitable for the young man's eyes. He also attempted to intercept the many letters that Alexis received from overly enthusiastic American women. But Possiet could not shield Alexis from everything; although the trip should have been a great diversion, the admiral admitted that the frequent letters from Zhukovskaya interfered with Alexis's ability to move past his grief.[61]

———————◆———————

While New Orleans prepared for the appearance of two royal guests, Alexis and Rex, the *James Howard* steamed down the Mississippi River with a party of about two dozen travelers.[62] Again, one of the few accounts of the trip down the Mississippi is from Libbie Custer, who again had been asked to recruit girls for this portion of the trip. Mrs. Custer describes how she approached the mothers with "great humility and great diplomacy" to persuade them to allow their daughters to travel to New Orleans. Apparently, a suitable number of mothers must have overcome their fears for Libbie reported, "We were successful . . . such a collection . . . I was able to present." The young people all had a marvelous time on the steamer, dancing and laughing, and overcoming the language barrier with the use of broken English, rusty French, and primitive sign language. With about three men for every young lady, the Kentucky belles were constantly surrounded and attended, and Alexis enjoyed the female company in particular. In the words of the *Memphis Daily Appeal*, "he may be an aristocrat by birth and lineage, but is the veriest [sic] republican in the midst of pretty girls." The dancing took a variety of forms, including Russian dances, which Mrs. Custer described as exhausting, "one gasping breathless rush around the room. . . . No lungs survived more than one turn around the hall of the ballroom." All of this occurred under the watchful eyes of the grand duke's "taskmasters," particularly Possiet, who was a bit more relaxed than usual; according to Libbie Custer, as "the immense steamer had no other passengers and as there was no one to criticize . . . [they] gave themselves a rest from espionage."[63] Alexis confirmed in a letter to his mother that the journey down the Mississippi was an enjoyable time, though he apparently told his father that the Mississippi itself was boring in comparison with the Volga. Possiet similarly recorded that the grand duke was healthy and had thoroughly enjoyed the journey down the Mississippi. More importantly, in Possiet's eyes, by the time they reached New Orleans, Alexis's mood had lifted and he rarely spoke about Zhukovskaya.[64]

After a brief and uneventful stop in Vicksburg, Mississippi, the *James Howard* continued down the Mississippi River and, according to several sources, paused for a brief stop at Belmont, a large plantation in St. James Parish, Louisiana, owned by the LeBourgeois family. Two days later the steamer stopped to spend the night tied up at Carrollton, a small area on the edge of New Orleans that at the time was still a separate town. Presumably, the steamer paused there so the grand duke's arrival in New Orleans would be a daytime event. At last on the morning of Monday, February 12, the *James Howard* puffed around the bend in the river at New Orleans. All along the shore and on the approach to the city, people watched and waved as the steamer went by, and the *Times* estimated that there were up to fifteen thousand people on the levee between Canal and Julia Street alone.[65]

When the *James Howard* came into view, nearby ships dipped their flags in salute and the waiting masses rushed onto nearby decks of steamboats and any other area that offered a better vantage point, standing on tiptoe and craning their necks. The thicket of steamboats made it difficult for the grand duke's steamer to make a landing, but eventually an opening was made at Girod Street; on shore, a squad of policemen struggled to keep the excited crowd from "carrying everything before them in their anxiety to get a glimpse at the son of royalty." When the steamer was securely tied, Mayor Flanders and Administrator Bonzano went on board to welcome the grand duke, and Flanders offered, "We have come in an informal manner, hearing of your well known dislike to public displays." There were introductions all around and pleasant small chat, during which Alexis expressed surprise that Flanders and Bonzano were not French, since he was under the impression that New Orleans was a French creole city and everyone would be speaking French. Dressed in a plain dark suit and a black silk hat, Alexis observed the waving and cheering crowd from the deck of the ship, though he seemed equally interested in the large stacks of cotton and other freight that were piled behind the levee. The *Daily Picayune* complimented city officials for the "entire absence of hobnobbing or toadyism."[66]

At about ten o'clock, the royal guests and their hosts disembarked amid the roar of cheers and cannons, but the crowd at the wharf was so thick that it took a full fifteen minutes to maneuver the carriages into a position where the party could access them. All along the grand duke's route from Poydras to Magazine, down Magazine to Canal, and up Carondelet to Common Street, the sidewalks were teeming. At the St. Charles Hotel, Alexis was immediately shown upstairs to his rooms, where he settled in and took a late breakfast, remaining indoors until the performance at the opera house later that evening. Alexis saw only a few visitors that afternoon, but he did receive a letter of welcome from Rex, the King of Carnival, who notified him that there would be a special audience for his reception at sunset on Mardi Gras day. Meanwhile, curious men and women milled about the parlors and halls of the hotel, so many that for a brief time it was necessary to station two patrolmen outside the duke's door until the initial excitement died down and the crowd dispersed.[67]

Built in 1851, after the previous structure of the same name had been destroyed by a spectacular conflagration, the newer version of the St. Charles Hotel was nearly identical to its namesake, with a projecting portico of six Corinthian columns and a winding marble staircase. Inside, the hotel featured an octagonal barroom of Ionic style and a billiard saloon in the Corinthian style. The St. Charles was considered one of the finest hotels in the South, offering deluxe accommodations for six hundred to seven hundred guests, a number of fine stores, and some thirty parlors of various types. For Alexis's visit, fourteen parlors and bedrooms had been set aside and redecorated for him and his entourage and, according to one description, no expense had been spared; if the reports are to be believed, the final cost of the grand duke's stay amounted to eleven thousand dollars.[68]

The grand duke's first evening in New Orleans began with an early dinner, a small affair exclusively for his suite and a few others, including the Custers. The hotel offered a variety of wine, featuring its own twenty-year-old St. Charles Hotel Sherry, and fine "Espenales" cigars were on hand as well. The dinner was a simple one, the conversation light and pleasant. Alexis apparently joked that his costume for the Mardi Gras ball the next day would be wide-top boots filled with little children. The dinner concluded at seven-thirty when the party climbed into carriages to head to the French Opera House at the corner of Bourbon and Toulouse. Opened in 1859, the opera house was considered one of the finest in the United States, with a spacious interior and a four-tiered performance hall capable of seating about twenty-eight hundred people.[69]

On the evening of February 12, the opera house was particularly beautiful, having been done up with special care for the imperial guest. The presence of the grand duke meant that the theater was full, and one local paper believed that "the brilliant and crowded display of beauty and fashion that greeted him in the auditorium might have rivaled New York." As Alexis and his suite entered the lavishly decorated proscenium box to the right of the stage, the orchestra under the direction of opera-house manager Edouard Calabresi struck up the Russian national hymn and the audience enthusiastically applauded. The *Daily Picayune* noted, however, that the behavior of the excited crowd was, nonetheless, dignified and respectful, and there was "neither noisy demonstration nor unseemly curiosity." The performance that evening was *Il Trovatore* (The Troubadour), by Giuseppi Verdi. At the conclusion of the opera, Alexis heartily applauded the performers and returned to his apartments at the hotel.[70]

Tuesday, February 13, 1872, dawned clear and fair, with a "sweet south wind," the perfect weather for Mardi Gras. The day's activities were not scheduled to begin until later in the day, but soon after lunch, crowds of women and children began to gather at City Hall on St. Charles Avenue (now known as Gallier Hall). A large platform stood in front of the building's main entrance, intended to hold some three thousand people. Inside City Hall, the corridors and halls, and even the mayor's parlor, were filled with ladies. The King of Carnival had ordered his followers to meet near the statue of Henry Clay on the corner of Canal Street and St. Charles Street at precisely three o'clock, but long before that appointed hour the streets in all directions near the statue were densely packed with "a surging sea of mortality." All along the parade route, the streets were crowded and the buildings were decorated with flowers, flags, and festoons, gas lights, and Chinese lanterns.[71]

Promptly at three o'clock, the sound of artillery fire indicated the start of the procession, which included a motley crew of men in a broad spectrum of costumes. There was the King of Carnival, twenty-three Lords of Yeomanry dressed as Bedouins, and a live cow, symbolic of the fatted calf. Behind them were three or four hundred men dressed as "kings and peasants, devils and saints, Indians and negroes, women of high and low degree, clowns and harlequins, birds, beasts and fishes." Many of the costumes reflected political satire, humorous versions of Grant, Horace Greeley, the "kleptomania of carpet-bagism," and, in the kind of role reversal that was typical of carnival celebrations, even the grand duke himself. There were also several bands, including Dan Rice's circus band.[72]

At four o'clock, Alexis and several members of his suite, accompanied by the mayor, arrived at City Hall and were introduced to Governor Henry C. Warmoth, Lieutenant Governor P. B. S. Pinchback, General James Longstreet, and several others. Alexis and Warmoth remained deep in conversation until the procession of Rex reached them, at which point they and the others went outside. A special seat of honor had been prepared for the young Russian, but he chose instead to take a chair next to the governor. When the procession reached City Hall, the parade halted and the band played the Russian national hymn. Alexis seemed to enjoy the parade, smiling, clapping, and raising his hat in appreciation of the various costumes and bands. He particularly enjoyed a wagon of children "fantastically dressed," bearing a placard that said, "The Grand Duke." When the parade was concluded, Alexis was taken inside and introduced to several senators and members of the House of Representatives, and then conducted out through a rear entrance to a carriage that quickly took him back to his hotel, while a large crowd continued to wait in front of City Hall for the royal visitor to reappear.[73]

Some hours later, Alexis returned to City Hall to see the procession of the Mistick Krewe of Comus, which that night was "incomparably grander and more beautiful than anything previously presented by that famous fraternity." The theme was that of *The Iliad* and *The Odyssey,* and it was a magnificent exhibition, illuminated by the light from the surrounding buildings. The procession, followed by the royal visitor and his entourage, then proceeded to the Varieties Theatre for the tableaux of the Krewe and the ball that would follow. The tableaux were a series of scenes presented onstage, in this case, representing "the Judgment, the Combat, the Olympian Deities in Council, and the Battle of the Frogs and Mice." Once the tableaux had been displayed, the ball began and the dancing continued into the morning hours. The grand duke enjoyed the tableaux and the ball, though reports varied on whether he engaged in dancing that evening. Subsequently, the Russian party went to the St. Charles Theatre, where another carnival ball was in full swing.[74]

On Wednesday, February 14, Alexis spent much of the day indoors, perhaps recovering from the previous day's carnival activities. In the early afternoon he received an assemblage of the foreign consuls residing in New Orleans, among them representatives from Austria, Argentina, Belgium, Spain, Venezuela, and

France. The committee of the foreign consuls introduced themselves to Alexis and welcomed him to the city. One of these, the Greek consul Nicholas M. Benachi, also appeared as part of a delegation from the St. Trinity Greek Church on North Dorgenois Street. Benachi, a businessman and diplomat, had founded the Greek Church in New Orleans in 1866–67. Benachi invited the grand duke to visit the chapel and requested that Alexis thank his mother for her generosity and support of the small Orthodox Church, to which she had given two icons and a Cyrillic Bible. Later in the afternoon, Alexis visited William Washburn's photo gallery on Canal Street, where he sat for six different individual photos. Subsequently, Washburn made the most of this particular addition to his resume, advertising himself as "the photographer to his Imperial Highness, the Grand Duke Alexis."[75]

In the evening, Alexis emerged from his apartments to attend a performance of *The Little Detective* starring Lotta Crabtree at the St. Charles Theatre. Often referred to as "Little Lotta" because of her diminutive size and youthful appearance, Crabtree was known for her ability to act, sing, and dance, and for her natural talent for mimicry. The week of the grand duke's visit, Lotta was scheduled to be in Memphis, but the temptation to perform for the young Russian was too great and so she extended her stay in New Orleans. Lotta Crabtree could attract a sizeable audience on her own and, with the anticipated presence of the grand duke, seats had sold quickly and none was available by the morning of the show. When Alexis arrived at eight o'clock that evening, his carriage was immediately consumed by the waiting crowd, preventing his egress for some ten minutes. Finally, the police succeeded in clearing a narrow path and Alexis was able to alight and proceed to a private box beautifully decorated with Russian and American flags and outfitted with sumptuous furniture for the occasion. The orchestra performed the Russian national hymn, and then the play began. As always, Lotta charmed the audience, including the grand duke, who smiled and applauded frequently. After the show, Alexis inquired about an introduction to the charming actress, a request that was made much of in the press. The *Daily Republican* claimed, for example, that the grand duke had fallen "a willing victim to the magnetic charm of the admired Lotta, who numbers her slaves by the thousands." Two days later, Alexis requested another meeting with Lotta, but by that time she had already departed for her next engagement. The grand duke left a gift for her, a bracelet of turquoise, small diamonds, black enamel, and two large pearls.[76]

Returning to his hotel, Alexis had no time to rest, for his hosts had arranged one more honor that evening, a serenade by fifty of the city's finest musicians under the direction of Professor Louis Mayer, the musical director of the St. Charles Theatre. The manager of the St. Charles Hotel had prepared for this midnight serenade, illuminating the large portico of the hotel with a double row of gas jets, creating "a scene of dazzling magnificence seldom seen in New Orleans." The orchestra performed several songs, including the overture from the opera *Reymond* and the "Grand Duke Reception March," which Mayer composed for Alexis to the tune of the Russian national hymn. When the serenade ended, Alexis retired to his bedchamber. There had been some speculation that Alexis would attend the performance of Dan Rice's circus in Congo Square earlier that day, but that did not transpire, postponed until a late date.[77]

Pleasant entertainment and private engagements consumed the remainder of Alexis's stay in New Orleans. For once, he was completely free from official receptions and, consequently, the local papers spent far less time reporting on his movements. In fact, according to several reports, members of the press were kept at bay from some of these events, making any detailed accounts of the grand duke's activities virtually impossible. On Thursday, February 15, Alexis was supposed to attend Dan Rice's circus at Annunciation Square, but once again he failed to appear, disappointing many who had come that day only to see the royal spectacle. Instead, the grand duke went for a long stroll through the streets around his hotel. That evening, Alexis stopped in once more at the French Opera House for a performance of Giacomo Meyebeer's *L'Africaine.* The house was full and particularly dazzling that evening, and the performance was a triumphant success, made clear by the enthusiastic applause and repeated curtain calls in which Alexis and his entourage heartily participated. Meanwhile, at the Academy of Music that same evening, Lydia Thompson and her company performed *Bluebeard,* the play which contained the popular song "If Ever I Cease to Love." The song had been adopted by Rex as the theme song of his new carnival krewe and was widely reported to be one of Alexis's favorite songs, but the grand duke failed to make an appearance at the academy that night, despite his much-rumored infatuation with Thompson.[78]

Friday, February 16, must have been a quiet day for the grand duke since the local papers gave no report on his activities. That evening, Alexis attended a private dinner at the Louisiana Jockey Club, a large and airy three-story mansion on Esplanade Street adjoining the Fair Grounds. The club had only recently been established in May 1871 for the purpose of promoting the sport of horse racing and improving the breeding of race horses. Though members of the press were not admitted, there were various reports that the dinner was sumptuous and well received by the imperial guests. Later, the *New Orleans Bee* reported that a number of members of the Jockey Club had refused to attend the dinner because Governor Warmoth, "the responsible author of the woes and indignities to which Louisiana has been subjected," would be there; however, according to the *Republican,* what kept them away was the requirement that every member attending had to pay his proportion of the expenses. Alexis was also expected to attend Lydia Thompson's farewell performance of *Kenilworth* at the Academy of Music that evening, and there were several reports that the grand duke had specifically requested that she incorporate "If Ever I Cease to Love" into the performance. It is unclear whether Alexis made it to the performance or not; the *Republican* reported that he appeared late, several hours into the performance, while the *Daily Picayune* claimed he never showed at all.[79]

On Saturday, February 17, the grand duke finally made it to a performance of Dan Rice's circus, accompanied by General Custer and Governor Warmoth. The performance took place in the nearby town of Jefferson, and Rice had arranged a large viewing platform, carpeted and draped with flags for his royal spectators. The *Daily Picayune* noted that, though the American circus is a "truly democratic institution," Alexis seemed to enjoy it nonetheless, taking particular interest in the trained horses, some of which he declared were the most beautiful he had ever seen. When Alexis left at the end of the performance, he reportedly remarked that it was "the first time in his life he had witnessed an arenic [sic] entertainment without being bored." Later that evening, Alexis went to the French Opera House one last time to see a performance of Meyerbeer's *The Huguenots*.[80]

When it was all over, the New Orleans papers deemed both Mardi Gras and Alexis's reception a sweeping success, noting the grand duke's approval of all the festivities. "Mardi Gras has come and gone," reported the *Daily Picayune,* "and our Imperial guest has seen the Crescent City in the zenith of her glory and to best advantage." In reality, Alexis's impressions of New Orleans were not all favorable. He wrote his mother that, on the one hand, the city's European flavor intrigued him, and he commented on the excellent French opera and the multitude of theaters. Mardi Gras, however, did not impress him. He recounted that the procession of maskers, on foot, on horseback and in carriages, was accompanied by music and screams, but observed that "all the same, some kind of stiffness governs all this happiness, as if someone ordered them to dress up and pretend to be happy," an ironic comment from the son of an absolute monarch, particularly one who had himself spent a great deal of time pretending to be happy.[81]

There is one final aspect of the grand duke's week in New Orleans that deserves comment. Amidst the theater performances and glittering balls, the problem of racism lurked just below the surface, thinly veiled, but omnipresent. The *New Orleans Times* noted that, though it had always been the "courteous custom" to invite members of the legislature to any reception or public event, Mayor Flanders had failed to include the legislators in the grand duke's reception. This change in practice led some to wonder if the mayor was "afraid that if the white members were invited he would also have to invite the colored members and their families." The *Bee* expressed concern that blacks should not be excluded from the special viewing platform on Mardi Gras day, advising, "the colored people should see to it that they are not cheated out of their share of an accommodation put up at the public expense, and for which they have to pay their share in taxation." In several places, the sheer novelty of African Americans in political office was highlighted in discussions of the grand duke's reception. In Memphis, it had been noted that Alexis would be shown "the only wonders that Memphis contains—great warehouses filled with countless cotton bales, steam power presses, oil mills," and "the colored councilmen." In New Orleans, the *Times* commented that, after seeing a pigeon shoot, hog killing, and a buffalo hunt, the only thing that remained for him to view was "a Southern Caucassio-African Legislature."[82]

———————◆———————

Alexis departed New Orleans on the evening of February 19, traveling by train to Mobile, where he boarded a steamer to take him to his fleet waiting at Pensacola. Pleading time constraints, the grand duke had declined the offer of Mobile city officials for a reception, but many remained hopeful that there would be some appearance of the royal visitor, and the local paper kept residents informed of his movements, "to quiet the nerves of those who are daily on the look-out for Alexis." One article suggested that a want of time was not the real reason the grand duke would forgo a reception in Mobile; rather, it was a disagreement with his father, the tsar. Hitting closer to home than it may have realized, the paper postulated that it was the extension of Alexis's trip through the Far East that made him unhappy and not in the mood to be feted. The near certainty that Alexis would spend no time whatsoever in Mobile did not prevent one business from using his name in its advertising; Grover and Baking Sewing Machine Company on Dauphin Street suggested that the grand duke would be stopping by to buy raffle tickets on an elegant dressing robe embroidered by the machines in the shop, and urged locals to do the same.[83]

At approximately six o'clock in the morning, the grand duke's train arrived in Mobile, greeted at the wharf by a small crowd and the Fire Department's brass band playing the Russian national hymn. There were no formal activities, and Alexis stayed hidden away in his train car until his boat arrived, at which point he "marched on board under a police guard, without casting his eye to the right or left, and not recognizing the common herd with a wink, blink or nod." Even the rousing blare of the brass band did not excite the grand duke. While Admiral Possiet acknowledged the melodic reception with a raise of his hat, Alexis gave no sign at all. The steamer, *St. Elmo,* took Alexis to Tensas, where he boarded a special train to Pensacola. Several newspapers reported a similar snubbing in Pensacola, where Alexis transferred to the *Svetlana* with no acknowledgment of the crowd that had come out to see him. Not everyone was left angered by the grand duke's final stops, however. The Russian fleet had purchased 450 tons of Alabama coal at twelve dollars a ton for the next leg of its trip. Also, in Mobile, Captain John Black of the steamer *St. Elmo* was given a diamond ring by the grand duke in appreciation for his service.[84]

Despite the unremarkable conclusion of Alexis's American excursion, Admiral Possiet could report to the tsar that overall the trip had been a success. In three months' time they had traveled approximately 8,500 versts (5,610 miles) by rail and 1,350 versts (891 miles) by river, fortunately without any real problems. He also noted that the grand duke had been enthusiastically received everywhere, and that the reception in the South had been every bit as warm as that in the North. Possiet admitted, however, that their itinerary had been exhausting, with nonstop receptions and celebrations, and that eventually all the new places ceased to interest them and the introductions became mechanical. By February 1872, even the seasoned admiral was ready for a less demanding schedule.[85]

Alexis's impressions of America were a mixed bag. He clearly enjoyed the buffalo hunt, his visit to Mammoth Cave, and his journey down the Mississippi, though he admitted to his mother that "American society gives me a strange impression." Alexis noted that he detected a difference between northerners and southerners, observing that southerners had completely different manners and more closely resembled Europeans. It was obvious, Alexis declared, that these southerners had been "old feudals," and they resembled the Russian nobility. He described American men as "smart and energetic, but entirely lacking in manners or even the most ordinary decencies, with the exception of soldiers and sailors."

Women fared slightly better in the grand duke's assessment. He confessed to his mother that he found American women to be smart and well educated, but "about religion their understanding is very liberal, although they often go to church." Alexis noted, however, that when American women first saw him, they stared at him "as one would stare at a crocodile or an unusually large monkey in a menagerie," but once they became accustomed to him, they regained their composure. He was struck by the number of beauties, especially in New York and St. Louis, though he assured his mother that his "success among American women," reported in the newspapers, was "entirely nonsense." To his brother, Vladimir, Alexis remarked that American women were lovely and, under different circumstances, he would have "fallen in love at every step."[86]

Alexis's comments on American women are particularly intriguing given the attention that they, and their antics, were given in the American press. In each city, newspapers commented on the excitement and preparations of the fairer sex. Women in particular were reported to have taken great lengths to see or be near the royal bachelor. In St. Louis, a girl of sixteen sat outside Alexis's apartments for thirteen hours before she was chased off by hotel staff. In New York, a young lady sent the grand duke a carrier dove with her card attached. The *Atlanta Constitution* reported that the rumor that Alexis liked small women had caused a frenzy among "the stately young ladies of fashion, who are knocking the high heels from their shoes, eschewing lofty coiffeurs, and otherwise seeking to reduce their stature within the limits supposed to be approved by the arrived scion of royalty." A number of papers also reported that a young lady near St. Louis had "fallen madly in love with Alexis" and followed him to Omaha, intent on becoming his wife."[87] These reports, coupled with the recruitment of attractive women for various events and the competitive crowing between cities over who had the prettiest girls, are a reminder that, despite the efforts of Lucy Stone, Elizabeth Cady Stanton, and others, in 1871–72, women were still viewed as accessories, not equals.

CONCLUSION
Buffalo Tales and Mardi Gras Myths

All hail to the Duke of the Russias—
Thou'rt now in the land of the free,
Whose laws, patriotic and noble,
Must stamp their impress upon thee.

—*Mobile Register,* February 11, 1872

A
S AMERICANS said farewell to Alexis and resumed their normal routines, the grand duke's journey had, in fact, only just begun. Admiral Possiet had much to do, as well. On their approach to New Orleans, he had taken Alexis's silence on Zhukovskaya as a hopeful sign, but his optimism was premature. As the grand duke departed the United States, he continued to agonize over his separation from his lover. In the middle of March 1872, Alexis received a letter from a friend, Count A. Perovski, which reveals much about his frame of mind. The grand duke had thanked Perovski for not turning his back on him and Zhukovskaya. Perovski responded, "I will never change towards my friends especially when they are unhappy. It is offensive to me to see how many of Zhukovskaya's former good friends now turn away from her and do not want to know her under the supposition that she is guilty because she is older than you. . . . even your brother Vladimir whom I love dearly (as a good, honest fellow) also said these things, though I think under the influence of others." On a lighter note, Perovski assured Alexis that Alexandra and the baby were both well and healthy, and that they had received the money that had been sent through Vladimir. Zhukovskaya apparently asked Perovski to visit her, but Perovski confided to Alexis that, though he would be happy to,

he did not have the money at the moment and suspected that he would not be permitted to visit her anyway. Perovski exhorted his friend to be brave.[1]

Meanwhile, the relationship between the tsar and his son remained strained. In March 1872, Alexander complained that, although Alexis knew that his mother was ill, his letters home displayed no concern for her fate. The emperor and empress interpreted this as a sign of Alexis's continuing anger and proof that, despite his age, Alexis still was not able to look at his life and responsibilities with sufficient seriousness. Instead, he sought only pleasure and diversion, and this irresponsible behavior made them worry about his future. Alexander's disappointment in his son was palpable; he added, "God grant that we will have no more reason to blush for you, after all the sorrow you have brought us over the last years. We cannot return to this." The tsar concluded with a stern reminder that Alexis should not cling to pointless hopes, nor continue a close friendship with Zhukovskaya, since he and the empress could not change their decision about her.[2]

Throughout this period, Admiral Possiet continued to keep a close eye on his ward and recorded his observations and suspicions in journal entries that also served as draft letters to the tsar. These entries make it clear that one of Possiet's gravest concerns was that Alexis and Zhukovskaya might attempt to meet at some point during the long journey. Conversations with the young man had led the admiral to believe that the couple was still intent on marriage, though Alexis had declared that, if there were any chance of receiving the tsar's blessing in the future, he would not even contemplate marrying in secret. The admiral knew, of course, that the tsar would never bless this union, and so he closely monitored Alexis's correspondence with Zhukovskaya, intercepting letters both to and from the grand duke. What these letters revealed is that the determined lovers had not yet given up on their hope of being together. They had discussed meeting somewhere in Europe, but Alexis, to his credit, had told Alexandra that he could not simply abandon his military post. In response, she had suggested they rendezvous in Singapore or China. They realized that if they did not marry while Alexis was abroad, it would be impossible to do so once he returned to Russia. As a consequence, Possiet pledged to the tsar that he would not allow Alexis to go ashore if he suspected that Zhukovskaya was there, but he worried that she might somehow evade his detection. Consequently, he enlisted the help of others to discover whether the troublesome woman was in a given port before Alexis could find out.[3]

Meanwhile, the grand duke continued his journey around the world with stops in Cuba, Brazil, the Cape of Good Hope, India, Singapore, Hong Kong, China and Japan. By the time Alexis reached the one-year mark of his long journey, he was clearly tired of traveling and growing a little bored with his company. In August 1872, Alexis wrote his brother Vladimir from Singapore, complaining about the heat and the cockroaches. He also expressed regret that he had been unable to hunt tigers or rhinoceroses. From Hong Kong, he confessed that, although he tried to hide it from everyone else, he was occasionally still gripped by terrible sadness. He was also tired of the company of "old men." Even his old tutor Possiet was beginning to irritate him. Apparently, all of the travelers were ready to get home; Alexis noted that all of the men were eager to return to the embraces of their wives, especially Possiet, who desperately missed his beloved Rosalee and, unlike the other men, did not take advantage of the female companionship that was available at each port. Several months later, writing from Nagasaki, Alexis asked his brother Vladimir to explain why he had encouraged Alexandra to break her tie with him the previous year. Alexis admitted that it still troubled him greatly whether his brother has done this of his own accord or had been following someone's orders. After a year and a half of travel away from Zhukovskaya, Alexis was still scarred by the event and felt betrayed by the reactions of his family. Once again, he asked Vladimir to send money to Zhukovskaya.[4]

Alexis may have successfully hidden his sadness from many of those around him, but Admiral Possiet knew that the young duke's love for Zhukovskaya was still intense. The admiral continued to remain vigilant for the remainder of the trip, still worried that Alexandra might appear in Singapore or some other place in the Far East. Possiet had already confronted Alexis about the couple's plans to meet and marry. He asked Alexis both to write Zhukovskaya and urge her to abandon these schemes, and to promise that he would not carry out such a plan, regardless of how much Zhukovskaya might insist otherwise. While still in Rio de Janeiro, Possiet pledged that he would demand this promise at every port if necessary, and assured the tsar that if upon arriving in Singapore he found out that Zhukovskaya was there, he would pull up anchor and, bypassing Hong Kong, continue on to Manila and Nagasaki.[5] The admiral's vigilance apparently paid off, for when the journey ended in July 1873, almost exactly two years after it began, Alexis was still a bachelor and Alexandra was in Europe raising their child without him.

Over the next years, Alexis traveled throughout Europe, making a number of state visits with or on behalf of his father. According to one contemporary, Alexis liked to have a good time, but "when necessary he could put on his grand-est airs, and could represent his country to perfection when called upon to do so on state occasions." Alexis even returned for a brief visit to the United States in 1877, during which President and Mrs. Rutherford B. Hayes allowed wine to be served at the White House, a notable exception to their no-alcohol policy.[6] His second American trip was cut short, however, by news of Russia's war with the Ottoman Empire. During that brief war, Alexis served as the commander of naval forces on the Danube, earning the Order of St. George. Three years later, in 1881, when his father died at the hands of terrorists, Alexis's older brother became the new tsar of Russia, Alexander III (1881–94).

Under Alexander III, Alexis served in several significant positions within the government. In 1881, he was appointed to the State Council, though his dedica-tion to this job was questioned by at least one contemporary who complained that Alexis seemed bored and could only think about how, "without infringe-ment of decency," he could escape to his lover's bed. Two years later, Alexis became general admiral of the Russian fleet. According to several sources, Alexis had no passion for this position either, repeatedly bumping heads with Naval Minister Ivan Shestakov, who complained incessantly about the grand duke's laziness, indifference, and resistance to modernization. Similarly, the vice-admiral and head of the Russian Naval Academy bemoaned Alexis's sluggish work ethic, while others complained that his supervision of the navy and the condition of the fleet was superficial, at best. Alexis's own nephew, Alexander Mikhailovich, known as Sandro, would later remark of his uncle, "His knowledge of naval affairs could not have been more limited. The very mention of pending naval reforms brought a hostile frown on his handsome face. [He was] not interested in anything that did not pertain to love-making, food and liquor." Among some of his contemporaries, he became known for "fast women and slow ships."[7]

The grand duke's professional life and reputation were further complicated by his personal life. Widely held to be the most handsome member of the im-perial family and very successful with women, Alexis remained a bachelor for life, but he always had a woman on his arm. His brother Alexander had hinted at this in a letter of 1875: "I heard that you are not bored in Venice, and that a little parrot flew there for a meeting with her cock!"[8] In the 1880s, he had a very public relationship with Zinaida Skobeleva, daughter of his favorite aunt, Grand Duchess Maria Nikolaevna, and wife of the Duke of Leuchtenberg. The cuckolded husband even complained to the tsar, who showed him no sympathy, and the affair continued until Zinaida's death in 1899. There were other mistresses, as well. A lover of ballet and music, Alexis was a frequent sight at the theater, nightclubs, and balls in St. Petersburg.[9]

Alexis also spent a great deal of time in Monte Carlo and Paris, where he purchased a home, entertaining and gambling with high rollers like the American steel magnate Charles Schwab.[10] Here, too, Alexis developed a reputation for his love of wine, women, and song, particularly in "lowlife" Paris. The *Washington Post* declared that Alexis was "fond of fun and not, they say, very scrupulous how or where he gets it." In fact, the antics of Alexis and his ducal companions became legendary in Paris and beyond. The favorite haunts of Alexis and his brother Vladimir became part of a tourist industry in this "mecca of hedonism." At the end of the nineteenth century, guidebooks recommended a number of these places as must-see sites in the "tour of the Grand Dukes." At least one guidebook still described this tour in the late 1920s.[11]

The Romanovs were known for their generous gifts to performers and others who found favor with them. For example, in January 1891, the Australian soprano Nellie Melba performed in St. Petersburg at the request of the tsar and for her troubles received a number of extravagant gifts from members of the royal family, including an exquisite diamond-and-sapphire bracelet from Alexis. A year later, when the American opera singer Sibyl Sanderson sang at the Marinsky Theatre in St. Petersburg, the tsar so enjoyed her performance that he ordered a shower of jewels be thrown to her on stage. Sanderson gave several more performances in the Russian capital, and the tsar's family rewarded her with various pieces of jewelry and jewel-encrusted items.[12] Even in this environment of opulence and conspicuous consumption, Alexis became known for his lavish spending. According to the records of the French jewelry house Boucheron, Alexis spent nearly 350,000 francs over two decades at the end of the nineteenth century. Many of these items, such as white- and black-pearl shirt buttons and stickpins, a gold reading light decorated with two miniatures, and a vase decorated with silver-gilt foliage, were likely for the grand duke himself. But other items were clearly for lady friends, including a diamond bracelet, sixty-one-carat sapphire earrings with diamond accents, a forty-four-carat round, yellow diamond, and a stunning emerald-and-diamond necklace in the shape of a peacock feather purchased for 14,000 francs. In the 1890s, Alexis bought extravagant gifts for his mistress, Zinaida: a shoulder ornament of three intertwined diamond rings (15,000 francs), a gold necklace of pearls and diamonds (25,000), and a tiara displaying fruit made of pearls and mistletoe of diamonds (6,800). Alexis was also a frequent client of Cartier's and purchased many items from the Fabergé firm. The performer Elise Baletta had a large collection of Fabergé animals and flowers, and many of these were gifts from the grand duke. A common joke in the Russian capital said that the women of Paris cost the Russian Navy a battleship a year. The humor was lost on many, however, and Alexis was widely criticized for his lack of attention to naval affairs and his extended stays in Paris, particularly later, when Russia found itself embroiled in war with Japan.[13]

Despite these concerns, Alexander III never seemed to lose faith in his favorite brother and continued to rely upon him to oversee the navy and to serve as Russia's representative abroad in various state obligations. In 1887, the same year that Alexis spent time in Vienna, Paris, Biarritz, and Bayonne, the tsar wrote his brother a letter praising his hard work with the navy, adding, "God willing that the time will soon come when we will be completely prepared for any sort of circumstances on our seas, so that we can firmly say to our enemies, 'As you like, we are ready!'"[14] When Alexander III died in 1894, Alexis was devastated, writing to his mistress, "It's impossible for me to express the pain I felt at that moment when they placed the body of my brother in the tomb. It was as if something inside me broke. The whole past, filled with the memories and friendship of youth . . . went with him to the grave!"[15]

Upon the death of Alexander III, his son inherited the throne as Nicholas II. As uncle to the new tsar, Alexis remained within the upper echelons of the government and continued in his position as general admiral. He also continued to travel on behalf of the crown. In 1895, Alexis represented Russia at the opening of the Baltic Canal, connecting the Baltic and North seas, and two years later, he helped greet the emperor and empress of Germany and President Félix Faure of France when they visited St. Petersburg only weeks apart. Despite his official duties and considerable time abroad, Alexis was on hand for family gatherings and obligations as well, both pleasurable and grim. In January 1895, he celebrated New Year's with his family, including his nephew, Tsar Nicholas II, and later that year he was at Tsarskoe Selo about the time that Nicholas and his wife, Alexandra, had their first child, Olga. Several years later, when his nephew George died, he accompanied his sister-in-law, Minni (Empress Maria Fedorovna), to retrieve her son's body in Batum and return it to the capital.[16]

Alexis was also present in 1896 for the coronation of Nicholas II, serving as escort for his sister-in-law, the mother of the new tsar. Sadly, while the official coronation had taken place inside the Kremlin, an outdoor public celebration at Khodynka Field had turned into a catastrophe when crowds stampeded, injuring over a thousand people and killing nearly fourteen hundred others. Alexis played a key role in the heated debates that followed the disastrous incident. Despite this tragedy, Alexis and his brothers, Vladimir and Serge, insisted that Nicholas and Alexandra should attend the ball being given that evening by the French ambassador. Nicholas's cousins, the Grand Dukes Nicholas and Alexander (Sandro) Mikhailovich and two of their brothers, attempted to persuade the tsar to forgo the ball. In the end, Nicholas took the advice of his uncles and attended the ball, a choice that was widely criticized at the time and has since been assessed harshly by historians as well.[17]

It was in his position as general admiral of the Russian fleet, however, that Alexis suffered the greatest blow to his reputation. In February 1904, Russia and Japan went to war. The conflict went badly for the Russians and led to popular discontent at all levels, feeding the hatred of Russia's revolutionary movement. In February 1905, Socialist Revolutionary terrorists assassinated Grand Duke Serge Alexandrovich, Alexis's brother who had served as governor general of Moscow and had been widely blamed for the Khodynka Field disaster. Alexis "sobbed like a child" over his brother's death, but was forbidden from attending the funeral for fear of his safety. Nicholas claimed to have irrefutable proof that Alexis was being tracked "like a wild beast" by terrorists and his life was in danger. Following Serge's murder, the tsar's family, including Alexis and the other grand dukes, moved with great caution, and a heavy atmosphere descended on the royal residences. American papers also reported that Alexis was being targeted by terrorists. In 1905, both the *Washington Post* and the *New York Times* declared that Alexis was, in fact, on the top of a list drawn up by Socialist Revolutionaries of those whom they intended to assassinate next and, according to a special cable from the *London Times,* a man loitering near Alexis's St. Petersburg palace had been found to be carrying a bomb.[18]

The grand duke's ill-timed appearances with his mistresses seemed only to make matters worse. In the spring of 1905, as Russia was sagging under the weight of the war, Alexis was hissed and booed out of a St. Petersburg theater for daring to show his face with the singer, actress, and demimondaine Elise Baletta. According to one report, though Baletta stuck her tongue out at the jeering crowd, Alexis blanched and hurried out of the theater. At this point, the *Washington Post* declared Alexis to be undoubtedly "the most unpopular of all the members of the imperial family of Russia."[19]

In late May 1905, Russia suffered a devastating defeat in the Battle of Tsu-shima—another serious blow to Alexis's professional and personal reputation. In the wake of this defeat, and confronted with charges of inefficiency, mismanagement, and corruption, as well as several public demonstrations against him, he resigned his position as head of the Russian Navy and moved to his home on Avenue Gabriel in Paris. His popularity suffered on American shores as well. Soon after the Battle of Tsushima, the *Washington Post* noted that Alexis's name evoked very different feelings at the present from those it had excited during his visit in 1871. Russia's recent defeat, the paper noted, had demonstrated that Alexis was never equipped for the enormous job with which he had been entrusted. The *Post* concluded, "The abject fall of Alexis whom Americans knew is one of the most striking features of the Russian debacle."[20]

Even in Paris, Alexis's popularity declined after the Russo-Japanese War. In August 1891, the *New York Tribune* had reported on the popularity of the tsar's brother in Paris, noting that "upon every occasion when he has shown himself to the public he has received hearty greetings." By 1906, however, there were reports that the bloom was off the rose. The *Washington Post* received news that Alexis and his nephew had to be smuggled out of Paris, the French police no longer willing to answer for their safety. Indeed, the *Post* noted that the frequency of assassination attempts by Russian revolutionaries both in Russia and abroad made the arrival of Russian royal guests an unwelcome sight across Europe, prompting other guests to find safer accommodations. In the spring of 1907, Alexis was run out of a restaurant and nearly mobbed for appearing with a Parisian woman of questionable reputation on the anniversary of the Battle of Tsushima. According to the columnist who relayed the story, "That he should have chosen this date of all others to banquet one of the most notorious women in Paris excited the utmost indignations of those present and has shocked not only the sense of propriety, but also the patriotic susceptibilities of the French."[21]

Ultimately, Alexis died of natural causes. In 1908, the year the grand duke turned fifty-eight, he suffered from several bouts of ill health, and in November he died of pneumonia at his home in Paris.[22] When news reached St. Petersburg, Tsar Nicholas II recorded in his diary, "My favorite uncle is dead." Alexis's body was taken to St. Petersburg, where a funeral procession made its way through crowded, snow-covered, and heavily guarded streets across the frozen Neva River to the fortress. The tsar followed behind the coffin. It was Nicholas's first appearance on the streets of the city in several years, a consequence of the constant fear of terrorist attack. American ambassador John W. Riddle attended the funeral. Alexis was interred in the Cathedral of St. Peter and St. Paul along with his Romanov ancestors.[23]

Americans received the news of Alexis's death with mixed feelings. Across the country newspapers published the grand duke's obituary and reported on his funeral. In many places, his death prompted fond reminiscences about his visit and the spectacular balls and banquets that had been held in his honor. However, the assessments of Alexis were not all kind. The *New York Times,* for example, noted that, while Alexis was remembered in the United States as a tall, handsome young man and a symbol of Russian friendship, he was also a hedonist upon whose shoulders "the burdens of authority rested lightly." Recounting the grand duke's life, the paper resurrected the story of Alexis's extended stay in Paris during the dark days of the Russo-Japanese War and the criticism he suffered for that choice. The *Times* concluded, "To say that he was never much more than a good-humored, overgrown boy is to judge him kindly."[24]

And what became of his son? Alexis Alexeevich, the son of Grand Duke Alexis and Alexandra Zhukovskaya, was born in November 1871 in Salzburg, Austria. Grand Duke Alexis, of course, was in America at the time of his son's birth, but he made every attempt to provide for the boy and his mother. In January 1872, Alexis requested that Vladimir send money to "you know who" in Salzburg, and nearly a year later, he asked his brother to send a similar sum to Venice. Vladimir honored his brother's wishes and helped him funnel thousands of rubles to Zhukovskaya. Even after Zhukovskaya married a guard's officer in Saxony in November 1875, Alexis still worked to provide for her and their son. That month, the tsar ordered that Zhukovskaya, now known as Baroness von Wohrmann, receive an annual pension for life of 25,000 rubles, in honor of her father's service. In reality, it is clear that Alexis arranged this for entirely different reasons. Earlier that year, in May, the tsar had issued a decree to give Alexis 500,000 rubles, an amount he withdrew from Alexis's share of his eventual inheritance to allow him to give it to Zhukovskaya in the form of an annual pension. In June, the tsar ordered 100,000 rubles in silver to be given to the child, Alexis Alexeevich, to remain intact until he reached the age of twenty-five.[25]

As a child, Alexis Alexeevich was known as Baron Seggiano, but in 1884 an imperial decree ordered that he should be given the name and title Count Alexis Alexeevich Belevski-Zhukovskii. The younger Alexis spent his childhood in Germany, but later he moved back to Russia and served as adjutant to his uncle, Grand Duke Serge. In 1894, he married Maria Petrovna Trubetskaya near Moscow at Ilinskaya, the palace of his Uncle Serge. According to one source, his mother Alexandra attended the wedding and was treated kindly by the members of the royal family. It is not known if Grand Duke Alexis was present or, indeed, how much contact he had with his son in the ensuing years, but some contemporary sources indicate that the elder Alexis publicly accepted his son and made it known that he was to be his heir. It is clear, however, that the other members of the royal family accepted and embraced Alexis Alexeevich and his growing family. The younger Alexis and his wife had four children—Elizaveta, Alexandra, Maria, and Sergei—and all of them had godparents from within the royal family, including Grand Duke Serge (godfather to Sergei) and the Empress Alexandra (godmother to Elizaveta). On visits to Tsarskoe Selo, these children often played with the tsar's daughters. Correspondence from various family members, including the empress herself, to Alexis Alexeevich's wife, Maria, reveals a genuine affection and concern for the health and welfare of the family.[26]

When Grand Duke Alexis died in November 1908, he failed to leave a will, yet he did leave behind a great deal of property, including his homes in St. Petersburg and Paris. In terms of movable property, his home in Paris contained a great deal of expensive furniture and serving pieces, as well as several dozen snuff boxes ornamented with rubies, diamonds, and enamel scenes and portraits. Alexis's property was divided, according to law, between his living brothers, Vladimir and Paul, and his nephew, Grand Duke Michael, the son of his deceased brother, Alexander. In addition, a commission in the spring of 1909 determined that one million rubles would be given to his son, Alexis Alexeevich.[27]

Not much is known about the younger Alexis's life after his father's death. According to one source, he was trained and worked as a biologist. When revolution struck Russia in 1917, Alexis Alexeevich's wife and children fled, first to Odessa, then to Italy and finally near Baden-Baden, Germany. Alexis, however, stayed behind and ultimately became a victim of the new regime, executed in Tbilisi, Georgia, in 1932 or 1933. His descendants reside in various places in the United States and Europe.[28]

———————◆———————

History has not been kind to the Grand Duke Alexis. When he died in 1908, in self-imposed exile in Paris, his name was still closely associated with Russia's disastrous defeat in the Russo-Japanese War, and his reputation as a ladies' man who preferred women to work only further damaged his memory in the annals of history. Contemporaries, and later historians, would label Alexis lazy, incompetent, and indecorous, exemplifying the kind of ineptitude and corruption that undermined the power and integrity of the Romanov Dynasty and led to its demise in 1917. Not only is this assessment an exaggeration and an oversimplification of the problems of the Russian monarchy, but it ignores Alexis's other contributions, particularly his visit to America in 1871–72.

Alexis spent only three months in the United States, and yet his visit has left a lasting mark on American history in a myriad of ways, large and small. In the immediate aftermath of the visit, the grand duke continued to be remembered through gifts he gave while here or those he sent later after returning to Russia. In other cases, proximity to Alexis conferred a certain level of celebrity on those who participated in this memorable episode or on the hotels and performance halls that housed his reception events. As the decades wore on and the visit passed from active recollection to distant memory, the grand duke's tour continued to be remembered through photographs and other types of ephemera, and commemorated in dinners and museum exhibitions. Finally, in several cases, Alexis has taken center stage in local history and mythology.

The legacy of Alexis's visit reaches beyond the realm of popular culture, however. The grand duke's trip to the United States came at a critical moment in the evolution of the Russian-American relationship, at a time when there were many threats to what had long been an unusual, but functioning, friendship. The appearance on American shores of this handsome, young grand duke who seemed so interested in American society, industry, and education did much to generate good will among the American people and to bolster confidence in the future of this complex relationship. In subsequent years, Alexis's visit was recalled fondly and cited as a reason for continued good relations with Russia. Ultimately, the romance of this odd pair of nations would wither and die over a range of insurmountable issues, the final straw being the October Revolution of 1917. But the American interest in Russia, its literature and culture, would survive even that most difficult of diplomatic challenges and continue in various ways throughout the Soviet period.

Alexis's visit holds a unique place in the story of the Russian-American relationship. Both the arrival of the Russian fleet in 1863 and the purchase of Alaska only a few short years later had placed Russia at the forefront of the American public's attention and imagination, but neither of these episodes had allowed the American people to engage with Russia in the same way that Alexis's visit did. In the first instance, while some Americans were able to interact with the Russian sailors and naval officers who visited in 1863, most did not. The men stayed in the cities where they had docked, and the balls and reception activities were limited to those places as well. The press did report on the exotic visitors, of course, but the best most people could hope for was to read about the dinners and dances in the papers. In the case of the Alaska Purchase in 1867, American newspapers published a great deal of information about Russian America, but again, the conversation took place at the highest levels, and the average American could only follow along from afar.

The visit of Alexis is differentiated from these other two highly publicized events by its broad appeal and democratic nature. Alexis traveled through nearly two dozen cities, creating a much larger media frenzy, geographically speaking, than the other Russian-related events of the previous decade. The grand duke's far-reaching itinerary prompted citizens across the country to want to know more about Russia and gave newspapers a reason to publish articles about this distant friend and its royal family. Everywhere Alexis traveled, and even in cities he never saw at all, the press both satisfied and stimulated curiosity about Russia by printing biographies of members of the Russian royal family and lengthy essays on Russian geography, history, climate, and the national traits of its people; many papers also included portraits of Alexis.[29] Meanwhile, some of the nation's illustrated papers such as *Puck, Harper's Weekly,* and *Frank Leslie's Illustrated* printed humorous cartoons about the grand duke and his enthusiastic admirers in America, as well as detailed and beautiful engravings that depicted events in Alexis's tour, Russian political figures, and scenes of

Russian life. Indeed, the *Louisville Courier-Journal* remarked that "the illustrated newspaper which at this time does not have a picture of Alexis will lose at least one hundred thousand subscribers."[30]

The American press acknowledged that the Russian visit had created a surge of interest in Alexis and his homeland. As one Philadelphia paper pointed out, "The visit of the Grand Duke Alexis will at least serve one good end.... It will popularize the history of Russia." A newspaper advertisement for a new publication entitled *A Russian Journey* declared that the arrival of Alexis "lends a special interest to any work that offers both fresh and valid information concerning Russia," while a *New York Herald* editorial concluded, "Russia and the Russians must be an interesting subject to every thinking American."[31] Several books resulted from the visit as well. Immediately after the grand duke's departure, a compilation of newspaper articles about his trip appeared in print under the title, *His Imperial Highness the Grand Duke Alexis in the United States of America During the Winter of 1871–72.* Over the next year, two more books included sections dedicated to Alexis and portions of his tour.[32]

As Alexis traveled across America, there were opportunities in every city for the "common man" to see him. These average Americans could not expect to dine or dance with him, but if they gathered along a parade route, at a train depot, or outside his hotel, they could see him, possibly more than once. They could certainly read about him in their city newspapers, and they might purchase photos or Alexis-themed items from local businesses eager to capitalize on the excitement. All of these possibilities allowed a broad spectrum of Americans to be part of this memorable event. For many who were directly involved with the grand duke's reception in some way, their participation would be remembered in memoirs and obituaries. For others, their brush with royalty was recalled in letters and family history. Ultimately, however, whether a person danced with Alexis, dined with him, or simply caught a glimpse of him passing in his carriage, the manner of the grand duke's visit, with its ambitious itinerary and its many public events, allowed for a broad sense of participation and engagement. It was a chance for individuals of all walks of life to say, "I was there."

The grand duke's visit also left behind many physical reminders that would help to entrench it in the collective memory of those who experienced it. As Alexis traveled through the United States, he gave away both a great deal of money and a substantial number of expensive gifts; in the words of Elizabeth Custer, "The royal purse had no string." He left cash donations for the poor in New York ($5,000) and Boston ($1,500), and while in Chicago he donated money for those who had suffered losses in the fire ($5,000). In New York, it was reported that Alexis gave the proprietors of the Clarendon Hotel the "furniture and fittings" of the apartments he occupied, valued at $20,000. In Philadelphia, he left $200 for the staff of the Continental Hotel; in St. Louis, he left $600 for those who attended him at the Southern Hotel; and in Denver, he left $300 for the employees of the American House. At Annapolis, Alexis gave the Naval Academy a handsome, Russian-made compass so large that it took two men to carry it, and in Milwaukee, Alexis gave the Milwaukee Light Guard an autographed photo of himself. Upon his departure from Mobile, he presented a diamond ring to the local steamer captain. These gifts alone would be worth nearly $750,000 today.[33]

The grand duke was particularly generous at the conclusion of the buffalo hunt. Spotted Tail and his men received red and green blankets and a large bag of silver dollars, and the mercantile firm of Otero and Sellar received a buffalo head, which remained a treasured memento for the firm and its successor, the Gross, Kelly mercantile firm. Later, the head was donated by the Kelly family to the Harvard Club in New York City, where it still resides on permanent display. Similarly, the National Museum of Natural History in Washington, D.C., possesses a buffalo skeleton from the Grand Duke Alexis buffalo hunt, though its precise provenance is unknown.[34] Alexis gave Buffalo Bill Cody several gifts, as well. One was the fur overcoat that he had worn on the hunt, and Cody treasured the coat so much that, when he subsequently wore it to a dance at the Riverside Hotel outside of Chicago, he refused to leave it in the check room, fearing that it would be stolen. He was content only when it was safely locked in the manager's private room.[35] Alexis also gave Cody a set of jewelry, a diamond-encrusted buffalo head stick pin and matching cuff links, which are now part of the collection at the Buffalo Bill Museum and Historical Center in Cody, Wyoming.

Alexis's particular generosity with female performers contributed to the persistent rumors that he had come to America to hunt more than buffalo. Alexis gave expensive bracelets to the burlesque star Lydia Thompson, the soprano Euphrosyne Parepa-Rosa, and the performer Lotta Crabtree. But the grand duke rewarded male performers as well; in St. Louis, he invited the composer and pianist Charles Kunkel to his chamber to perform for him, and in a show of gratitude Alexis gave Kunkel a gold ring with a large emerald surrounded by twelve diamonds valued at $450. In Louisville, Kentucky, Alexis gave the performer J. W. Fuller a beautiful gold ring set with a large topaz surrounded by twelve diamonds.[36]

Even after he had returned home, Alexis ordered gifts to be sent to various individuals and institutions. In the fall of 1873, at the grand duke's request, Admiral Possiet sent a parcel of books to the University of Michigan for placement in the campus library that included over fifty volumes on Russian history and law. Possiet assured the president, "We have all a most agreeable recollection of our tour in the United States, and particularly of the stay we had the pleasure of passing with you in Detroit." In 1874, Alexis sent grape cuttings to the Park of Fruits near St. Louis, as promised, and a collection of books to the Mechanic's Association in Lowell, Massachusetts. Some individuals also received special honors from the Russian government. General John Adams Dix was awarded the Star and Cross of the Military Order of St. Stanislaus by the emperor for his part in the reception of the grand duke.[37] Albert Bierstadt received the same award and, according to one source, Alexander II ordered that one of his paintings be displayed in the Hermitage.[38] In November 1872, Hamilton Fish recorded in his diary that the Russian minister Baron Heinrich Offenberg had inquired about the protocol for the Russian government to grant special decorations to a number of individuals who had played a role in the grand duke's visit.[39]

Alexis also invited several individuals to visit Russia, and some took him up on his offer. The English cornetist Jules Levy spent twenty months in Russia in 1871–73 after an invitation from the grand duke, who had heard him play as a soloist in Jim Fisk's band in New York. It was also reported in several places that, while dining with the New York Yacht Club, Alexis had invited a squadron of the club's best yachts to visit Russia, and the owners of these vessels had planned to make the journey in the immediate future.[40]

The grand duke's visit also left behind a great deal of ephemera—photographs, invitations, menus, and train schedules generated during his stay. As Alexis traveled, he served as a subject for some of the country's top photographers, men like Mathew Brady, Jeremiah Gurney, Eadric Eaton, and James Scholten. Consequently, by the time Alexis departed, there were many photographs of him in existence and, fortunately for historians, many of these are still extant today. The Library of Congress, for example, holds a stereograph of Alexis with a group of dignitaries outside the home of Gustavus Vasa Fox in Lowell, Massachusetts, while the Minneapolis Institute of Arts has a portrait of

Alexis in its Jeremiah Gurney collection. Other photos, including stereoscopic views and *cartes de visite* exist in various other libraries, museums, and historical societies, and a great many are in private hands.[41]

The same can be said for ball and reception invitations, admittance cards or tickets, and train schedules. In each city, reception and ball committees printed special invitations and tickets, and since most of these events were quite large, thousands of these items would have been floating around after the grand duke's visit. Many of these have survived to the present day. Again, some of these are held in libraries, museums, and historical societies—the New York Historical Society, the Milwaukee Historical Society, the Atwater Kent Museum in Philadelphia, the Historical Society of Pennsylvania—but many others are in private collections and periodically appear for sale in public auctions and other places.[42] Train schedules are also hot commodities for collectors. Each leg of Alexis's trip was commemorated with specially printed train schedules, some of them gilded and quite ornate, and many of these are preserved in libraries and similar facilities. Drexel University holds the papers of train manager Frank Thomson, which include seventeen schedules, along with other documents relating to the grand duke's train travel.[43] Many train schedules are held in private collections as well. Finally, there were several widely circulating illustrated newspapers—*Harper's Weekly* (American), *Frank Leslie's Illustrated* (American), *The Graphic* (British), and *Canadian Illustrated News*—that reported on the grand duke's progress through the United States and included beautiful engravings of the grand duke himself and certain memorable moments in his trip, such as the reception aboard the *Mary Powell,* the naval ball in Brooklyn, and the trip to Niagara Falls.

The visit of the "Russian Cub" also generated creative innovations. In many cities along the grand duke's route, special music was composed in honor of the royal visitor. There were, for example, two pieces entitled the "Prince Alexis March," one composed in Philadelphia, the other in New York, as well as a "Grand Duke Alexis Galop" from Brooklyn, a "Prince Alexis Galop" from New York, and "Prince Alexis Waltzes," composed in Philadelphia. There were even several pieces composed after the grand duke's visit had ended, including the "Alexis Grand Russian Polka" and the "Yankee Maiden Love Song by Alexis." Charles Ranhofer, the longtime chef of Delmonico's in New York, created a dish called Lobster Duke Alexis which was a featured item on the menu for at least two decades, and in New Orleans, a local bakery sells a "Russian Cake" that is reported to have originated at the time of Alexis's visit. In Bridgeport, Connecticut, the Ives, Blakeslee, and Williams Company, one of the foremost "mechanical clockwork" toymakers in the world, named one of its toy locomotives the "Grand Duke" to commemorate the 1871 visit.[44]

Alexis left his mark in other ways as well. One small town in Illinois, previously named Alexander, decided to rename itself Alexis in honor of the young visitor. In New York City, bootblacks and newsboys founded their own theater on Baxter Street south of the Five Points intersection, and after Alexis visited there during his time in the city, it became known as "The Grand Duke's Opera House." The name stuck—in his 1874 novel, *Julius the Street Boy,* Horatio Alger had a chapter called "The Grand Duke's Oprea [sic] House."[45] On a more humorous note, quite a few cattlemen decided to name bulls after the grand duke. The herd registries from the period show that, while breeders were often creative in their choice of names, christening new calves with names like "Abe Lincoln," "General Grant," and "General Sheridan," in the fall of 1871 and the first half of 1872, the names "Alexis," "Duke Alexis," and "Grand Duke Alexis" began to appear in noticeable numbers.[46]

Alexis's presence also left its impact in less tangible forms. Those who had interacted with Alexis in some way, either as his hosts or his dance partners, often clung to those memories and resurrected them throughout their lives. Being a part of the grand duke's visit, after all, was something worth remembering and recounting to others. Consequently, a number of people described their encounters with the royal visitor, however brief or distant, in letters, diaries, and memoirs. Even men and women of political and literary fame thought their interaction with the grand duke worthy of note; Louisa May Alcott recalled the ducal ball in Boston in her diary, and both William Lloyd Garrison and Henry Wadsworth Longfellow recorded their meetings with Alexis. Many others also commented on the visit in letters to friends and relatives.[47] Sally Spottiswood Mackin née Britton of St. Louis recalled her encounter with Alexis in her memoir, *A Society Woman on Two Continents,* eschewing all false modesty to note that, not only had Alexis sought her out repeatedly during his first visit to the United States, but had asked for her as well in his subsequent visit in 1877.[48]

The buffalo hunt, not surprisingly, appears in a number of memoirs and recollections. J. J. Dickey, general superintendent of the Western Union Telegraph company in 1871, recounted the hunt in Kansas to a journalist from the *Denver Times* in 1899. The various memoirs and recollections of Buffalo Bill almost all include his version of the Grand Duke Alexis buffalo hunt, and Cody used his brush with Russian royalty to promote himself in other ways as well. In 1880, Cody staged a new drama called "The Prairie Waif," and the poster advertising the show included a small image of a buffalo head with diamond eyes, clearly a reference to the jewelry he had received from the grand duke. Behind the buffalo head is what looks like a medal with the largely obstructed phrase about its presentation to "Bill" by "[Duk]e Alexis."[49]

Contact with the grand duke was also considered sufficiently noteworthy to be mentioned in obituaries. In December 1885, the *New York Times* reported that Mrs. E. Riley, "the woman who a few years ago made herself famous by visiting all the large cities in America looking for the Grand Duke Alexis," had died. When the famous restaurateur Lorenzo Delmonico died in 1881, his lengthy obituary noted Grand Duke Alexis among the famous names he had served. Similarly, when Junius Kingsley, owner of the Continental Hotel in Philadelphia, died in 1890, he was remembered, among other things, for entertaining the Prince of Wales, Dom Pedro, and Grand Duke Alexis. Joseph Sharland, prominent in the music world of Boston, died in 1909, and the *New York Times* deemed his organization of the musical performance for the grand duke important enough to mention in his obituary of only eighteen lines. Other obituaries mentioned an association with Alexis as well.[50]

The grand duke's name was also invoked when one of his many fair dancing partners got married. In 1875, the wedding announcement of Ida Demorest described her as one "whom the Grand Duke Alexis considered the handsomest woman in the United States." The following year, when Mollie Morton married, the newspaper called her "the Louisville belle with whom the Grand Duke Alexis fell so madly in love." There were other mentions such as these in subsequent years. As late as 1905, an article in the *New York Times* on Sally Spottiswood Mackin's recent engagement recalled her time on the dance floor with Alexis.[51] Even animals were remembered for their connection with the famous Russian visitor. In October 1887, when a valuable stallion died in Baltimore, the *Times* noted that the horse had been purchased from the stables of the Grand Duke Alexis in Russia, and even as late as 1914, six years after the grand duke's death, a story in the *New York Tribune* about the Westminster Kennel Club show noted that one of the winners was a Russian wolfhound, "straight from the hunting pack of Grand Duke Alexis." In fact, when the Westminster Kennel Club held its first show in 1877, two of the winners, staghounds named Stanley and Madgie, had been gifts from Alexis to Custer.[52]

Finally, in an early version of celebrity endorsement, hotels and other entertainment facilities recalled their connection to the young Russian visitor to attract new customers. Hotels used the grand duke's stay as a point of pride in advertising to demonstrate the superior quality of their accommodations and services. The Spencer House at Niagara Falls, for example, mentioned the grand duke's stay in its travelers' guides and promotional materials.[53] Similarly, even over a century later, when New York's Clarendon Hotel was described in publications of various sorts, Alexis was almost always mentioned.[54] When such buildings were later destroyed, by fire or demolition, newspapers usually mentioned if the grand duke had danced, dined, or slept there. After the historic Revere House in Boston succumbed to flames in early 1912, and when the Plankinton House in Milwaukee was slated for demolition in 1913, the newspapers noted their long histories and one of their most famous guests, Grand Duke Alexis.[55] Similarly, when the steamboat *Mary Powell* was retired in 1913, surpassed by newer, larger ships, her illustrious history as the boat that bore a grand duke was recalled with great sentiment.[56]

This popular element of the grand duke's visit—its place in the collective memory—stimulated a growing interest in Russia and news about Russia. In the wake of the grand duke's tour of the United States, and in the two decades following his departure, there was an increase in the number of publications specifically related to Russia. A quick survey of American newspapers during the period in question reveals that the number of articles dedicated to Russia grew in some cases by as much as 300 percent between 1860 and 1880.[57] George Kennan (the elder) facilitated this growth as he began to write for popular magazines, as did Eugene Schuyler who, in addition to general articles about Russia, published a translation of Leo Tolstoy's *The Cossacks* in 1878, the first translation of Tolstoy to appear in North America. At the same time, many American travelers wrote of their experiences in Russia, and in 1878, *Harper's Weekly* commissioned a travel guide for "Europe and the East" that dedicated a section to Russia.[58]

Alexis's visit and the interest in Russia it inspired also led to more serious and philosophical discussions. The grand duke's visit, then, has an important place in the general narrative of American perceptions about itself and Russia. Historian David Engerman has demonstrated that American writings on Russia, and later, the Soviet Union, were shaped by several ideas, including the belief that every nation had its own unique character. Until the 1920s, Americans writing about Russia described that enormous nation as apathetic and lethargic, characteristics often associated with Asian culture. Both admirers and critics believed that these negative traits limited Russia's ability to change and modernize. Others, however, argued that, despite the deep-rooted nature of the Russian character, the possibility of change was alive under the right circumstances. David Foglesong has examined America's desire to reform Russia in his fascinating study, *The American Mission and the "Evil Empire."*[59]

Alexis's visit prompted some of the first discussions about Russia's ability to improve itself and America's opportunity to serve as a model. In this dialogue it is clear that, for many Americans, Russia was both "the other" and "like us." Newspapers joked about Russian names that were difficult to pronounce and frequently remarked that Alexis looked like any handsome young man of good culture and education (implying, it would seem, that he was expected to look different because he was Russian). Alexis's own comment that people stared at him like a monkey in a zoo indicates he was aware of his "otherness" in American eyes. At the same time, much was made of Russia's recent abolition of serfdom and its parallel to the emancipation of slaves in America, and the names of Lincoln and Alexander II were frequently invoked in the same breath. The *Cleveland Daily Plain Dealer,* for example, referred to the Russians as "that people which, in many respects, especially energy and enterprise, resembles the people of the United States." The *Pittsburgh Gazette,* in an article entitled "Progress in Russia," praised Russian railroad development and emphasized that Alexander II was not an "unbending autocrat," but rather an educated, energetic, and capable leader. Though some questioned the purpose, sincerity, and depth of this friendship and denounced "this absurd love-making, which can never result in a match," the bulk of American opinion-makers focused on the positive elements of the friendship, on the similarities rather than on the differences.[60]

There was also the sense, in speeches and newspaper articles, that America had much to show the young Russian, and that the Russian nation might learn from America's example. The *Missouri Republican* explained that the grand duke's visit was "one of inquiry and investigation—to learn the customs of our people and note the wonderful development of our country, and the working of our institutions." This is an early example of an attitude toward Russia that many Americans would adopt over the coming years, that of benevolent guid-ance. Throughout the Russian visit of 1871–72, politicians and newspapermen noted the possibility that Russia could learn from the United States. In his speech at the Revere House banquet in Boston, for example, George Hillard made a reference to what would become a common theme in late-nineteenth-century Russian-American relations: "Surely, if we think the institutions of Rus-sia are not democratic enough, how can we better bring about the improvement we desire than by causing a member of the imperial family to think kindly of a country which has made such splendid progress under democratic institu-tions?" The *Milwaukee Sentinel* expressed a similar sentiment later that month, urging Alexis's American hosts to show him factories and intelligent workers, schools and teachers, publishing houses and the Patent Office. There are many additional examples of this notion.[61]

The grand duke's visit was not the only source of American exposure to Russia, of course. There were Russians who had come to the United States after the Civil War, traveling and, in some cases, establishing Russian communities in a number of American cities. Russians had also moved from Alaska to the West Coast after 1867, and in the decade after Alexis's visit nearly one thousand Russian Mennonite families emigrated to the United States, dismayed by their declining status back home. In the 1880s, Russian Jews began to arrive in America as well, fleeing intensifying anti-Semitism and violent pogroms. Americans also could learn about Russian life and Russian national identity through the imperial government's participation in the 1876 Centennial Ex-hibition in Philadelphia, where objects in the "Russian style" predominated, incorporating historical themes and peasant motifs. In the aftermath of that exhibition, several American firms, such as Tiffany and Company, marketed Russian decorative items in the United States, such as bronzes, silvers, enamels, and porcelains.[62] By this point, Russian literature had also begun to appear in American bookstores, largely due to the efforts of Isabel Hapgood, an educated Bostonian who became "one of Victorian America's most prolific Russophiles." Hapgood's championing of Russian literature, particularly Tolstoy, contributed to a surge of American interest in Russian authors. Indeed, Americans not only read Tolstoy, but also wrote to him and visited him. Subsequently, Hapgood would also be instrumental in the establishment of Russian studies programs at American universities; both Harvard and the University of Chicago would hire scholars with a focus on Russia in the 1890s.[63]

There were, of course, other events that kept Russia in the American line of vision. The Russo-Turkish War of 1877–78 garnered much attention in the American press, and the viewpoint was, for the most part, sympathetic to Russia and its desire to protect fellow Christians.[64] Another major event was the Russian famine of 1891–92. Americans became aware of the famine soon after it began and, by November 1891, there were already efforts in the United States to offer assistance, both private endeavors and others led by Clara Barton of the American Red Cross. In the end, five American vessels traveled to Russia in the spring of 1892 carrying flour, cornmeal, and grain.[65] Though some Americans complained about the passivity, fatalism, and inertia of Russians, in the end the famine also resurrected that sentiment repeated so often during Alexis's visit, that Russia and America were friends. The *New York Times* emphasized that American generosity had "stimulated a feeling between the two nations which will last so long as they both endure." As one historian wrote, "In 1892, we still clung to this cherished myth of traditional friendship despite a growing antipathy to autocracy and all it stood for in our eyes."[66]

This may, however, have been the last gasp in the Russian-American romance, and the way that Americans reacted to the famine demonstrates that public opinion was changing about Russia and Russian autocracy. While under Alexander II, there was mutual interest and mutual admiration—expressions of gratitude (for Russia's support during the Civil War); congratulations (for Alexander's escape from an assassination attempt); and condolences (on Lincoln's assassination)—in subsequent years, the situation would change dramatically. It was more difficult to find common ground with the more repressive government of Alexander III. This allowed for the less generous assessments of Russia to drown out those that had focused on similarities and Russia's ability to change.[67] Now, American public opinion viewed Russia not as a friend, but as a repressive state.

In the years between 1881 and 1905, American activists embarked upon a crusade to free Russia from the religious persecution and political oppression of the tsarist empire. Russia's famine of 1891–92 had already caused many Americans to assess the Russian government, if not the Russian people, more harshly. Another issue that dampened the ardor of the United States for Russia was the latter nation's treatment of its Jewish population. This problem already had been a subject of American concern in 1869–71, and it had even been suggested that Alexis might be addressed about the problem during his visit. Finally, in 1903, after the violent pogrom at Kishenev, Ukraine, the United States government under Theodore Roosevelt decided that it could no longer stand by, and it sent a petition signed by prominent citizens from around the country to Nicholas II; the tsar refused to accept it. According to Russian officials, "the Emperor whose will is the sole law of this land had no need of information from outside sources as to what is taking place within his dominions."[68]

There would certainly continue to be interaction between the two nations, and even interest and admiration by certain groups in the years before and after the Revolution of 1917. Many Russian Marxists, including Vladimir Lenin, admired America's industrial capabilities and technology, and embraced the industrial models of Frederick Winslow Taylor and Henry Ford. Early Soviet leaders also praised American initiative and efficiency, and urged Russians to "work like an American."[69] At the same time, Soviet promises of a communist utopia appealed to some Americans who had become disenchanted with the greed and ruthlessness of capitalism. Not only did American communism thrive during this period (1920s–30s) but a number of Americans went to Russia to experience Soviet Communism firsthand. Communism and life in the Soviet Union were particularly attractive to African Americans who sought an escape from racism and discrimination in the United States. A number of African Americans traveled to the Soviet Union during this period, including the poet Langston Hughes.[70] There was also a great appreciation for Russian art, music, and ballet in America, as well as a fruitful interaction in the theater world. Russian opera singers and composers came to the United States to perform and, in some cases, remained for years.[71] Russian actors also came to the United States in touring troupes or with the hope of finding fortune in Hollywood, and many American actors embraced the method-acting school of Constantin Stanislavki.[72]

On political and diplomatic levels, however, there was no love lost between the two nations in the years after the October Revolution, and if there were moments of détente and cooperation, these moments were driven largely by self-interest, ulterior motives, and need, not the feeling of mutual good will that had been palpable in the 1860s and 1870s. This shift to a more negative view of Russia makes Alexis's visit important for one other reason. Though no one would know it then, the era between the end of the Civil War and the

226 ALEXIS IN AMERICA

beginning of the more repressive era that followed the assassination of Alexander II in 1881 was the heyday of Russian-American diplomatic relations. The grand duke's visit was the last time Russia and America viewed one another as friends, and the success and popular appeal of that meeting of two very different peoples would live on in popular memory and diplomatic nostalgia.

Despite the cooling of diplomatic relations after the Russian Revolution and the later tensions of the Cold War, the visit of Grand Duke Alexis has continued to be remembered, celebrated, and commemorated in a variety of ways. For example, the Fair Grounds in New Orleans hosted a horse race in 1924 called the "Grand Duke Alexis Handicap." Eleven years later, the Association of Former Imperial Russian Naval Officers in New York City held a charity ball modeled on the one given to Alexis in New York sixty-four years earlier. In 1967, supporters of the Waldemar Medical Research Foundation in New York City held a Mardi Gras ball to raise money for cancer and leukemia research, and the highlight of the evening was a tableau based on the visit of Alexis to New Orleans. In Memphis, the Peabody Hotel hosted a special dinner in 1998 to welcome Prince Nikita Romanov, great nephew of the last Russian emperor, Nicholas II. Organizers decided that the perfect way to honor their special guest was to recreate the eleven-course meal prepared for Alexis in 1872.[73]

The Russian visit has also been commemorated by museum exhibits. In 1996, an exhibition entitled "Jewels of the Romanovs," designed to commemorate the 125th anniversary of the first state visit by a member of the Russian imperial family, began at the Corcoran Gallery of Art in Washington, D.C., traveling to Houston, San Diego, Memphis, and Brooklyn. The installation displayed over two hundred items, including jewels, paintings, court gowns, ecclesiastical garments and objects, and several dozen items pertaining to Alexis's visit. These items included photographs of the grand duke and his party, as well as telegrams and letters he sent to his parents during his travels. The exhibition catalog also contained an introductory essay that dedicated several pages to the grand duke's visit and its significance in the larger story of Russian-American relations. In 2001, the Captain Frederick Pabst Mansion in Milwaukee, Wisconsin, staged an exhibition entitled "At the Grand Duke's Table," displaying a cup and saucer from the Grand Duke Alexis service made at the Imperial Porcelain Factory in St. Petersburg, along with a portrait of Alexis, a brief biography, and an overview of his trip to the United States. Finally, in 2008–9, the American-Russian Cultural Cooperation Foundation presented an exhibit, "The Tsar and the President: Alexander II and Abraham Lincoln, Liberator and Emancipator," that appeared in several states. The exhibit itself contained several items related to Alexis's American visit, and the accompanying catalog dedicated a chapter to it as well.[74]

The visit of the grand duke was also referenced during the Cold War in newspaper and magazine articles in discussions of the halcyon days when Russia was America's friend and supporter. In August 1945, as World War Two drew to a close and the fragile alliance between the Soviet Union and the United States ceased to be a necessity, *Life* magazine published an article on the future of American-Soviet relations, examining the history of the Russian-American friendship and including, among other images, an engraving of the grand duke's ball in Brooklyn. In that significant year and in subsequent years, others would also reference the grand duke's visit in discussing the current state of affairs. In January 1949, the *Louisville Times* recalled Alexis's time in that city with the opening observation, "Today when the machinations of the Politburo make for uneasy slumber, and U.S.-Soviet relations are strained, to put it mildly, it is hard to imagine Louisville turning over the keys of the city to a young traveler from Russia." In the 1950s, a number of other publications highlighted the Russia visit as well.[75]

———————◆———————

Two episodes of the grand duke's visit in particular have received the greatest amount of attention in popular literature—his participation in the buffalo hunt and his presence at Mardi Gras. The dramatic and exciting hunt on the snowy plains of Nebraska and Kansas has been repeated in memoirs, newspapers, and books, often with exaggeration and errors. It is not difficult to imagine why this should be true. The story embodies many of the people and elements that fascinate modern Americans about this period of American history, and reaches beyond the narrow confines of academics and specialists. The images of the Wild West capture the imagination, as do the dashing and memorable figures of Buffalo Bill and Custer. Articles about the hunt have appeared in a wide variety of popular publications, including *The American West, The American Rifleman,* and *Field and Stream.* Many other publications mention the Russian buffalo hunt in other contexts, ranging from the history of the West to the history of guns or hunting, and virtually every book about Custer, Sheridan, or

Cody makes some reference to this memorable event.[76] There have also been several self-published accounts by amateur historians.

The grand duke's hunting expedition has also worked its way into American popular culture. In his novel *Hickok and Cody,* Matt Braun uses the Russian buffalo hunt as the opening for a murder mystery in which those two legendary frontiersmen become the heroes who rescue a pair of kidnapped orphans. The grand duke's time in America's Wild West has been remembered in television and movies as well. A television series called *Colt .45* that aired between 1957 and 1960 featured an episode in November 1959 called "A Legend of Buffalo Bill" that incorporated the Russian royal visit. Similarly, the 1994 movie *Maverick* starring Mel Gibson and Jodie Foster features a Russian visitor to the American West who, though not identified as Grand Duke Alexis, is clearly inspired by that actual historical figure.[77]

The most elaborate celebration of the grand duke's visit has taken place in Hayes Center, Nebraska, a tiny town of two hundred about five hours from the nearest major airport. There on a stretch of land near a small lake, history buffs and local enthusiasts gathered for ten years to recall and commemorate the royal buffalo hunt in an annual three-day event known as the Grand Duke Alexis Rendezvous. Between 1999 and 2010, the local chapter of the Lion's Club hosted this event, funding it through donations, raffles, and the sale of food on-site. A local rancher donated a buffalo each year, which became the main dish on the menu, served in various ways, from burgers to stew.

The highlight and centerpiece of the Grand Duke Alexis Rendezvous, however, were the presentations of the living historians. Dressed in handmade costumes based on careful historical research, the men who played the roles of Alexis, Buffalo Bill, Custer, and Spotted Tail stood before the crowd and told their slightly different versions of the buffalo hunt and shared humorous stories about one another. The reenactors were joined by black-powder shooters and other enthusiasts in period costumes, most of whom set up tents and spent the weekend living like settlers on the frontier. Some of the tents, such as that of the grand duke, were loosely based on the descriptions of the actual accommodations at the hunt of 1872, while others were just imaginative renderings of what the campsite tents might have looked like. In addition, buses ran regularly to a monument that marks the location of the original campsite, allowing visitors to stand on the same ground once walked by the grand duke and his famous guides.

Though little physical evidence remains of the hunt, a team of archaeologists has worked at the hunt campsite, conducting a surface excavation for artifacts and attempting to map the precise location of the various tents. The team has found clasps, nails, and remnants of champagne bottles. These archaeologists have poignantly observed that, while the other places that Alexis visited have changed dramatically over the years, with new buildings taking the place of old and streets becoming wide and busy with cars, "the site and landscape on which Camp Alexis resides may be the only tangible place where the grand duke, Sheridan, Custer, Cody and others once trod that can be identified with certainty."[78] The authenticity of the experience in Hayes Center surely accounts for the enthusiasm so many felt, and continue to feel, for this historic site. In fact, the Lion's Club only reluctantly decided to disband the rendezvous in 2011, hampered by the club's small and aging membership. Fortunately, in 2014 the Lincoln County Historical Museum initiated plans to revive the event.

In the case of Mardi Gras, the commemoration of Alexis's visit has been as much about misremembering as remembering, but has been more consistent and long-lasting. Grand Duke Alexis's presence during the carnival festivities of February 1872 has become a staple of the historical literature of Mardi Gras. Most histories of Mardi Gras make some mention of Alexis, and many credit his visit as the inspiration for the birth of Rex, the mythical monarch who issued edicts creating the organization known as the Krewe of Rex and the tradition of the daytime Mardi Gras parade.[79] Others go even further, arguing that Alexis traveled to the Crescent City in pursuit of Lydia Thompson, and that it was his fascination with her which prompted Rex to play, and later adopt as its theme song, one of her musical pieces, "If Ever I Cease to Love."[80] The lack of any evidence to support this legend has done nothing to hinder its dissemination; attempts by Mardi Gras writers and others to dispel the myth have had limited impact on the popular literature.[81] The strength and perpetuation of this myth is testimony to the power and influence of public memory on written history. Much like the story of George Washington and the cherry tree in American history, the idea of a lovesick Russian prince pursuing a burlesque performer across America has so firmly implanted itself in Mardi Gras history that its extraction may be impossible. In fact, Alexis has been so tightly entwined in Mardi Gras history that several carnival krewes have been named after him.

The central role of Alexis in Mardi Gras history has been tied to two separate, but connected, questions about the carnival events of February 1872—what was the inspiration for the creation of the Krewe of Rex, and what prompted that group of men to choose "If Ever I Cease to Love" as the theme song for their new organization? Although the edicts that Rex published in local newspapers made no specific mention of Alexis, much of the secondary literature on Mardi Gras has concluded that the grand duke's visit prompted the appearance of Rex in February 1872.[82] In fact, the origins of Rex are far more complicated.

On the most basic level, the wealthy white men who founded Rex wanted to bring some sense of order, as well as an element of privilege and exclusivity, to a celebration that had by some accounts grown increasingly disorderly in previous years. There is also strong evidence that order for the sake of promoting tourism may have been a consideration. Invented traditions often emerge when a society undergoes a rapid transformation that weakens or destroys the social patterns for which older traditions had been created. In a time of social, political, and racial upheaval, when the primacy of the elite was perceived to be under threat, it hardly seems surprising that these men chose to create a new tradition which emphasized social preference. In fact, racial, social, and religious discrimination became standard features of the oldest Mardi Gras krewes, and because these groups tended to admit only family members and close friends to their ranks, they necessarily excluded all those who could not afford to socialize with them.[83]

The creation of Rex can also be associated with Reconstruction and the racial and political tensions of the post–Civil War era, which were especially acute in New Orleans. Though Henry Clay Warmoth had been a powerful governor, by 1870 his power was fading and his Republican Party was split, which led to increasing disorder, violence, and corruption within the legislature, the misuse of both federal troops and local police by governing officials, and, ultimately, a disputed gubernatorial election. These conflicts caught the notice of the northern newspapers, which reported on the political chaos in Louisiana with harsh and condescending language about "the decay of New Orleans."[84]

In the midst of this chaos, it can easily be understood why certain individuals would have sought to improve the image of Louisiana and New Orleans. The visit of Russian royalty during Mardi Gras served as the perfect opportunity to make a variety of statements about New Orleans, Louisiana, and the South.[85] Rex's organizers understood that, apart from Mobile, New Orleans was unique in its tradition of Mardi Gras, and thus this festival offered a rare opportunity for the Crescent City to distinguish itself, attracting positive journalistic attention and delivering a message of southern pride and self-confidence to the North. Local papers also repeatedly linked the presence of the grand duke with Mardi Gras, calling it a "double event" and a "two-edged sword" which offered a more substantial reason for celebration and an enticement to visitors. In all of these articles there is a distinct tone of pride, often aimed directly at the North. "Mardi Gras is a festival with which our brethren of more Northern climes have little or no acquaintance," wrote the *Daily Picayune.* Indeed, when the New York *Herald* called for the young men of that city to conceive of something that might eclipse New Orleans's Mardi Gras celebration, the *Picayune* responded confidently, "It cannot be done. New Orleans is the only city on the continent that can reach perfection in this elegant and classical pageant."[86] None of this, however, proves that Alexis's visit was the inspiration for Rex.

Nor is there any truth behind the persistent story of Alexis, Lydia Thompson, and her famous song, "If Ever I Cease to Love." First, Alexis was not in love with Thompson. Though his American hosts may not have known it, Alexis was still pining for Alexandra Zhukovskaya, as his own letters and those of his family members make clear. The American press fabricated the infatuation with Thompson to sell papers. As for the song, it came from Thompson's burlesque musical *Bluebeard* and was enormously popular in the United States and abroad long before either Alexis or Lydia set foot in the city. Indeed, all over the country, many people had already found the song to be amusing and easy to adapt for other purposes. In mid-November, Waggener's clothing emporium of Memphis used the song to promote its fine selection: "May I never get a suit I' full, From Wag'ner, which is beautiful, If ever I cease to love!" A few days later, a Cleveland newspaper, in writing about the friendship between Russia and the United States, declared, "we hope that Alexis may have the happiest kind of a time; and that the United States may never 'cease to love' Russia."[87] It is far more plausible that the founders of Rex selected this song because of its general popularity than its specific connection to Alexis and his rumored fascination with Thompson. Nonetheless, the fabricated bond between Alexis, Lydia, and the theme song of Rex has persisted for over a century and shows no signs of weakening.

Alexis continues to be remembered in New Orleans in one other way, through the organization known as the Krewe of Alexis. There has actually been more than one Krewe of Alexis, the first operating between 1924 and 1928. Dedicated to the memory of Alexis, the first ball's program declared, "The late Grand Duke Alexis Alexandrovitch of the imperial house of Romanoff was a gai oiseau—and that's us. He was a bachelor, we not, but . . . it's why we admire him." The reigning officials of the ball bore the titles of "Duke Alexis," "Tzaritza," and "Tzarevnas," but the ball itself did not always have a Russian theme. When this organization disbanded, it would be some fifty years before another one would emerge to take its place. Also named the Krewe of Alexis, the new organization emerged in 1973 and followed in the footsteps of its predecessor with a queen, now called the "Tsarina," and "Grand Duchesses." Each year, the organization chooses a Russian theme for its ball—"At the Court of Ivan the Great, 1472," "Hall of St. Vladimir," "A Russian Fairy Tale," and "St. Petersburg, The Winter Palace, 1903"—and members of the organization dress in costumes to coordinate with the theme. Finally, the krewe favor that is given to special guests each year incorporates the Romanov double-headed eagle; in 2012, for example, the ball favor was a set of wine glasses etched with the Romanov coat of arms and the words, "Alexis 2012."[88]

—————————◆—————————

The grand duke could never have imagined in 1871–72 that his short visit would have such a lasting place in American history and popular memory and earn him a permanent place alongside some of America's most treasured folk heroes and traditions. Above all, that curious episode when Grand Duke Alexis, the product of centuries of autocracy, and Buffalo Bill, the frontiersman and rugged individualist par excellence, rode the western plains together gave birth to a memorable image that would capture the American imagination, and his participation in Mardi Gras guaranteed that his visit would never be forgotten. Later, this pleasant image of a Russian grand duke comfortably interacting with American citizens would be co-opted by those who wished to recall or recreate that period when Russia and America were friends. Even now, in certain circles, the memory of Alexis and his remarkable visit lives on.

NOTES

INTRODUCTION: THE EAGLE, TODAY, NESTLES CLOSE TO THE BEAR

1. William Seward to Henry Clay, February 27, 1865, and July 2, 1867, Hamilton Fish to Andrew Curtin, March 22, 1870, and to Andrew Curtin, June 9, 1871, all in Diplomatic Instructions of the Department of State (DIDS), National Archives and Records Administration, Washington, DC (NARA), Record Group 59, M 77, roll 137; Andrew Curtin to Hamilton Fish, June 11, 1871, and George Pomutz to Hamilton Fish, September 10, 1871, with attachments, Despatches from U.S. Ministers to Russia, 1808–1906 (DUSM), NARA, M 35, roll 23; *Philadelphia Inquirer,* August 23, 1871.

2. Catacazy to Gorchakov, 9–21 March 1871, f. 133, op. 470, d. 123 (1871) and Catacazy to Gorchakov, 2–14 July 1871, f. 133, op. 470, d. 123 (1871), Arkhiv Vneshnei Politiki Rossiiskoi Imperii (AVPRI) (Archive of Foreign Policy of the Russian Empire), Moscow, as cited in Norman Saul, *Concord and Conflict: The United States and Russia, 1867–1914* (Lawrence: University Press of Kansas, 1996), 55; Diary of Possiet, Rossiskii Gosudarstvennyi Arkhiv Voenno-Morskogo Flota (RGA VMF) (Russian State Naval Archive), f. 1247, op. 1, d. 41, ll. 13.

3. Gordon Hendricks, *Albert Bierstadt: Painter of the American West* (New York: Harry N. Abrams, Inc., 1974), 206–8; *New York Times,* July 2, 1871.

4. *New Orleans Daily Picayune,* January 25, 1872; *New Orleans Republican,* January 10, 1872; *New Orleans Times,* January 11, 1872; *New Orleans Bee,* January 11, 1872; *Journal of the Select Council of the City of Philadelphia: From July 1, 1871, to January 1, 1872* (Philadelphia: E. C. Markley & Son, 1872), 212, 239–40, 394; *Journal of the Common Council of the City of Philadelphia. For the Year 1871* (Philadelphia: King & Baird, 1871), vol. 2: 250–52, 263–64, 282–85, 333.

5. *New York Herald,* October 8, 1871.

6. *The Papers of Hamilton Fish, Diaries, 1869–76,* reel 1 (vol. 1), January 26, 1870, and reel 1 (vol. 2), April 6, 1871, Microfilmed from manuscript collection in the Library of Congress, Manuscript Division, MSS 17, 634; William S. McFeely, *Grant: A Biography* (New York: W. W. Norton & Co., 1981), 335.

7. *Brooklyn Daily Eagle,* September 2, 1868; October 23, 1871. *Kansas Daily Commonwealth,* January 21, 1872. *Cleveland Daily Plain Dealer,* November 23, 1871. This rumor appeared in countless articles; *Memphis Daily Appeal,* November 24, 1871.

8. Alan Trachtenberg, *The Incorporation of America: Culture and Society in the Gilded Age* (New York: Hill and Wang, 1982), 5–8, 73–81; Sean Dennis Cashman, *America in the Gilded Age: From the*

Death of Lincoln to the Rise of Theodore Roosevelt, 3rd ed. (New York: New York University Press, 1993), 23–25, 135–50.

9. Marc Pachter and Frances Wein, *Abroad in America: Visitors to the New Nation, 1776–1914* (Reading, MA: Addison-Wesley Publishing Co., 1976), 82–91, 124–33; John Oliver, *Louis Kossuth's Visit to Pittsburgh, 1852* (Pittsburgh: University of Pittsburgh, 1928), 3–21; Noble Frankland, *Witness of a Century: The Life and times of Prince Arthur Duke of Connaught, 1850–1942* (London: Shepheard-Walwyn, 1993), 34–39.

10. Anne C. Loveland, *Emblem of Liberty: The Image of Lafayette in the American Mind* (Baton Rouge: Louisiana State University Press, 1971), 4–5, 26, 38–40, 51–53; Stephanie Kermes, *Creating an American Identity: New England, 1789–1825* (New York: Palgrave Macmillan, 2008), 117–31.

11. Loveland, *Emblem of Liberty,* 35–38, 52–53, 75, 99; Kermes, *Creating an American Identity,* 117–31.

12. *Milwaukee Sentinel,* January 5, 1872.

1. BORN IN THE SHADOW OF AN IMPERIAL CROWN

1. Zoia Iosifovna Beliakova, *Velikii kniaz' Aleksei Aleksandrovich: za I protiv* (St. Petersburg: Logos, 2004), 15–16; I. Starkovskii, *Ego Imperatorskoe Vysochestvo Velikii Kniaz' Aleksei Aleksandrovicha shef' Leib-Gvardii Moskovskogo Polka* (St. Petersburg, 1900), 5–9.

2. Beliakova, *Velikii kniaz' Aleksei Aleksandrovich,* 18–19; Starkovskii, *Ego Imperatorskoe,* 9–11.

3. Beliakova, *Velikii kniaz' Aleksei Aleksandrovich,* 23–31; childhood letters of Grand Duke Alexis, Gosudarstvennyi Arkhiv Rossisskaia Federatsiia (GARF) (State Archive of the Russian Federation), Moscow, Russia, f. 704, op. 1, d. 5, str. 3–4.

4. Beliakova, *Velikii kniaz' Aleksei Aleksandrovich,* 23, 32.

5. Ibid., 47–48; schedule of studies for Alexis and brothers, GARF, f. 704, op. 1, d. 9.

6. Letters from Alexander II to Alexis, July 6, 1860; September 22, 1861; December 9, 1862; October 17, 1863; September 26, 1864; and June 8, 1866, GARF, f. 681, op. 1, d. 17, str. 4–5, 12–13, 16–17 ob., 18–19 ob., 20–21, 28–29 ob. Beliakova, *Velikii kniaz' Aleksei Aleksandrovich,* 48, 54–55, 59–60, 66; Richard S. Wortman, *Scenarios of Power: Myth and Ceremony in Russian Monarchy* (Princeton, NJ: Princeton University Press, 1995), vol. 1: 345–50.

7. Starkovskii, *Ego Imperatorskoe,* 8, 19; GARF, f. 641, op. 1, d. 18; Beliakova, *Velikii kniaz' Aleksei Aleksandrovich,* 13–14, 17, 57, 74–75; *Puteshestvie velikogo kniazia Alekseia Aleksandrovicha* (St. Petersburg: Oshchestvennaia Pol'za, 1868), 3–13; *Russkie Vedomosti,* June 13, June 17, June 20, 1867.

8. Beliakova, *Velikii kniaz' Aleksei Aleksandrovich,* 77; *Harper's Weekly,* September 30, 1871.

9. Starkovskii, *Ego Imperatorskoe,* 20–21; Alexander Mikhailovich, Grand Duke of Russia, *Once a Grand Duke* (New York: Farrar & Rinehart, 1932), 139.

10. *London Daily News,* March 10, 1869.

11. Letter of Nicholas to Alexis, January 2, 1865, GARF, f. 681, op. 1, d. 38, str. 9–12; Beliakova, *Velikii kniaz' Aleksei Aleksandrovich,* 69; I. V. Zimin, "Bolezn's I smert' tsarevich Nikolaia Aleksandrovicha," *Voprosy istorii* 9 (2001), 140–47.

12. Beliakova, *Velikii kniaz' Aleksei Aleksandrovich,* 69–72, 86–87.

13. Wortman, *Scenarios of Power,* vol. 1: 357; Beliakova, *Velikii kniaz' Aleksei Aleksandrovich,* 78–80.

14. Joseph Wieczynski and George N. Rhyne, eds., *Modern Encyclopedia of Russian and Soviet History* (Gulf Breeze, FL: Academic International Press, 1987), vol. 46: 67–70; Beliakova, *Velikii kniaz' Aleksei Aleksandrovich,* 85; Diary of Grand Duke Alexis, Fond of Nikolai Borisovich Yusupov, Rossiiskaia Gosudarstvennaia Biblioteka (RGB) (Russian National Library), f. 890, op. 1, d. 83, ll. 83–85.

15. Diary of Alexis, RGB, f. 890, op. 1, d. 83, ll. 184–234.

16. Journal of Alexis, GARF, f. 681, op. 1, d. 1, ll. 3–3 ob., 8, 11.

17. Ibid., ll. 14 ob.

18. Beliakova, *Velikii kniaz' Aleksei Aleksandrovich,* 92–93; interview with Elizabeth Sverbeyeff Byron, great-great-granddaughter of Alexis, New York, May 4, 2011. See also, for example, *Chicago Tribune,* January 7, 1894; *New York Tribune,* September 29, 1901; *Washington Post,* December 31, 1908.

19. *Kansas State Record,* December 20, 1871; *Appleton's,* December 30, 1871; *Birmingham Daily Post,* August 29, 1871; *Brooklyn Daily Eagle,* September 20, 1870; *Brooklyn Daily Eagle,* July 22, 1871; *Cleveland Daily Leader,* March 8, 1872; *Buffalo Commercial Advertiser,* November 2, 1871.

20. Beliakova, *Velikii kniaz' Aleksei Aleksandrovich,* 72, 85–92. On the story of Nikolai Nikolaevich and Chislova, see Greg King, "Grand Duke Nicholas Nikolaievich (1831–1891)," in *The Grand Dukes: Sons and Grandsons of Russia's Tsars since Paul I,* ed. Arturo E. Beéche (East Richmond Heights, CA: Europhistory.com, 2010), vol. 1: 71.

21. Beliakova, *Velikii kniaz' Aleksei Aleksandrovich,* 72, 85–92; Ioann Rozhdestvenskii to Alexis, October 18, 1871, GARF, f. 681, op. 1, d. 63, ll. 1–4.

22. Sally Britton Spottiswood Mackin, *A Society Woman on Two Continents* (New York: Continental Publishing Co., 1897), 37–43; Alexis to Vladimir, September 1, 1872, GARF, f. 652, op. 1, d. 385, ll. 20 ob.

2. GOD BLESS THE EMPIRE THAT LOVES THE GREAT UNION

1. I am enormously grateful for Dr. Norman Saul's two-volume history of Russian-American relations. It is thorough, detailed, and well researched. This chapter draws much material from it, particularly the first volume. See Saul, *Concord and Conflict,* and *Distant Friends: The United States and Russia, 1763–1867* (Lawrence: University Press of Kansas, 1991). Other sources on the Russian-American relationship are N. N. Bolkhovitinov, *The Beginnings of Russian-American Relations, 1775–1815* (Cambridge, MA: Harvard University Press, 1975), and N. N. Bolkhovitinov, *Russko-amerikanskie otnosheniia: 1815–1832* (Moscow: Nauka, 1975).

2. Saul, *Distant Friends,* 3–18. See also, David M. Griffiths, "Nikita Panin, Russian Diplomacy and the American Revolution," *Slavic Review* 28, no. 1 (March 1969): 1–24, and N. N. Bolkhovitinov, *Russia and the American Revolution* (Tallahassee: Diplomatic Press, 1976) and *The Beginnings of Russian-American Relations,* 1–78.

3. Saul, *Distant Friends,* 22–28. See also Lincoln Lorenz, *The Admiral and the Empress: John Paul Jones and Catherine the Great* (New York: Bookman Associates, 1954).

4. Saul, *Distant Friends,* 48–51, 74–78; Bolkhovitinov, *The Beginnings of Russian-American Relations,* 304–33.

5. Saul, *Distant Friends,* 80–81.

6. Ibid., 111–16.

7. Ibid., 119–22. See also Walther Kirchner, *Studies in Russian-American Commerce, 1820–1860* (Leiden: E. J. Brill, 1975).

8. Saul, *Distant Friends,* 132–41; 184; Albert L. Weeks, *Russia's Life-Saver; Lend-Lease Aid to the U.S.S.R. in World War II* (Lanham, MD: Lexington Books, 2004), 68–69; Alexandre Tarsaidze, "American Pioneers in Russian Railroad Building," *Russian Review* 9, no. 4 (October 1950): 286–95.

9. Saul, *Distant Friends,* 198–200; 209–10, 217–18; Frank Golder, "Russian American Relations during the Crimean War," *American Historical Review* 31, no. 3 (April 1926): 462–76; Richard W. Van Alstyne, "John F. Crampton, Conspirator or Dupe?" *American Historical Review* 41, no. 3 (April 1936): 492–502.

10. Saul, *Distant Friends,* 210–215; 218–23; Eufrosina Dvoichenko-Markov, "Americans in the Crimean War," *Russian Review* 13, no. 2 (April 1954): 137–45; Albert Parry, "American Doctors in the Crimean War," *South Atlantic Quarterly* 54, no. 4 (October 1955): 478–90.

11. Saul, *Distant Friends,* 235, 237, 243, 251–57, 264.

12. Ibid., 316–17, 321; Frank Golder, "The American Civil War through the Eyes of a Russian Diplomat," *American Historical Review* 26, no. 3 (April 1921): 454–63.

13. Saul, *Distant Friends,* 333.

14. Ibid., 336–39; Harold Blinn, "Seward and the Polish Rebellion of 1863," *American Historical Review* 45, no. 4 (July 1940): 828–33.

15. Saul, *Distant Friends,* 340–52; William E. Nagengast, "The Visit of the Russian Fleet to the United States: Were Americans Deceived?" *Russian Review* 8, no. 1 (January 1949): 46–55; Frank A. Golder, "The Russian Fleet and the Civil War," *American Historical Review* 20, no. 2 (1915): 801–12; Thomas A. Bailey, "The Russian Fleet Myth Re-Examined," *Mississippi Valley Historical Review* 38, no. 1 (June 1951): 81–90.

16. Saul, *Distant Friends,* 360–70. For more on Kennan, see George Kennan, *Tent Life in Siberia* (Honolulu: University Press of the Pacific, 2001); Frederick F. Travis, *George Kennan and the American-Russian Relationship, 1865–1924* (Athens: Ohio University Press, 1990).

17. Saul, *Distant Friends,* 370–77.

18. Mark Twain, *The Innocents Abroad,* ed. Shelley Fisher Fishkin (New York: Oxford University Press, 1996), 390–98.

19. Saul, *Concord and Conflict,* 18, 103; Charles L. Lewis, *David Glasgow Farragut: Admiral in the Making* (Annapolis, MD: U.S. Naval Institute, 1980), 339–42.

20. Saul, *Distant Friends,* 388–96; Saul, *Concord and Conflict,* 2–13. See also Ronald Jensen, *The Alaska Purchase and Russian-American Relations* (Seattle: University of Washington Press, 1975); Paul Holbo, *Tarnished Expansion: The Alaska Scandal, the Press and Congress* (Knoxville: University of Tennessee Press, 1983); N. N. Bolkhovitinov, *Russian-American Relations and the Sale of Alaska, 1834–1867* (Fairbanks, AK: Limestone Press, distributed by University of Alaska Press, 1996); Thomas Bailey, "Why the United States Purchased Alaska," *Pacific Historical Review*

3 (1934): 39–49; Frank Golder, "The Purchase of Alaska," *American Historical Review* 25 (1920): 411–25; William Dunning, "Paying for Alaska," *Political Science Quarterly* 38 (1912): 385–98; and David H. Miller, "Russian Opinion on the Cession of Alaska," *American Historical Review* 48 (April 1943): 526–31.

21. The most thorough retelling of this episode can be found in Saul, *Concord and Conflict,* 20–39. The primary sources give more details; see *Claim of Captain Benjamin W. Perkins against the Government of Russia, in the Matter of Two Contracts Entered into in the Years 1855 and 1856* [Washington, DC, 1860], 1–7, 9–11, 15–20, 22. Also, there are numerous documents in the following collection that helped me reconstruct the story of the Perkins Claim: Records of Boundary and Claims Commissions and Arbitrations, 1716–1979, RG 76, NARA. These include: Summons for a money demand on contract, to Lilienfeldt, Supreme Court, City and County of New York, June 7, 1856; court order for cost bond, New York, June 18, 1856; Offer of Judgment between Perkins and Lilienfeldt, New York, March 21, 1857; Acceptance of Judgment between Perkins and Lilienfeldt, New York, March 21, 1857; judge's order to enter judgment in Supreme Court of New York, March 21, 1857.

22. Saul, *Concord and Conflict,* 21; *Petition of Anna B. Perkins, of Worcester, Mass, administratrix of the late B. W. Perkins: praying that out of the sums of money to be paid to the Imperial Government of Russia, under the terms of the recent treaty between the government and the United States…* (Washington, DC: Intelligencer Printing House, 1867); *Journal of the Senate of the United States of America* 60: July 9 and 17, 1867; *Journal of the House of Representatives of the United States* 66: December 11, 1867, and January 14, 1868. See also Thomas A. Bailey, *A Diplomatic History of the American People* (New York: Appleton-Century-Crofts, 1964), 370; Golder, "The Purchase of Alaska," 422–24; Jensen, *The Alaska Purchase,* 102–19, 126–39.

23. *Hamilton Fish Diaries,* reel 1 (vol. 1), September 19 and 24, 1869, and reel 1 (vol. 2), November 19, 1870; Saul, *Concord and Conflict,* 27–39; *Harper's Weekly,* November 27, 1869.

24. Letter from Catacazy to Fish, New York, August 12–24, 1870; Notes from the Russian Legation in the United States to the Department of State, 1809–1906, NARA, RG 59, roll 5.

25. He also declared that, if Russia were to pay out on such fabricated claims, she would be inundated by dishonest opportunists, and reminded Clay that there were many claims by Russian citizens against the U.S. government, but that his government had abstained from getting involved in these; letter from B. Stewart, lawyer for Mrs. Perkins, to Secretary of State, Hamilton Fish, Washington, April 24, 1870, Notes to Foreign Legations in the United States from the Department of State, 1834–1906: Russia, NARA, RG 59, M 99.

26. Dispatch of February 17, 1870, qtd. in letter from B. Stewart to Fish, Washington, April 24, 1870, NARA, RG 59, M 99; *Hamilton Fish Diaries,* reel 1 (vol. 2), February 26, 1871, and (vol. 3), April 29, 1871.

27. William Marvel, *The Alabama and the Kearsarge* (Chapel Hill: University of North Carolina Press, 1996); Adrian Cook, "A Lost Opportunity in Anglo-American Relations: The Alabama Claims, 1865–1867," *Australian Journal of Politics and History* 12, no. 1 (1966): 54–65; Maureen M. Robson, "The Alabama Claims and the Anglo-American Reconciliation, 1865–1871," *Canadian Historical Review* 42, no. 1 (March 1961): 1–22; *London Times,* December 6, 1871, qtd. in *Buffalo Commercial Advertiser,* December 22, 1871.

28. Saul, *Concord and Conflict,* 27; *Kansas City Times,* December 14, 1871, January 17, 1872; *Leavenworth Daily Commonwealth,* November 28, 1871; *Cincinnati Daily Enquirer,* November 25, 1871.

29. For example, *New Orleans Daily Picayune,* January 18, 1872; *New Orleans Times,* January 17, 1872.

30. Chester W. Clark, "Prince Gorchakov and the Black Sea Question, 1866: A Russian Bomb That Did Not Explode," *American Historical Review* 48, no. 1 (October 1942): 52–60; W. E. Mosse, "The End of the Crimean System: England, Russia and the Neutrality of the Black Sea, 1870–1," *Historical Journal* 4, no. 2 (1961): 164–90; *New York Sun,* November 16, 17, 18, and 21, 1870; Hannis Taylor, *A Treatise on International Public Law* (Chicago: Callaghan and Co., 1901), 124–25, 400–401.

31. Curtin to Fish, December 19, 1870, DUSM, NARA, RG 59, M 35, roll 23.

3. WHERE EVERY MAN IS A SOVEREIGN

1. *New York Times,* May 7, June 6, September 12, and November 9, 1871; David McCollough, *The Great Bridge: The Epic Story of the Building of the Brooklyn Bridge* (New York: Simon and Schuster, 1972), 289–90, 298; George Lankevich, *American Metropolis: A History of New York* (New York: New York University Press, 1998), 1–116; *New York Illustrated: Containing Illustrations of Public Buildings, Street Scenes, and Suburban Views, with a Map, and General Stranger's Guide* (New York: D. Appleton & Co., 1870), 2.

2. Steven Johnson, *The Ghost Map* (New York: Riverhead Books, 2006); War Department, Surgeon-General's Office, *Cholera Epidemic of 1873 in the United States* (Washington, DC: Government Printing Office, 1875), 345–47; *Charleston Daily Courier,* November 17, 1871; *Philadelphia Press,* November 15, 1871.

3. Donald R. Hopkins, *The Greatest Killer: Smallpox in History* (Chicago: University of Chicago Press, 2002), 276–83; *Philadelphia Inquirer,* November 11, 1871; *Charleston Daily Courier,* November 30 and December 16, 1871; *Mobile Register,* January 17 and 31, 1872, February 4, 1872.

4. *Charleston Daily Courier,* September 11 and 14, 1871, December 1 and 16, 1871.

5. Ibid.; Molly Caldwell Crosby, *The American Plague: The Untold Story of Yellow Fever, the Epidemic That Shaped Our History* (New York: Berkeley Books, 2006), 9–12; qtd. from Margaret Humphreys, *Yellow Fever and the South* (New Brunswick, NJ: Rutgers University Press, 1992), 10.

6. Grant's speech qtd. in the *Boston Herald,* December 5, 1871; Claudia Lauper Bushman and Richard Lyman Bushman, *Building the Kingdom: A History of the Mormons in America* (Oxford, UK: Oxford University Press, 2001), 63–67; Richard Lyman Bushman, *Mormonism: A Very Short Introduction* (Oxford, UK: Oxford University Press, 2008), 94–97; *Boston Herald,* November 9, 1871, November 29, 1871; *Louisville Courier-Journal,* December 6, 1871.

7. Brian S. Wills, "Ku Klux Klan," in *Encyclopedia of the Reconstruction Era,* ed. Richard Zuczek (Westport, CT: Greenwood Press, 2006), vol. 1: 362–65; *Boston Herald,* November 14, 1871. Saul indicates that Klan activity caused the Grand Duke's itinerary to be altered; Saul, *Concord and Conflict,* 63.

8. *New York Herald,* November 13 and 14, 1871.

9. *New York Times,* April 21 and 27, 1871; *New York Herald,* October 3, 1871.

10. *New York Times,* May 16, June 12, October 29, and November 18, 1871.

11. *New York Times,* January 19, 1875, February 23, 1890; *American National Biography,* ed. John A. Garraty and Mark C. Carnes (New York: Oxford University Press, 1999), 22, s.v. "William Henry Vanderbilt"; Don C. Seitz, *The James Gordon Bennetts, Father and Son* (Indianapolis: Bobbs-Merrill Co., 1928), 203; *American National Biography* 9, s.v. "Horace Greeley."

12. *American National Biography* 7, s.v. "Cyrus West Field"; Samuel I. Prime, *The Life of Samuel F. B. Morse, LL.D., Inventor of the Electro-Magnetic Recording Telegraph* (New York: D. Appleton and Co., 1875), 739–40; *New York Times,* July 14, 1890; *American National Biography* 2, s.v. "Henry Ward Beecher"; Valerie K. Angeli, "140 Years of Compassion: The ASPCA, Its History, Its Archives, Its Legends," internal presentation, acquired from the ASPCA, New York.

13. *New York Times,* June 12, October 27, November 2 and 20, 1871.

14. *New York Times,* September 16, October 22, and November 12, 1871; *The Grand Duke Alexis: His Grand Reception, the Magnificent Ball, Gorgeous Scenes, How He Dances, Looks, Walks, and Talks* (New York: Ornum & Co., 1871), 25–26.

15. Melvin Holli and Peter d'A. Jones, eds., *Biographical Dictionary of American Mayors, 1820–1980: Big City Mayors* (Westport, CT: Greenwood Press, 1981), 146–47; *New York Times,* June 16, 1871; *Philadelphia Bulletin,* November 22, 1871; *Cleveland Daily Leader,* December 7, 1871; *New York Times,* June 16 and October 20, 1871.

16. *New York Times,* November 12, 1871; *Boston Herald,* November 29, 1871; *Philadelphia Public Ledger,* November 21, 1871; *Philadelphia Inquirer,* November 3, 1871.

17. George Templeton Strong, *The Diary of George Templeton Strong: Post War Years, 1865–1875,* ed. Allan Nevins and Milton Halsey Thomas (New York: Macmillan Co., 1952), 394, 401; *New York Times,* October 31 and 22, 1871.

18. *New York Times,* November 25, 26, and 28, 1871.

19. *New York Sun,* June 2, 1871; *Philadelphia Public Ledger,* November 22, 1871; *Philadelphia Press,* November 15, 1871; *Philadelphia Bulletin,* November 20, 1871. See also *Philadelphia Bulletin,* December 12, 1871; *Philadelphia Press,* November 24 and 25, 1871.

20. Edwin G. Burrows and Mike Wallace, *Gotham: A History of New York City to 1898* (New York: Oxford University Press, 1999), 1219–20; *Brooklyn Eagle,* October 23, 1871.

21. Edmund G. Olszyk, *The Polish Press in America* (Milwaukee, WI: Marquette University Press, 1940), 7; Ninth U.S. Census, June 1, 1870 (Washington, DC: Government Printing Office, 1872), vol. 1: 390–91; Saul, *Distant Friends,* 337-338.

22. *New York Times,* October 27, 1871; *New York Herald,* October 22, 1871.

23. Catacazy to Fish, September 16–28, 1871, Notes from the Russian Legation in the United States to the Department of State, 1809–1906, NARA, RG 59, M 39, roll 5; J. B. Stewart to Fish, November 3, 1871, Hamilton Fish Papers, LOC, Container 83, Doc. 13125-13126; Fish to Catacazy, October 3 and 31, 1871, Notes to Foreign Legations, NARA, RG 59, M99, roll 83; *New York Tribune,* October 15, 1871.

24. *Chicago Times,* November 24, 1871; *Kansas Daily Commonwealth,* November 25, 1871; *Chicago Times,* January 7, 1872; *Cleveland Daily Leader,* December 9, 1871; *Cincinnati Daily Enquirer,* December 1, 1871.

25. *Golos,* February 4, March 15, and May 16, 17, and 28, 1871; *New York Times,* November 20, 1871; Beliakova, *Velikii kniaz' Aleksei Aleksandrovich,* 96–97; *Boston Courier,* October 29, 1871.

26. Alexis to Maria Alexandrovna, September 12 and November 19, 1871, GARF, f. 641, op. 1, d. 34, ll. 110–17 ob.; Diary of Constantin Possiet, c. January 1872, RGA VMF, f. 1247, op. 1, d. 41, l. 9 ob.–11 ob.

27. Beliakova, *Velikii kniaz' Aleksei Aleksandrovich,* 119; Vladimir to Alexis, September 17, 1871, GARF, f. 681, op. 1, d. 36, str. 9–10 ob.

28. *New York Times,* October 26, 27, and 28, November 2 and 4, 1871; *New York Herald,* October 26, 1871.

29. *New York Times,* October 24 and 25, November 2, 3, 5, and 13, 1871; *Detroit Free Press,* November 17, 1871.

30. *New York Times,* November 4, 5, and 12, 1871; *Overland Monthly and Out West Magazine* 7, no. 6 (December 1871); *Charleston Daily Courier,* November 7, 1871; *Cincinnati Daily Enquirer,* October 29, November 2, and December 8, 1871.

31. *New York Herald,* November 13, 17, and 21, 1871.

32. *New York Herald,* November 13 and 17, 1871.

33. *New York Times,* November 20, 1871; *New York Herald,* November 22, 1871.

34. Donald C. Ringwald, *The Mary Powell: A History of the Beautiful Side-Wheel Steamer Called the "Queen of the Hudson"* (Berkeley, CA: Howell-North Books, 1972), 41–42, 47, 50, 69–71; *Washington Daily Morning Chronicle,* October 26, 1871.

35. *New York Times,* November 20 and 21, 1871.

36. Ibid.

37. Strong, *The Diary of George Templeton Strong,* 401; *New York Times,* November 20 and 21, 1871.

38. *New York Times,* November 22, 1871.

39. Mary Clemmer Ames, *Outlines of Men, Women and Things* (New York: Hurd and Houghton, 1873), 57, 60; *New York Times,* November 22, 1871.

40. New York City Landmarks Preservation Committee, Equitable Building Designation Report, June 25, 1996, Designation List 273, LP-1935, www.nyc.gov/html/lpc/downloads/pdf/reports/equitable.pdf (accessed September 28, 2011); *New York Times,* November 20, 1871; *Philadelphia Public Ledger,* December 6, 1871; Edward Chester, *Sectionalism, Politics, and American Diplomacy* (Metuchen, NJ: Scarecrow Press, 1975), 184.

41. Evan W. Cornog, "To Give Character to Our City: New York's City Hall," *New York History* 69, no. 4 (October 1988): 421–22; *New York Times,* November 20, 1871; *Prairie Farmer,* November 25, 1871; W. W. Tucker, comp., *His Imperial Highness the Grand Duke Alexis in the United States of America during the Winter of 1871–72* (1872; rpt. New York: Interland Publishing Inc., 1972), 23.

42. *New York Times,* November 22, 1871.

43. Patrick Bunyan, *All around Town: Amazing Manhattan Facts and Curiosities* (New York: Fordham University Press, 1999), 201; Richard Edwards, ed., *New York's Great Industries* (New York: Historical Publishing Co., 1884), 282; Henry Collins Brown, ed., *Valentine's Manual of Old New York,* no. 7, new series (New York: Valentine's Manual, Inc., 1923), 201; James Trager, *Park Avenue: Street of Dreams* (New York: Atheneum, 1990), 38; *New York Times,* November 20 and 3, 1871.

44. *New York Times,* November 22, 1871.

45. Eugene Schuyler to Fish, July 17, 1870, DUSM, NARA, RG 59, M 35, roll 22; Catacazy to Fish, February 17, 1871, Hamilton Fish Papers, LOC, Container 76, Doc. 11690–91; *New York Times,* November 22, 1871; *New York Herald,* November 14, 21, and 22, 1871.

46. *New York Herald,* November 22, 1871. For a full account of Fisk's business dealings, see Kenneth D. Ackerman, *The Gold Ring: Jim Fisk, Jay Gould, and Black Friday, 1869* (New York: Dodd, Mead & Co., 1988); *Cleveland Daily Leader,* November 28, 1871. On his personal life, see Fisk's *Romantic Incidents in the Life of James Fisk, Jr.* (Philadelphia: Clarke and Co., 1872).

47. Newspapers qtd.: *Chicago Evening Journal,* January 5, 1872; *New Orleans Times,* November 13, 1871; *Washington Daily Morning Chronicle,* November 20, 1871; *Weekly* (Prescott) *Arizona Miner,* October 28, 1871. For other examples, see *Pittsburgh Gazette,* November 29, 1871; *Leavenworth Daily Commercial,* November 29, 1871; *Baltimore Sun,* November 23, 1871; and *Washington Evening Star,* November 28, 1871. Other comments about the toadyism of New Yorkers can be found in the *Trenton State Gazette,* November 24, 1871, and the *Washington Evening Star,* November 23, 1871.

48. *New York Times,* November 23, 1871; Tucker, comp., *His Imperial Highness the Grand Duke Alexis,* 29.

49. *Philadelphia Enquirer,* July 13, 14, 15, and 25, 1871; *Baltimore Gazette,* Wharton Murder Trial reports, 1872, mdhistory.net/msaref04/msa-sc-5339–68–192/html/bg-wharton-trial-0177.html (accessed September 28, 2011).

50. *New York Times,* November 23, 1871; Thomas Carrier, *Washington, D.C.: A Historical Walking Tour* (Charleston, SC: Arcadia, 2005), 77.

51. *New York Times,* November 24, 1871; Betty C. Monkman, *The White House: Its Historic Furnishings and First Families* (New York: Abbeville Press, 2000), 120, 143–44.

52. *New York Times,* November 24, 1871; Monkman, *The White House,* 30, 38, 101, 132, 150; Julia Dent Grant, *The Personal Memoirs of Julia Dent Grant,* ed. John Y. Simon (New York: G. P. Putnam's Sons, 1975), 187.

53. *Hamilton Fish, Diaries,* reel 1, November 23, December 7, 19, and 20, 1871; Fish to Gorlov, December 19, 1871, Notes to Foreign Legations, NARA, RG 59, M99, roll 83; Gorlov to Fish, December 26, 1871, Notes from the Russian Legation in the United States to the Department of State, 1809–1906, NARA, RG 59, M 39, roll 5.

54. RGA VMF, f. 1247, op.1, d. 41, ll. 18.

55. *Louisville Courier-Journal,* January 25, 1872; *Memphis Daily Appeal,* February 5, 1872, January 11, 1871; *Mobile Register,* February 11, 18, and 24, 1872; *Charleston Daily Courier,* January 19, 1872. See also January 17, 1872; *Atlanta Daily Constitution,* November 16, 1871.

56. *Boston Courier,* November 5, 1871.

57. *New York Times,* November 25, 1871; Tucker, comp., *His Imperial Highness the Grand Duke Alexis,* 34.

58. "The Conquest of Hell Gate," report from U.S. Army Corps of Engineers, www.nan.usace.army.mil/whoweare/hellgate.pdf (accessed September 28, 2011); *New York Times,* November 26, 1871.

59. "Governor's Island," U.S. Department of the Interior, National Park Service, National Register of Historic Places Inventory—Nomination Form, pdfhost.focus.nps.gov/docs/NHLS/Text/85002435.pdf (accessed September 28, 2011); *New York Times,* November 26, 1871.

60. *New York Herald,* November 27, 1871; *New York Times,* November 27, 1871.

61. John Hannavy, ed., *Encyclopedia of Nineteenth-Century Photography* (Oxford, UK: Routledge, 2007), vol. 1: 67, 567; Barbara McCandless, "The Portrait Studio and the Celebrity: Promoting the Art," in *Photography in Nineteenth-Century America* (Fort Worth, TX: Amon Carter Museum and Harry N. Abrams, 1991): 48–75; *New York Times,* November 28, 1871.

62. *New York Times,* November 28, 1871.

63. Ibid., November 27 and 28, 1871.

64. Beliakova, *Velikii kniaz' Aleksei Aleksandrovich,* 113; Sergei to Alexis, December 16, 1871, GARF, f. 681, op. 1, d. 40, ll. 7–8 ob., f. 681, op. 1, d. 30, ll. 10–11 ob.

65. A. A. Tolstaya to Alexis, October 18, 1871, GARF, f. 681, op. 1, d. 64, ll. 1–3 ob.; Ioann Rozhdestvenskii to Alexis, October 18, 1871, GARF, f. 681, op. 1, d. 63, ll. 1–4.

66. Alexis to Vladimir, November 23, 1871, GARF, f. 652, op. 1, d. 385, ll. 4–5 ob.

67. Alexander II to Alexis, December 17, 1871, GARF, f. 681, op. 1, d. 18, ll. 1–2 ob.

68. *New York Times,* November 29, 1871; James D. McCabe Jr., *Lights and Shadows of New York Life; or, the Sights and Sensations of the Great City. A Facsimile Edition* (New York: Farrar, Straus and Giroux, 1970), 439; Augustine Costello, *Birth of the Bravest: A History of the New York Fire Department from 1600 to 1887,* abridged by Brian Thomsen (New York: T. Doherty Associates, 2002), 382, 469–70.

69. *New York Times,* November 24 and 27, 1871.

70. *New York Times,* November 29, 1871; *Harper's Weekly,* December 17, 1871; *Brooklyn Eagle,* November 29 and December 2, 1871.

71. *New York Times,* November 30, 1871.

72. Ibid., November 27 and 30, 1871.

73. Ibid., November 23, 1871.

74. Ibid., November 30, 1871.

75. Ibid.

76. Ibid.; *New York Herald,* November 30, 1871.

77. *New York Times,* November 30 and December 1, 1871; *New York Tribune,* July 30, 1895; *Graphic,* December 30, 1871; *Hartford Daily Courant,* December 15, 1871; *New York Times,* June 17, 1870, September 30, 1874; James Fuld, *The Book of World-Famous Music: Classical, Popular and Folk,* 5th ed. (New York: Dover Publications, 2000), 196–99.

78. *New York Times,* November 30 and December 2, 1871.

79. *New York Times,* December 2, 1871.

80. *New York Times,* July 18 and September 16, 1871; *Appleton's Cyclopaedia of American Biography,* ed. James Grant Wilson and John Fiske (New York: D. Appleton and Co., 1889), vol. 4, s.v. "Page, William"; *Harper's Weekly,* August 12, 1871; document sent to Hamilton Fish, September 14, 1869, Hamilton Fish Papers, Library of Congress (LOC), Washington, DC, container 56, doc. 7025; *New York Times,* December 3, 1871; Eliot Clark, *History of the National Academy of Design, 1825–1953* (New York: Columbia University Press, 1954), 84.

81. Peter Andrews, "Delmonico's—The Restaurant That Changed the Way We Dine," *American Heritage Magazine* 31, no. 5 (August–September 1980): 96–101; Lately Thomas, *Delmonico's: A*

Century of Splendor (Boston: Houghton Mifflin Co., 1967), 26–28; Judith Choate and James Canora, *Dining at Delmonico's* (New York: Stewart, Tabori and Chang, 2008), 11–25.

82. Telegram from J. L Loubat, New York, to Gustavus Vasa Fox, Lowell, November 28, 1871, G. V. Fox Collection, Manuscript Department, New York Historical Society, New York; *New York Times,* December 3, 1871; Arthur Bartlett Maurice, *Fifth Avenue* (New York: Dodd, Mead and Co., 1918), 111; *Fifth Avenue Events: A Brief Account of Some of the Most Interesting Events Which Have Occurred on the Avenue* (Printed for Fifth Avenue Bank of New York, 1916), 16–18; John Parkinson, *History of New York Yacht Club from Its Founding through 1973* (New York: New York Yacht Club, 1975), vol. 2: 530.

83. Christian A. Peterson, *Chaining the Sun: Portraits by Jeremiah Gurney* (Minneapolis: Minneapolis Institute of Arts, 1999), 9, 82, 95–96; *New York Times,* December 4, 1871.

84. *Washington Daily Morning Chronicle,* November 23, 1871; *Cleveland Daily Leader,* November 24, 1871; *Kansas State Record,* November 29, 1871; see also Mary Gabriel, *Notorious Victoria* (Chapel Hill, NC: Algonquin Books, 1998).

85. *New York Times,* December 12, 1871.

86. Ibid., November 4, 1871; *Graphic,* December 16, 1871; *New York Herald,* November 30, 1871; Daniel Pope, *The Making of Modern Advertising* (New York: Basic Books, 1983), 133; Frank Presbrey, *The History and Development of Advertising* (New York: Greenwood Press, 1968), 228–31, 256.

87. *New York Times,* December 16, 1871; *New York Tribune,* December 16, 1871; *Missouri Democrat,* January 6, 1872; *Brooklyn Eagle,* December 27 and 29, 1871; February 19, 1872; *Ottawa Citizen,* November 24, 1871.

88. *New York Herald,* October 26, 1871; *Harper's Weekly,* September 30, 1871; *Wellman's Miscellany,* September 1871; *Philadelphia Public Ledger,* December 11, 1871; *Missouri Democrat,* December 2, 1871; *Philadelphia Public Ledger,* December 9, 1871.

4. LEAVING HIS RUSSIAN STEPPES BEHIND

1. *Philadelphia Inquirer,* July 22 and 28, August 3 and 23, November 14, 1871; *Philadelphia Public Ledger,* November 6, 1871; *Journal of the Select Council of the City of Philadelphia: From July 1, 1871, to January 1, 1872,* 212, 239–40, 394; *Journal of the Common Council of the City of Philadelphia. For the Year 1871* 2: 250–52, 263–64, 282–85, 333.

2. *Philadelphia Inquirer,* November 20, 1871.

3. Ibid., November 23, 24, 25, 27, and 29, 1871; *Philadelphia Public Ledger,* November 24, 25, and 27, 1871.

4. *Biographical Encyclopaedia of Pennsylvania in the Nineteenth Century* (Philadelphia: Galaxy Publishing, 1874), 129–30, 190, 368, 640; *Men of America: A Biographical Album of the City Government of Philadelphia in the Bi-Centennial Year* (Philadelphia: American Biographical Publishing Co., 1883), 41–42; Charles Morris, ed., *Makers of Philadelphia* (Philadelphia: L. R. Hamersly & Co., 1894), 79, 182; George Morgan, *The City of Firsts, Being a Complete History of the City of Philadelphia from Its Founding, in 1862, to the Present Time* (Philadelphia: Historical Publication Society, 1926), 167; Moses King, *Philadelphia and Notable Philadelphians* (New York: Moses King

Publishers, 1901), 100; Joseph Jackson, *Encyclopedia of Philadelphia* (Harrisburg, PA: National Historical Association Telegraph Building, 1931), vol. 2: 673.

5. Ezra Warner, *Generals in Blue: Lives of the Union Commanders* (Baton Rouge: Louisiana State University Press, 1964), 315–17; George Gordon Meade, *The Life and Letters of General George Gordon Meade: Major General United States Army* (New York: Charles Scribner's Sons, 1913), 300–303.

6. King, *Philadelphia*, 97; James Ward, *J. Edgar Thompson: Master of Pennsylvania* (Westport, CT: Greenwood Press, 1980), 16; Jackson, *Encyclopedia of Philadelphia*, vol. 1: 211–12; *Biographical Encyclopaedia of Pennsylvania in the Nineteenth Century*, 380–82.

7. *Philadelphia Public Ledger,* February 24, 1880; *Philadelphia Bulletin,* November 17, 1871; Howard Gilletee Jr., "Philadelphia's City Hall: Monument to a New Political Machine," *Pennsylvania Magazine of History and Biography* 97 (April 1973), 233–49; *Philadelphia Bulletin,* December 1 and November 29, 1871.

8. *Philadelphia Inquirer,* November 28 and 29, December 2 and 4, 1871; *Philadelphia Public Ledger,* November 29 and 30, 1871; *Philadelphia Press,* December 2, 1871.

9. *Philadelphia North American and United States Gazette,* November, 30, 1871; *Philadelphia Inquirer,* December 4, 1871; *Philadelphia Public Ledger,* December 2, 6, and 8, 1871; *Philadelphia Bulletin,* November 29, 1871.

10. *Philadelphia Inquirer,* December 1 and 2, 1871; *Philadelphia Press,* December 1, 2, and 5, 1871; *Philadelphia North American and United States Gazette,* November 25, 1871.

11. *Philadelphia Inquirer,* December 4, 1871; *Philadelphia Public Ledger,* December 4, 1871.

12. George W. Edwards, letter to John Rice concerning "bogus subscribers" to the Butler House Hotel Co., Philadelphia, 1857, Historical Society of Pennsylvania; see also, *Hotel Folly. A Series of Letter in Reference to the Building of a Monster Hotel in the City of Philadelphia, by a Corporation, Originally Written over the Signature of "Franklin," and Published in the Philadelphia Evening Journal* (1857); *Illustrated Philadelphia: Its Wealth and Industries,* 2nd ed. (New York: American Publishing and Engraving Co., 1889), 160.

13. *Philadelphia Inquirer,* December 5, 1871; *Philadelphia Public Ledger,* December 5, 1871; *Philadelphia Inquirer,* December 6 and 8, 1871.

14. Jackson, *Encyclopedia of Philadelphia,* vol. 2: 726; Roger Butterfield, "George Lippard and His Secret Brotherhood," *Pennsylvania Magazine of History and Biography* 79 (July 1955): 294; Board of Directors of City Trusts, Philadelphia, www.citytrusts.com (accessed August 16, 2010).

15. *Philadelphia Inquirer,* December 5, 1871; *Philadelphia Public Ledger,* December 5, 1871; Charles Keyser, *Fairmount Park and the International Exhibition at Philadelphia* (Philadelphia: Claxton, Remsen & Haffelfinger, 1876), 136.

16. Thomas Richard Butler, "Belmont through the Years," Remarks delivered at a meeting of the Numismatic and Antiquarian Society of Philadelphia at Belmont Mansion, Fairmount Park, Philadelphia, Monday, May 24, 1954, 3–16; Richard Peters Jr., "Belmont Mansion," read to the Numismatic and Antiquarian Society of Philadelphia, October 12, 1923.

17. *Philadelphia Inquirer,* December 4 and 5, 1871.

18. John K. Brown, *The Baldwin Locomotive Works, 1831–1915* (Baltimore: Johns Hopkins University Press, 1995), xxv, 1–7, 20, 184; Malcolm C. Clark, "The Birth of an Enterprise: Baldwin

Locomotive, 1831–1842," *Pennsylvania Magazine of History and Biography* (October 1966): 423–44. *Philadelphia Public Ledger,* December 5, 1871.

19. *Philadelphia Inquirer,* December 5, 1871.

20. Destroyer History Foundation, Information about the Philadelphia Navy Yard, www .destroyerhistory.org/destroyers/philadelphiany.html (accessed January 30, 2011).

21. Dictionary of American Naval Fighting Ships, Biographical information on Emmons, www .history.navy.mil/danfs/e3/emmons.htm (accessed February 7, 2011); *Journal of the U.S.S. Ossipee,* found at vilda.alaska.edu/cdm4/results.php?CISOOP1=all&CISOBOX1=journal ossipee&CISO FIELD1=CISOSEARCHALL&CISOOP2=exact&CISOBOX2=&CISOFIELD2=CISOSEARCHALL& CISOOP3=any&CISOBOX3=&CISOFIELD3=CISOSEARCHALL&CISOOP4=none&CISOBOX4= &CISOFIELD4=CISOSEARCHALL&CISOROOT=all&t=a (accessed January 30, 2011).

22. *Philadelphia Inquirer,* December 5 and 6, 1871.

23. Irvin R. Glazer, *Philadelphia Theatres, A–Z: A Comprehensive, Descriptive Record of 813 Theatres Constructed since 1724* (New York: Greenwood Press, 1986), 53–54; Jackson, *Encyclopedia of Philadelphia,* vol. 1: 8–11; John Francis Marion, *Within These Walls: A History of the Academy of Music in Philadelphia* (Philadelphia: Academy of Music, 1984), 76.

24. *Philadelphia Inquirer,* December 5, 1871; *Philadelphia Public Ledger,* December 5, 1871.

25. *Philadelphia Inquirer,* December 5, 1871; *Philadelphia Press,* December 5, 1871.

26. Alexander K. McClure, *Old Time Notes of Pennsylvania* (Philadelphia: John C. Winston Co., 1905), vol. 2: 244–49.

27. *Philadelphia Bulletin,* December 6, 1871; *Philadelphia Inquirer,* December 5 and 6, 1871; *Philadelphia Public Ledger,* December 6, 1871; *Saturday Evening Post,* December 16, 1871; J. Thomas Scharf and Thompson Westcott, *History of Philadelphia* (Philadelphia: L. H. Everts & Co., 1884), vol. 1: 621.

28. *Philadelphia Press,* December 5, 1871; *Philadelphia Evening Bulletin,* December 4, 1871; *Philadelphia Inquirer,* December 5, 1871; *Saturday Evening Post,* December 16, 1871; news clipping dated December 10, 1871, Geary Family Papers, vol. 23, "Scrapbook," Historical Society of Pennsylvania, Philadelphia; Alexis's intent also noted in *Boston Courier,* December 10, 1871.

29. *Philadelphia Evening Bulletin,* December 4, 1871.

30. News clipping, December 10, 1871, Geary Family Papers, vol. 23, "Scrapbook," Historical Society of Pennsylvania, Philadelphia.

31. *Detroit Free Press,* December 12, 1871.

32. Qtd. in Roger Lane, *William Dorsey's Philadelphia and Ours* (New York: Oxford University Press, 1991), 113. Lane's footnote attributes the letter to the private collection of Dorsey's great-great-grandson, Dr. Preston Johnson. A version of the letter was also printed in the *New Orleans Daily Picayune,* December 22, 1871.

33. John N. Ingham and Lynne B. Feldman, *African-American Business Leaders: A Biographical Dictionary* (Westport, CT: Greenwood, 1993), 226; W. E. B. Du Bois, *The Philadelphia Negro: A Social Study* (Philadelphia: University of Pennsylvania, 1899), 35; *New York Times,* December 7, 1871.

34. *Detroit Free Press,* December 12, 1871; *New York Times,* December 7, 1871; *Baltimore Sun,* December 7, 1871; R. J. M. Blackett, ed., *Thomas Morris Chester, Black Civil War Correspondent: His Dispatches from the Virginia Front* (Baton Rouge: Louisiana State University Press, 1989), 3–91.

35. William Woys Weaver, *Encyclopedia of Food and Culture* (New York: Charles Scribner's Son, 2003), vol. 3: 40–41; *Philadelphia Press,* July 31, 1874.

36. James Wood Parkinson, *American Dishes at the Centennial* (Philadelphia: King & Baird, 1874), 2–7.

37. U.S. Census Bureau, www.census.gov (accessed July 2009); *Hartford Daily Courant,* December 6 and 8, 1871.

38. *Hartford Daily Courant,* December 6 and 8, 1871.

39. Joseph Bradley, *Guns for the Tsar: American Technology and the Small Arms Industry in Nineteenth-Century Russia* (DeKalb: Northern Illinois University Press, 1990), 105–16; *Boston Herald,* December 8, 1871; *Hartford Daily Courant,* December 8 and 11, 1871.

40. *Hartford Daily Courant,* December 8 and 11, 1871.

41. Julia Keller, *Mr. Gatlin's Terrible Marvel: The Gun That Changed Everything and the Misunderstood Genius Who Invented It* (New York: Viking, 2008), 136–37, 160, 181; *Hartford Daily Courant,* December 8 and 11, 1871.

42. *Boston Herald,* December 8, 1871.

43. Massasoit House, *Massasoit House, M. Chapin, E. S. Chapin Bill of fare, Monday, March 17, 1851* ([Springfield, MA]: H. S. Taylor's Power Press, 1851).

44. *Springfield Daily Republican,* December 8, 1871; *Boston Herald,* December 8, 1871.

45. *Philadelphia Inquirer,* November 27, 1871; *Proceedings of the Common Council,* September 28, 1871 (Boston: Municipal Printing Office, 1871), 276; *Chicago Times,* November 25, 1871; *Detroit Free Press,* November 25, 1871; *Boston Herald,* November 11, 1871.

46. Francis Palfrey, "Memoir of the Hon. George Stillman Hillard," *Proceedings of the Massachusetts Historical Society* (Boston: Massachusetts Historical Society), vol. 19 (1882): 339–45; *Memorial Biographies of the New-England Historic Genealogical Society* (Boston: Published by the Society, 1907), vol. 8 (1880–89): 41–42; D. Hamilton Hurd, comp., *History of Essex County Massachusetts, with Biographical Sketches of Many of Its Pioneers and Prominent Men* (Philadelphia: J. W. Lewis & Co., 1888), vol. 2: 1490–91; *New York Times,* December 7, 1871.

47. *Farmer's Cabinet,* December 6, 1871; *Boston Herald,* December 5, 6, 7, and 8, 1871.

48. *City of Boston, Proceedings of the Board of Aldermen,* December 4, 1871; *Boston Herald,* December 5 and 7, 1871.

49. *Boston Herald,* December 8, 1871.

50. Edwin M. Bacon, ed., *Boston Illustrated, Containing Full Descriptions of the City, and Its Immediate Suburbs, Its Public Buildings and Institutions, ... Etc.* (Boston: Houghton Mifflin and Co., 1886), 83; *Revere House, Bowdoin Square. Boston. Wrisely, Wetherbee & Co. proprietors... Dinner on Friday, August 19, 1870* (Boston, 1870); *Boston Herald,* December 8, 1871.

51. Edward Everett Parker, *History of the Town of Brookline* (Published by the Town, 1914), 322–24.

52. *Boston Herald,* December 8, 1871; James L. Bruce, *The Old State House* (Boston: Bostonian Society, 1965), 7, 9, 22–23, 25; Richard Herndon, comp., *Boston of To-day: A Glance at Its History and Characteristics, with Biographical Sketches and Portraits of Many of Its Professional and Business Men* (Boston: Post Publishing Co., 1892), 34–36; *Saturday Evening Post,* December 23, 1871.

53. *Louisville Courier-Journal,* November 22, 1871.

54. *Saturday Evening Post,* December 23, 1871; *Philadelphia Public Ledger,* December 9, 1871.

55. *Saturday Evening Post,* December 23, 1871; *Milwaukee Sentinel,* December 15, 1871.

56. *Massachusetts Ploughman and New England Journal of Agriculture,* December 16, 1871; *Harper's New Monthly Magazine* 52 (December 1875 to May 1876): 199; John Langdon Sibley, *John Langdon Sibley's Diary, 1846–1882,* transcription, Harvard/Radcliffe Online Historical Reference Shelf, December 8, 1871, hul.harvard.edu/huarc/refshelf/Sibley.htm (accessed September 1, 2009); *Saturday Evening Post,* December 23, 1871; Alfred Claghorn Potter and Charles Knowles Bolton, *The Librarians of Harvard, 1667–1877* (Cambridge, MA: Library of Harvard University, 1897), 39–42; Samuel Longfellow, *Life of Henry Wadsworth Longfellow: With Extracts from his Journal and Correspondence* (Boston: Houghton Mifflin, 1893), 190–91.

57. Justin Winsor, ed., *The Memorial History of Boston Including Suffolk County, Massachusetts, 1630–1880* (Boston: James R. Osgood and Co., 1881), vol. 3: 335–36, 367.

58. *Saturday Evening Post,* December 23, 1871.

59. Douglass Shand Tucci, "The Boston1Realto: Playhouses, Concert Halls and Movie Palaces," Boston: Boston Public Library, 1977, 4; Herndon, comp., *Boston of To-day,* 96; Eugene Tompkins, *The History of the Boston Theatre, 1854–1901* (Boston: Houghton Mifflin Co., 1908), 2–10; newspaper clipping, December 8, 1871, from Scrapbook X, 82–84, Bostonian Society, Boston; *Saturday Evening Post,* December 23, 1871; *Boston Herald,* December 7, 1871; Tucker, comp., *His Imperial Highness the Grand Duke Alexis,* 72–73.

60. *Boston Courier,* December 10, 1871; Scrapbook X, 82–84, Bostonian Society, Boston; *Saturday Evening Post,* December 23, 1871; *Boston Herald,* December 8 and 9, 1871; Tucker, comp., *His Imperial Highness the Grand Duke Alexis,* 71.

61. *Boston Courier,* December 10, 1871; Scrapbook X, 82–84, Bostonian Society, Boston; *Saturday Evening Post,* December 23, 1871; *Boston Herald,* December 8, and 9, 1871.

62. Ednah D. Cheney, ed., *Louisa May Alcott: Her Life, Letters and Journals* (Boston: Roberts Brothers, 1889), 261.

63. Scrapbook X, 82–84, Bostonian Society, Boston; *Boston Herald,* December 5, 1871.

64. *New York Times,* December 20, 1871; *Chicago Republican,* December 20, 1871; Timothy J. Regan, *The Lost Civil War Diaries: The Diaries of Corporal Timothy J. Regan* (Victoria, BC: Trafford, 2003), 310.

65. *Boston Herald,* December 19, 1871; *Massachusetts Reports: Cases Argued and Determined in the Supreme Judicial Court of Massachusetts, June–October 1876* (Boston: Houghton, Mifflin and Co., 1876), vol. 118: 234–36. This case would be recalled years later in a report on a similar case involving injury to a guest at a facility rented by a third party; *New York Tribune,* May 2, 1880.

66. For an account of Fox's trip, see, John D. Champlin Jr., ed., *Narrative of the Mission to Russia, in 1866, of the Hon. Gustavus Vasa Fox, Assistant-Secretary of the Navy* (New York: D. Appleton and Co., 1873).

67. *Boston Courier,* December 10, 1871.

68. Ibid; diary entries from December 4 and 5, 1871, Gustavus Fox Collection, Series II: Personal Papers, box 14, folder 1, Diaries (1866–72) and miscellaneous correspondence, October–Decem-

ber 1871, Gustavus Fox Collection, Series I: Correspondence (1838–83), box 12, folder 9, Naval History Society Collection, New York Historical Society, New York; Champlin, ed., *Narrative of the Mission to Russia,* 442–44.

69. *Boston Courier,* December 10, 1871; Scrapbook, H.80.124, Rare Books and Manuscripts, Boston Public Library; *Order of Exercises at the Musical Entertainment in Honor of His Imperial Highness, the Grand Duke Alexis of Russia,… At the Boston Music Hall… December 9, 1871* (Boston: Rockwell and Churchill, 1871); *Boston Commonwealth,* December 16, 1871.

70. *Boston Courier,* December 10, 1871; *Boston Herald,* December 11, 1871.

71. *Boston Courier,* December 10, 1871; *Menu to the Complimentary Dinner to H. I. H. the Grand Duke Alexis at the Revere House, Boston, December 9, 1871,* Rare Books and Manuscripts, H.80.124 bdsd, Boston Public Library.

72. *Boston Courier,* December 10, 1871.

73. Ibid.; Tucker, comp., *His Imperial Highness the Grand Duke Alexis,* 104; *Philadelphia Bulletin,* December 16, 1871.

74. Longfellow, *Life of Henry Wadsworth Longfellow,* 190–91.

75. *Boston Herald,* December 11, 1871; *New York Times,* December 7, 1871.

76. *Boston Herald,* December 11, 1871; *New York Times,* December 7, 1871.

77. Bessie Zaban Jones and Lyle Gifford Boyd, *The Harvard College Observatory: The First Four Directorships, 1839–1919* (Cambridge, MA: Harvard University Press, 1971), 40–57, 184–89; *Boston Herald,* December 11, 1871.

78. *Boston Herald,* December 12, 1871; Tucker, comp., *His Imperial Highness the Grand Duke Alexis,* 106.

79. Geraldine E. Rodgers, *The History of Beginning Reading: From Teaching by "Sound" to Teaching by "Meaning"* (LaVergne, TN: First Books, 2009), vol. 1: 525–44.

80. Program of special performance at the Globe Theatre, December 12, 1871, Scrapbook H. 80.124, Rare Books and Manuscripts, Boston Public Library; Lisa Merrill, *When Romeo Was a Woman* (Ann Arbor: University of Michigan Press, 1999), xv, 21, 38–39, 124–27, 197, 235, 239–42; *Boston Herald,* December 11 and 13, 1871.

81. *Proceedings of the Massachusetts Historical Society, 1871–73* (Boston: Published by the Society, 1873), 174; Robert Waterson, "Memoir of George Sumner," *Proceedings of the Massachusetts Historical Society, 1880–1881* (Boston: Published by the Society, 1881), 193–98.

82. *Boston Herald,* December 12, 1871.

83. *The Great Organ in the Boston Music Hall* (Boston: Ticknor and Fields, 1865), 7–41; David A. Wells, ed., *Annual of Scientific Discovery or, Year-Book of Facts in Science and Art for 1864* (Boston: Gould and Lincoln, 1864), 42–43; *New York Times,* April 12, 1883, May 13, 1897.

84. *Boston Herald,* December 14, 1871.

85. Ibid.

86. *Catholic Encyclopedia* (New York: Robert Appleton Co., 1910), s.v., "Louis Hennepin"; John F. Sears, *Sacred Places: American Tourist Attractions in the Nineteenth Century* (New York: Oxford University Press, 1989), 4, 12; Karen Dubinsky, *The Second Greatest Disappointment: Honeymooners, Heterosexuality, and the Tourist Industry at Niagara Falls* (New Brunswick, NJ: Rutgers Univer-

sity Press, 1999), 31–35; Jeremy Elwell Adamson, *Niagara: Two Centuries of Changing Attitudes, 1697–1901* (Washington, DC: Corcoran Gallery of Art, 1985), 9.

87. Ginger Strand, *Inventing Niagara: Beauty, Power, and Lies* (New York: Simon and Schuster, 2008), 77–80; Dubinsky, *The Second Greatest Disappointment,* 85–87.

88. *Toronto Globe,* December 23, 1871; *New York Times,* December 25, 1871; *Buffalo Commercial Advertiser,* December 23, 1871.

89. *New York Times,* December 25, 1871; *Buffalo Commercial Advertiser,* December 21 and 23, 1871; *Niagara Falls* (Buffalo, NY: Matthews, Northrup & Co., 1890), 76; Spencer House, A. Cluck, and Cosack & Co., *Spencer House, Niagara Falls, N.Y. . . .* (Niagara Falls, NY, 1870).

90. *New York Times,* December 25, 1871.

91. *Buffalo Commercial Advertiser,* December 12, 1871.

92. *New York Times,* December 24, 1871; *Buffalo Commercial Advertiser,* December 22 and 23, 1871.

93. *Buffalo Commercial Advertiser,* December 23, 1871.

94. Ibid.; *New York Times,* December 24, 1871; *Horner's Buffalo and Niagara Falls Guide and Encyclopedia of Useful Knowledge* (Buffalo: W. T. Horner, 1874), 50; *Buffalo City Directory for the Year 1873* (Buffalo: Wakren, Johnson & Co., 1873), 68, 566.

95. *Buffalo Commercial Advertiser,* December 26, 1871.

96. Rebecca McDougall Graves, *The North Presbyterian Church* (Buffalo, 1922), 15–10; *Buffalo Commercial Advertiser,* December 26, 1871; *New York Times,* December 26, 1871; Daniel J. Sweeney, comp., *History of Buffalo and Erie County, 1914–1919,* 2nd ed. (Buffalo: Committee of One Hundred, 1919), 128.

97. Richmond Hill, *A Thespian Temple: A Brief History of the Academy of Music and Review of the Dramatic Events of Over Fifty Years in the City of Buffalo, N.Y.* (Buffalo: Courier Co., 1893), 16–18; George Ripley and Charles A. Dana, eds., *The American Cyclopaedia: A Popular Dictionary of General Knowledge* (New York: D. Appleton and Co., 1875), vol. 14: 430–31; *New York Times,* September 2, 1895, January 23, 1874.

98. *Buffalo Commercial Advertiser,* December 26, 1871.

99. Ibid., December 23 and 26, 1871.

5. "ROAMIN' OFF" TO THE MIDWEST

1. Robert I. Vexler, comp. and ed., *Cleveland: A Chronological and Documentary History, 1760–1976* (Dobbs Ferry, NY: Oceana Publications, Inc., 1977), 1–30; Carol Poh Miller and Robert A. Wheeler, *Cleveland: A Concise History, 1796–1996,* 2nd ed. (Bloomington: Indiana University Press, 1997), 7–9, 14, 31, 47–48, 53–69; J. Disturnell, comp., *The Great Lakes, or Inland Seas of America; . . . Giving a Description of Cities, Towns, Etc.* (New York: American News Co., 1868), 56.

2. *Cleveland Daily Leader,* November 29 and December 4, 1871; *Cleveland Daily Plain Dealer,* September 4, October 26, December 8 and 13, 1871.

3. *Cincinnati Daily Enquirer,* November 2, 1871. See also *Cincinnati Daily Enquirer,* November 20, 1871; *Cheyenne Daily Leader,* December 9, 1871; *Cleveland Daily Plain Dealer,* December 26, 1871.

4. *Cleveland Daily Plain Dealer,* December 18 and 26, 1871; see also *Detroit Free Press,* November 25, 1871.

5. David D. Van Tassel and John J. Grabowski, eds., *Dictionary of Cleveland Biography* (Bloomington: Indiana University Press, 1996), 27, 126, 433; Stephen Peet, *The Ashtabula Disaster* (Chicago: J. S. Goodman–Louis Lloyd & Co., 1877), 15, 207–8.

6. *Cleveland Daily Leader,* December 6, 9, 21, and 23, 1871.

7. Letter of Samuel L. Mather, January 1, 1872, Cleveland, to Samuel Mather, Samuel Mather Family Papers, container 1, folder 1, Western Reserve Historical Society, Cleveland; *Cleveland Daily Leader,* December 27, 1871; *Cleveland Daily Plain Dealer,* December 27, 1871.

8. William Ganson Rose, *Cleveland: The Making of a City* (Cleveland: World Publishing Co., 1950), 267, 335; *Historic Sites of Cleveland: Hotels and Taverns,* prepared by Ohio Historical Records Survey, Project Survey Division, Work Projects Administration (Columbus: Ohio Historical Records Survey, 1942), 366–67, 412–22, 436; *Cleveland Daily Leader,* December 27, 1871.

9. *Cleveland Daily Leader,* December 27 and 28, 1871.

10. Encyclopedia of Cleveland History, ech.cwru.edu/ech-cgi/article.pl?id=N and ech.cwru.edu/ech-cgi/article.pl?id=CH8 (accessed October 3, 2012).

11. *Cleveland Daily Leader,* December 28, 1871; *Cleveland Daily Plain Dealer,* December 28, 1871.

12. *Cleveland Daily Leader,* December 27, 1871.

13. Ibid., December 28, 1871.

14. Ibid.; *Cleveland Daily Plain Dealer,* December 28, 1871.

15. Robert Ross and George Caitlin, *Landmarks of Detroit: A History of the City* (Detroit: Evening News Association, 1898), 445–46; *Detroit Free Press,* December 30, 1871; Bruce F. Adams, *The Politics of Punishment: Prison Reform in Russia, 1863–1917* (DeKalb: Northern Illinois University Press, 1996), 52–64; *Ninth Annual Report of the Board of State Charities of Massachusetts* (Boston: Wright and Potter, 1873), 5–6; *Milwaukee Sentinel,* January 5, 1872.

16. Catacazy to Gorchakov, March 9–21, 1871, f. 133, op. 470, d. 123 (1871) and Catacazy to Gorchakov, July 2–14, 1871, f. 133, op. 470, d. 123 (1871), AVPRI, as cited in Saul, *Concord and Conflict,* 55; Ross Miller, *American Apocalypse: The Great Fire and the Myth of Chicago* (Chicago: University of Chicago Press, 1990), 18; *Chicago Times,* December 19, 1871.

17. Erik Larson, *Devil in the White City* (New York: Vintage Books, 2003), 16.

18. Lisa Kristoff Boehm, *Popular Culture and the Enduring Myth of Chicago, 1871–1968* (New York: Routledge, 2004), 1–2, 16–19. For more on antimodernism and the distrust of cities, see Henry Nash Smith, *Virgin Land: The American West as Symbol and Myth* (Cambridge, MA: Harvard University Press, 1978), and T. J. Jackson Lears, *No Place of Grace: Antimodernism and the Transformation of American Culture, 1880–1920* (Chicago: University of Chicago Press, 1994.)

19. *Missouri Democrat,* October 11, 14, 15, 16, 17, 20, and 21, 1871; *Daily Milwaukee News,* October 11 and November 23, 1871.

20. *Chicago Times,* December 28, 1871; *Chicago Tribune,* December 31, 1871; Marc Levinson, *The Great A&P and the Struggle for Small Business in America* (New York: Hill and Wang, 2011), 30–31; *Joseph Medill: A Brief Biography and an Appreciation* (Chicago: Tribune Co., 1947).

21. *Biographical Sketches of Leading Men of Chicago* (Chicago: Wilson & St. Clair, 1868), 25–46, 117–20, 177–80, 227–29, 433–34, 445–46, 583–89. See also M. L. Ahern, *The Great Revolution: A History of the Rise and Progress of the People's Party in the City of Chicago and County of Cook with Sketches of the Elect in Office* (Chicago: Lakeside Publishing and Printing Co., 1874), 241.

22. *Chicago Tribune,* December 31, 1871; *Chicago Evening Journal,* January 2, 1872.

23. Stephen M. Davis, "'Of the Class Denominated Princely': The Tremont House Hotel," *Chicago History* 11 (Spring 1982): 26–35.

24. *Chicago Tribune,* December 31, 1871; *Chicago Evening Journal,* January 2, 1872.

25. *Chicago Times,* January 1, 1872.

26. *Chicago Evening Journal,* January 2, 1872; *Chicago Times,* January 3, 1872.

27. Richard Storr, *Harper's University: The Beginnings; A History of the University of Chicago* (Chicago: University of Chicago Press, 1966), 3–6.

28. Thomas Hoyne, *Chicago Astronomical Society, Meeting of April 16, 1874. Full Report of the Secretary and History of Organization, with the Proceedings (so far as recollected) of the Society …* (Chicago, 1874); *Chicago Times,* January 3, 1872.

29. Donald L. Miller, *City of the Century: The Epic of Chicago and the Making of America* (New York: Simon and Schuster, 1997), 114–17; *Chicago Times,* January 3, 1872.

30. *Chicago Times,* January 3, 1872.

31. Ibid.; *Time table of special train tendered to His Imperial Highness, the Grand Duke Alexis of Russia and Suite: Tuesday and Thursday, January 2d and 4th, 1872* ([Chicago]: Chicago and North Western Railway Co., 1872).

32. *Chicago Times,* January 3 and 6, 1872; *Chicago Evening Journal,* January 6, 1872.

33. Bayrd Still, *Milwaukee: The History of a City* (Madison: State Historical Society of Wisconsin, 1948), 3–41, 72, 106–11, 186; Disturnell, comp., *The Great Lakes,* 82; *Milwaukee Sentinel,* November 30, 1871.

34. *Daily Milwaukee News,* December 12, 1871; *Milwaukee Sentinel,* December 12, 13, and 14, 1871.

35. H. B. Segel, "Sienkiewicz's First Translator, Jeremiah Curtin," *Slavic Review* 24, no. 2 (1965): 190–91; Joseph Schafer, ed., *Memoirs of Jeremiah Curtin* (Madison: State Historical Society of Wisconsin, 1940), 209; *Milwaukee Sentinel,* December 21, 22, and 27, 1871.

36. *Milwaukee Sentinel,* December 16 and 28, 1871.

37. Holli and Jones, eds., *Biographical Dictionary of American Mayors,* 223–24; *History of Milwaukee, Wisconsin, from Pre-Historical Times to the Present Date, …* (Chicago: Western Historical Co., 1881), 1150–51; Charles Tuttle, *An Illustrated History of the State of Wisconsin Being a Complete Civil, Political, and Military History …* (Boston: B. B. Russell, 1875), 797; *Dictionary of Wisconsin Biography* (Madison: State Historical Society of Wisconsin, 1960), 125.

38. Hanni Holzman, "The German Forty Eighters and the Socialists in Milwaukee: A Social Psychological Study of Assimilation," MA thesis, University of Wisconsin–Madison, 1948, 8, 26; Phil Drotning, *Milwaukee: A Salute to Yesterday and Today* (1946), 13, 20; Still, *Milwaukee,* 259; Carl Heinz Knoche, "The German Immigrant Press in Milwaukee," PhD diss., Ohio State University, 1969, 104–8; J. H. U. Lacher, *The German Element in Wisconsin* (Milwaukee: Milwaukee Steuben Society, 1925), 78–79.

39. *Daily Milwaukee News,* December 15, 1871; Lacher, *The German Element in Wisconsin,* 78; Milwaukee Public Museum, www.mpm.edu/about/ (accessed March 2, 2009); John Gregory, *A New and Vastly Improved Edition of the Industrial Resources of Wisconsin, Containing Numerous New Subjects,…* (Milwaukee: See-Bote Job Print, 1870), 189; Gregory, *A New And Vastly Improved Edition…,* 3rd ed. (1872), 90–93.

40. *Milwaukee Sentinel,* December 18, 1871.

41. Ibid., December 18, and 19, 1871; *Daily Milwaukee News,* December 15 and 19, 1871.

42. Knoche, "The German Immigrant Press in Milwaukee," 104–8, 257; *Der Seebote* (Abend), March 4, 1872.

43. *Milwaukee Sentinel,* January 3, 1872.

44. Ibid., January 3, 1872.

45. *Chicago Times,* January 4, 1872; *Milwaukee Sentinel,* January 4, 1872.

46. *Burning of the Newhall House* (Milwaukee: Bleyer Brothers, 1883); Larry Widen, "A Fiery End," *Greater Milwaukee Today,* March 9, 2005; *Invitation to Reception and Ball Given by the Citizens of Milwaukee at the Newhall House to His Imperial Highness Grand Duke Alexis,* Jeremiah Curtin Collection, Milwaukee County Historical Society, Milwaukee.

47. *Milwaukee Sentinel,* January 4, 1872; *Chicago Times,* January 4, 1872; John Jacob Schlicher, "Hans Balatka and the Milwaukee Musical Society," *Wisconsin Magazine of History* 27, no. 1 (1943–44): 40–55; Still, *Milwaukee,* 115.

48. *Milwaukee Sentinel,* January 4, 1872.

49. Ibid., January 4 and 5, 1872, January 6, 1871, January 10 and 11, 1872.

50. Ibid., December 16, 1871; *Cleveland Daily Plain Dealer,* January 4, 1872.

51. *Chicago Tribune,* January 4, 1871; *Chicago Times,* January 5, 1872.

52. *Milwaukee Sentinel,* January 6, 1872; *Daily Milwaukee News,* January 7, 1872.

53. *American Education Monthly,* April 1872; *Missouri Democrat,* January 6, 1872; *Chicago Times,* January 5 and 6, 1872.

54. Eric Sandweiss, *St. Louis: The Evolution of an American Urban Landscape* (Philadelphia: Temple University Press, 2001), 28; Selwyn K. Troen and Glen E. Holt, eds., *St. Louis* (New York: New Viewpoints, 1977), xvii–xx; David Lossos, *St. Louis: Then and Now* (Charleston, SC: Arcadia Publishing, 2005), 18; "The City of St. Louis," stlouis-mo.gov/visit-play/stlouis-history.cfm (accessed December 20, 2011).

55. *Missouri Democrat,* December 17, 1871.

56. Ibid., December 11, 16, 17, and 25, 1871.

57. Holli and Jones, eds., *Biographical Dictionary of American Mayors,* 43; St. Louis Commercial Club, Address of Colonel George E. Leighton, Vice-President, at the Autumnal Meeting of the Club, October 29, 1887, Duke University Library and Wisconsin Historical Society; Edward J. Gallagher, *Stilson Hutchins, 1838–1912: A Biography of the Founder of the Washington Post* (Laconia, NH: Citizen Publishing Co., 1965), 60–76; "The Pulitzer Prizes," www.pulitzer.org/biography (accessed April 4, 2011).

58. *Missouri Democrat,* January 5, 7, and 11, 1871.

59. Ibid., January 5, 1871.

60. *St. Louis Globe Democrat,* February 15, 1918, December 2, 1933.

61. *St. Louis Times,* February 10, 1930; *Missouri Democrat,* January 5 and 7, 1872; Southern Hotel and William Mackwitz, *Southern Hotel, Laveille, Warner & Co., Proprietors. Southern Hotel, St. Louis, Mo.... Bill of fare, One o'clock dinner St. Louis, Monday, September 9th, 1867* (Saint Louis, 1867).

62. *Missouri Democrat,* January 7, 1872.

63. Ibid.

64. Ibid.

65. Ibid.

66. John M. Callahan, "A History of the Second Olympic Theatre of St. Louis, 1882–1916," *Missouri Historical Society Bulletin,* July 1975; *Missouri Democrat,* January 3, 4, 5, 6, 7, and 8, 1872. See also *Atlanta Constitution,* January 19, 1872.

67. *Missouri Democrat,* January 8, 1872.

68. Ibid.; *Philadelphia Inquirer,* January 15, 1872.

69. *Missouri Democrat,* January 9, 1872.

70. David McCullough, *The Great Bridge* (New York: Simon and Schuster, 1983), 180–87; *Missouri Democrat,* January 9, 1872.

71. Letter of Henry Wicker, St. Louis, January 7, 1872, Wicker Collection, Missouri Historical Society, St. Louis.

72. *Missouri Democrat,* January 9, 1872.

73. Ibid.; Mackin, *A Society Woman on Two Continents,* 37–43.

74. *Missouri Democrat,* January 10, 1872.

75. Ibid., January 11 and 26, 1872.

76. Ibid., January 12, 1872.

77. Ibid.

78. *Missouri Democrat,* January 11, 1872; letters of Henry Wicker, January 14 and 28, 1872, Wicker Collection, Missouri Historical Society, St. Louis.

6. SO HAPPY TO BE HUNTING AGAIN

1. Cody's article in *The Cosmopolitan,* for example, incorrectly dates the Russian buffalo hunt as taking place in January 1873; see William F. Cody, "Famous Hunting Parties of the Plains," *The Cosmopolitan* 17, no. 2 (June 1894): 141. For a nicely written overview of the hunt, see Suzanne Massie, "The Grand Duke Alexis in the U.S.A.," *Gilcrease Magazine of American History and Art* 6, no. 3 (July 1984): 1–38.

2. Douglas Scott, Peter Bleed, and Stephen Damm, *Custer, Cody, and Grand Duke Alexis: Historical Archaeology of the Royal Buffalo Hunt* (Norman: University of Oklahoma Press, 2013), 40–44; Belknap to Sherman, November 1, 1871, and Sheridan to Townsend, November 22, 1871, Records of the Adjutant General's Office (RAGO), 1871, NARA, RG 94, Microfilm 666, obtained through Kansas State Historical Society. For more on Sheridan, see David Coffey, *Sheridan's Lieutenants: Phil Sheridan, His Generals, and the Final Years of the Civil Wars* (Wilmington, DE: Rowman & Littlefield Publishers, 2005), and *Phil Sheridan and His Army* (Lincoln: University of Nebraska Press, 1985).

3. Donald E. Worcester, "Spotted Tail: Warrior, Diplomat," *American West* 1, no. 4 (Fall 1964): 38–46; *Washington Daily Morning Chronicle,* June 9, 1870.

4. Scott, Bleed, and Damm, *Custer, Cody, and Grand Duke Alexis,* 45–47; *New York Herald,* January 14 and 15, 1872.

5. William F. Cody, *The Life of Hon. William F. Cody* (Hartford, CT: Frank E. Bliss, 1879), 295–98; Cody, *An Autobiography of Buffalo Bill (Colonel W. F. Cody)* (New York: Cosmopolitan Book Corp., 1928), 227–29; Cody, "Famous Hunting Parties of the Plains," 140; Helen Cody Wetmore and Zane Grey, *Last of the Great Scouts* (Chicago: Duluth Press Publishing Co., 1899), 192–94.

6. Fish to Belknap, December 20, 1871, and Sheridan to Townsend, January 3, 1871, RAGO, NARA, RG 94, Microfilm 666, obtained through Kansas State Historical Society; Scott, Bleed, and Damm, *Custer, Cody, and Grand Duke Alexis,* 43–45.

7. Scott, Bleed, and Damm, *Custer, Cody, and Grand Duke Alexis,* 44–47.

8. Ibid., 67. For more on Custer, see Paul Andrew Hutton, ed., *The Custer Reader* (Norman: University of Oklahoma Press, 2004), and Robert Marshall Utley, *Cavalier in Buckskin: George Armstrong Custer and the Western Military Frontier* (Norman: University of Oklahoma Press, 1988).

9. Scott, Bleed, and Damm, *Custer, Cody, and Grand Duke Alexis,* 44–45.

10. *Leavenworth Daily Commercial,* January 12 and 23, 1872.

11. *New York Herald,* January 13, 1872; Scott, Bleed, and Damm, *Custer, Cody, and Grand Duke Alexis,* 5, 17; *Kansas City Times,* January 14, 1872.

12. *Leavenworth Daily Commercial,* January 17, 1872.

13. *New York Herald,* January 13 and 14, 1872.

14. Ibid., January 14, 1872.

15. Ibid.; Wetmore and Grey, *Last of the Great Scouts,* 195.

16. Scott, Bleed, and Damm, *Custer, Cody, and Grand Duke Alexis,* 137–39; Henry E. Davies, *Ten Days on the Plains,* ed. Paul Andrew Hutton (Dallas: Southern Methodist University Press, 1985); *New York Times,* April 27, 1904.

17. Scott, Bleed, and Damm, *Custer, Cody, and Grand Duke Alexis,* 81–105; *New York Herald,* January 14, 1872; *Denver Times,* March 31, 1899.

18. *New York Herald,* January 14 and 16, 1872.

19. Ibid., January 16, 1872; Scott, Bleed, and Damm, *Custer, Cody, and Grand Duke Alexis,* 87–104, 144–55; Cody, *The Life of Hon. William F. Cody,* 298.

20. *New York Herald,* January 16, 1872.

21. Ibid.; Scott, Bleed, and Damm, *Custer, Cody, and Grand Duke Alexis,* 90–92; Alexei Alexandrovich Romanov to Maria Alexandrovna Romanov, January–February 1872, GARF, f. 641, op, 1, d. 34, ll. 120–120 ob.

22. *New York Herald,* January 16, 1872. This version of the grand duke's first kill has been widely repeated: Judge Bayard H. Paine, *The Famous Buffalo Hunt of Grand Duke Alexis of Russia, as Given at the Second Annual Picnic Held at Camp Duke Alexis, Hayes County, Nebraska, August 13, 1932;* James Albert Hadley, "A Royal Buffalo Hunt," *Transactions of the Kansas State Historical Society* 10 (1907–8): 564–74.

23. Cody, *The Life of Hon. William F. Cody,* 301; Cody, *Autobiography,* 231.

24. *Saturday Evening Post,* February 17, 1872; *Denver Times,* March 31, 1899; *Cleveland Daily Leader,* January 15 and 18, 1872; Cody, *The Life of Hon. William F. Cody,* 302; Cody, *Autobiography,* 232.

25. *New York Herald,* January 16, 1872; Cody, *The Life of Hon. William F. Cody,* 302; Cody, *Autobiography,* 232–33.

26. Cody, *Autobiography,* 233; Davies, 111.

27. *New York Herald,* January 16 and 17, 1872; Wetmore and Grey, *Last of the Great Scouts,* 197; Tucker, comp., *His Imperial Highness the Grand Duke Alexis,* 170.

28. *New York Herald,* January 17 and 18, 1872; Wetmore and Grey, *Last of the Great Scouts,* 197.

29. *New York Herald,* January 18, 1872; Cody, *The Life of Hon. William F. Cody,* 300.

30. Wetmore and Grey, *Last of the Great Scouts,* 197; Cody, *The Life of Hon. William F. Cody,* 302; Cody, *Autobiography,* 233; Cody, "Famous Hunting Parties of the Plains," 141; *New York Herald,* January 17 and 18, 1872.

31. Alexis to Vladimir, January 24, 1872, GARF, f. 652, op. 1, d. 385, ll. 7 ob-8.

32. *New York Herald,* January 18, 1872; Cody, *The Life of Hon. William F. Cody,* 304–5; Cody, *Autobiography,* 235–36; Wetmore and Grey, *Last of the Great Scouts,* 198.

33. *New York Herald,* January 18, 1872.

34. Ibid.; *Denver Post,* December 17, 1933.

35. *New York Herald,* January 18, 1872.

36. Ibid.; *Denver Times,* March 31, 1899.

37. *New York Herald,* January 18 and 20, 1872; *Denver Times,* March 31, 1899.

38. *New York Herald,* January 22, 1872; Chalkley Beeson, "A Royal Buffalo Hunt: Chalkley Beeson's Account," *Transactions of the Kansas State Historical Society* 10 (1907–8): 574–80; Miguel Antonio Otero, *My Life on the Frontier, 1864–1882* (New York: Press of the Pioneers, 1935), 51.

39. Otero, *My Life on the Frontier,* 51–53.

40. Beeson, "A Royal Buffalo Hunt," 578.

41. *New York Herald,* January 22 and 23, 1872.

42. Alexis to Maria Alexandrovna, January–February, 1872, GARF, f. 641, op. 1, d. 34, ll. 120–22; Alexis to Vladimir, January 24, 1872, GARF, f. 652, op. 1, d. 385, ll. 6–9 ob.

43. *Missouri Democrat,* January 24, 25, and 29, 1872.

44. Ibid.; January 30, 1872.

45. Peter E. Palmquist and Thomas R. Kailbourn, *Pioneer Photographers from the Mississippi to the Great Divide: A Biographical Dictionary, 1839–1865* (Palo Alto, CA: Stanford University Press, 2005), 536; Thomas J. Scharf, *History of St. Louis City and County* (Philadelphia: Louis H. Everts and Co., 1883), vol. 2: 1334; *Missouri Democrat,* January 26 and 27, 1872; Scott, Bleed, and Damm, *Custer, Cody, and Grand Duke Alexis,* 80–81.

46. *New York Herald,* January 13, 18, 22, and 24, 1872; *Philadelphia Inquirer,* January 13, 1872; see also *Mobile Register,* January 31, 1872.

47. *A Bill Restricting the Killing of the Bison, or Buffalo, upon the Public Lands,* H.R. 157, 42nd Cong., 1st sess., March 13, 1871; *Cleveland Daily Leader,* January 30, 1872; *A Bill Restricting the Killing of the Bison, or Buffalo, upon the Public Lands, to the Committee on the Public Lands,* H.R. 1728, 43rd Cong., 1st sess., February 2, 1874; *A Bill Restricting the Killing of the Buffalo upon the*

Public Lands, S. 655, 42nd Cong., 2nd sess., February 16, 1874; William Temple Hornaday, *Thirty Years War for Wildlife* (North Stratford, NH: Ayer Publishing, 1970), 247; *Congressional Globe and Appendix,* 42nd Cong., 2nd sess., part 6 (Washington, DC: Office of the Congressional Globe, 1872), 179–80. In his memoirs, W. T. Sherman expressed his view that the Indian problem was solved by the disappearance of the buffalo; see William Tecumseh Sherman, *Memoirs of W. T. Sherman* (New York: Literary Classics of the United States, Inc., 1990), 902–3, 926.

48. *New York Times,* January 26, February 7, and July 22, 1872.

49. W. E. Webb, *Buffalo Land: An Authentic Account of the Discoveries, Adventures and Mishaps of a Scientific and Sporting Party in the Wild West* (Cincinnati: E. Hannaford & Co., 1872); *New York Times,* July 22, 1874; Albert Bierstadt, *The Last of the Buffalo* (1888), Corcoran Gallery, Washington, DC; Hornaday, 248.

7. THIS YOUNG DUCK OF MUSCOVY

1. Qtd. in *Louisville Courier-Journal,* February 2, 1872.

2. *New Orleans Times,* December 22, 1871; Alexis to Maria Alexandrovna, January–February 1872, GARF, f. 641, op. 1, d. 34, l. 123.

3. Paul Gaston, *The New South Creed: A Study in Southern Mythmaking* (New York: Knopf, 1970), 3–7. See Lee A. Farrow, "Grand Duke Alexei and the Origins of Rex, 1872: Myth, Public Memory and the Distortion of History," *Gulf South Historical Review* 18, no.1 (Fall 2002): 6–30.

4. *Richmond Whig,* April 28, 1871; *New Orleans Republican,* November 26 and December 7, 1871; *New Orleans Times,* December 16, 1871, January 17, 1872. For other examples of negative and sarcastic references to the North, see *New Orleans Republican,* February 4 and 12, 1872; *New Orleans Times,* January 5, 1872; *New Orleans Semi-Weekly Louisianian,* February 15, 1872; *New Orleans Daily Picayune,* February 15, 1872.

5. *Memphis Daily Appeal,* February 1, 1872; *Charleston Daily Courier,* November 27, 1871; *Savannah Advertiser* qtd. in the *Charleston Daily Courier,* December 2, 1871.

6. *New Orleans Times,* December 5 and 8, 1871, January 15, 1872; *New Orleans Republican,* November 26, 1871.

7. John E. Kleber, ed., *The Encyclopedia of Louisville* (Louisville: University Press of Kentucky, 2001), xv–xxi.

8. *Memphis Daily Appeal,* January 26, 1872; *Louisville Courier Journal,* October 22, 1871, and January 26, 1872.

9. Biographical Dictionary of the United States Congress, bioguide.congress.gov/scripts/biodisplay.pl?index=P000517 (accessed February 24, 2011); Kleber, ed., *The Encyclopedia of Louisville,* 67, 368, 960; *History of the Ohio Falls Cities and Their Counties with Illustrations and Biographical Sketches* (Cleveland: L. A. Williams & Co., 1882), vol. 1: 593–96; *Biographical Encyclopedia of Kentucky of the Dead and Living Men of the Nineteenth Century* (Cincinnati: J. M. Armstrong & Co., 1878), 13–14; M. Joblin & Co., *Louisville Past and Present: Its Industrial History as Exhibited in the Life-labors of Its Leading Men* (Louisville: John P. Morton and Co., 1875), 120, 288–90; Frederick Wallis and Hambleton Tapp, eds., *A Sesqui-Centennial History of Kentucky* (Hopkinsville, KY: Historical Record Assoc., 1945), 1300–1304.

10. Kleber, ed., *The Encyclopedia of Louisville*, 198–99; Joe Drape, ed., *To the Swift: Classic Triple Crown Horses and Their Race to Glory* (New York: MacMillan, 2008), 7–9.

11. *Louisville Daily Ledger,* January 24, 1872; *Louisville Courier-Journal,* January 27, 28, 29, and 30, 1872.

12. *Louisville Daily Ledger,* January 24, 28, and 31, 1872, February 1, 1872; *Louisville Courier-Journal,* January 26 and 28, 1872.

13. *Louisville Courier-Journal,* January 29 and 30, 1872; *Louisville Daily Ledger,* January 30, 1872.

14. *Louisville Courier-Journal,* January 31, 1872; *Louisville Daily Ledger,* January 31, 1872; Ann Bodley to Temple Bodley, February 29, 1872, Bodley Family Papers, 1773–1939, Filson Historical Society, Louisville, KY.

15. Kleber, ed., *The Encyclopedia of Louisville,* 327–28; *Louisville Courier Journal and Times Magazine,* August 6, 1872; *New York Times,* April 25, 1869; *Louisville Courier-Journal,* January 26 and February 2, 1872.

16. *Louisville Courier-Journal,* January 31, 1872.

17. Martha Bodley to Temple Bodley, February 16, 1872, and Ann Bodley to Temple Bodley, February 29, 1872, Bodley Family Papers, 1773–1939, Filson Historical Society, Louisville, KY; *Louisville Daily Ledger,* January 31, 1872; *Louisville Courier-Journal,* January 31 and February 1, 1872.

18. Alexis to Maria Alexandrovna, January–February 1872, GARF, f. 641, op. 1, d. 34, l. 123 ob.

19. *Louisville Daily Ledger,* February 1, 1872; Louisville Water Co., www.louisvilleky.gov/LWC/Out+of+the+Archives/Building+the+Louisville+Water+Works.htm (accessed October 21, 2013); Kleber, ed., *The Encyclopedia of Louisville,* 581.

20. Kentucky Historical Society, migration.kentucky.gov/kyhs/hmdb/MarkerSearch.aspx?mode=Subject&subject=161 (accessed October 19, 2013); Kleber, ed., *The Encyclopedia of Louisville,* 467, 938–39; *Louisville Daily Ledger,* February 1, 1872.

21. *Virginia City Territorial Enterprise,* January 30, 1868; *New York Times,* August 10 and 12, 1899.

22. *Louisville Courier Journal,* February 1 and 2, 1872; *Louisville Daily Ledger,* February 1 and 2, 1872.

23. *Louisville Daily Ledger,* February 2, 1872.

24. Elizabeth B. Custer and John Manion, "Custer, Cody and the Grand Duke Alexis," *Research Review: The Journal of the Little Big Horn Associates* 4 (January 1990): 12.

25. Qtd. in Marguerite Merington, ed., *The Custer Story: The Life and Intimate Letters of General George A. Custer and His Wife Elizabeth* (Lincoln: University of Nebraska Press, 1987), 247.

26. John J. Wagoner and Lewis D. Cutliff, *Mammoth Cave* (Arlington, VA: Interpretive Publications, Inc., 1985), 30–36.

27. *Louisville Courier Journal,* February 2 and 3, 1872; *Louisville Daily Ledger,* February 2 and 3, 1872; Alexis to Maria Alexandrovna, January–February 1872, GARF, f. 641, op. 1, d. 34, l. 124.

28. John E. Harkins, *Metropolis of the American Nile: An Illustrated History of Memphis and Shelby County* (Oxford, MS: Guild Bindery Press, 1991), 26, 30, 36, 41, 53–55, 70–86, 88–91.

29. *Memphis Daily Appeal,* January 7, 8, 9, and 26, 1872; *City of Memphis Mayor and Board of Aldermen Minute Book,* January 10, 1870, to June 22, 1874, 373, Shelby County Archive, Memphis;

O. F. Vedder, *History of the City of Memphis and Shelby County Tennessee, with Illustrations and Biographical Sketches of Some of Its Prominent Citizens* (Syracuse, NY: D. Mason and Co., 1888), vol. 2: 30, 31, 81, 159, 174, 175, 208.

30. *Memphis Daily Appeal,* January 17 and 20, 1872, February 2, 1872.

31. Ibid., January 14, 1872.

32. Ibid., January 2, 5, 6, 11, and 21, 1872.

33. Ibid., January 31, 1872, February 2 and 3, 1872; *New Orleans Republican,* February 1, 1872.

34. *Memphis Daily Appeal,* February 3, 1872; "A History of the Peabody Hotel, Memphis," unpublished document obtained from Peabody Hotel, Memphis.

35. "How a River Town Grew into a City" (Memphis) *Commercial Appeal,* December 5, 1920, "Memphis—City Hall—History," Clippings Files, Memphis Public Library; *Memphis Daily Appeal,* February 4, 1872.

36. (Memphis) *Press Scimitar,* March 30 and November 24, 1932, Clippings Files, "Memphis—Visitors—Alexis, Grand Duke of Russia," and (Memphis) *Commercial Appeal,* March 23, 24, and 25, 1936 (Memphis) *Press Scimitar,* March 23, 1936, Clippings Files, "Memphis—Biography—Pinson, Sina Duke (Mrs. R.A.)," Memphis Public Library; *Memphis Daily Appeal,* February 3 and 4, 1872; *New Orleans Bee,* February 4, 1872.

37. Joe Walk, "Memphis and Shelby County Government Buildings: County Courthouses, Jails and Workhouses City Halls, The Early Years: 1820–1880" (1996), manuscript in Shelby County Archive, Memphis; Joan Hassell, ed., *Memphis, 1800–1900,* comp. Carole M. Ornelas-Struve (New York: Nancy Powers & Co., 1982), vol. 3: 63; *Memphis Daily Appeal,* February 5, 1872.

38. *Memphis Daily Appeal,* February 5, 1872.

39. Diary of Constantin Possiet, February 1872, RGA VMF, f. 1247, op. 1, d. 41, ll. 19 ob-20.

40. *Cincinnati Daily Gazette,* January 15, 1871; *New Orleans Times,* February 3, 1872; *Memphis Daily Appeal,* February 7 and 8, 1872; Lewis C. Baird, *Baird's History of Clark County, Indiana* (Indianapolis: B. F. Bowen, 1909), 330, 338.

41. Thomas Smith, *Southern Queen: New Orleans in the Nineteenth Century* (London: Continuum, 2011), 6–19, 121–25; see also Joan B. Garvey and Mary Lou Widmer, *Beautiful Crescent: A History of New Orleans* (New Orleans: Garmer Press, 1982).

42. James K. Hogue, *Uncivil War: Five New Orleans Street Battles and the Rise and Fall of Radical Reconstruction* (Baton Rouge: Louisiana State University Press, 2006), 2–8, 40–45.

43. *The Papers of Ulysses S. Grant: June 1, 1871–January 31, 1872* (Carbondale: South Illinois University Press, 1998), 340–41; Robert W. Coakley, *The Role of Federal Military Forces in Domestic Disorders, 1789–1878* (Darby, PA: Diane Publishing, 1996), 317–21.

44. *New Orleans Daily Picayune,* November 25, 1871, December 3 and January 13, 1872; *New Orleans Republican,* November 25, 1871; *New Orleans Bee,* January 14, 1872.

45. *New Orleans Times,* January 30, 1872; *New Orleans Daily Picayune,* December 31, 1871, February 9, 11, 13, and 14, 1872.

46. *New Orleans Daily Picayune,* January 27, 1872; *New Orleans Times,* January 31, 1872.

47. *New Orleans Daily Picayune,* January 31, 1872; *New Orleans Times,* January 29, 1872.

48. *New Orleans Times,* February 1, 1872.

49. Errol Laborde, *Krewe: The Early New Orleans Carnival, Comus to Zulu* (Metairie, LA: Carnival Press, 2007), 13, 35, 48–49; *New Orleans Times,* February 1, 1872; *New Orleans Bee,* February 14, 1872; *New Orleans Republican,* February 12, 1872.

50. *New Orleans Bee,* February 1, 2, and 3, 1872; *New Orleans Daily Picayune,* February 1, 3, and 7, 1872; *New Orleans Republican,* February 6 and 7, 1872; Laborde, *Krewe,* 43.

51. *New Orleans Bee,* February 2, 1872; *New Orleans Daily Picayune,* February 2, 1872; *New Orleans Times,* February 7 and 8, 1872.

52. *New Orleans Times,* February 2, 3, 4, 8, and 11, 1872.

53. *New Orleans Daily Picayune,* February 11, 1872; *Atlanta Constitution,* January 18 and 31, 1872; *New Orleans Republican,* February 13, 1872.

54. *Wichita Eagle,* May 22, 1901; *Topeka Capital,* May 25, 1901; *Field and Farm,* August 19, 1905; *New Orleans Republican,* February 11, 1872; *New Orleans Daily Picayune,* February 11, 1872.

55. Ella Lonn, *Foreigners in the Confederacy* (Chapel Hill: University of North Carolina Press, 2002), 145–46, 223–28; Valery Sulakowski, "The Visit of the Grand Duke Alexis, of Russia, to New Orleans." Sulakowski's pronouncement is undated, but is referred to in the *New Orleans Republican,* February 10, 1872, so it had to have appeared before then.

56. *New Orleans Times,* February 6, 1872. See, for example, the disgust expressed in the articles in the *New Orleans Times,* December 15 and 16, 1871.

57. *Memphis Daily Appeal,* February 4 and 5, 1872; Sam Kinser, *Carnival, American Style: Mardi Gras at New Orleans and Mobile* (Chicago: University of Chicago Press, 1990), 78–89, 107.

58. *Hartford Daily Courant,* October 20, 1871; *Memphis Daily Appeal,* February 4 and January 28, 1872; *Weekly Louisianian,* February 15, 1872; *New Orleans Republican,* December 7, 1871; *New Orleans Daily Picayune,* February 14, 1872; *Philadelphia Inquirer,* November 29, 1871. For other examples, see *Every Saturday,* December 23, 1871; *Baltimore Sun,* November 21, 1871.

59. *Toronto Globe,* November 4, 1871. See, for example, *Vienna Tageblatt,* qtd. in *Washington Daily Morning Chronicle,* December 18, 1871; *Dublin Freeman's Journal and Daily Commercial Advertiser,* September 2, 1872; *Belfast News-Letter,* December 16, 1871; *Pall Mall Gazette,* December 9, 1871; *Cleveland Daily Leader,* December 22, 1871.

60. Rpt. from *New York Tribune* in *Philadelphia Bulletin,* December 8, 1871.

61. Diary of Constantin Possiet, February 1872, RGA VMF, f. 1247, op. 1, d. 41, ll. 20–24 ob.

62. *New Orleans Daily Picayune,* February 11, 1872.

63. Custer and Manion, "Custer, Cody and the Grand Duke Alexis," 12; *Memphis Daily Appeal,* February 6, 1872.

64. Alexis to Maria Alexandrovna, January–February 1872, GARF, f. 641, op. 1, d. 34, l. 124 ob.; Beliakova, *Velikii kniaz' Aleksei Aleksandrovich,* 126; Diary of Constantin Possiet, February 1872, RGA VMF, f. 1247, op. 1, d. 41, ll. 20–24 ob.

65. Herman DeBachelle Seebold, *Old Louisiana Plantation Homes and Family Trees* (1941; rpt. Gretna, LA: Pelican Publishing, 2005), 111–15; Lillian C. Bourgeois, *Cabanocey: The History, Customs and Folklore of St. James Parish* (1957; Gretna, LA: Pelican Publishing, 1999), 141; Adèle le Bourgeois Chapin, *"Their Trackless Way": A Book of Memories,* ed. Christina Chapin (London: Constable & Co., 1931), 28–29; *New Orleans Bee,* February 13, 1872; *New Orleans Daily Picayune,* February 13, 1872.

66. *New Orleans Times,* February 13, 1872; *New Orleans Daily Picayune,* February 13, 1872; *New Orleans Republican,* February 13, 1872.

67. *New Orleans Times,* February 13, 1872; *New Orleans Daily Picayune,* February 13, 1872; *New Orleans Republican,* February 13, 1872.

68. *Historical Sketchbook and Guide to New Orleans and Environs, with Map* (New York: Will H. Coleman, 1885), 71; *New Orleans Republican,* February 27, 1872.

69. *New Orleans Daily Picayune,* February 13, 1872; *The Picayune's Guide to New Orleans,* 6th ed. (New Orleans: The Picayune, 1904), 18; *Visitor's Guide to New Orleans* (New Orleans: J. Curtis Waldo, 1875), 110; Andre Lafargue, "The New Orleans French Opera House: A Retrospect," *Louisiana Historical Quarterly* 3 (1922): 368–72.

70. *New Orleans Daily Picayune,* February 13 and 14, 1872.

71. *New Orleans Republican,* February 9, 13, and 14, 1872; *New Orleans Daily Picayune,* February 14, 1872; *New Orleans Bee,* February 14, 1872.

72. *New Orleans Republican,* February 9, 13, and 14, 1872; *New Orleans Daily Picayune,* February 14, 1872; *New Orleans Bee,* February 14, 1872.

73. *New Orleans Republican,* February 14, 1872; *New Orleans Semi-Weekly Louisianian,* February 15, 1872.

74. *New Orleans Republican,* February 14, 1872; *New Orleans Bee,* February 14, 1872.

75. *New Orleans Times,* June 13, 1867; *New Orleans Daily Picayune,* February 15 and 18, 1872; *Picayune's Guide,* 58–59.

76. Edward T. James and Janet Wilson James, *Notable American Women: A Biographical Dictionary* (Cambridge, MA: Harvard University Press, 1972), 395–96; *New Orleans Republican,* February 15, 1872; *New Orleans Daily Republican,* February 18, and 20, 1872.

77. *New Orleans Daily Picayune,* February 13 and 14, 1872.

78. Ibid., February 16, 1872; *New Orleans Republican,* February 16, 1872.

79. *Visitor's Guide to New Orleans,* 42; *New Orleans Republican,* February 16, 17, and 21, 1872; *New Orleans Daily Picayune,* February 16, 17, and 20, 1872.

80. *New Orleans Daily Picayune,* February 18, 1872.

81. Ibid., February 15, 1872; Alexis to Maria Alexandrovna, January–February 1872, GARF, f. 641, op. 1, d. 34, l. 125.

82. *New Orleans Times,* January 5 and February 14, 1872; *New Orleans Bee,* February 11, 1872; *Memphis Daily Appeal,* January 17, 1872

83. *Mobile Register,* February 13, 14, 15, 17, and 20, 1872.

84. *New Orleans Daily Picayune,* February 23, 1872; *New Orleans Republican,* February 27 and 28, 1872; *Mobile Register,* February 21 and 25, 1872.

85. Diary of Constantin Possiet, February 1872, RGA VMF, f. 1247, op. 1, d. 41, ll. 20 ob–22.

86. Alexis to Maria Alexandrovna, January–February 1872, GARF, f. 641, op. 1, d. 34, ll. 121–24; Alexis to Vladimir, January 24, 1872, GARF, f. 652, op. 1, d. 385, ll. 8–8 ob.

87. *Atlanta Constitution,* December 15, 1871; *Kansas City Times,* January 19, 1872. See also *New Orleans Republican,* January 25, February 1 and 18, and March 13, 1872; *New Orleans Times,* December 23, 1871; *Saturday Evening Post,* February 24, 1872.

CONCLUSION: BUFFALO TALES AND MARDI GRAS MYTHS

1. Count A. Perovskii to Alexis, March 17, 1872, GARF, f. 681, op. 1, d. 62, 1–4 ob.

2. Alexander II to Alexis, March 16, 1872, GARF, f. 681, op, 1, d. 18, str. 3–4 ob.

3. Diary of Possiet, RGA VMF, f. 1247, op. 1, d. 41, ll. 30 ob–33 ob.

4. Alexis to Vladimir, December 1872, GARF, f. 652, op. 1, d. 385, ll. 69–72.

5. Diary of Possiet, RGA VMF, f. 1247, op. 1, d. 41, ll. 51 ob–53 ob.

6. Catherine Radziwill, *Behind the Veil at the Russian Court* (New York: John Lane Co., 1914), 126; *Washington Post,* October 7, 1907; Saul, *Concord and Conflict,* 111–16.

7. Beliakova, "Grand Duke Alexis Alexandrovich (1850–1908)," in *The Grand Dukes,* 128; Beliakova, *Velikii kniaz' Aleksei Aleksandrovich,* 160–68; A. Novikoff-Priboy, *Tsushima,* trans. Eden and Cedar Paul (New York: Alfred A. Knopf, 1937), 34; Sergei Witte, *The Memoirs of Count Witte,* ed. Sidney Harcave (Armonk, NY: M. E. Sharpe, 1990), 153; quote from Sandro in Andrei Maylunas and Sergei Mironenko, *A Lifelong Passion: Nicholas and Alexandra, Their Own Story* (New York: Doubleday, 1997), 314; Charlotte Zeepvat, "Fast Women and Slow Ships," *Royalty Digest* 7 (May 1988): 322–27.

8. Alexander to Alexis, November 18, 1875, GARF, f. 681, op. 1, d. 31, ll. 1–2 ob.

9. Mikhailovich, *Once a Grand Duke,* 151; Beliakova, *Velikii kniaz' Aleksei Aleksandrovich,* 178–80. The affair with Zina was reported in western papers, as well. See *New York Times,* June 23 and October 6, 1889.

10. F. C. Philips, *My Varied Life* (London: Ballantine and Co., 1914), 49; Beliakova, *Velikii kniaz' Aleksei Aleksandrovich,* 174–88; *New York Times,* September 21, 1902; *New York Tribune,* June 22, 1900.

11. *Washington Post,* March 10, 1907; Charles Rearick, *Paris Dreams, Paris Memories: The City and Its Mystique* (Palo Alto, CA: Stanford University Press, 2011), 30–31, 53–54; David Chavchavadze, *The Grand Dukes* (New York: Atlantic International Publishers, 1990), 113–17. The *New York Tribune,* on December 20, 1891, reported that Grand Dukes Alexis and Vladimir were "doing" the slums of Paris, as well.

12. Ann Blainey, *Marvelous Melba: The Extraordinary Life of a Great Diva* (Chicago: Ivan R. Dee, 2009), 105–7; Nellie Melba, *Melodies and Memories* (Cambridge, UK: Cambridge University Press, 2011), 103–4; Jack Winsor Hansen, *The Sibyl Sanderson Story: Requiem for a Diva* (Pompton Plains, NJ: Amadeus Press, 2005), 161–70.

13. Inventory obtained from Boucheron, Paris, May 2012; Vincent Meylan, *Boucheron: The Secret Archives* (Woodbridge, Suffolk, Eng.: Antique Collectors' Club Ltd., 2009), 106; Hans Nadelhoffer, *Cartier* (San Francisco: Chronicle Books, 2007), 104, 344; *The Fabergé Menagerie* (London: Philip Wilson Publishers, 2003), 25.

14. Documents relating to Alexis's travels abroad in 1887, GARF, f. 681, op. 1, d. 81, ll. 1–331; Alexander III to Alexis, December 31, 1887, f. 681, d.33, ll. 7–7 ob. In a letter from 1889, he informs Alexis that he should be prepared to go to Vienna for the coronation ceremony there; Alexander III to Alexis, January 19,1889, GARF, f. 681, op. 1, d. 34, ll. 3.

15. Alexis to Zinaida Leuchtenberg, November 19, 1894, GARF, f. 681, op. 1, d. 13. ll. 1–3.

16. *New York Tribune,* May 27 and June 21, 1895, August 8 and 24, 1897; Maylunas and Mironenko, *A Lifelong Passion,* 103, 132, 186–87.

17. Maylunas and Mironenko, *A Lifelong Passion,* 143–47.

18. Ibid., 267–68, 273; *New York Times,* February 21, 1905; *Washington Post,* February 21, April 1, 16, and 27, March 23, 1905.

19. *Washington Post,* April 27, 1905; *Chicago Tribune,* March 2, 1907.

20. *Washington Post,* June 23, 1905.

21. *New York Tribune,* August 14, 1891; *Washington Post,* May 13 and November 28, 1906; *New York Tribune,* July 1, 1907.

22. Papers relating to the illness and death of Alexis, 1908, GARF, f. 652, op. 1, d. 1009, ll. 2–28.

23. Invitation to funeral to John W. Riddle, Flandrau Family Papers, 1856–1969, box 75, folder 90, Arizona Historical Society, Southern Division, Tucson.

24. *New York Times,* November 15, 20, and 22, 1908; *Denver Republican,* November 15, 1908; *Washington Post,* November 23, 1908; *New York Tribune,* November 22, 1908; *San Francisco Call,* December 20, 1908.

25. Alexis to Vladimir, January 24, 1872, GARF, f. 652, op. 1, d. 385, str. 9 ob, 76; letter of January 16, 1873 ordering money to be sent to Zhukovskaya, f. 652, op. 1, d. 909, str. 5, 16–22; Beliakova, *Velikii kniaz' Aleksei Aleksandrovich,* 99–101.

26. Documents pertaining to the distribution of capital to Count Belevski and his family, GARF, f. 681, op. 1, d. 80, 1–20; Beliakova, *Velikii kniaz' Aleksei Aleksandrovich,* 101–3; Belevski-Zhukovskii Collection, New York Public Library; *New York Tribune,* January 7, 1894; *Chicago Tribune,* September 29, 1901; *Washington Post,* December 31, 1908;

27. List of property remaining after the death of Alexis, 1908, GARF, f. 652, op. 1, d. 1008, ll. 24–36; documents pertaining to the distribution of capital to Count Belevski and his family, GARF, f. 681, op. 1, 80, 41–43; Beliakova, "Grand Duke Alexis Alexandrovich (1850–1908)," 131; Rosemary and Donald Crawford, *Michael and Natasha: The Life and Love of Michael II, the Last of the Romanov Tsars* (New York: Scribner, 1997), 166.

28. Beliakova, *Velikii kniaz' Aleksei Aleksandrovich,* 103–4.

29. For example, for historical information on Alexis and his family, see *Every Saturday,* October 28, 1871; *Memphis Daily Appeal,* October 29, 1871; *Missouri Democrat,* November 4, 1871; *New Orleans Times,* November 15, 1871; *San Francisco Chronicle,* November 18 and 21, 1871; *Milwaukee Sentinel,* November 20 and 21, 1871; *Detroit Advertiser and Tribune,* November 21, 1871; *Kansas State Record,* November 22, 1871; *Kansas Daily Commonwealth,* November 22, 1871, and January 21, 1872; *Scribner's Monthly Magazine* 3, no. 2 (December 1871); *Washington Evening Star,* December 9, 1871; *Appleton's,* December 16, 1871; *Weekly Louisianian,* December 28, 1871; *(New Orleans) Semi-Weekly Louisianian,* December 28, 1871; *Kansas Daily Commonwealth,* January 21, 1872; *Louisville Courier-Journal,* January 28–31, 1872; *Louisville Daily Ledger,* January 31, 1872; *Overland Monthly and Out West Magazine* 8, no. 2 (February 2, 1872); *Memphis Daily Appeal,* February 2, 1872, and February 4, 1871; *New Orleans Daily Picayune,* February 14, 1871. For articles on Russia and Russian society, see *New Orleans Times,* November 7, 1871; *Missouri Democrat,* November 12, 1871; *Weekly Louisianian,* December 14, 1871; *Memphis Appeal,* February 3, 1872.

30. *Louisville Courier-Journal,* October 30, 1871.

31. *Philadelphia Press,* November 21, 1871; *Philadelphia Bulletin,* November 6, 1871; *New York Herald,* November 11, 1871; *Boston Commonwealth,* December 9, 1871.

32. Tucker, comp., *His Imperial Highness the Grand Duke Alexis;* J. W. Goodspeed, *The Life of Col. James Fisk, Jr., "The Prince of Erie,"… Together with a Sketch of the Grand Duke Alexis, of Russia, his Home and Family* (Chicago: H. S. Goodspeed, 1872); Ames, *Outlines of Men, Women and Things.*

33. Custer and Manion, "Custer, Cody and the Grand Duke Alexis," 11; *Toronto Globe,* December 15 and 29, 1871; *Brooklyn Eagle,* December 19, 1871; *Washington Daily Morning Chronicle,* December 16, 1871; *Saturday Evening Post,* December 16, 1871; *Missouri Democrat,* January 12, 1871; *Cheyenne Daily Leader,* January 25, 1872; *New York Times,* October 25, 1872; James Russell Soley, *Historical Sketch of the United States Naval Academy* (Washington, DC: Government Printing Office, 1876), 178; *Milwaukee Sentinel,* February 15, 1872; *New Orleans Republican,* December 15, 1871, January 12 and February 28, 1872. He also left $1,000 for the poor in Montreal; *Toronto Globe,* December 29, 1871.

34. Daniel T. Kelly, *The Buffalo Head: A Century of Mercantile Pioneering in the Southwest* (Santa Fe, NM: Vergara Publishing Co., 1972), 15. The buffalo skeleton can be found at the National Museum of Natural History, Washington, DC (Catalog number USNM 269169). In a list of accessions for the fiscal year 1939–40, the donation is attributed to Professor Paul B. Sawin of Brown University; Smithsonian Institution, *Report on Progress and Condition of the United States National Museum for the Year Ended June 30, 1940* (Washington, DC: Government Printing Office, 1941), 79. Of course, not all mementos were genuine: for over two decades, the Harlem Club in New York City claimed to have in its reception area a bear shot by Alexis during the hunt, though there is no record of the Grand Duke shooting bear in the United States; *New York Tribune,* February 2, 1902.

35. *Riverside: A Village in a Park* (Riverside, IL: Frederick Law Olmstead Society of Riverside, 1970), n.p.

36. *Missouri Democrat,* January 8 and 12, 1872; *Louisville Courier-Journal,* February 1 and 2, 1872.

37. *New York Times,* December 28, 1873; *Proceedings of the Board of Regents, University of Michigan (1870–1876),* 322–23, name.umdl.umich.edu/ACW7513.1870.001 (accessed October 18, 2013); *The Chronicle* (University of Michigan), vol. 5 (1874): 75; *New York Tribune,* March 31 and October 9, 1874; Morgan Dix, comp., *Memoirs of John Adams Dix* (New York: Harper and Brothers, 1883), vol. 2: 161–62.

38. Letter from Albert Bierstadt to William Stoddard, December 29, 1872, Accession No. 68x101.1, and letter from Albert Bierstadt to M. Bodisco, Imperial Consulate of Russia, December 29, 1872, Accession No. 69x53a, Collection 276 (Albert Bierstadt), Joseph Downs Collection of Manuscripts and Printed Ephemera, Winterthur Library, Henry Francis du Pont Winterthur Museum, Winterthur, Delaware. The reference to the Hermitage can be found in Phillip Drennon Thomas, "Bierstadt of Dusseldorf, Painter of America's Western Vision," *Magazine of Western History* 26, no. 2 (Spring 1976): 15.

39. The list included General Philip Sheridan, Vice-Admiral Stephen Clegg Rowan, Captain Henry K. Davenport, Captain Fitzhugh, Captain H. A. Adams, Captain Chester Hatfield, Vice-Commodore Henry Robeson, General John A. Dix, and William H. Aspinwall; *Hamilton Fish Diaries,* reel 1, vol. 3: November 11, 1872.

40. Edward H. Tarr, *East Meets West: The Russian Trumpet Tradition from the Time of Peter the Great to the October Revolution* (Hillsdale, NY: Pendragon Press, 2003), 85; *Cleveland Daily Plain Dealer,* December 30, 1871; *Daily Alta California,* January 22, 1872.

41. See, for example, the New York Public Library; the National Portrait Gallery of the Smithsonian; the Buffalo Bill Historical Center; the Denver Public Library, the Golden Spike/Promontory Photograph Collection at the Utah State History Society; the Manuscripts, Archives and Special Collections division of the Washington State University Library in Pullman; the Center for Southwest Research at the University of New Mexico; the Special Collections of the Fine Arts Library at Harvard University; and the Utah State Archives.

42. Other facilities that possess dinner and ball tickets are the New Jersey Historical Society and the Museum of the City of New York.

43. Other places that possess train schedules or passes are the National Library and Archives of Canada in Ottawa; the Abraham Lincoln Presidential Library; the Thomas J. Dodd Research Center at the University of Connecticut; the Litchfield Historical Society, Litchfield, Connecticut; and the William L. Clements Library, University of Michigan.

44. Charles Ranhofer, *The Epicurean* (New York: Charles Ranhofer, 1894), 79, 273; haydelbakery.com/Russian-Cake (accessed October 15, 2013); Virginia Tuttle Clayton, Elizabeth Stillinger, and Erika Lee Doss, *Drawing on America's Past: Folk Art, Modernism, and the Index of American Design* (Chapel Hill: University of North Carolina Press, 2002), 193–94.

45. Alexis, Illinois, www.alexisonline.com (accessed August 7, 2012); *New York Times,* October 10, 1937; Tyler Anbinder, *Five Points: The 19th-Century New York City Neighborhood That Invented Tap Dance, Stole Elections, and Became the World's Most Notorious Slum* (New York: Free Press, 2001), 190–91.

46. See Lewis F. Allen, *The American Herd Book, Containing Pedigrees of Short-Horn Cattle* (Buffalo: Thomas, Howard and Johnson), vol. 8 (1868), vol. 9 (1870), vol. 10 (1871), vol. 12, pt. 1 (1873), and vol. 13 (1874); James Buckingham, *American Devon Record: Containing the Pedigrees of Pure Bred Devon Cattle in the United States and the Dominion of Canada to January 1, 1880* (Frankfort, KY: Major, Johnston and Banett, 1881), vol. 1; H. M. Sessions, ed., *American Devon Herd Book, Containing the Names and Pedigrees of Devon Cattle, and the Prizes They Have Gained, with the Names of Their Breeders and Owners* (Springfield, MA: Clark W. Bryan and Co., 1872), vol. 3; *American Jersey Herd Book, Association of Breeders of Thorough-Bred Neat Stock,* 2nd ed. (Worcester: Tyler and Seagrave, 1873), vol. 1.

47. John Langdon Sibley, *John Langdon Sibley's Diary, 1846–1882;* Hollis Horatio Hunnewell, ed., *Life Letters, and Diary of Horatio Hollis Hunnewell*... (privately printed, 1906), 65; Ednah D. Cheney, ed., *Louisa May Alcott: Her Life, Letters and Journals* (Boston: Roberts Brothers, 1889), 261; William Lloyd Garrison, *The Letters of William Lloyd Garrison: To Rouse the Slumbering Land, 1868–1979* (Cambridge, MA: Harvard University Press, 1981), 20; Longfellow, *Life of Henry Wadsworth Longfellow,* 190–91. In addition to the memoirs which are quoted elsewhere in the text, see Lee Merriwether, *Afterthoughts: A Sequel to My Yesteryears* (Webster Grove, MO: International Mark Twain Society, 1945), 407; Chapin, *"Their Trackless Way,"* 28–29. For more letters that mention the Russian visit, see C. D. Emory to Henry F. Brownson, December 7, 1871, Henry F. Brownson Papers, University of Notre Dame Archives, Notre Dame, IN; Mary Mason Fairbanks to

Mark Twain, February 28, 1872, in Lin Salamo and Harriet Elinor Smith, eds., *Mark Twain's Letters* (Berkeley: University of California Press, 1997), vol. 5, *1872–1873*: 50; William Bodley to Temple Bodley, February 8, 1872, Martha Bodley to Temple Bodley, February 16, 1872, and Ann Bodley to Temple Bodley, February 29, 1872, all in Bodley Family Papers, 1773–1939, Filson Historical Society, Louisville, KY; Mary Eliza Reeves to Ms. Thomas A. Marshall, February 15, 1872, Marshall Family Papers, Filson Historical Society, Louisville, KY; and *Samuel F. B. Morse, His Letters and Journals* (Boston: Houghton Mifflin, 1914), vol. 2: 497.

48. Mackin, *A Society Woman on Two Continents*, 37–43.

49. *Denver Times*, March 31, 1899; poster, object I.D. no. 1.69.2646, Buffalo Bill Museum and Historical Center, Cody, WY; Sandra Sagala, *Buffalo Bill on Stage* (Albuquerque: University of New Mexico Press, 2008), 149.

50. *New York Times*, September 4, 1881, June 22, 1890, March 23, 1909; *New York Tribune*, October 5 and 18, 1893; *New York Times*, September 30, 1897, November 17, 1901, April 7, 1906; *New York Tribune*, July 23, 1912; *New York Times*, March 6, 1931, February 5, 1933; *Milwaukee Journal*, March 11, 1940. Similarly, the obituary of Luther Crocker, "Inventor of Ticket Punches," mentioned his creation of the special ticket punch used for the train of Grand Duke Alexis, which displayed the Romanov family coat of arms; *Boston Journal*, April 8, 1895.

51. *Daily Constitution* (Middletown, CT), November 20, 1875; *San Francisco Bulletin*, August 19, 1876; *New York Times*, June 18, 1905. See also *Sun*, June 6, 1877. In the case of Miss Alexandra Patricia Bjerring, it was not her interaction with the grand duke but her father's that was mentioned in the announcement of her engagement; her father was the late Reverend Nicholas Bjerring, chaplain of the Russian Orthodox Church at the time of the royal visit; *New York Times*, July 6, 1932.

52. *New York Times*, December 24, 1885, October 8, 1887; *New York Tribune*, February 26, 1914; William Stifel, *The Dog Show: 125 Years of Westminster* (New York: Westminster Kennel Club, 2001), 27.

53. *Niagara Falls* (Buffalo, NY: Matthews, Northrup, & Co., 1890), 76. The famous New York institution Delmonico's has had much written about it over the years, and the grand duke's banquet is almost always offered as one of the most spectacular moments in the restaurant's long history. See for example, *Fifth Avenue Events*, 8; Maurice, *Fifth Avenue*, 111; Thomas, *Delmonico's*, 96–101.

54. For a sample of such references, see Edwards, ed., *New York's Great Industries*, 282; *Century Illustrated Monthly Magazine* 79 (Nov. 1909–April 1910): 702; Brown, ed., *Valentine's Manual of Old New York*, 201; Trager, *Park Avenue*, 38; Bunyan, *All around Town*, 201.

55. *New York Tribune*, January 16, 1912; *Milwaukee Daily News*, April 23, 1913. See also, on the American House in Denver, *Rocky Mountain News*, December 3, 1890; on the demolition of the Delmonico's building, *New York Times*, August 20, 1925.

56. *New York Tribune*, July 27, 1913. Even as late as 1957, the Louisiana Tourist Bureau mentioned in one of its promotional brochures on plantation tours that one of the mementos of "The Cottage" in St. Francisville was a set of china and gold flatware used to entertain the grand duke during his visit to New Orleans; Louisiana Department of Commerce and Industry Tourist Bureau, *Louisiana Plantation Homes* (Baton Rouge, 1957), 60–62. Another travel magazine credits the home with having Russian candlesticks from the visit; see Jennifer Quayle, "The Cottage," *Travel Holiday* (January 1980): 30–33.

57. Using the search term "Russia," the ProQuest newspaper database revealed the following number of articles: *New York Times,* 1860—409 articles, 1880—909 articles; *Chicago Tribune,* 1860—160 articles, 1880—695 articles; *Baltimore Sun,* 1860—226 articles, 1880—381 articles; *San Francisco Chronicle,* 1860—41 articles, 1880—196 articles. This search was conducted in August 2011.

58. David Engerman, *Modernization from the Other Shore* (Cambridge, MA: Harvard University Press, 2003), 28–55; Marion Moore Coleman, "Eugene Schuyler: Diplomat Extraordinary from the United States to Russia 1867–1876," *Russian Review* 17, no. 1 (Autumn 1947): 40–45; Saul, *Concord and Conflict,* 168–69, 180–88.

59. Engerman, *Modernization from the Other Shore,* 3–6, 28–40; David Foglesong, *The American Mission and the "Evil Empire"* (Cambridge, UK: Cambridge University Press, 2007), esp. 1–35. See also Saul, *Concord and Conflict,* 189–96.

60. *Cleveland Daily Plain Dealer,* December 26, 1871; *Pittsburgh Gazette,* November 24, 1871; *Washington Evening Star,* January 17, 1872.

61. *Missouri Republican,* January 8, 1872; *Boston Courier,* December 10, 1871; *Milwaukee Sentinel,* December 28, 1871; *Philadelphia Press,* November 30 and December 7, 1871.

62. Saul, *Concord and Conflict,* 51, 76–83, 138–41, 207–29, 253–57; Karen Kettering, "Decoration and Disconnection: The *Russkii stil'* and Russian Decorative Arts at Nineteenth-Century American World's Fairs," in *Russian Art and the West: A Century of Dialogue in Painting, Architecture, and the Decorative Arts,* ed. Rosalind P. Blakesley and Susan E. Reid (DeKalb: Northern Illinois University Press, 2007), 62–68.

63. Engerman, *Modernization from the Other Shore,* 28–55. For American interest in Tolstoy, see Saul, *Concord and Conflict,* 323–30; Robert T. Whittaker, "Tolstoy's American Mailbag: Selected Exchanges with His Occasional Correspondents," *TriQuarterly* 95 (Winter 1995–96): 7–44; Whittaker, "Tolstoy's American Disciple: Letters to Ernest Howard Crosby, 1894–1906," *TriQuarterly* 98 (Winter 1996–97): 210–50; Whittaker, "Tolstoy's American Translator: Letters to Isabel Hapgood, 1888–1903," *TriQuarterly* 102 (Spring 1998): 7–65; Whittaker, "Tolstoy's American Preachers: Letters on Religion and Ethics, 1886–1908," *TriQuarterly* 107–8 (Fall 2000): 561–629; Whittaker, "Tolstoy's American Visitors: Memoirs of Personal Encounters, 1868–1909," *TriQuarterly* 110–11 (Fall 2001): 213–73.

64. *Harper's Weekly,* May 26, 1877; Saul, *Concord and Conflict,* 116–23.

65. Richard Robbins, *Famine in Russia, 1891–1892* (New York: Columbia University Press, 1975), 2–10; Charles Emory Smith, "The Famine in Russia," *North American Review* 154, no. 426 (May 1892): 541–51; George S. Queen, "American Relief in the Russian Famine of 1891–1892," *Russian Review* 14, no. 2 (April 1955): 140–50; *New York Times,* January 30, 1892; see also Harold F. Smith, "Bread for Russians: William C. Edgar and the Relief Campaign of 1892," *Minnesota History* 42, no. 2 (Summer 1970): 54–62.

66. *New York Times,* December 25, 1892; Queen, "American Relief in the Russian Famine," 147. Even in 1917, albeit before the worst excesses of the Russian Revolution had occurred, Francis Reeves wrote about the famine and warmly referred to the continuing friendship between the two nations. See *Russian Then and Now, 1892–1917: My Mission to Russia during the Famine of 1891–1892 with Data Bearing upon Russia of Today* (New York: G. P. Putnam's Sons, 1917).

67. Saul, *Concord and Conflict,* 281–98.

68. Foglesong, *The American Mission and the "Evil Empire,"* 7; *Washington Daily Morning Chronicle,* December 2, 1869, January 19 and February 1, 1870; letter from M. Y. Isaacs to Hamilton Fish, January 31, 1870, Hamilton Fish Papers, container 67, doc. 9500–9501, Library of Congress, Manuscripts Division, Washington, DC; *New York Herald,* October 29, 1871; Taylor Stults, "Russian Persecution of Jews, and American Public Opinion," *Jewish Social Studies* 33, no. 1 (January 1971): 13–22.

69. Alan M. Ball, *Imagining America: Influence and Images in Twentieth-Century Russia* (Lanham, MD: Rowman & Littlefield, 2003), 24–28; Richard Stites, *Revolutionary Dreams: Utopian Vision and Experimental Life in the Russian Revolution* (New York: Oxford University Press, 1989), 146–49.

70. See, for example, Guenter Lewy, *The Cause That Failed: Communism in American Political Life* (New York: Oxford University Press, 1990); John Scott, *Behind the Urals: An American Worker in Russia's City of Steel* (Bloomington: Indiana University Press, 1973); Joy Gleason Carew, *Blacks, Reds, and Russians: Sojourners in Search of the Soviet Promise* (New Brunswick, NJ: Rutgers University Press, 2008); Tim Tzouliadis, *The Forsaken: An American Tragedy in Stalin's Russia* (New York: Penguin, 2008); Margaret Wettlin, *Fifty Russian Winters: An American Woman's Life in the Soviet Union* (New York: Pharos Books, 1992); Mary M. Leder, *My Life in Stalinist Russia: An American Woman Looks Back* (Bloomington: Indiana University Press, 2001); Barbara Keys, "An African-American Worker in Stalin's Soviet Union: Race and the Soviet Experiment in International Perspective," *The Historian* (2009): 31–54; Mark I. Solomon, *Red and Black: Communism and Afro-Americans, 1929–1935* (New York: Garland Publishing, 1988).

71. Also, Robert C. Williams, "The Quiet Trade: Russian Art and American Money," *Wilson Quarterly* 3, no. 1 (Winter 1979): 162–75.

72. See, for example, Harlow Robinson, *Russians in Hollywood, Hollywood's Russians: Biography of an Image* (Boston: Northeastern University Press, 2007); Laurence Senelick, ed., *Wandering Stars: Russian Émigré Theatre, 1905–1940* (Iowa City: University of Iowa Press, 1992).

73. *Washington Post,* February 24, 1924; *New York Times,* November 10 and 16, 1935, March 7, 1967. Invitation and copy of menu in hands of author, obtained from Peabody Hotel, Memphis.

74. Nicholas B. A. Nicholson, *Jewels of the Romanovs: Treasures of the Russian Imperial Court* (Washington, DC: Corcoran Gallery of Art, 1997); copies of exhibition display items in hands of author, obtained from Pabst Mansion, Milwaukee, Wisconsin; Marilyn Pfeifer Swezey, ed., *The Tsar and the President: Alexander II and Abraham Lincoln, Liberator and Emancipator* (Washington, DC: American-Russian Cultural Cooperation Foundation, 2008), 59–66.

75. Joseph Freeman, "Russia and the U.S.," *Life* (August 27, 1945): 88–100; Melville O. Briney, "Grand Doings in Louisville for a Grand Duke," *Louisville Times,* January 13, 1949. See also *Sikeston (Mo.) Herald,* February 15, 1945; Albert Parry, "A Grand Duke Comes to America," *American Mercury* (September 1948): 334–41; Caroline Bancroft, *Buffalo Bill and the Grand Duke Alexis* (Denver: Westerners, Denver Posse, 1951); John Stuart Martin, ed., *A Picture History of Russia* (New York: Crown Publishers, 1956), 154–55; Joseph Balmer, "The Famous Buffalo Hunt of Grand Duke Alexis," *English Westerners' Brand Book* 3, no. 5 (March 1957): 3–8; Alexander Tarsaidze, *Czars and Presidents: The Story of a Forgotten Friendship* (New York: McDowell/Obolensky, Inc., 1958), 258–81.

76. For example, *The American Rifleman* (1952), *The American West* (1972), *Wild West* (1988), *Field and Stream* (1999), *Stereo World* (2000), *Ephemera News* (2005), *American History* (2010), and *Persimmon Hill* (1991), the magazine of the National Cowboy and Western Heritage Center

in Oklahoma City. There are far too many publications that mention the buffalo hunt to list them all here. See, for example, Dan Beard, "Make Your Own Sleeping Poke," *Boys' Life* (October 1936): 19; Durward Allen, "The Stone Age Lingers On," *Boys' Life* 49, no. 11 (November 1959): 55, 84–85; Newton B. Drury, "The Comeback of the Bison," *Rotarian* 69, no. 6 (December 1946): 20–22; Mari Sandoz and Michael Punke, *The Buffalo Hunters: The Story of the Hide Men* (Reno: University of Nevada Press, 2008), 117–24; George Black, *Empire of Shadows: The Epic Story of Yellowstone* (New York: St. Martin's Press, 2012), 382.

77. There is even a French comic book in the "Lucky Luke" series, *Le Grand Duc,* that features a Russian Grand Duke who visits America for diplomatic reasons and travels out West.

78. Scott, Bleed, and Damm, *Custer, Cody, and Grand Duke Alexis,* xi–xii.

79. There are so many publications on Mardi Gras that give some version of the claim that Alexis inspired Rex that only a few will be cited here. See Charles Dufour and Leonard V. Huber, *If Ever I Cease to Love: One Hundred Years of Rex, 1872–1971* (New Orleans: School of Design, 1970), 5; Errol Laborde, *Mardi Gras! A Celebration* (New Orleans: Picayune Press, 1981), 55; Garvey and Widmer, *Beautiful Crescent,* 130; Henri Schindler, *Mardi Gras: New Orleans* (New York: Flammarion, 1997), 47; and James Gill, *Lords of Misrule: Mardi Gras and the Politics of Race in New Orleans* (Jackson: University Press of Mississippi, 1997), 94. New Orleans travel guides have also contributed to the myth. See, for example, Honey Naylor, *The Insider's Guide to New Orleans* (Boston: Harvard Common Press, 1994), 99; *Frommer's New Orleans 2001,* 10; Becky Retz and James Gaffney, *Insider's Guide: New Orleans* (Helena, MT: Falcon Publishing, Inc., 2000), 210.

80. There are numerous examples. See Perry Young, *Carnival and Mardi Gras in New Orleans* (New Orleans: Harmanson's 1939), 44–45; Robert Tallant, *Mardi Gras* (Garden City, NY: Doubleday and Co., 1948), 130–37; Arthur B. LaCour, *New Orleans Masquerade, Chronicles of Carnival* (New Orleans: Pelican Publishing Co., 1957), 41; Schindler, *Mardi Gras: New Orleans,* 48; Gill, *Lords of Misrule,* 96–100; Garvey and Widmer, *Beautiful Crescent,* 130; Naylor, *The Insider's Guide to New Orleans,* 99; *Frommer's New Orleans 2001,* 10; Retz and Gaffney, *Insider's Guide: New Orleans,* 210.

81. There have been a few attempts to question the traditional legend about Alexis, Lydia, and Rex. See, for example, Reid Mitchell, *All on a Mardi Gras Day* (Cambridge, MA: Harvard University Press, 1995), 55; Arthur Hardy, *Mardi Gras in New Orleans: An Illustrated History* (Metairie, LA: Arthur Hardy Enterprises, 2001), 16–19; Errol Laborde, *Marched the Day God: A History of the Rex Organization* (New Orleans: School of Design, 1999), 17; Theodore P. Mahne, "Carnival Anthem Is Love Story with City, not Duke," *Times Picayune,* February 25, 2001, E-10; Don Lee Keith, "Siren's Song," *Arthur Hardy's Mardi Gras Guide,* 13th ed. (Metairie, LA: Arthur Hardy Enterprises, 1989): 13–17; Farrow, "Grand Duke Alexei and the Origins of Rex." Again, this is not intended to be a comprehensive list.

82. Gill, *Lords of Misrule,* 94; Kinser, *Carnival, American Style,* 102; Leonard J. Huber, *Mardi Gras: A Pictorial History of Carnival in New Orleans* (Gretna, LA: Pelican Publishing, 1994), 13–15.

83. *New Orleans Republican,* February 12, 1872; "First Rex Tells How It Began," *Times-Picayune,* February 25, 1938; Eric Hobsbawm, "Introduction: Inventing Traditions," in *The Invention of Tradition,* ed. Eric Hobsbawm and Terence Ranger (New York: Cambridge University Press, 1983), 4, 10; Gill, *Lords of Misrule,* 35–44, 93–97, 13.

84. Joe Gray Taylor, *Louisiana Reconstructed, 1863–1877* (Baton Rouge: Louisiana State University Press, 1974), 209–41; Bennet H. Wall, ed., *Louisiana: A History,* 3rd ed. (Wheeling, IL: Harlan Davidson, 1997), 187–93; *New Orleans Times,* December 5 and 8, 1871. See also *Kansas City Times,* January 5, 1872; *New Orleans Times,* January 8 and 15, 1872.

85. *New Orleans Republican,* January 25, 1872.

86. Ibid., February 12 and 13, 1872; *New Orleans Daily Picayune,* February 14 and 22, 1872.

87. *Memphis Daily Appeal,* November 19, 1871; *Cleveland Daily Plain Dealer,* November 24, 1871.

88. There is no written history of the Krewe of Alexis. The description here is compiled from documents located at Tulane University, the New Orleans Public Library, the Louisiana State Museum, and the Historic New Orleans Collection. Alexis continues to appear in newspaper articles and other sources on a regular basis. In 1998, a poem about his trip appeared in the *New Orleans Review.* See Louis Gallo, "The City Care Forgot, or Duke Alexis Alexandrovitch Romanoff Meets Buffalo Bill, after Which He Travels to New Orleans for Mardi Gras," *New Orleans Review* 24, no. 3 (Summer 1998): 6–8.

INDEX